MW01616472

Two Years on Malekula
Living in a Different Universe

Stan Combs

Manples Publishing

Cover photo: Man in south Malekula Small Nambas kastom village of Imarao blows "bubu", or Triton shell trumpet, to call villagers together.

Manples Publishing
20A Pear Tree Road, Ashford, Middlesex, TW15 1PW

First published in the UK by Manples Publishing in 2021

Stan Combs
scombs@telus.net
www.ruralvanuatu.net

Two Years in Lakatoro/ Stan Combs. -- 1st ed.
ISBN 978-1-5272-5900-3

This memoir is dedicated to my love, Holly Morgan, who followed me out to Vanuatu and still pays for our great time there because of the loss of six pensionable years in Canada (although well worth it). Holly took many of the photos in this memoir. Also, our daughters Heather and Laurel, who soldiered bravely through six years of their youth without McDonalds or Halloween.

And, of course, the people of Vanuatu.

Thanks are owed to Wendy Burton, who initiated and taught the course on Hornby Island that started me on this project. Wendy also edited my manuscript and made many useful suggestions. Cornelia Hoogland taught further terms of the course and strove to improve my writing skills. And, special thanks go to Norman Shackley of the British Friends of Vanuatu, who encouraged me to publish this manuscript and formatted it for publication.

Holly on Malekula, Christmas 1988
Wearing a boar's tusk on right arm.

Me shortly after our arrival in
Lakatoro in my Magnum, P.I. shirt.

Table of Contents

Maps   x
    The South Pacific   x
    Vanuatu   xi
    Malekula   xii

A Note on Bislama Pronunciation   xiv
Glossary of Terms   xv

FOREWORD   xviii

PART 1—GETTING TO LAKATORO   1
    How I ended up as a CUSO in Lakatoro, Malekula   1
    Our Arrival in Vanuatu   3

PART 2—ABOUT VANUATU   9
    Vanuatu's History and Condominium Legacy   9
    Bislama, Vanuatu's National Language   12
        Using Bislama when others didn't expect it.   15
    Vanuatu and World War II   15
    Vanuatu Politics Following Independence   21
    Religion in Vanuatu   22
    Elder Cernis of the South Malekula Presbyterian Church   28
    Relations Between Westerners and ni-Vanuatu   31
    Geological Phenomena   33
        Sea Levels   33
        Earthquakes and Tsunamis   35
        Volcanoes   35
    The Jon Frum Society   37
    Nakaemas   39
    Kava   40
    A Typical Evening at a Commercial Nakamal in a Town   45
    Is Kava Addictive?   46
    Kava and North American Law   47
    Kava In Another Society Where It Is Not A Tradition   47
    My First Experience With Kava   47
    Kava at Club Hippique   50
    Kava Sent Home to My Sister   50

Stories of Sharks   50
    Custom Sharks   50
    Initial Exposure to Malekula Sharks   51
    Shark Attacks on Malekula   53

Sexual Assault   55
Vanuatu Inter-Island Flights   57
Port Vila's Bus System   58
The Port Vila Riot, May 16, 1988   59

PART 3—WORKING ON MALEKULA   61
Underdevelopment in Vanuatu   62
Regional Development Planner Work   68
    Working Relationships   69
Financial Analyses and Pricing of Services and Goods   70
    The LGC Minibus   70
    Public Phones   72
    Corrugated Iron Roofing Sheets and Concrete Blocks   73
    Resthouses   74
    Village Fisheries Project   74
    The Lakatoro Bakery   76
    Women's Business Workshop   77
    The Litzlitz Wharf   78
    Emergency Food Relief   83
    Staff Education   89
    Rural Water Supplies   89
    Rural Sanitation   94
    Community Relations   96
    Roads   97
    Regional Development Planner Work—The Reality   97
    Final Word on Technical Assistance to Vanuatu   98
A Trip to the Southeast Corner of Malekula   99
On Tour With the Acting Prime Minister   105
Metenesel Estates Limited   109
    Angry Ground at MEL   110
Visiting a Small Nambas Kastom Village   111
Circumnavigating Malekula   119
The New Patrol Boat   124
Regional Development Planners Conference   126
The New Aid Post   129

The Proposed Brenwe Falls Hydroelectricity Project   130
Relations with National Planning and Statistics Office   131
The Game   133

Logging on Malekula   133
    The Taiwanese   133
    Small Scale and Local Logging   135

Personnel Issues   135
    Dealing With Fully-Funded (Well-Paid) Consultants   136
    A Unique Consultant   137
    CUSO Cooperant Issues   137
    Volunteers Suffering in Vanuatu   142
South Pacific Travel—Not What the Brochures Promised!   143

PART 4 -THE CUSO COOPERANT LIFE ON MALEKULA   147
Lakatoro: Home, Sweet Home   148
Domestic Life   158
Life for Heather and Laurel   170
Norsup French Elementary School—"Groupe Scolaire
Edmond Caillard" and the Lakatoro Kinder   174
Health Issues   183
Relations With Other Malekula Expatriates   191
Interactions With Other CUSO Cooperants   192
Interactions With Animals   194
    Goat   194
    Cattle   198
    Crabs   198
       Land Crab (Cardisoma carnifex)   198
       Coconut Crab (Birgus latro, family Paguridae)   200
       Caledonie Crab (Scylla serrate)   203
    Spiny Lobster (Panulirus longipes bispinosus)   203
    Broadclub Cuttlefish (Sepia latimanus)   204
    Giant Clam (Tridacna gigas)   204
    Fruit Bat or Vanuatu Flying Fox (Pteropus anetianus)   205
    Dugong, or "Kaufis" (Dugong dugon, family
    Dugongidae)   205
    Palolo Worm (Palola viridis)   208
    Pigs' Tusks (Sus scrofa domesticus)   210
    Chicken (Gallus gallus domesticus)   214
    Coconut Lorikeet (Trichoglossus haematodus Massena)   217
    Rat (Rattus exulans)   219

Ants (Who Knows; there's a zillion species)   220
Cockroaches (Again, Who Knows the species)   221
The "White Man's Rat" (Cavia porcellus)   222

Personal Transportation (aside from Shank's Mare)   223
    Bicycles   223
    Motorcycle   224
    Renting a Truck From the LGC   225
    Canoe   227
    Fireball Racing Sailing Dinghy   228
    Land Cruiser   231

Charismatic Religion Next Door   240
Stan vs. the BBC World Service   243
Other Short-Wave Radio Services and News Media   244
    Radio Canada International news broadcasts: 245
    Other short-wave news services: 245
    Local Vanuatu Media: 246

The Custom Cave   246
Labour Day Festivities At The Norsup Catholic Church   254
Bush Leaves in Port Vila   259
Walking Across Southern Malekula   263
White Ladies Make Wedding Cakes   282
Stan Gets Blessed by a Cardinal   285
Basil and Hanson's Wedding   294
Cyclone Bola   302
Heather Visits Uripiv Island   304
Stan DJs a Dance   307
At a Previous Met-Met Club Dance   309
Stan MCs and Competes in a Music Contest   309
An Expedition to the Brenwe River Falls   311
Crisis at the Lakatoro Branch of the Vanuatu Co-operative
Credit Union   316
Daniel's Nakamal   317

Two Christmas and New Year's Seasons in the
Combs/Morgan Household   319
Our first Christmas in Vanuatu: 319
    Our second Christmas on Malekula: 320
    Our second New Year's Eve on Malekula, about
    a month before we left: 324

PART 5 - LEAVING 327
Leaving Malekula and Vanuatu 327

EPILOGUE 331
What Did Vanuatu Gain from My Time in Lakatoro? 331
What Did I Gain from My Time in Vanuatu? 331
Our Poor, Abused Children 336
Holly's Career 336
My Further International Aid Advisor Career 337
My CUSO Termination Report 337
CUSO Since 1992 338

APPENDIX 339

CUSO COOPERANT - TERMINATION REPORT 339

    1. YOUR JOB 339
    2. TIPS FOR NEW COOPERANTS 341
    3. PERSONAL AND SOCIAL 343
    4. PERSONAL OBJECTIVES 344
    5. CUSO AND YOU 345
    6. YOUR FUTURE 350
    7. PROFESSIONAL CONTACTS 350
    8. RESOURCES 350
    9. GENERAL 351

MAPS

The South Pacific

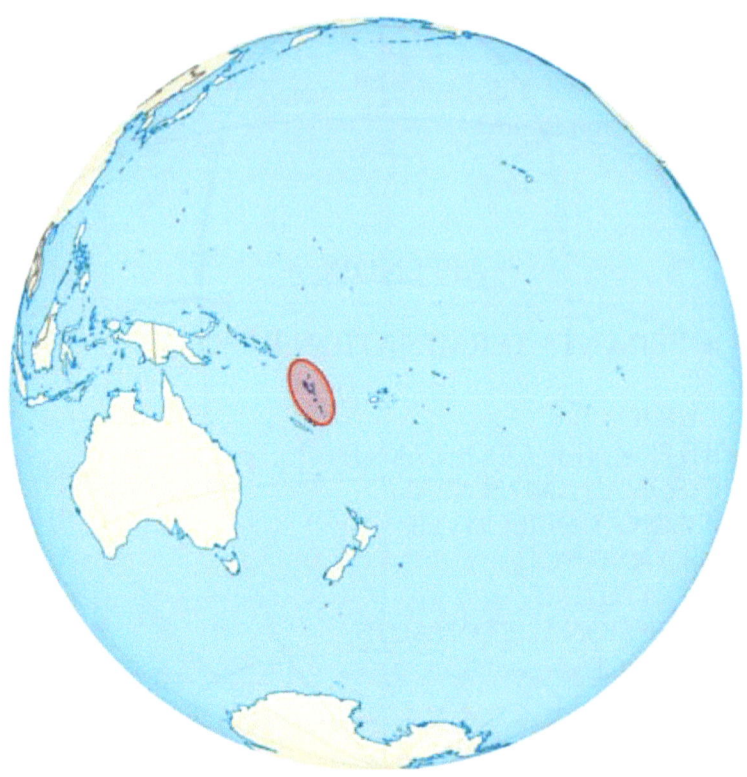

The Pacific is a big ocean with a few very widely scattered islands. Vanuatu is circled; a sliver of Canada is in the upper right.

Republic of Vanuatu

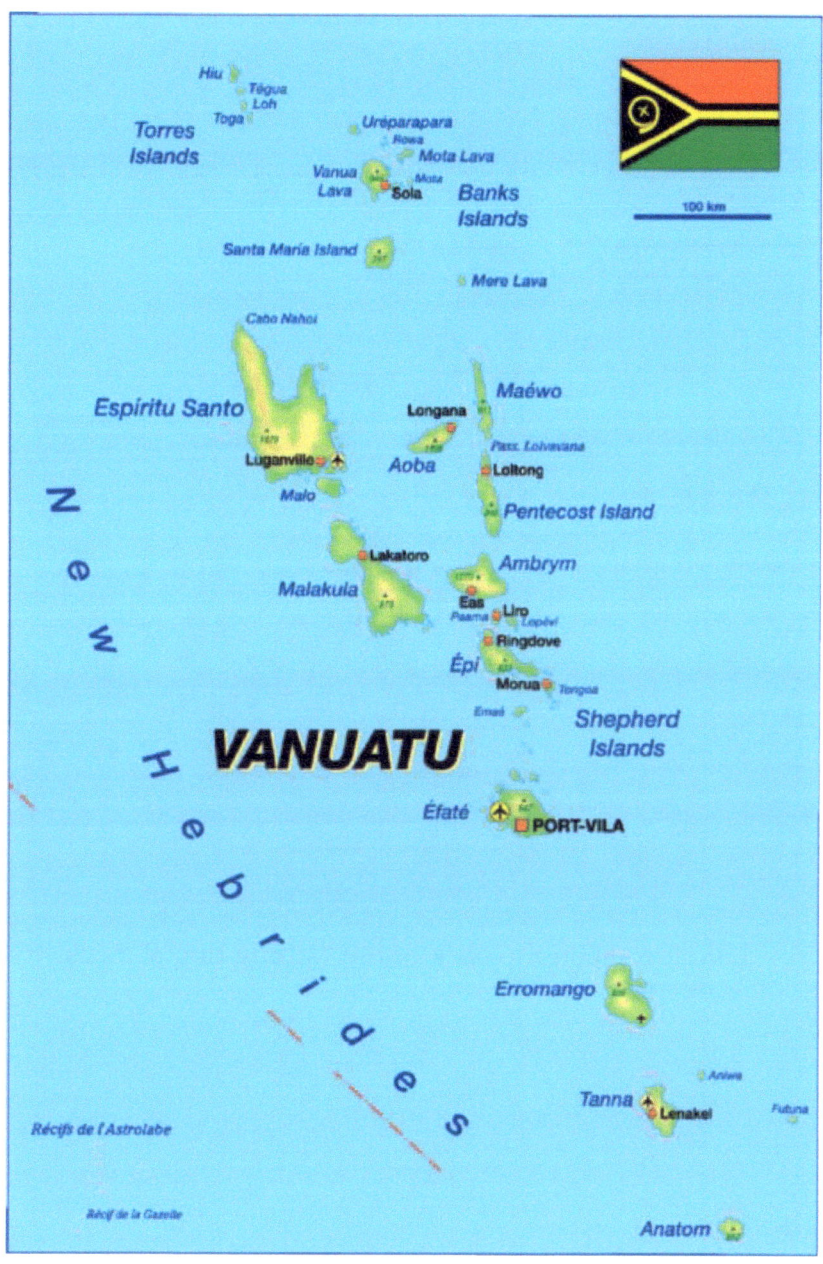

The island of "Malekula" has different spellings, "Malakula" on this map.

Malekula

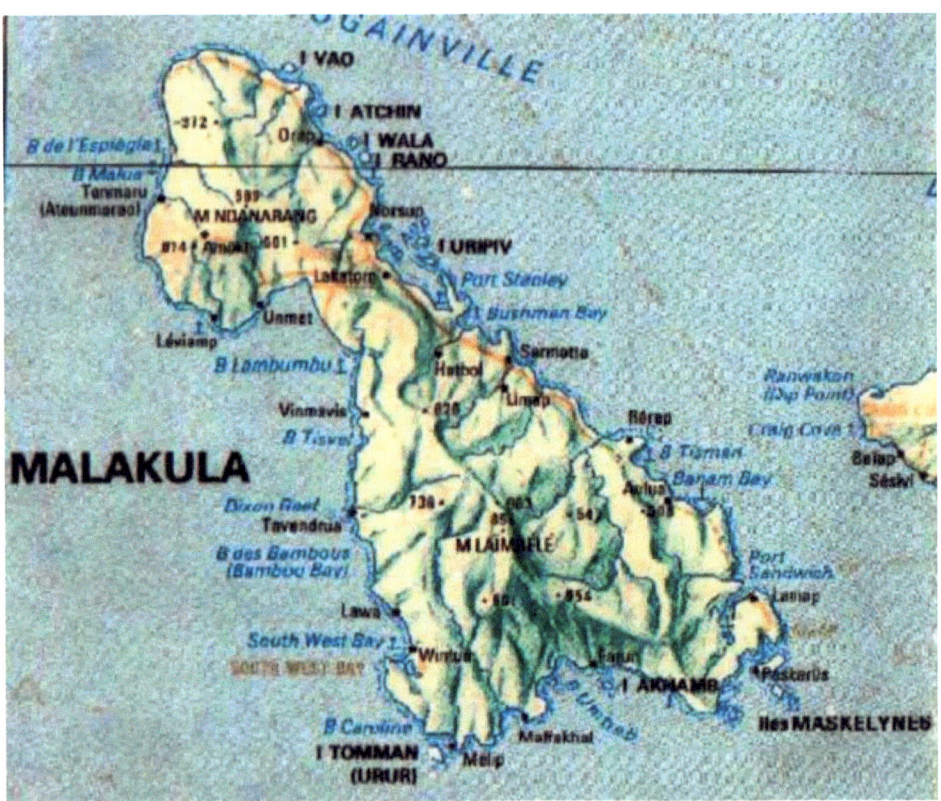

Lakatoro is on the back of the "sitting dog's" neck.

A Note on Bislama Pronunciation

When I speak or write about Vanuatu, I scatter in the odd word or phrase of Bislama, Vanuatu's pidgin lingua franca. The consonants are pronounced as in English, except "s" is lisped a bit as in the English word "sip". Depending on what island the speaker is from, they may interchange some vowels, like g and k or p and b. My counterpart was amazed I couldn't differentiate accents from different islands, but I could not.

Vowels are pronounced European-style:

a—ah
e—ay as in weigh
i—ee
o—oh
u—ou as in whoo

and, a few additions:

ae—eye
au—ow as in ouch.

Bislama has two prepositions one will see in many phrases:

> Blong—"belonging to", pronounced "blow" [1]
> Long—everything else a cat can do to a box (i.e., all other prepositions), pronounced "low"

As many of the words are derived from English, pronouncing them out loud often reveals their English meaning, for example:

Rod—road
Sip—ship
Bagarap—break
Basket blong titi—bra

OK; native English speakers find various Bislama phrases amusing. A plane doesn't land, "i fol daun". See the book "Evri Samting Yu Wanem Lanem Long Bislama Be Yu Fraet Tumas Blong Askem "[1] for more of this.

---

[1] *A CUSO friend, upon his return to Canada, had to learn to stop telling waitresses which dish was his by saying, "Blong mi".*

[1] *"Everything You Want to Know About Bislama, But Are Afraid to Ask"*
by Darrell Tryon.

Glossary of Terms

Bislama	Vanuatu's pidgin lingua franca. Listed in its constitution as Vanuatu's "National Language" as opposed to the "Official Languages" of English and French. There are also more than one hundred "Village Languages"; Vanuatu has the world's largest number of languages per capita. Bislama is a mixture of English, French, Village Language, and other words set to a Melanesian syntax.
Busnaef	Bushknife, or Machete. The essential rural all-purpose tool, used for cutting vines and bushes, clearing paths and gardens, working the soil, and occasionally as a weapon.
Cargo	Western material goods. Often used in the context of receiving these goods without working or paying for them.
Contact	Contact with the West, starting with Western navigators in the 17th and 18th century, and continuing in the 19th century with sandalwood and sea slug traders, missionaries, labour recruiters, traders, planters, and colonial government administrators.
Cooperant	CUSO-ese for "volunteer".
Copra	Dried coconut meat, Vanuatu's main export, which is sent to Europe to be crushed for coconut oil—that stuff that either kills you or cures all, depending on which book you've recently read.
CUSO	Meaningless acronym (formerly Canadian University Services Overseas) for Canada's semi-official overseas volunteer organization. When we were in Lakatoro, CUSO had morphed from its beginnings of sending new university graduates to teach English in Africa to sending experienced professionals to many types of jobs in numerous third-world countries. Also used to indicate CUSO cooperants.
Fason blong ...	Pronounced "Fason blow". "The way things are done by...".
FSO	Field Staff Officer. The officer administrating all the CUSO cooperants in Vanuatu. We had two, a husband and wife, but I mainly refer to the woman, with whom I interacted the most.
Major Islands of Vanuatu	From north to south: Banks and Torres groups, Gaua (Santa Maria), Espiritu Santo (Santo), Maewo, Ambae (Aoba), Pentecost, Malekula, Ambrym, Epi, Paama, Shepherds group, Efate, Erromango [1], Aniwa, Tanna, Futuna, Aneityum (Anatom), and Mathew and Hunter (the last two depending on if you ask Vanuatu or France).
Kastom	"Custom", referring to tradition, or in many cases, sorcery.

---

[1] *A CUSO who had lived on Erromango and learned the local language told me that Captain James Cook had the habit of learning the name of each new island he visited by picking up a handful of soil when he asked what the island's name was. Here, he was told "dirt", or in the local language, "erromango".*

Kumala	Sweet potato. The only pre-contact crop in Vanuatu to originate in the New World, which gives hope to those who like to insist (often for religious reasons) that Melanesians came from the Americas. If so, they must have come via Southeast Asia, because that's where their languages, pottery, and everything else in pre-contact Vanuatu originated.
LGC	Local Government Council.
Luganville	Vanuatu's second-largest urban centre, on Espiritu Santo Island. Known throughout Vanuatu as "Santo", except on Espiritu Santo Island, where it is known as "Kanal".
Malekula [1]	Sometimes spelled "Malakula", or in French, "Malicollo"
Masta	Adult white male.
Misis	Adult white female.
Nakamal	Traditional men's meeting building in villages; commercial kava bar in urban areas.
New Hebridean	Melanesian indigenous resident of the New Hebrides, as Vanuatu was known before independence in 1980.
New Hebrides	Pre-independence (1980) name of Vanuatu. Apparently, the islands reminded James Cook of the Hebrides Islands of Scotland.
Ni-Vanuatu	Melanesian citizen or citizens of Vanuatu. Sometimes, erroneously in my view, used to indicate Vanuatu citizens of any race. Canadians, unlike ni-Vanuatu, have an aversion to classifying people by race. Believing that "we are all the same under the skin" is a major cause of failure to be effective in Vanuatu. I believe one must respect everyone equally, but acknowledge cultural, psychological, and sociological differences.
NPSO	National Planning and Statistics Office, of which the NP part was nominally responsible for liaising between central government departments and international aid donors.
Pikinini	Child. Also applies to inanimate objects with a connection to something larger, as in "pikinini blong kanu" — "outrigger" and "pikinini blong wil" —inner tube inside "mama blong wil" —"tire".
PRV	Plantation Reunion de Vanuatu, a large French-owned coconut plantation. Its headquarters were located at Norsup, 8km north of Lakatoro.
Resthouse	Travelers' Hostel.
Santo	Espiritu Santo Island; also used outside of that island to indicate Luganville.
Smol Misis or Masta	Juvenile white female or male.

---

[1] *A French joke says the island got its name after an explorer used the leaves of nangalak, a stinging plant, for toilet paper and reported to his compatriots that "mal au cul, la" or loosely "pain in the ass, that".*

Storian	Discuss something; chat.
Vanua'aku Pati	The ruling political party when we lived in Lakatoro. In power since independence, it was an Anglophone party and tightly controlled everything in Vanuatu.
Vanuatu—A Canadian's Perspective	My website about what I learned about rural Vanuatu while I lived in Vanuatu. http://ruralvanuatu.net .
Vatu, or vt	Vanuatu's unit of currency, at the time of this memoir close enough for practical purposes to $CAN 0.01.
Vila	Common term for Port Vila, Vanuatu's capital.
Waetman	Whiteman. Non-Melanesian, including Caucasians, South Asians, and Japanese, but excluding Chinese (man Jaena or Shinwa) and Vietnamese (Sinoa).

Two Years on Malekula, 1987-88
Living in a Different Universe

Foreword

Vanuatu is a different universe than Canada. People in Vanuatu take in the same sensations and information as Canadians and then perceive that entirely different things have happened based on different causes. Westerners think ni-Vanuatu are nuts, and ni-Vanuatu know we are crazy.

Because Vanuatu is an unknown universe to Westerners, I have included some background as to how that universe developed. I've read several books written by Westerners in the New Hebrides during the 19th century, and not much has changed over time in Vanuatu. OK—they don't strangle widows any more. I think. A high fence had to be built around the Vila cemetery soon after our arrival, however, because bodies were being dug up in order to suck the marrow out of a certain bone to obtain magical powers. On the subject of cannibalism, Holly's co-workers at the Norsup Hospital told her that the best bits are the insides of the upper arms and thighs.

During our two years on Malekula, February 1987—February 1989, I kept my eyes open for interesting occurrences, of which there were many. I included them in my letters home, this being prior to the advent of the Internet and email. I also took a lot of photos, and labeled them on their backs. These, as well as my writings on my Rural Vanuatu website, are the primary sources for this memoir.

Excerpts of those letters home, some recovered from humidity-ravaged magnetic media floppy disks, are indented and highlighted in this memoir.

The key to learning about Vanuatu is to live for at least a couple of years in a rural area; not the towns of Port Vila or Luganville. And, keeping one's mind open and treating ni-Vanuatu with respect, which includes respecting their view of the world. Most of their traditional knowledge is secret and not shared with expatriates. Even amongst ni-Vanuatu, knowledge is a commodity that is sold, not shared freely. During my two years in rural

Vanuatu, I just scratched the surface; I am nowhere near an expert on Vanuatu kastom.

After leaving Malekula and spending several months travelling and in Canada, we returned to Vanuatu in August 1989. We lived in the capital, Port Vila, for 39 months while I worked for the central government's National Planning and Statistics Office as Vanuatu's first Regional Development Planning Advisor. I characterized Vila at that time as an expat Disneyland without much connection to the world back home. It also didn't bear much relation to the actual Vanuatu, which is less a nation than a collection of villages on isolated islands. Most villages have their own language, and villagers live what is termed an "affluent subsistence" lifestyle, growing their own food with only a few days' labour per week. They have limited contact with the money economy, perhaps earning a bit of money each year laboriously making copra and spending it on such luxuries as sugar, tea, tobacco, and beer. Port Vila is a big shock for villagers who, because "every day is the same" in the village, move to town. In Vila, they find that money is needed to purchase the necessities of life and money is not easy to obtain, even if full-time work can be secured. They are then loath to return home where people will mock them for failing to "make it" in town.

One of my major disappointments in Vila was eventually realizing that most of the expatriates there, including aid-funded technical advisors, knew next-to-nothing about Vanuatu. They had the misconception that Vila was Vanuatu, when Vanuatu was really the rural areas where 85% of the population lived in small rural villages.

In the mid-1990s, when the Internet first became widespread, I posted "Vanuatu—a Canadian's Perspective"[1] containing what I had learned about what I called the real—i.e. rural—Vanuatu. My objective was to provide a resource for non-ni-Vanuatu who would be making decisions affecting Vanuatu. Back then a search on Alta Vista, the premier search engine of the time, brought up three sites about Vanuatu, including mine. Now a Google search brings up millions, but the last time I checked, I was relegated to Page 5 of a search for "rural Vanuatu"—Page 9 if the parentheses were omitted. Not bad for two decades later, I guess.

In those days I had many interesting email conversations with people who read my site, but now I'm not sure any of my intended audience read it.

Two decades later, I'm retired on Hornby Island, B.C., Canada. I took a course on writing memoirs, spent a winter dry-camping on a Mexican beach writing this one up, and the next few years editing and improving it.

---

[1] http://ruralvanuatu.net

My motives in writing this memoir are to:

- Educate about Vanuatu, which is both fascinating and unfamiliar to Westerners.
- Present some of the realities of foreign aid work, which are little known aside from a Western government budget line that makes voters feel good.
- Entertain with tales of our life in Lakatoro, including various stumbles made by us newbies.

Readers will find it useful to read "PART 2—ABOUT VANUATU—The different Universe" first so that the rest of the memoir will make more sense.

I hope I have succeeded in making it entertaining and educational.

Keep in mind these events, while as true as I can recall them, occurred three decades ago; things in Vanuatu have changed since, although I doubt if the essentials are all that different.

Stan Combs
August, 2019

Two Years on Malekula

PART 1—GETTING TO LAKATORO

How I ended up as a CUSO in Lakatoro, Malekula

I enjoyed traveling in Australia and Europe as a late teenager in the early '70s. Shortly after I returned from Australia at age 20, my father morphed his career into international aid work; this looked to me like a good way to travel, help people, and get paid for it.

A few years later, when my job lending to Alberta farmers for the Bank of Nova Scotia didn't look like it was going where I wanted it to, I started investigating international aid work. "Sorry", I was told, "You don't have a Master's Degree". So, with the clichéd wife working to put me through, I determined to take an MSc in agricultural economics. But, which university?

The University of Guelph was suggested. Their literature in that pre-internet age trumpeted their international agricultural economics programme. Off I went, their token Western Canadian as I later concluded. Of a class of 12, 11 of us were eager young international aid aspirants. As we all soon learned, Guelph's international programme consisted of professors who went off on well paid international contracts, refusing to take students with them and, indeed, leaving some students in the lurch waiting for their return in order to take their oral exams and graduate.

I persevered, and to get rid of a pesky student who challenged the system, they gave me a few letters after my name and showed me the door. At this point, those who decide these things informed me that, "No; we can't hire you for aid work—you have no overseas experience." This wasn't going as planned.

Offered a job in Vermillion, Alberta with two weeks' annual vacation or one in Victoria, BC with twice as much vacation and 33% more pay, off I went to British Columbia.

What was then known as Canadian University Students Overseas, a programme which sent volunteers to what we then called the Third World, seemed like a good way to gain said experience. But, CUSO and I soon developed a major

1

personality clash. I applied and was accepted for a position in Papua New Guinea, but when advised CUSO would hold my passport until arrival in PNG, I told them this wasn't going to happen. At this point, PNG decided they wanted someone with more experience, anyway, so this appointment fell through. This was a bullet dodged, I later learned—PNG is a dangerous place, and most CUSOs I met who were sent there returned early.

Nevertheless, I was in the CUSO's Pacific Desk's bad books, and my further applications were ignored. I did meet a CUSO cooperant that had returned from a post with the Agriculture Department in Vanuatu, a place I'd never heard of. In order to beef up my application for his old position, I phoned Vanuatu, mentioned his name, and asked for some inside information. Years later, I mentioned this call to a colleague in Vanuatu who told me, "Were you that guy who phoned? Your contact had been a giant pain in the ass, and we figured anyone he knew had to be just as bad, so we refused your application!" There is an element of randomness in these things.

I gave up on CUSO. In 1986, though, I saw a CUSO ad in the Globe and Mail, read the University of Victoria library's sole book on Vanuatu, and couldn't help but send in another application. A month or two went by without any reply, so in September, Holly and I gathered up our two young daughters and our camping equipment and embarked on our fateful first stay on Hornby Island, where my wife and I now live.

Four weeks later, we returned home to a telegram[1] from CUSO. As he later told me in our Lakatoro living room, the new Pacific Officer had found my application on his desk and not knowing the history, had asked himself, "Why haven't we grabbed this guy?"[2] Randomness again reared its ugly head, and four months later, in early February 1987, we stepped off the plane in Port Vila into the teeth of Uma, a Category Five cyclone—i.e., "Catastrophic damage will occur". There is no Category Six.

---

[1] The antique predecessor of email.

[2] While in Ottawa for pre-departure orientation, I ran into the Director of CUSO, who told me I had the longest application process of any cooperant.

Two Years on Malekula

Our Arrival in Vanuatu

After a week's orientation in Ottawa and a four-day layover in Nandi, Fiji, I flew with the family[1] to Port Vila on Friday, February 6, 1987. I knew we were going to die when our Air Pacific 737 pilot put the spoilers up on the wings while we were still over the ocean miles away from the runway, rolled over on one wing, dropped that thing like a rock while coming around a sharp turn to line up with the runway, and just plunked us right down at the runway's end. We managed to stop at its extreme end.

Years later, when tourism was part of my National Planning Office responsibilities, I learned that Bauerfield, which was built as a bomber base in WW II, had an approach angle over the nearby hills greater than allowed under international commercial airline standards. The airport is allowed to operate under a special dispensation by international air transport authorities.

We caused a minor sensation amongst our fellow arrivals at the airport when they saw us take our four bicycle boxes and four hockey goalie pad bags—the extreme baggage limit I'd carefully researched—through customs without paying duty. They may not have known that aid workers were allowed to bring in their initial belongings duty-free.

It had been raining in Nandi, and in Vila we learned that Cyclone Uma was approaching. We were supposed to receive a further week's orientation in Vila, but in the early evening the CUSO Field Staff Officer showed up at our hotel room door, threw a stack of paper at us, and announced that the plane that flew us in was the last commercial flight in prior to Uma. It was leaving 12 hours early in order to avoid the cyclone, and she was going to catch it shortly to go on her annual leave.

The next day, the power went out at 1230, and I went to a nearby store to stock up on that essential, beer, only to get my first lesson about Vanuatu—liquor sales are cut off from noon Saturday to Monday morning. The radio was still broadcasting, though, and our second lesson was that Vanuatu is a small pond, as our arrival was announced on the national news. It was also announced where people should go to wait out the cyclone if they lived in housing that wouldn't withstand it.

By 1600,[2] the wind had picked up. We were in the top (second) floor of a long concrete block hotel building, second unit from the south end, with our strictly Francophone CUSO travelling companions, Daniel and Simone, next to us on the end. Access was from an external walkway. At 1730 things were really howling, and a large tree fell on the corner of Daniel and Simone's unit, taking out their only door. I climbed around the wall separating our balconies and helped them move their luggage to our unit before assisting them over.

---

[1] My wife Holly (33 years old) and daughters Heather (5) and Laurel (3). I was 35.

[2] The 24-hour clock will be used throughout.

Two Years on Malekula

Their stove's butane bottle outside what had been their door was hissing gas, and all six of us—Daniel, Simone, Holly, I, and our daughters Heather and Laurel evacuated to the hotel bar, which we thought would be stronger and safer. There we learned the New Zealander manager hadn't been seen since the morning, and nobody was in charge of the hotel. The scheduled dinner celebrating New Zealand's national holiday, Waitangi Day, had for some reason been cancelled. The true state of the bar's sturdiness was revealed when a door blew in on me, with Laurel on my lap. I managed to raise my right arm quickly enough so that the door hit my forearm rather than Laurel's head. A ni-Vanuatu staff member ushered us into a hotel room, but it was obvious it was flimsier than the bar. Out the window, we could see the roots of a large tree upwind from the room were lifting the ground on its opposite side. That room didn't seem a good place to shelter.

An Australian and I went back to what was left of Daniel and Simone's entrance to turn off the butane bottle, and our party returned to the Combs room. We put the girls to bed and sat in the living room watching the storm through the sliding glass doors until 2200, when the glass doors started to bulge inwards.

We grabbed the kids and all of us fled to the bathroom, which we later learned is the traditional refuge in these circumstances because of the strength of the high ratio of walls to floor area. Fortunately, I had a flashlight. From there, we could hear the glass doors shattering and glass shards blowing into the rooms we had just left. We later learned that standard cyclone preparation in Vanuatu included taping all windows with packing tape so if they broke they wouldn't explode into the house. None of this was done at the Solaise Hotel because the manager abandoned us in the morning, and most ni-Vanuatu staff do nothing that their boss hasn't told them to.

Between us and the kitchen was a wood frame wall, and it wasn't long until it was bowed in so much from the force of the wind coming in the now-missing sliding glass doors that Daniel and I had to shoulder the door to keep it closed. Then the bathroom ceiling started moving up and down, and we decided it was time to vacate.
There was a small high window to the outside walkway. Holly and Simone crawled through first, and then Daniel passed through Heather and Laurel while I kept the door shut. Last, I let the door spring open and followed everyone out. We all went down to the ground level, which was in the storm's lee. Now I noticed that the girls, wearing only diapers and underwear, were shivering. We needed better shelter.

I knocked on the nearest door, after a moment it opened a crack, and I slipped in. A window happened to break at this time, which was perhaps due to the door opening for me and releasing the room's internal air pressure. Unfortunately, my shorts caught in the door as it immediately slammed shut. Inside, there was some light, and I could see that the unit was occupied by two ni-Vanuatu female hotel

4

staff and a Whiteman. It soon became evident that the man was an Australian who had unsuccessfully attempted to alleviate his panic with alcohol. He started shouting at me, "YOU FUCKING ASSHOLE! WHAT THE FUCK DO YOU THINK YOU ARE DOING?" I was standing there unsuccessfully trying to get my pants loose from the door so I could defend myself in case he attacked, which he fortunately didn't. Finally, one of the women, for whom cyclones were normal, albeit inconvenient, weather, opened the door latch, and I escaped outside.

Holly had heard all this and unsuccessfully tried to open the door from the outside. After I got out, I told her I wasn't going to try another door. So, I shined my flashlight out over the parking lot and saw a white subcompact. I went over to it, but the doors were locked. I shined my light further and saw another small white car. Not only were its doors unlocked, the keys were in its ignition. So, I brought everyone over, and we piled in; Daniel behind the wheel, me in the front passenger seat with Laurel on my lap, and Simone, Holly, and Heather in the back.

A few occurrences that night remain in my memory. As cyclones move along, the wind at any one spot changes direction. Daniel started the car and moved us a few times to be as far as possible from the nearest upwind tree threatening to fall on us. At one point, I got out to take a leak keeping in mind the adage against "pissing against the wind". Later I awoke from a doze when someone said, "Here it comes!", and the roof of the unit to the right of ours flew over us and landed on the first car I'd tried to get us into. Sometimes luck runs your way.

During the worst of the storm, I saw a light flashing at us from the unit under Daniel and Simone's. Aha! Some kind soul was offering us shelter! Once again, I ventured into the storm over to the unit's window. I didn't get the full story from him until a few years later, but Alan McPhail later told me he had seen our red brake lights as we manoeuvered away from a tree, and thought we had come to rescue his family! At the time, though, he explained that water was coming through their ceiling in every room, and the only dry spot he could find for himself, his wife Jackie, and their nine-month-old child, Andrew, was the shower. He invited us to join them, but I told him I didn't think six more of us would fit in that shower and returned to the car.
By 0300, Cyclone Uma had moved away, and the wind died down. A British physician in the undamaged bottom unit next to my friend the drunk Aussie— oh, why hadn't I knocked on her door? —invited us in, and we got a few hours' sleep. At dawn, she fed us before leaving for the hospital to see if she was needed.
OK. Here I was with my wife and two toddlers in a strange town where 90% of the buildings had been destroyed or damaged, and where I knew nobody. There was no water available except in our toilet tank. Still no sign of the hotel manager, whose neighbour later told me had spent the afternoon after Uma drinking beer in his back yard.

Two Years on Malekula

What was I going to do?

Then, a young British man came along and said he was sightseeing because he'd heard the Solaise Hotel had been destroyed. I explained our situation, and he gave us directions to the apartment across town of another CUSO, Heather McDermott. We wandered over there through downtown streets blocked with debris, with a few business people cleaning up. I think this was when I first heard the mournful plaint of the urban Vanuatu expatriate, "You should have been here before independence." Fortunately, all of these whingers seemed to leave after Uma, as I stopped hearing this wail after a year or so.

Heather McDermott's high-rise apartment was unscathed, and she was unaware any serious damage had occurred elsewhere. She had heard that the Intercontinental Hotel a short distance out of town was still open, so off we went to find transport. Out on the street, I learned every taxi was full of the driver's family gawking at all the damage, in the usual way of things after a cyclone. An expat lady sweeping up glass in front of her shop told us that she had seen Captain Klaus in a jeep with empty seats, and he had headed behind the Hotel Rossi across the street. Off we went to find Klaus, and there he was—pissing against a wall. He graciously gave us a ride to the Intercontinental. Captain Klaus was a local character, a Swede well over 190cm tall and of substantial girth. He ran a local shipping office; more of him later. I had a beer with him when we spent a few days in Vila in 2009, and he had no recollection of these events.

At the hotel, I replayed the scene in the old American Express commercial, walking up to the front desk in torn shorts and T-shirt wearing thongs. I pulled out my first credit card, which I had brought for this sort of eventuality, and they took me in. The hotel had power from a generator and trucked-in water running through their pipes. Life was good, although there was an elderly Australian in the lobby complaining that the bar was closed. What was it with these Australians and their drink? I eventually learned to appreciate their greater consumption and propensity to party than my more moderate Canadian countrymen.

The hotel lent me a truck, and I retrieved all our luggage from the Solaise. It was soaked, except a partial letter I left on top of the fridge, which was for some reason untouched by the storm. We spread everything out over our room and broke the hotel rule prohibiting outside clotheslines, hanging our wet clothing out there on the verge of the golf course.

Cyclone Uma broke the Vanuatu weather service's anemometer early on, but it was estimated that the wind speed had been 270kph, making Uma a Category 5 cyclone (There is no Category 6), like Katrina that hit New Orleans in 2005. Our FSO's excuse for leaving us high and dry (not) was that "Nobody expected it to be so bad." Only one person was killed in Vila, a man hit by flying corrugated roofing iron, but about 50 people were lost in two ships that inexplicably (to me) went out to sea just prior to the storm.

Two Years on Malekula

The Hotel Solaise the morning after Cyclone Uma. The right-most upper window is the one we left our unit from, and the car is the one in which we spent the night.
Photo by Alan McPhail, used by permission.

My $35 Chinese guitar, selected as the only one with an un-warped neck in various Chinese stores in Santo. It had a wide neck like a folk guitar, so I replaced the steel strings with nylon ones I'd brought from Canada. Then I cut down the bridge to "lower the action", as I'm told those who know what they're doing call it. I did the same two-and-a-half years later with a similar instrument I bought when, after an interlude traveling and in Canada, we moved to Port Vila.

Two Years on Malekula

Another CUSO heard of our arrival and came each day to give us Bislama lessons. It had been planned for us to visit a fellow CUSO Regional Development Planner on Tanna Island for a week in order to learn the ropes of my new position. Unfortunately, he was busy organizing long-term food relief on Tanna Island, which besides also being hit quite hard by Uma had poor food crops due to an abnormal amount of dust emitted from the Yasur Volcano over the past few months. So, after a week in Vila, we flew up to Luganville for a few days, where we bought our cooking utensils and other necessities, including a cheap Chinese guitar, before finally flying to our ultimate destination, Lakatoro.

Once there, I wrote a letter to the Solaise Hotel owner and father of the manager, asking what he thought of a hotel manager who left his clients without assistance before and during a cyclone. He replied with a short and abusive letter. The CUSO FSO expressed her annoyance to me for writing him, and caved to his demand that CUSO pay for the nights after the cyclone that CUSO had reserved for us, but we hadn't used—because the hotel had been destroyed! a) Our FSO had been on the job too long, and it was time for her to move on, and b) At the time, businessmen who couldn't make it elsewhere drifted to Vanuatu where there was only room for one of each business, and despite any incompetence they could exist without competition.

For what it's worth, the Solaise owner rebuilt the hotel bigger and grander. Then, reportedly because this had been financed through insurance fraud, he lost ownership. Because he had given up his New Zealand citizenship to obtain that of Vanuatu, perhaps to avoid income taxes in his home country, he was stuck in Vanuatu. The last time I saw him, several years later, he was driving one of Vila's many minibuses around town. Karma.

Seven years later, in Kelowna, British Columbia, Canada, I picked up a reference book in a used bookstore. Leafing through it, I came upon the section on Vanuatu. I was surprised that when I read the words "Cyclone Uma", the hairs on the back of my head spontaneously stood up. Mild Post Traumatic Stress Disorder, I suppose.

PART 2 — About Vanuatu

Vanuatu's History and Condominium Legacy

The archipelago that would become Vanuatu was first populated about 3,300 years ago by Lapita Culture people originating in Taiwan, who later mixed with Papuan people from Papua New Guinea. In the south, there was some Polynesian influence from the east or New Zealand. Unlike the Polynesians and Micronesians who undertook regular epic sea voyages of exploration and colonization, the Melanesians remained primarily island-bound once they expanded south to New Caledonia and east to Fiji. This is evidenced by Melanesian languages being very localized geographically, often village-by-village in Vanuatu, whereas due to regular contact across the Pacific, Polynesian languages are similar throughout Polynesia.

European explorers such as Pedro Fernandez de Queirós in 1606 from Spain, Louis Antoine Bougainville from France in 1772 and James Cook from England in 1776 briefly visited, with Cook naming the islands The New Hebrides.

Significant contact, though, did not occur until the early 19th century, when sandalwood and sea slugs, the former for incense and the latter as an aphrodisiac, were harvested for the lucrative Chinese market. Whalers visited and used Aneityum Island, for one, as a base. Permission from the landowners and village chiefs had to be obtained for these resource extractions. Melanesians were recruited as labour and sailors, and fatal conflicts occurred. European diseases such as influenza, smallpox, and gonorrhea were introduced and began to ravage the population, culminating in a nadir of 35,000 prior to WW II before recovering to about 120,000 when we lived there and about double that now. Estimates of the New Hebrides pre-contact population range up to two million when a politician is attempting to justify extracting more aid from foreign donors; an anthropologist I respect estimates 600,000. The true number is not known; a demographer I worked with told me that someone like Captain Cook would sail up to a place and count everyone. Then he'd sail down the coast and count again. Of course, everyone at the first place would have in the meantime run down to the second place to once again witness these strange men in their huge boat, so a lot of double-counting took place.

Two Years on Malekula

Catholic, and then Protestant, missionaries started appearing in mid-century to compete for souls and speed their own passage to heaven. A few of them were killed and eaten for their troubles, including three Canadians on Erromango Island—George Nicol Gordon and his wife, Ellen Catherine Powell on 20 May, 1861, and Gordon's brother, James Douglas on 7 March, 1872. Two English missionaries, John Williams and James Harris, were also martyred in November, 1839. In November, 2009, a traditional reconciliation ceremony was held on Erromango between the descendants of these two English dinees and the diners. The Erromangans hoped this would stop a run of bad fortune they had been suffering.

Part of this religious rivalry manifested itself in efforts by both sides to get their home nations of France or England to declare sovereignty over the New Hebrides and remove their religious competitors.

From a November 20, 1987 letter home:

> I haven't met any missionaries here; they all came and did their damage long ago. A couple of weeks ago, I attended a ceremony marking the 60th Anniversary of the landing of the first missionary on Malekula. He was a Scottish Presbyterian from the famed London Missionary Society. I may have told you my standard line on the subject, which I haven't tested on a local audience: "Everyone would be better off if they had eaten a few more Missionaries on the beach." I have heard that there is some New Zealander on a small island off Lakatoro learning the local language so he can translate the Bible. Seeing as how, depending on whom you listen to, there are 35 or 54 separate and distinct languages on Malekula alone (population approximately 17,000) and about 110 languages in Vanuatu (world's highest number per capita), you'd think he could think of a more profitable use of his time.

I shouldn't have been so hard on him. In actual fact, the Summer Institute of Linguistics' work does have the side effect of preserving many of these languages.

Meanwhile, towards the end of the 19th century sugar planters, mainly from Queensland, began recruiting labour from Melanesia, including the New Hebrides. This is now popularly seen as a slave trade, in which New Hebrideans were kidnapped and sent to Queensland where many labourers died in horrible conditions. I'm not so sure of this, although some kidnapping probably did take place. Motives for New Hebrideans to sign on included their best chance to obtain Western goods, escape from chiefly authority, and avoid the consequences of a kastom crime. According to the account of one of the traders, William T. Wawn[1], at each village where he recruited he had to negotiate with the chief and

---

[1] "The South Sea Islanders and the Queensland Labour Trade", Edited by Peter Corris, 1973. The original copyright date of the book is 1893, and part of its dedication is "To the SUGAR PLANTERS OF QUEENSLAND… and those BOLD PIONEERS… who have done more towards the PRACTICAL CIVILIZATION of the CANNIBAL AND THE SAVAGE than all the Well-intentioned but Narrow-Minded Enthusiasts of the SOUTHERN PACIFIC…".

give him a musket to compensate him for the loss of young warriors. Some recruits would sneak onto the ship as it left. Also, many labourers returned for another period of indenture. And, although many New Hebrideans no doubt died during their contracts, the death rate on the islands was also high.

The Protestant missionaries were at the forefront of the anti-labour trade movement. They sent accounts of trader and sugar planter misdeeds back to Great Britain in order to influence public and political opinion, having several motives. They wanted Great Britain to colonize the New Hebrides and expel the French Catholic priests competing with them. Also, they detested the returned labourers, who had experienced first-hand the reality of the Whiteman's world and knew that few Whitemen behaved as the missionaries told villagers they should. The returned labourers told their fellow villagers about what they had learned and undermined the missionaries' authority, which had been absolute in some areas.

By 1887, the French and British had decided that the New Hebrides were not worth fighting over and decided to share them. First they negotiated a Joint Naval Commission to administer the New Hebrides, which eventually morphed into a formal Condominium Protocol in 1914, ratified by both powers in 1922. This resulted in longstanding rivalries and confusion that had both comic and tragic consequences for the Melanesian people of the New Hebrides, extending past 1980's independence to ni-Vanuatu of the present.

British and French Commissioners set up office in Port Vila, with a Spanish judge who did not speak either language to resolve disputes. Every government service was duplicated, with French and English police departments, prisons, hospitals, school systems, agriculture departments, and on and on. There was one set of laws for French expatriates, one for English, and none for New Hebrideans. Expatriates changed sides as it suited their legal positions. Both metropolitan governments competed for the hearts and minds of New Hebrideans with a flow of gifts and favours. Neighbouring villages chose one side or the other.

This mess continued officially until independence in 1980 and in reality until today. Just before independence was scheduled to take place, a civil war broke out. The rebels were supported tacitly by France and explicitly by the extremist libertarian Phoenix Foundation from the United States, who wanted to establish their own nation of Vemarana on Espiritu Santo. French and English troops were brought in, but their governments couldn't agree on military action. Finally the Vanuatu government-in-waiting asked in Papua New Guinean troops, who shot two people and restored order. During the insurrection government and civil property was destroyed, and on Malekula at least one Anglophone ni-Vanuatu woman died because a roadblock prevented her from reaching the hospital in the Francophone village of Norsup. When independence finally occurred the French authorities, in the fit of pique common to their departure from other colonies, destroyed all their land tenure records that recorded from which New

Hebrideans Frenchmen had obtained land parcels. This contributed to land ownership confusion which reigns until today, blocking much economic development and causing social chaos.

Vanuatu continues to be greatly divided by language and religion, with the addition of a few more sects such as Seventh Day Adventists, evangelical, Baha'i, and Latter-day Saints. When we lived in Vanuatu, political parties were very much divided into Francophone and Anglophone. Two school systems, French and English, remained; we chose French for our girls so they would learn a second Western language.

When I later worked for the NPSO, I visited many islands throughout the archipelago and met with people to ask what they wanted from development. An older man in Tanna told me that he just wanted the French to return.

From an October 30, 1987 letter home:

> I see a lot of people here in Vanuatu who have dumped their traditional cultures because someone told them they were incompatible with Christianity. A lot of these people have decided, after two generations, that custom can coexist with the Church, and they want their cultures back. It's sad, but they can't find their cultures. The thread was broken when their grandparents died, so now they are attempting to put back together some semblance of their real selves. Their churches are suffering a lot of guilt over killing these cultures. Some ni-Vanuatu are still trying to stamp out tradition, and what are they? Melanesians trying to copy some Whiteman. It's pitiful. They haven't a chance of becoming mental Whitemen—they haven't got anything like all the generations of the same cultural knowledge I have in my head. It's just the same if I were to try to live like a ni-Vanuatu: believe it when I tell you there is no way you or I will ever completely understand the ni-Vanuatu point of view. As far as you or I are concerned, some of the decisions they think are perfectly logical might as well come from outer space.
> The Italian priest I met at Lolopoipoi, Ambae is pretty wise. His church is full of symbols from the locals' custom beliefs. Doesn't bother him a bit; he was proud to point them all out to me and explain the beliefs behind them.

Bislama, Vanuatu's National Language

When we lived there Vanuatu had about 110 languages for its 120,000 inhabitants, the world's highest concentration of languages. Scores more must have been lost during the New Hebrides' depopulation by introduced Western diseases, when many entire villages, with their distinct languages and cultures, were exterminated. Historically most villages had very limited contact with each other, and most developed their own languages. Contact with the West brought trade, Christianization, and colonization, forcing the villages to communicate with each other. Throughout much of Melanesia (from Papua New Guinea through the Solomon Islands to Vanuatu) a more-or-less common pidgin developed. Vanuatu's variant of this pidgin is called Bislama.

Melanesian Pidgin got its start in the 19th century when Europeans harvested sandalwood and sea cucumbers (this reputed aphrodisiac, named "bicho do mar" in Portuguese, became "bêche-de-mer" in French and then "Bislama") for trade with China. (The word "pidgin" is Chinese Pidgin for "business".) The development of Melanesian Pidgin accelerated in the late 1800's when Melanesians were recruited as labourers for Queensland's sugarcane plantations. Men with mutually unintelligible village languages found themselves living and working together, as well as needing to communicate with their English-speaking supervisors. Melanesian Pidgin developed out of necessity, and returning labourers brought their new language back to Vanuatu. There, Bislama's development continued when men began working on European-owned plantations in the early 1900's, when they were recruited to work on the large American bases during WW II, and when the urban centres of Port Vila and Luganville began growing in the 1960's.

Bislama is a mixture of English, French, and Melanesian words set to a Melanesian syntax. Words tend to represent general concepts, rather than specific things. For example, the noun "han" means "upper extremity", as in "arm" (anywhere from fingertip to shoulder), "sleeve", "tree branch", etc. The verb "harem" means "sense", as in "hear", "feel", "smell", or "taste". (We still tease our younger daughter about the time, mixing up her languages, she poked her mother and asked, "Can you hear this?" and the time she wailed that "A hornet ate me!") Concepts expressed in conversation can be a bit vague and are usually expressed several different ways, with examples given and gestures made. Misunderstandings are not unusual. Spelling is phonetic and fluid, especially since several consonant sounds are considered equivalent; for example, "k" and "g", or "b" and "p".

Many newly-arrived expatriates, or expatriates whose experience with ni-Vanuatu does not extend far beyond giving orders to a housegirl, think Bislama is simply a form of baby-talk which can be mastered without effort, and understanding of which can be enhanced by raising one's voice. This is not true, as Bislama is a language in its own right.

On my first day of work with the Malekula Local Government Council, my boss Keith Mala gathered his staff and told us that I was allowed three days of speaking English, after which I was to be communicated with in Bislama only. Despite my week of Bislama tutelage in the aftermath of Cyclone Uma after my arrival in Port Vila, I found that I really only started to understand people face-to-face after three weeks, and over the telephone (no facial or body-language clues) after three months. When I left Malekula after two years, I was just gaining an idiomatic facility with the language.

Two Years on Malekula

Our children played with the neighbourhood kids for a few months, seemingly without a common language, until one day we noticed them chattering away in Bislama; Laurel came home and proudly announced, "Puss-kat" — that's Bis-a-lama, you know!"[1]

By the time we left they spoke English only with us, and they continued to bicker in Bislama while we toured Australia on the way home until they noticed that they were the only people on the continent speaking it and stopped.

We all continue to attract each other's attention in the ni-Vanuatu way by hissing, though. Even in a noisy crowded Canadian situation it is a unique sound and works.

Urban ni-Vanuatu, especially those who often communicate with a mass audience, often take shortcuts and use English or French phrases to substitute for several Bislama sentences, a language variant known as "politician's Bislama".

A common language was essential for Vanuatu's transformation from a collection of villages to a nation. As a homegrown lingua franca, Bislama is one of Vanuatu's few unifying forces, as well as a source of national pride.

Here is a familiar Christmas quote in Bislama:

"Tufala i stap yet long Betlehem, nao i kam kasem stret taem blong Meri i bonem pikinini. Nao hem i bonem fasbon pikinini blong hem we hem i boe. Hem i kavremapgud long kaliko, nao i putum hem i slip long wan bokis we oltaim ol man oli stap putum gras long hem, blong ol anamol oli kakae. Tufala i mekem olsem, from we long hotel, i no gat ples blong tufala i stap."—Luk 2:6-7.

The style of Bislama in this Bible passage is relatively simple (see the long passage that means "manger"), because most of the intended audience is rural, with less exposure to Bislama (and Western concepts such as cutting fodder to feed livestock) than residents of town, where the language continues to develop. (To be fair, how many modern Western non-horsemen would know what a "manger" was if not for these famous verses?) A loose literal translation is:

"The two of them were in Bethlehem, now it came the exact time for Mary she births child. Now him he born firstborn of her that him he boy. She she cover up (him) good in cloth, now she put him he lay in one box where always all men they are putting grass in him, for all animals they eat (it). The two of them they made same, because at hotel, it no got place for the two of them to stay."—Luke 2:6-7

---

[1] Which led to more teasing, and a long-standing family tradition of, whenever speaking a non-English phrase, exclaiming, "That's [whatever language], you know!" You had to be tough to survive the Combs/Morgan household.

Two Years on Malekula

Using Bislama when others didn't expect it.

Years later, in Kelowna, I was in a Video Shop[1] where I heard two white guys conversing in South Pacific pidgin. I asked them, "Wea yu tufala lanem toktok ia?" (Where did you two learn that language?). After a double take they told me they were University of British Columbia anthropologists who had spent six months in Papua New Guinea. Well, so much for their secret language.

Another time Holly and I spent 24 hours in the Brisbane airport waiting for a flight to Port Vila. A group of young ni-Vanuatu men spent much of the time storianing—they didn't say anything derogatory about us. When we got to Vila I spoke to the immigration officers in Bislama. "Yu save tok Bislama?!" (You can speak Bislama?!) one asked. I explained we'd lived in Lakatoro for two years and a further three years in Vila.

When we moved to Vila in '89, ni-Vanuatu I met early on were also very surprised that a waetman could speak Bislama.

And, when we spoke our common language, Bislama, with a French-Canadian CUSO couple, ni-Vanuatu present were amused.

Vanuatu and World War II

Because the Japanese never invaded Vanuatu aside from the odd uncontested reconnaissance landing from submarines, and combat was limited to a small number of Japanese bombing missions and a few shells from their submarines, not many people know the New Hebrides was the site of the United States' largest South Pacific Base. It was from here that the Solomons campaign was launched and supported. The effects on Vanuatu of the American occupation were massive and lasting.

In 1940, when Germany invaded France, most expatriates in the New Hebrides were French. Like other overseas French they faced the choice of pledging their loyalty to the Nazi Germany-backed Vichy regime of Marshal Petain in the south of France, or to General De Gaulle's London-based Free French. French Indochina went with the Vichy regime, with business proceeding as usual under its Japanese conquerors. There is a plaque in Port Vila's Catholic Cathedral commemorating the date on which the French of Vanuatu decided to side with De Gaulle; the first French colony to do so. They did not, however, get along especially well with the American military—more on this at the end of this chapter.

---

[1] For any youngsters reading this, before we old folk had Netflix and you learned how to steal movies from the Internet, there were these "video shops" where we would rent movies on tape or DVD.

Two Years on Malekula

In May, 1942, the Americans showed up seemingly from nowhere, massively overwhelmed everything for four years, and suddenly left. Things were never again the same though. Besides the infrastructure left behind, once again the ni-Vanuatu universe had changed. They had witnessed a relationship between white and black people that was markedly different from their relationship with the British and French colonialists, even though the American military was segregated with black troops restricted to construction and stevedore work. For example, ni-Vanuatu saw black and white people eating in common mess halls, and even ate there themselves. Eating together is an expression of social bonding between equals in Vanuatu, and was rare between the races before the war. As well, black Americans drove trucks, a responsible activity that had always been denied ni-Vanuatu. Trains of thought about how inter-racial relationships could change germinated, culminating in Independence thirty-five years after WWII in 1980.

The New Hebridean men who served with the American forces were fiercely proud of their association with that powerful nation and their contribution during its time of need. They contributed not only their labour, but their local knowledge and, as one narrator relates, kastom magic powers.[1] I met one such man on Malekula, and he brought out and showed me his war memento—the rusty old metal parts of an American rifle that he had found in the bush and hand-carved a stock for.

Vanuatu's colonial planters, mostly French, also had their world disrupted by the American occupation. Their New Hebridean labourers became accustomed to higher wages. They learned new ways by mixing with American troops and learning that the black Americans, although the victims of systemic discrimination, had privileges and responsibilities that were being denied to New Hebrideans.

After V-J Day the Americans wound down their activities and went home, leaving what are now the airports at Port Vila and Luganville as well as several fighter strips that are no longer used. The perforated planking that covered these airstrips became fencing all over Vanuatu. The tailgate of an old Land Cruiser I bought was made of aluminum from an abandoned bomber. They also left roads—the main drag in Luganville is wide enough for two Sherman tanks to pass each other—and many Quonset huts that were repurposed for decades. The ruins of the "Dancing Bear Club", with red silhouettes of its namesakes painted on its white outer walls, remained on that street. I explored it once; its warren of small rooms with single iron bedframes attested to its former role as a bordello. When visiting Luganville we often saw its former Madam, always in a black dress, pedaling her bike around town. Her girls, however, had been replaced with several goats kept in the courtyard.

---

[1] See my translation of Stelio Giovanni's memories of WW II at:
http://ruralvanuatu.net/wol_stel.html.

Perhaps the remains of a Jeep at Million Dollar Point.

Rather than haul all of their trucks and equipment back to the United States, the Americans offered to sell it to the French Planters. They refused, shrewdly planning to just take it for free after the Americans left. The Americans, not wanting to play along with this game, built a ramp into the ocean east of Luganville and drove all of that equipment into the sea at what is now know by Whitemen as "Million Dollar Point" and by ni-Vanuatu as "Poin Doti", or "Garbage Point". Enterprising Whitemen then salvaged and sold as much as they could from the site.

Today, it is a popular snorkeling and SCUBA diving location. Personally, I didn't find it all that interesting—just a bunch of junk encrusted with sea growth.

Another popular dive site left from the war is the wreck of the "SS President Coolidge". The Coolidge was a luxury liner that plied the US-Orient route for the Dollar and then President lines during the thirties; General Douglas MacArthur met his wife on board. In '42 it was leased by the US military, converted to a troop ship, and loaded with 5,000 soldiers and their equipment en route to the Solomons campaign. Unfortunately, the US military did not tell the ship's civilian captain where the safe passage through the minefield protecting the Luganville harbor was, and the Coolidge struck two mines. The captain ran her up on shore and all aboard, save one sailor, Fireman Robert Reid, killed in the initial explosions and one soldier, Artillery Captain Elwood J. Euart, were saved. Captain Euart heroically returned into the ship and helped three soldiers evacuate up a rope before going down with the ship; his remains were not recovered until 2015. During the ensuing enquiry Admiral Nimitz tried to pin the blame on the Coolidge's civilian Captain Henry Nelson, but a U.S. Navy Military Commission exonerated him.

"The Lady" with my diving partner whose bubbles go magically horizontal. Shortly after this photo was taken, as I wrote to Peter Stone, the author of a book about the Coolidge: "I confirmed down there by grope that her nipples were exposed. Sick, I know, but I just had to do it. Blame the nitrogen. " Peter asserted that her nipples are not exposed, and it was nitrogen narcosis at 45m that gave me that impression. Dang.

Ninety minutes after it was grounded the ship fell over on its port side and slid backwards down the reef with its bow resting at about 20 metres depth. During the hasty evacuation all of the men's equipment was abandoned, with the wreck later becoming a popular dive site, protected by the Australian Alan Power—one of the salvors, and the primary dive operator on the site for decades.

Two Years on Malekula

Remaining from her liner days were a fancy chandelier, a fountain, a swimming pool ringed with gold tiles, and "The Lady"[1] —a statue of an Elizabethan gentlewoman with a unicorn. I eventually saw all of these things, but as I described my first dives on the Coolidge with ex-CUSO Hamish Inksetter:

Helmet, rifle, and other equipment on the SS President Coolidge wreck.

January 15, 1988:

Largely because the dives were tailored to inexperienced me, we never went right into the lower parts of the ship, and some of the interesting stuff will have to wait for future dives. There is a lot to see everywhere, though. On the Promenade Deck, there are helmets, boots, rifles, side arms, binoculars, etc. right where they were dropped. In the forward hold, there is a jumble of tanks, jeeps, and trucks. Holes have been cut into the upward starboard side for salvage, and you can look at the electric motors that powered it (she was steam turbine-electric drive). They have set up little stashes of morphine ampoules and rifle ammunition for you to look at. On the sea bed near the bow, there are typewriters and bunches of anti-tank shells. The bridge is full of electric fans, and there are still light bulbs floating up at the end of their wires; you would think that the pressure would crush them. I got a little nervous about handling all that live ammunition, but survived. I only went inside once, through the dining room (shreds of tacky linoleum on the floor, even though it was a luxury liner— maybe they took up the carpets for the troops), to the door of the galley. Not all that exciting, but you sure hope your equipment works well.

---

[1] Pg 182, "The Lady and the President—The Life and Loss of the S.S. President Coolidge". 1999, ISBN 0 9586657 2 9.

Even without the artefacts, there is a lot of fish life around. Lots of big Lion Fish, so you don't want to grope around too much. Turtles like to wedge themselves under pieces of junk and sleep, but they swim away when you approach. A large grouper showed up the first day after an absence of 8 months and shadowed us a lot during the week. A big one-eyed moray eel lives down near the engine room (gee, what with the

Hamish feeds Boris.

Divemaster Alan Power tickles Greenie at the 10-ft. decompression stop.

morphine, this was just like the movie "The Deep", but no Jacqueline Bisset in a transparent wet T-shirt), and a green one at the 10-ft. decompression stop. They leave one-eye alone, but Hamish liked to pet the green moray and pinch his skin. He would snuggle up like a cat. I tried to pet that eel, but he wouldn't let me. One-Eye was about as thick as a thigh and Greenie a bit smaller.

Vanuatu Politics Following Independence

In my view, Vanuatu is more a geographic group of villages than a nation. Common loyalties and priorities were expressed by one Member of Parliament as he changed parties: "The governing party has done nothing for me, my family, or my village".

Parliamentarians glory in looking for minute, often misinterpreted, rules to use to each other's disadvantage. For example, Vanuatu may be the only place in the world where, thanks to a compliant British Chief Magistrate, 50% is a majority.

Vanuatu is governed by a President with limited powers and a single-chamber parliament with a Prime Minister as the head of the governing party.

After independence, the government was formed by the Anglophone Vanua'aku Pati with Father Walter Lini, an Anglican priest with church dispensation to enter politics, as the Prime Minister. The opposition was made up of Francophone parties. This arrangement provided stability until soon after we arrived in early 1987, when Father Lini suffered a debilitating stroke. Even so, he managed to keep things in line until about 1990.

My theory is that after ten years of independence, ni-Vanuatu started to figure out that being released from the yoke of colonization wasn't going to provide them with the power and material wealth they had thought the colonial masters had been denying them. In fact, they and the country were slipping back to a level that was sustainable without English and French support. The Vanua'aku Pati began to fragment, with the ailing Father Lini starting to act like a third-world rather than developed-country politician. Lini's cabinet ministers started jostling for power, and stable government ended.

In the early '90s, a group of Francophone parties gained power, and since then Vanuatu has been governed by a succession of short-lived coalitions. Politicians change sides depending on what they have been promised by whomever is on the other side of the chamber.

Corruption started to increase—if a politician living in relative wealth in the capital loses his position, he is instantly transformed into a villager wearing tattered shorts and T-shirt and living in a bamboo hut. There is a strong incentive to do anything to stay in power while building a nest egg to maintain an urban standard of living if one should lose one's position.

Government has been in chaos since then to the present; fortunately whatever happens in the capital, Port Vila, has little influence on the outer islands where most of the population lives in a largely-subsistence economy.

Religion in Vanuatu

Vanuatu's true universal religion is animism. What Westerners consider inanimate objects have similar motives to humans and supernatural means of acting on their motives. So, after a boulder moved during a cyclone, it was said to be a male boulder that had shifted to be nearer to a female boulder that had moved earlier. An outboard motor that had fallen overboard and been retrieved was more likely to fall off again now that it had learned to escape. It was dangerous to wear the colour red when crossing Malekula's Pankumu river because the river didn't like that colour. Men with supernatural powers could use certain leaves or stones for good or evil purposes.

"Pagan" magic stones and potions collected by an Evangelist during
a Revival Meeting on Paama Island. My guess is that everyone went
home and made more.

Two Years on Malekula

One of my ni-Vanuatu co-workers once told me that there were two reasons ni-Vanuatu had accepted Christianity so readily: 1. It was the key to obtaining material goods, and 2. Christian spirits would protect them from the evil spirits used by enemies to harm them. (There are exceptions, as I relate in Viene's Vao shark attack explanation in "Stories of Sharks" below.) I add a third: The multitude of Christian denominations and sects allows every village to choose one that is different from that of their rival neighbours. If part of a village converted to a new denomination, that was a symptom and cause of a great schism with far-reaching social and political consequences.

Western Religion in Vanuatu is serious business. It is regulated by the Vanuatu Christian Council, which like everything else in the country was run by the ruling Vanua'aku Pati. In theory, only churches that were members of the VCC were allowed in the country; these were the Catholic, Church of Melanesia

The Seventh Day Adventist Church certainly got their adherents to, so to speak, toe the line. This is a sight I never thought I'd see—ni-Vanuatu villagers dressed identically and doing close-order drill to the beat of a drum. My boss wouldn't be caught dead at an occasion held by any church but his own, so I was assigned to represent the LGC at these types of ceremonies.

(Anglican), Presbyterian, Apostolic Church, and Churches of Christ, with associate members Seventh Day Adventist and Assemblies of God. The Seventh Day Adventist Church in particular, although not a full VCC member, had many members and dominated many villages in Vanuatu. The Holiness Fellowship, an evangelical sect, was also quite active. There was also a smattering of Baha'i and Latter-day Saints adherents. One day an expatriate Jehovah's Witness lady knocked on our door in Port Vila; not the way I would spend my tropical vacation.

Pretty well everyone belonged to one Christian church or another, although there were a few "kastom" villages here and there that nominally adhered to their pre-contact beliefs. Although, perhaps it would be more accurate to say that the entire country except these kastom villages nominally adhered to Christianity.

Vao Mainland Catholic Chapel with slit drums.

From a 23 June, 1988 letter to a sister toying with the idea of becoming a foreign missionary:

You've mentioned missionary work in your last couple of letters, so I'll just offer a few comments based on my experiences and observations here. Everyone here is into some variety of Christianity in a big way, but it's a pretty thin veneer. I mean, they all pray loud and long at the drop of a hat and go to church every Sunday, but I can't think of one instance of "love your neighbour" or "turn the other cheek". Everyone believes all the old custom beliefs more than the Christian ones.

All of the clichés about missionaries on power trips making everyone feel guilty are really true. Ni-Vanuatu definitely wear clothes now—won't even take them off to bathe or shower—I kid you not! The missionaries really laid a big guilt trip on them about previously eating each other. It is still in a religious tract we were given a couple of weeks ago. A couple of times, I've asked people if they really think the Whiteman's religion is appropriate for them and got the same answer: "But, we used to eat each other, you know." Actually, they all only joined up because the missionaries were white and had lots of material goods—they thought the new magic would make them rich, too. This mentality still applies to development. In general, everyone is baffled that, without working (as white people apparently don't—ni-Vanuatu have no idea that we work in factories to produce things), they don't just get rich (i.e. accumulate lots of "cargo" or material goods), too.

The worst is, they all use religion as another excuse for dividing communities and hating each other. When a community splits over an issue, one half goes looking for a new denomination. You can imagine what happens when someone from a different denomination shows up in an area and makes a few converts. This is happening right here in Lakatoro, where my boss's church, a charismatic denomination, is raiding local churches. Open warfare is barely beneath the surface. Maybe our Treasurer has it right—he's chucked them all and joined the Bahai faith. People like to hedge their bets, though. Chief Virhambat, the last Big Nambas living the custom way, died of blood poisoning a few months ago—why did I bother hauling up a nurse, penicillin, and soap to him four months ago, when he had an infected knee? He did a John Wayne and had a priest come up and baptize him at the last minute.

Chief Virhambat of Amok Village, north Malekula, four months before his death in April, 1988. He was the last of the Big Nambas people living the custom lifestyle. Note the leaf over the recovering infection on his left leg. He always charged for photos, but let me take this one for free because I had brought up thatch roofing materials and medical care to him. This wife was one of six.

Two Years on Malekula

There is maybe one worse thing about the religious scene here. All ni-Vanuatu are really into American televangelists like Jimmy Swaggart and Oral Roberts. They buy all kinds of videos and song cassettes, and I fear they also send money to those bloodsuckers. It is pitiful to see a bunch of barefoot, dirt-poor ni-Vanuatu huddled around a TV watching a video of a guy with a $1,000 suit and styled hair shouting at an auditorium of expensively dressed white Americans in a posh TV studio. I mean, big band playing in the background and US football stars being announced as the special guests (I saw this one last Sunday night, as I passed by the Lakatoro chapel). Most of these people don't even understand English well enough to understand what is being said.

When sacks of sea mail come in, they are 90% "The Plain Truth" magazines, which everyone subscribes to because it is free (thank goodness for that, anyway). It is the only reading material anyone gets here, except expats.

So, that's the background. Oh, I forgot. The reason there are so many denominations, and therefore so many unnecessary divisions, here is that European churches had a free-for-all here in the late 1800's-early 1900's, with every church staking out their territory as fast as they could. The first church that came to a village won all the souls there.

Anyway, if you go with an established mainstream church to an area where everyone is already a member, good luck and have a good time. I'll be blunt—the damage is already done. Missionaries who come to start new denominations, however well meaning, just end up causing divisions and hate to spread. People here just don't think like we do. They really fear and hate other people who are in any way different. Sadly (to us), they see no inconsistency in being Christian and hating their Christian cousins in another church.

I'm a real missionary-lover compared to some people here. You should hear the curator of the national museum and cultural centre in Vila (an Anglo/American) go on about them, even at public lectures. Basically, I believe each culture develops a religion that is right for it, but they don't work well in other cultures. They are always transferred in order to gain cultural, economic, and political power over the recipients.

From another letter:

Our friend Sister Judith, a New Zealand nun at the Walarano mission, was disgusted because the ni-Vanuatu priest was showing a video last month about a monk who predicted (hundreds of years ago) that the world would end in May 1988, in order to get people to convert quickly. She was saying this near the end of the month. I told her that maybe these things worked on the Julian calendar[1] so I guess we're safe now. This video, provided by the French Embassy, was the topic of lots of discussion around here.

When the first nuns from New Zealand came to Walarano, the community rejected them because their Priests, competing with English Anglicans and Presbyterians, had always told them that French was the only Christian language. A special letter had to be sent from the Vatican to advise that this was not true.

---

[1] I got this backwards; the old Julian Calendar, still used by Orthodox Christian Churches, is actually behind our Gregorian Calendar by thirteen days.

Two Years on Malekula

Elder Cernis of the South Malekula Presbyterian Church

One day, I noticed a flurry of activity in the LGC main office. The typist was typing away on Gestetner stencils, someone was hand-cranking the machine, and stacks of copied pages were spread about waiting to be collated. For those readers of a younger persuasion, in the Olden Days (which extended into the late 1980s in Lakatoro), we didn't have Xerox machines, and copies of documents such as school handouts were made on what were known as "mimeograph machines". There were a few types, but all of them required that each page be typed onto a special stencil, which was then fastened onto a drum in a machine. The drum was then rotated by hand or electric motor, picking up ink on the typed letters, and putting the ink on one page of paper per rotation. The Gestetner Company made one type of mimeograph, but most of our schoolwork was printed by the cheaper spirit printer process, which usually came out in light purple ink. The ink gave off a distinct odour, and every kindergarten kid quickly picked up a life-long habit of, as soon as the copies were distributed, holding them up to their nose and sniffing it.

A Xerox machine was sent to the LGC in 1988, but in the Vanuatu way was sent back to Port Vila to replace the toner when it ran out, rather than a toner cartridge just being sent to Lakatoro. On the way back to Lakatoro, the machine got flipped over a few times in transit, and the toner spilled all over its interior. The LGC went back to the Gestetner. Fason blong Vanuatu.

But, I digress. Back at the LGC office, I inquired as to what was going on, and was informed that the LGC was being paid to print the History of the Presbyterian Church in South Malekula, written in Bislama. So, with permission I appropriated a copy, which made very interesting reading.

The central character of this history was Elder Cernis. Cernis, whose birth was foretold by a woman sorcerer, was born early in the 20th century in a small village in the interior of southern Malekula. At age 12 he went with his father to work for a year on a plantation on Espiritu Santo, and upon his return he was mentored by English missionary Fred J. Paton (son of the well-known missionary John Paton of Tanna) for some time before receiving further religious instruction at the Church's Teachers' Training Institute on Tongoa Island during 1919-20. He then returned to south Malekula and was appointed by Paton as a Church Elder against the wishes of the local congregation, who did not want a "man bus" (rural bumpkin) as an Elder in their church.
One of Elder Cernis's major tasks was touring the interior of Malekula, visiting heathen villages and persuading their residents to come down to the coast where the missionaries were or to build churches in their villages. This could be somewhat risky if a village, such as Amok in the interior of northern Malekula, was not receptive to the new religion, but the Elder was quite successful over the years.

Two Years on Malekula

Elder Cernis performed various miraculous acts during this time, including:

- Killing a snake in a tree by pointing his bible at it.
- Causing his wife to die when she went, against his wishes, to a celebration and slept with another man. (Perhaps this one wasn't quite what Westerners would consider strictly "Christian".)
- Helping a villager by killing an unwanted mango tree that stubbornly wouldn't die, by placing his hand on it.
- Successfully warning a man not to take two wives in the heathen fashion, demonstrating his powers by causing a tree to die overnight.
- Sternly telling a male papaya tree near his house to start growing fruit instead of only flowers. It did. (When I told a multi-generational French plantation owner friend about this, he told me anyone could do this by pounding nails into the base of a male papaya tree. So, I tried it with a male tree next to my house by pushing my bushknife through its base twice at right angles—it worked.)
- When a Chinese copra buyer cheated villagers, successfully praying to cause the buyer's ship to run aground.
- When two men gave him poison, they died instead.
- When the Pankumu River was too deep to cross, speaking severely to the river while his companion prayed. A large stone appeared in the riverbed and made the river shallow enough for the two to wade across safely, the stone then disappearing. (Too bad I didn't have Elder Cernis along when a pickup I was driving started drifting sideways down the Pankumu River another time it was swollen. Fortunately, a bunch of young men from a truck behind me jumped out and pushed my truck to a shallower spot where the wheels found purchase.
- Most spectacularly, bringing a dead woman back to life by putting his tongue in her mouth and praying, as well as bringing two men killed by gunshot back to life by putting his finger in the bullet holes.
- In 1967, curing a man who had been ill for seven years despite trying traditional and Western medicine.
- Helping, by prayer, two men attain satisfactory results in land ownership disputes.

Elder Cernis died on 18 November, 1975 at an undetermined age; older ni-Vanuatu usually do not know in what year they were born.

Elder Cernis's recorded accomplishments may seem unlikely to Westerners, but I've always taken the position that if the missionaries told New Hebrideans about a man who walked on water, turned water into wine, and raised people from the dead, there isn't any reason the Melanesian Presbyterians of south Malekula shouldn't believe that one of their own had similar powers. And, there isn't any reason that ni-Vanuatu transcriptions of oral histories years after the principal character died, as did the biblical Gospels, shouldn't include Elder Cernis's accomplishments.

Papaya tree I changed from male to female; note fruit with longer stems than normal. Close-up of bushknife scars in inset.

Two Years on Malekula

Relations Between Westerners and ni-Vanuatu

Walarano Catholic Cathedral Centenary Celebration, 15 August, 1987. This is a re-enactment of villagers paddling the first Catholic missionary in a canoe.

From a July 3, 1988 letter to a friend who had worked in Central America:

> I recently read "Zen and the Art of Motorcycle Maintenance", which was heavy going at times, but said some of the things I've learned here about different people fitting the same information into completely different mental frameworks and people operating outside the framework of the surrounding population being classified as insane. I don't know how your Panama experience went, but now I really understand Kipling when he said, "East is East, and West is West, and never the twain shall meet."[1]

Europeans have very little common ground with Melanesians. We were a bit prepared for this, but another couple who came over in March told me a couple of weeks ago that they felt quite disappointed. They knew they were going to live in an area with very few Europeans, but figured that "people are people; some good, some bad", and they would make ni-Vanuatu friends. So far, like us, they have no contact outside of working hours. CUSO doesn't help matters by implying at orientation that people who don't assimilate socially are not quite racist jerks, but are not real volunteers.

---

[1] Mind you; they did meet later in the poem.

Two Years on Malekula

It's not quite fair, because CUSO's medical wing is more realistic and brings home people who have "gone bush" (i.e. started operating outside the Canadian mental framework).

It was very easy for male CUSOs to form liaisons with ni-Vanuatu women. The attraction was that, besides giving access to Western material riches, Whitemen usually didn't beat their women like ni-Vanuatu men did. These couplings could be hazardous though; one woman from Malekula gave three CUSO men (one married) from different islands gonorrhea. To quote Bill Clinton, "I did not have sexual relations with that woman." Or the one who, a few years after we left Malekula, named her son "Stankombs".

There was a woman who worked at the Lakatoro branch of the Credit Union who was friendly, and I asked her to dance a couple times at various public affairs. The next time I ran into her, she addressed me as "Sir" and wouldn't meet my eye. I strongly suspect that her boyfriend had given her the word, or worse.

One time at the Saturday Norsup market, we noticed a young woman dressed in Western fashion drive up in the passenger seat of a pickup. She came up to Holly and me and chatted about how she had just returned from working in Vila. The next week, she came in an island dress seated in the truck bed. She didn't speak to us again. Fason blong village social pressures.

Two Years on Malekula

Geological Phenomena
Sea Levels

Lately, rising sea levels from global warming melting the earth's icecaps have been covered extensively in the media. I don't doubt this is happening. What gets my goat is the misinformation about Vanuatu being one of the nations severely impacted by this. The Canadian Broadcasting Corporation broadcast a report on this in the 2000s, submitted by a woman who evidently never left the capital's island, Efate. She reported that a village on Vanuatu's northernmost Torres Islands was forced to move due to rising seas. Maybe it was, because some of Vanuatu's northern islands are low-lying, as opposed to most of its islands, which are volcanic mountains rising steeply from the sea. Nevertheless, Vanuatu villages get moved for all sorts of reasons, and she didn't go up there to determine exactly why this one was relocated. Then, she talked with a man on Efate's north coast who showed her some erosion at the mouth of a stream and claimed it was due to rising seas—I'd say it was much more likely to be caused by the yearly wet season or a recent cyclone. I emailed the correspondent: no response.

Vanuatu politicians and even ni-Vanuatu in general will always tell a visiting journalist that Vanuatu is suffering from some pressing issue that requires large injections of cash into the country. They also like to feel they are affected by the same issues as the rest of the world.

Here, in a letter, I wrote about what I later realized was why rising sea levels are unlikely to seriously affect Vanuatu—Vanuatu itself is rising!

August 10, 1988

We had a couple of Americans come through Monday, which is a rarity. I couldn't believe it when they opened their mouths and started speaking. They are geologists studying earthquakes and claim that, next to Japan, Vanuatu is the world's most geologically active area. They are measuring the rate at which the northern half of Malekula is rising.

Can you imagine the G-forces generated by our average rise of 3.5 millimetres per year? That strikes me as a pretty rapid rate, in geological terms, but get this: we go up in jerks, and the island went up 1 metre on 11 August, 1965! We've sunk back about 30 centimetres since. We'd heard all about this and been shown where the water line used to be in some places, but nobody here could tell us the precise year (nobody here knows his age, either). This uplift also screwed up the surface water drainage in spots.

These guys sample dead coral at the present and previous high water marks and date it by the amount of uranium left compared to that in new coral (it decays after being incorporated into the coral). The last previous uplift was in 1729. They also plan to measure our rate of drift towards New Caledonia (on the Australian plate) with a satellite navigation system. Right now, they estimate that we are cruising along at the speed of 8.5 centimetres per year. You should see the wake we are throwing out.

The main problem caused by this rising island stuff is that most Vanuatu islands, including Malekula, are ringed by shelves of dead intertidal coral reefs, rather than beaches. It's hard to find a good beach, and I fear that despite the illusions of politicians and planners, Vanuatu will never be a major tourist destination.

Later, when my NPSO desk in Vila was handling geological matters, the Australians insisted on installing a sensitive ocean level meter in Vila to measure the oceans' rise. I fruitlessly informed them of the above. Later in Canada, I exchanged emails with an Australian on that project who told me that, in essence, their project included a set number of monitoring stations, and Vila was going to be one come hell or high water (so to speak). Yep, fason blong development agency.

Coral steps from periodic geological uplifts, Unmet Malekula.

Two Years on Malekula

Earthquakes and Tsunamis

From letters:
August 10, 1988:

> Unfortunately, we've only had little earthquakes, like 5.4 on the Richter Scale, since we've arrived. In the biggest ones, the place shakes and sways for ten-twenty seconds. I was dreaming one night a few weeks ago, when my dream became all confused and disjointed. I woke and realized this was because the dream was being given the cocktail shaker treatment inside my head.
>
> Fortunately, we're 80 metres above sea level, so the Tsunamis can crash in without inconveniencing us. Holly has heard some tsunami eyewitness accounts from local women. Everyone runs out on the sea floor to gather fish when the water goes out and tries to beat the following wave back to safety. The concept of risk does not exist in the Melanesian psyche.
>
> I'd like to see a Tsunami, from the top of a big hill. We had a warning on Vancouver Island once, and if you can believe it, TV crews all rushed down to the beach to film it! It was a false alarm, fortunately for them.

One day when we were shopping in Vila while on a bush leave, we heard a radio in a Chinese store broadcasting a tsunami warning for the Banks Islands. The next time we ran into a CUSO who was stationed up there, I asked him about it. He told me everyone ran uphill for safety, but when the wave came, it was only 30cm or so high and sloshed around a bit in the Sola harbour.

Up on Efate's north-east coast, there was a small resort which, when we lived in Vila, we sometimes visited for drinks or snorkelling. I noticed that many of the trees there were surrounded with rings of coral rocks and asked a local man if the coral had been thrown up by a tsunami and later placed around the trees. He replied that it had. The wave had come in the middle of the night and bent his house over so that the door was jammed shut. Then, the water rushed back to the sea, straightening out his house so he could open the door and get out.

Volcanoes

When we arrived at Lakatoro, an underwater volcano south of us had recently erupted, and a lot of pumice stone washed up on the beach we frequented.

The nearest volcano to Lakatoro was on Ambrym Island.

Two Years on Malekula

Yasur Volcano, Tanna Island

The sun rising through ash from the Ambrym volcano.We could see nearby islands only after a rain had cleared the air of ash, and everything in our house was continually bathed in a light layer of ash.

The John Frum Society

"Jon Frum" is often mistranslated by Whitemen as "John From", with the erroneous explanation that it refers to "John from America"; in Bislama, that would be "Jon i kam long America" or "Jon man America", not "John Frum". It is properly pronounced as "Joan Froom", and it's pretty sure it doesn't refer to an American.

The Jon Frum Society is perhaps the best known of the Cargo Cults that sprang up in the south Pacific after contact. Rather than being "cute" primitive behavior by "savages", cargo cults are, to the islanders, logical responses to Western invasion and economic hegemony.

Cargo cults are anti-Westerner movements based on the concept that material goods are made in the heavens by people's ancestors and sent to earth to be equally shared among all people. Westerners, however, work magic that selfishly diverts the cargo to themselves. It was thought by some that the key to this Whiteman magic lay in his Bible, but the Whitemen were not revealing the relevant pages of the Bible to New Hebrideans. In some cases, people have tried to conjure up cargo by repeating the actions of Whitemen, such as sitting at village-made desks, shuffling papers, and speaking into boxes.

Vanuatu's colonial powers implemented the classic tactic of requiring the natives to pay annual cash head taxes so they would be forced to enter the money economy by working for colonial employers. Ni-Vanuatu soon recognized that Westerners were controlling their real wages by setting pay rates as well as the prices of goods in the stores. Not caring much about Western notions about the relative value of management vs. labour, they felt it was grossly unfair that they sweated long hours and still received a small fraction of the store-bought goods that their bosses got for simply telling them what to do.

So, when Jon Frum appeared to certain Tanna Islanders in the late Thirties he found a ready audience for his message: If the New Hebrideans threw all their money into the sea and quit wage-work for Westerners, he would return with plenty of cargo for all. The British and French colonial administrations recognized this as a direct threat to Western economic dominance of Tanna, the rest of the New Hebrides, and their other Pacific colonies. A more charitable interpretation might be that they felt it would inhibit the "development" of Tanna. In any case, they jailed the Jon Frum leaders for many years during the '40s and 50's.

In the meantime, World War II occurred and suddenly out of nowhere ships and planes arrived disgorging hundreds of thousands of men with millions of tons of food, trucks, radios, buildings, and you name it. The Jon Frum cult gained impetus and adopted the US military medic symbol of a red cross in a white circle. Westerners started assuming Jon Frum must have been an unknown American Marine Medic, despite his first appearance having pre-dated the War.

Two Years on Malekula

The original leaders of the Jon Frum cult were eventually released from prison, and they continued to report the occasional visitation from Jon Frum until their deaths over the past couple of decades. The cult members continue to hold regular services in their base at the village of Sulphur Bay, Tanna at the base of Yasur Volcano. They also perform traditional dances and march in uniforms carrying wooden guns under the American flag, waiting for Jon Frum to return with the cargo they deserve. If a Westerner asks if they are discouraged that Jon Frum hasn't returned yet, Jon Frum members simply point out that Westerners are still waiting for Jesus to return after two millennia.

Sulphur Bay, the base of the Jon Frum movement, with
rough imitations of American Flags.

When the first air service was started in the New Hebrides, Jon Frum villagers were recruited to help build the first airstrip, which they were willing to do because it was in line with their beliefs.

The Jon Frum Society has, since we left Vanuatu, fielded and elected members of parliament; it is a serious philosophical and political force.

The Vanuatu government took a dim view of Americans joining in Jon Frum ceremonies. While we were there, a man was deported for playing his flute and marching along with the villagers.

Two Years on Malekula

Nakaemas

From a September 13, 1987 letter home:

I made an error a while back when I told you that half the people here believe in custom sharks. Everybody does. I had a chat on the subject with Kalosak Masing, my new counterpart, the other day, and with a guy in Lamap on my recent cruise around Malekula. The ability to assume the form of an animal and work other spiritual magic is nakaemas (pronounced na-ky'-mas). I think it is inherited. It isn't all fun and games, because if you don't use it, it will kill you. Also, while your spirit inhabits another body, your own body looks like you are asleep. If anyone tries to wake you, you die. The same if someone kills the animal whose form you have taken. Kalosak tells me that there used to be lots of men with nakaemas on Malekula, but not so many anymore. Ambrym, on the other hand is "fulap" (has lots of them). Everyone in Vanuatu is afraid to go to Ambrym. Government workers who are assigned there often refuse to go, or leave shortly after moving there. Kalosak said that if a man Ambrym wants to kill you, he does the deed. Then he guts you and fills the cavity with kastom lif (custom leaves) and his spirit enters your body. He then returns to your home and lives with your family, sleeping with your wife (this always enters into the picture), for some predetermined time until abandoning your body and returning to his own. You can tell such a dead man because he passes green stools (from the leaves). Kalosak (relatively well educated with Grade 10 and Public Health Officer training) told me that "Mifala olgeta lanem saens long skul, be save I giaman nomo" or "We all study science in school, but know it is just lies". In response to his inquiry about my belief in nakaemas, I gave him my standard response when a ni-Vanuatu tested me on my belief in supernatural kastom: that because I was a Whiteman, I had trouble believing in nakaemas; his attitude seemed to be that, well what can you expect—that was my problem.

One day when some of us LGC staff were driving along an area populated by people originally from Ambrym, we passed some people walking and one of my co-workers exclaimed, "There's that man we passed a ways back; he's used his powers to get ahead of us!"

In another incident, our CUSO physician friend, Brendan, performed an appendectomy on a man whom I was told had been killed and his body taken over by a man Ambrym. I asked my ni-Vanuatu counterparts, "So, why didn't the doctor find leaves inside the abdomen when he made his incision?" The response was that the man Ambrym had, immediately prior to the surgery, abandoned the body to its original owner and used his powers to remove the leaves.

Brendan Hanley, CUSO Physician at Norsup Hospital.

Kava

Kava was the recreational drug of choice in Vanuatu.

It is a drink prepared from the roots of the domesticated kava plant (piper methysticum), which is related to the pepper plant (the vine that provides peppercorns that are ground into black pepper). Unlike pepper, kava is a bush with branches that radiate up from a central mass of roots. Domesticated cultivars can only be propagated vegetatively, by planting pieces of stem back into the ground after a mature plant (two to five years old) has been harvested. There are several different domesticated cultivars of kava. Some have stronger effects than others, and the effect of some is reputed to last longer (tu-de kava;

two-day kava). I have seen the results of scientific tests that show that different cultivars have different kava ketones (the active ingredient, a fat-soluble compound found within the root cells) that stay in the bloodstream different lengths of time.

Kava plant

Although it was not used in some parts of the archipelago before Western contact, kava drinking is an age-old tradition in most of Vanuatu. I was not a nightly kava drinker, as are many expatriates, but I did drink the occasional shell in village nakamals and at traditional ceremonies. I also gained some familiarity with the commercial nakamals of Port Vila and Luganville.

It must be kept in mind that a great number of Vanuatu's villages comprise their own language groups with their own customs and traditions, and generalizations are dangerous. Nevertheless, it is safe to say that in most areas where kava use is traditional, only adult men may drink it. Many of them drink it every night. My wife and I were told in one village that kava drinking was not an old tradition there, and she was invited to join in that evening. Nevertheless, I suspect kava is not a regular woman's drink there, either.

In the towns of Port Vila and Luganville, and to a lesser extent in Norsup, Malekula and Lenakel, Tanna,[1] commercial nakamals (kava bars) were present.

---

[1] The only four places in Vanuatu where the money economy existed to any extent.

Two Years on Malekula

Expatriate and even ni-Vanuatu women were allowed to drink kava here, as long as the latter were not from the same village as the nakamal owner, who was generally not too concerned with the misdeeds of women from villages other than his own.

In villages, kava is always prepared from fresh roots. Each afternoon, someone digs up a root ball from his garden, replanting several of the stalks so that a perpetual supply is assured. He then shakes the soil off the root and carries it to the nakamal. About dusk, men start gathering, and one or two of them clean the roots, scrape the skin off, and cut the roots into small pieces about 2cm long. The root is then pulverized or ground by one of several methods, depending on the region. Some places pound the roots, often with an old truck axle in an anti-aircraft shell casing left from WW II. Others put the roots in their hands and rotate a cylinder of coral rock in the hand, and in Tanna the roots are often ground by chewing them.

Cleaning kava roots.

42

Pounding Kava.

The ground kava is then mixed with water before the liquid is squeezed out one shell[1] at a time by hand and strained through a cone of fibrous "cloth" from a coconut palm trunk. Sometimes, it is strained all at once through a piece of woven polypropylene rice bag fabric. It is important not to strain the kava too thoroughly, because the fine kava particles containing the active ingredient must be left suspended in the liquid.

---

[1] Half a coconut shell, the official volume measure of kava.

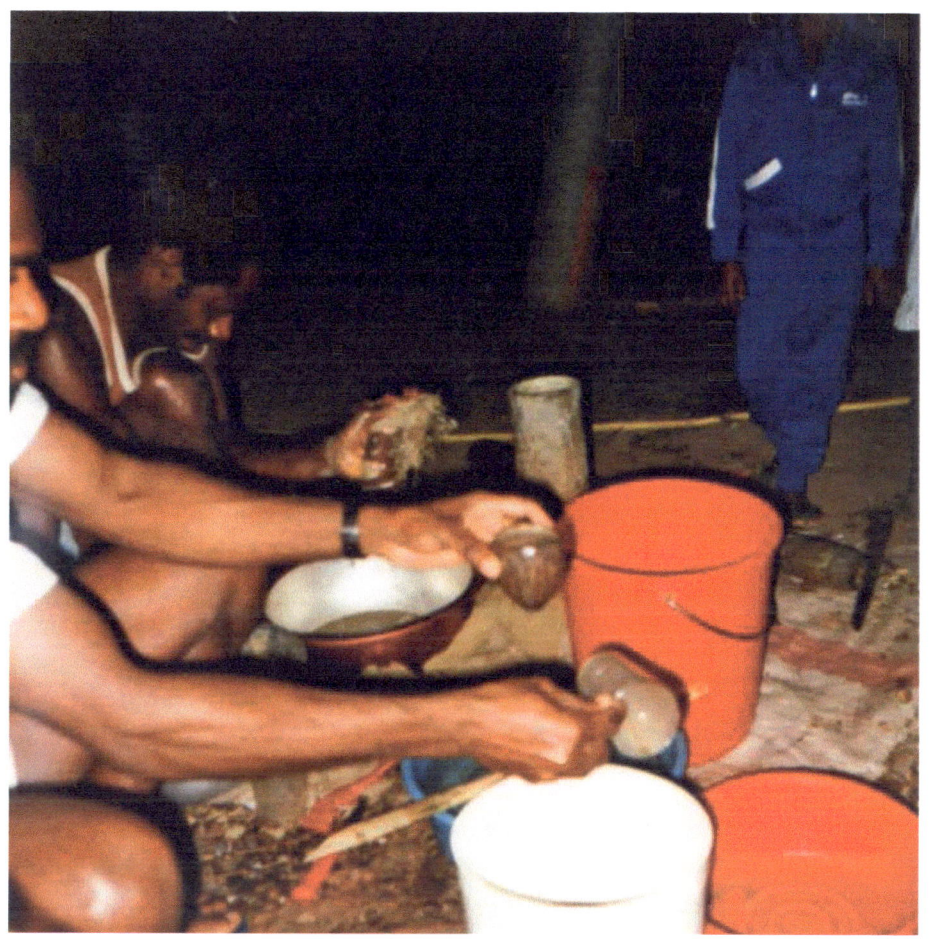

A shell of kava ready to drink.

By this time, it is well dark and all the kava drinkers have drifted in. None have eaten yet, so as to get the greatest effect from the kava. The actual act of drinking each shell is solitary, performed at the nakamal's outer wall facing outwards, sometimes while calling out to the kava's spirit. It is drunk with reverence, and then the men sit quietly, "listening to the kava". In many traditional village nakamals, speech is forbidden. By a couple of hours past nightfall, the men will have left the nakamal to have their evening meal, finish their day, and sleep. Vanuatu kava is reputed to be the world's strongest, and is used almost exclusively as an intoxicant. This is not the weaker Fiji kava made from kava stems rather than roots, which I am told is served during coffee breaks in offices. I was once at a Vanuatu government conference that was broken up by a kava ceremony; nobody was at all inclined to do any work for the remainder of the morning.

Kava's appearance is a bit like thin pea soup. To me, it tastes like dirty water with a hint of clove. Its first effect (after a successful effort to keep it down) is a slight numbing of the back of the throat, which probably accounts for the hawking and spitting that often follows drinking a shell. It is not like alcohol, in that one doesn't feel the systemic effects immediately, but after about ten minutes it can suddenly hit your mind with a bang. This is especially true for experienced drinkers, as they have learned what to look for in the kava. First-timers can be lulled into a false sense of impunity by the lack of immediate apparent effect, quickly have a couple more shells, and fall on their faces when they stand up. I have heard and read many times that kava does not cause a hangover, but it always gave me one as soon as its intoxicating effects wore off. I heard of occasional deaths caused by mixing excessive amounts of kava and alcohol.

Unlike alcohol, which was not present in Vanuatu pre-contact, kava does not cause aggressiveness. Ni-Vanuatu women prefer their men to drink kava because they come home, want sex, and then fall asleep, while a night of alcohol drinking can end with a wife-beating. While some Christian denominations have attempted to stamp out kava drinking since the arrival of their first missionaries, others quietly encourage its use as a less-harmful substitute for alcohol. In fact, one of my early experiences with kava was with the Catholic Bishop of Vanuatu.

As a development adviser, I was favourably impressed by kava because its commercial trade is the only sector of Vanuatu's money economy that is completely controlled by ni-Vanuatu. The urban nakamals are run along family lines, with the kava roots being grown by relatives back on the islands. They are sent to town on the coastal traders that buy copra. In town, nakamal businesses fail and re-open according to management ability and social distractions, but there are always many open at any one time. The commercial kava trade is a good way to get money out to the outer islands, and money spent on kava circulates among ni-Vanuatu. It is much less expensive than domestic or imported beer, and it is culturally and socially appropriate.

I always hoped that fresh food root crops could be imported into Vanuatu's towns by the same mechanisms as kava, but the villages that own the land where the towns are situated maintain a tight monopoly on the fresh food trade. Locally-raised food is very expensive in town, and most urban ni-Vanuatu are forced to subsist on white rice imported from Australia. I never learned why rice wasn't imported from less expensive sources, like Thailand. Perhaps there was no incentive to do so, since a Vietnamese businessman had the exclusive license to import rice.

A Typical Evening at a Commercial Nakamal in a Town

A commercial nakamal is usually a rough shed made of woven bamboo, galvanized iron, lumber scraps, and whatever is available, with an earth floor. A simple counter at one end serves as a bar, and benches ring the outer wall;

perhaps some more benches are outside. Lighting is provided by a single kerosene wick lamp or maybe a low-wattage bulb hanging from a wire near the bar. A similar arrangement hung out by the road advertises the nakamal's presence.

Late in the afternoon, the nakamal owner starts preparing the fresh kava by washing the roots and scraping off the skin. Commercial kava is usually ground with a large hand-cranked meat grinder into a plastic basin. It is then mixed with water and the kava drink is squeezed out through a woven plastic rice bag or a coarse cloth.

About sundown, the customers, both ni-Vanuatu and expatriate, start to arrive. As in the villages, they have not eaten, as kava is always drunk on an empty stomach. Women are allowed to buy and drink kava if they are not from the village of the nakamal owner, although I have heard bitter complaints that Whitemen spoil (in a cultural sense) ni-Vanuatu women by taking them to kava bars.

Whatever lighting is available is turned on, and business commences. Each customer goes up to the bar and gives 50 vatu (1992 price, about CAN$0.50) to the owner. After the kava is stirred with a stick to keep the particles mixed with the water, the customer is given a half-coconut shell of kava (or, disappointingly often, a glass). The customer then quietly goes out of the nakamal to the edge of its yard, faces outward, and downs the kava in one draw. The dregs are usually poured on the ground, and a bout of hawking and spitting often follows. The customer goes back to the bar, where he returns the shell to the owner. The shell is then rinsed in a bucket of water, refilled, and balanced in an old tuna tin on the bar to await the next customer.

The customer may linger at the bar to purchase some locally-grown and roasted peanuts or bits of meat on a spit, or hard candies to eat and take away the kava taste. He then quietly returns to a bench, where he sits with his companions. Depending on the nakamal's location and his preference, he may sit inside the nakamal's twilight, or he may go to a bench outside and watch the stars appear over Port Vila harbour. He and his companions quietly converse, almost at a whisper, and discuss the day's events. Some just sit in quiet contemplation, "listening to the kava".

Usually, a person waits a half-hour or so, and perhaps has another shell. That is usually it. By 20:00, about two hours after they have opened, most nakamals are empty and shut down. The customers have drifted off for supper somewhere.

Is Kava Addictive?

There are certainly many ni-Vanuatu men who drink kava in their village every night. Many expatriates, especially single men with no reason to get home early in the evening, also drink kava every night. Some of them become somewhat emaciated because they habitually forget to eat properly after visiting the nakamal with an empty stomach. When it comes time to leave Vanuatu, however, all the nakamal regulars just up and go, giving up kava with no withdrawal symptoms. It is generally agreed along the nakamal bench that kava can be psychologically addictive, but not physically.

Kava and North American Law

Kava is not an illegal substance in North America; I have declared it at both United States and Canada Customs. I understand that relatively small amounts are imported by ethnic Pacific communities. Dried kava powder can be purchased in Port Vila and Luganville and mailed overseas. Some westerners have urged the Government of Vanuatu to get into large-scale production of freeze-dried kava and export it to Europe and North America for sale in health and grocery stores. My guess is that North America probably wouldn't welcome large volumes of yet another intoxicating drug, and the first kava-induced automobile fatality would lead to tight regulation.

Kava in Another Society Where it is Not a Tradition

I have heard that missionaries have introduced kava to some Australian Aboriginal settlements as a substitute for socially-destructive alcohol. Without Vanuatu's traditional social constraints against over-indulgence, though, it just became another abused drug.

My First Experience With Kava

March 5 is Vanuatu's Malvatumauri, or Custom Chief's Day, holiday. Government policy is to encourage respect for Custom, including the chiefs, who run kind of a parallel authority and are integrated into Local Governments. Because Lakatoro, an artificially-established government centre where people only live for employment, isn't a traditional village, nothing was shaking there. We heard on the radio that a big festivity was happening at Lingarak, about 12 km S of here, and my boss Keith Mala offered us the LGC Landcruiser ("Oh, yeah—Don't forget to pump the brakes to stop."—an understatement), so off we went.

We gave a ride to the LGC Minibus driver, who lives near there, and when we arrived, he asked the Lingarak chief if it was OK if we came—an essential bit of protocol I had forgotten. It soon became evident that we were the only visitors, which wasn't all bad, because we saw the real thing, which wasn't all that spectacular, just interesting. We had timed our arrival to miss the 10:30 church service and arrived at 11:45. Well, probably due to a combination of "Vanuatu Time" and a long service, most everyone was in the church, a medium-sized bamboo building, when we arrived. A bunch of children and women (probably wouldn't fit inside) were sitting in the shade of a tree near the church, so we joined them. Of course, the chief, a nice old man, went into the church, kicked a bunch of worshipers off a bench, and carried it out for us to sit on (everyone else was on the ground), so there we were, perched on a bench playing what I called "white king", or "bwana". It wasn't long before I learned that anywhere I went, I was an "honoured guest" who received special treatment, including being seated in front on any stage. I found this embarrassing, but eventually accepted it.

Church finished about 13:00—we spent our time watching the kids play with a huge rhinoceros beetle (a serious coconut palm pest) and smiling back and forth—and we were told that food was coming up next. After a while, we all went to the Nakamal (a building used for a men's club or town hall), where it became apparent that we were "honoured guests".

Before we ate, they had a traditional kava ceremony. Frankly, I had been avoiding kava and had already turned down a few invites for "boys' night out". I had been warned that occasionally the big sport was to get a new Whiteman to overindulge, get real drunk, and vomit and I had been advised to stick to one shell the first time.

Well, here I was, honoured guest, and they lined me up with all the dignitaries and gave a speech, in which I was introduced (speaker had to come over and ask my name again—everyone knows what I do because I'd been announced on the national radio news). I figured I'd just watch what the others did first, because I knew there is a definite protocol to follow, but of course I had to go with the first batch of 3 very high chiefs. I just kept my eye on them and tried to imitate them. We went up front and stood in a line side-by-side (so I had to watch them out of the corner of my eye). The kava was poured out of the traditional container (a big aluminium kettle) into enamel mugs (part of the speech had been an apology for the lack of coconut shell cups), and the mugs were ceremoniously handed to us one by one, using 2 hands wrapped around the mug. I'm not sure if you are supposed to put your hands over the other guys or vice-versa, or not, so I just faked it. My closest experience to date was the University of Alberta convocation ceremony, where I had to put my hands inside those of the Chancellor's before receiving my diploma—my mortar-board fell off at that point, and I had to grab it.

Then, we all knelt on one knee and drained the mug with one long, slow draw. I managed to do that—it didn't taste that bad, sort of like pounded roots with a bit of dirt and a faint air of pepper and cloves—and then I noticed with horror that everyone else, heads bowed, had saved some dregs which they were pouting onto the dirt floor! I thought, "What if there isn't any more in my mug?" and tipped it down. Luckily, a few drops ran out. Then we solemnly walked back to the line-up (shoulder-to-shoulder ringing the room) and waited while the other men went through the same ceremony.

The kava, this being a church-supervised occasion, I guess, had been kept pretty weak and really didn't have much effect, except to numb the back of my throat a bit. Perhaps I didn't yet know what to "listen" to.

Afterwards, the "old" pastor (retired 2 years before, but returned for the festivities) said grace, and we all ate. They had 3 long tables with benches (all built on legs sunk into the ground) with lap-lap spread down the centre of each on banana leaves. Lap-lap is grated banana, manioc (cassava or tapioca), or root crop mixed with coconut milk and (often) meat that is wrapped in big leaves and cooked on hot rocks. It is the national dish here. We also had rice and naura (fresh-water shrimp). Actually, the whole thing reminded me of an Arvin[1] Congregational Church potluck.

They had a list posted of who was assigned to do what. Later, I asked a bunch of questions about local crops, and they showed me their cacao trees and different types of palms (coconut and thatch). One guy showed us that if you cut open a sprouted coconut, the interior is filled with a crisp spongy sweet stuff that bears some resemblance to cotton candy. I asked how to plant bananas, so they told me you dig up a sucker and plant it, then for a going-away present, gave us 2 banana shoots to plant. I specified my favourites, little sweet "lady-finger" eating ones, and planted them out back of our house when we got home. All in all, a worthwhile day.

The Lingarak banana plant, two years later, complete with crabby five-year-old who didn't want to be in the photo. If that bunch of bananas turning yellow isn't harvested today, flying foxes will eat them tonight. To harvest a banana bunch, you just cut down the plant they are growing on; it is not a tree and only fruits once. New plants sprout from its roots.

---

[1] California, home village of my branch of the Combs clan.

Kava at Club Hippique

When we lived in Port Vila, we belonged to the "Club Hippique" riding club. We financed the club by tapping into the hordes of tourists that flooded town most weeks on cruise ship day. The ship would charge each tourist $50 to visit the club, paying $30 to the Vanuatu tourism board, which would bus the tourists to us. We got $20 each from the tourism board. Add $15 to what the ship charged and what we got for the one of three groups each tourist day that we sold lunch to. Fason blong tourism industry. Every club member was required to make their horse available for the tourist rides, and this income kept the Combs family's bill for the board of four horses, twice-weekly lessons for four riders, and bar bill to CAN$300 per month.

Many of the tourists, especially the women, needed assistance saddling up, which we would provide with a hand or two to the butt—we called this "mounting the tourists".

When our Australian manager wasn't available, I often led the rides and gave a talk on coconuts and kava in our little nakamal where we gave the tourists the opportunity to try kava at double the local price.

One day, for whatever reason, our usual source of liquid kava wasn't available. Before the tourists arrived, I entered the nakamal to find several of our Tannese staff chewing away on kava roots and spitting the mass into a bowl. Not on my watch, I thought, and sent the mystified head man off into town to find some drink made from ground kava. I don't want to think how often we served chewed kava to tourists (and perhaps even me) when I hadn't stumbled onto the process.

Kava Sent Home to my Sister

From a letter:

> I think if you wrote to my hero, Miss Manners, she would advise you that it is perfectly acceptable to flush kava that was sent to you at great expense down the toilet. It is, however, inexcusable to tell the donor about it. These situations are best handled with vague lies, like: "Well, I tried it, but it ended up in the 'big white telephone', if you know what I mean." Holly told me you wouldn't like the kava, but I didn't want to give you the same thing that I gave Cindy.

Stories of Sharks

Custom Sharks

No discussion of sharks in Vanuatu can make any sense to a Westerner without a quick review of the topic of "Kastom Sak", or "Custom Sharks", "custom" referring to traditional or supernatural beliefs. Almost all ni-Vanuatu are nominal

Two Years on Malekula

Christians of various denominations. Under the skin though are strongly-held animist beliefs—non-human animals and what Westerners consider inanimate objects have human-like consciousness, motivations, and abilities.

Ni-Vanuatu know that sharks that attack people are custom sharks, or men who have transformed themselves into sharks in order to avenge a wrong or slight inflicted by the victim of the attack. This is a sub-set of "nakaemas", or a man's power to transform oneself into an animal; I never heard of women with this power. Because custom knowledge is not readily shared, I only learned some of the details.

One use of shark nakaemas is rape, a common assault in Vanuatu.

From an October 19, 1987 letter:

> John Kamphorst has put the proper interpretation on these incidents of CUSO women waking up in bed at night beside their husbands with some ni-Vanuatu guy on top of them trying to (as they put it here) "intercourse[1] them". These guys think they have Nakaemas and have put a spell on the couple so that the husband remains asleep and the woman doesn't remember the experience the next day. I have heard first-hand of two such incidents, both from CUSO women within a few miles of each other on Ambae, which fit in with the theory. Tales of guys who turn themselves into sharks at night, swim to another island, and intercourse unsuspecting women are popular guy talk here. Everybody knows someone who has an uncle who does this all the time. The other belief, or maybe an associated one, is that if you use the proper leaves, you can gain the same type of power. I asked Kalosak, my counterpart, how anybody knows that this happens, since the victims don't remember it. He says that the women wake up with their clothes off or rearranged. One of John's workers says that his uncle or whatever writes his name on the insides of the women's thighs with a ball-point pen. Anyway, we always lock our veranda and house doors at night.

The people of some villages, for example Vao, believed that they were descended from sharks and therefore never ate them. Litzlitz believed that it was descended from pigs and never ate female pigs—males were OK to eat.

Initial Exposure to Malekula Sharks

When we arrived at Malekula, I was nervous about the possibility of shark attack for some time. I intended to enjoy water activities like snorkeling, so in order to lengthen my odds of survival, I made it my business to accumulate as much knowledge on this subject as possible. I was told that Paama Island was rife with

---

[1] Rape; let's be frank.

Two Years on Malekula

shark attacks, Efate Island never had them, and Malekula was in the middle with the occasional attack. Locals also told us that shark attacks were much more likely in water over black sand; I did observe that ni-Vanuatu would not enter the sea at black sand beaches.

I was also told that sharks never attacked SCUBA divers; only snorkelers and swimmers. Nevertheless, ni-Vanuatu spear fishers, who reported sharks would take fish from the ends of their spears, would hang their catch on their belts while they continued fishing. I could only theorize that they had clear consciences and didn't fear retribution from custom sharks.

Most of Vanuatu's island shorelines are made of dead coral that is very sharp and not at all suitable for swimming, but the lovely Aop Beach was just north of Lakatoro. Aop Beach was fringed with large trees that provided a lot of shade, and the water's edge contained fingers of staghorn coral that tinkled in the small surf; it was a great place. Soon after moving to Lakatoro, we rode our bicycles down there for the first of many Sunday picnics and swims. I was surprised that Heather (5) and Laurel (3) absolutely refused to follow me into the ocean. No Way—"There's sharks in there!" I didn't know that, just before we left Victoria, they had watched a National Geographic TV programme that featured sharks jumping onto rocks to snatch up seals. It was weeks before they would swim in the ocean.

After two years on Malekula, the girls' fear of sharks diminished. On our way back to Vanuatu in August, 1989, we had a layover in Fiji. I was snorkeling with Heather on my back peeking over my shoulder with her mask and snorkel, when a shark swam past along the ocean floor, clearly visible about 4 metres under us in the clear water. I expected Heather to panic and run across the surface of the water to the dive boat, but there was no reaction. Back on board, I asked her why. "Oh, that was just a Blacktip Reef Shark like we saw at the Honolulu Aquarium last week. They don't eat people."

One Sunday at Aop, we watched our French friends, Daniel and Michelle, sailing their Fireball dinghy out in the bay. Shortly afterwards we learned that their boat was up for sale; while we were watching them and swimming, the 5-metre boat had been circled by a 6-metre tiger shark. Michelle had announced flatly that she would never go out again. I bought the Fireball.

Mark, a British friend from Metenesel Plantation across the island, once told me that he had decided to catch a shark at Aop Bay. He welded a chain with a large hook to a floating 200-litre barrel, baited it with a cow's head, and left it at the end of a rope in the bay overnight. Next morning, chain, hook, and cow's head were gone. So, he made repairs and tried again. Success, but he had to get a tractor to drag the shark on shore. He cut the jaws out, stood side by side with another man, and passed them over their shoulders. A big one!

Shark Attacks on Malekula

Only one shark attack occurred while we lived on Malekula, a couple of months after our arrival.

From an April 7, 1987 letter:

> Before noon, we stopped at Atchin Mainland (across from Atchin Island) where a Swedish tourist was killed by a shark four years ago (details below), so I asked about it and got the whole story. I ask these things of as many people as I can, because I'm trying to get the real story—all the expats won't go near the water, but the locals insist that there's no problem (of course, I've yet to see one of them actually swimming).

> A few minutes later, we picked up a farmer a few km north (30 km north of Lakatoro), and he told us that a boy had just then been dragged out to sea by a shark. I guess (wait for it...) he must have had dandruff, because they later found his head and shoulders on the beach[1]. Actually, they found his head, arm, and leg. Poor kid; what a way to go. Luckily, we've gotten better at Bislama, because the radio gives two versions of local news here, one in Bislama and one in English. The English version just said he was "swimming in two metres of water, when tragedy struck", but the Bislama version included all of the gory details, along the lines of how he was swimming (generic word here that includes everything from taking a shower or sponge bath to scuba diving) with some friends at lunch hour after school (he was eight), and a girl held on to his hand (i.e. somewhere between fingertips and shoulder) after the shark struck, but he was dragged under anyway. His friends went to get some adults, but when they returned, they found only blood. They like their news spicy here. Thank goodness they don't have TV, or we'd get "film at eleven".

In a later letter:

> I heard on the radio that they caught the shark that killed the boy here—it was 4.3 metres long and had a dog and cat in its stomach. I'd say that they caught a shark—there are probably more 4.3 metre sharks around here than you can shake a stick at.

23 April, 1987:

> The traditional story on shark attacks here is that someone who is spiritually powerful transforms himself into a shark and eats an enemy. I think they still

---

[1] Reference to old sick joke about the lady in the opening scene of the film "Jaws".

half believe it[1] —it was brought up in a half-joking manner today when I was discussing the incident with a bunch sitting outside my office. I guess that's why they don't worry—you can't fight that kind of power anyway. From now on, I'm keeping Heather or Laurel on the outer side of me when I go snorkelling. Once again, my co-workers all told me that there're lots of sharks down here, but they only attack on the far side of the islands off of Malekula. We go to the beach every Sunday and snorkel.

A year later a visitor took our girls swimming in front of the large bright red cross on Vao Island that marks the spot. When discussing this with a ni-Vanuatu, I was assured that it was perfectly safe—real sharks never went there; only custom sharks.

One day, I was sitting across the water from Vao Island with Viene, an intelligent and knowledgeable fieldworker for the Vanuatu Cultural Centre. I asked him about the custom shark who had killed the boy. Viene pointed at a house on the island and told me that the boy's uncle had stolen some stones from the nasara, or sacred family dancing ground, of the house's owner in order to build a bread oven. The offended man had then changed into a shark and killed the boy in revenge. "But, Viene", I said, "that house is right next to the Catholic Church. Surely that man is Christian and wouldn't have done that." Viene replied, "Yes, but his custom magic spirit is stronger than the Christian one."

Some months after the attack I bought the canoe that was used to recover the boy's body.

Being curious about such things, during my time in Lakatoro, I asked the details of earlier Malekula shark attacks. For example, in 1983, that Swedish tourist had landed at Norsup airstrip and got a ride north to Atchin Mainland. Half-an-hour after landing on Malekula, he ran into the ocean and was immediately attacked by a shark. A witness told me the Swede's arm and shoulder were missing and he had packed the wound with sand to stop the bleeding before taking him to the CUSO doctor at the Norsup hospital. Unfortunately, the Swede soon died. So, I asked my informant on custom shark attacks, "This man had not been here long enough to make any enemies. Why did the custom shark attack him?" "Oh", he said, "Another man was supposed to enter the water there at that exact time, but the tourist ran in ahead of him, and the custom shark bit him by mistake".
`

Actually, when we got to Lamap, we did get a different answer: Two years ago in 1985, an American tourist on a yacht put her small child in a swim ring or something in the ocean, and a shark came and ate it. That would kind of put a damper on your vacation, wouldn't it?

---

[1] I was still learning at this point; everyone believes it completely, independently of education level or religious affiliation.

True to form when getting second-hand stories in Bislama, we eventually got several versions of this tragedy. In one, the mother's friend was playing with the baby by dipping it in and out of the water, and came up with half a child—how to break up a friendship. Another account had an older child attacked while swimming from the boat to the shore.

I asked my co-worker informant on these matters—how this child could have made an enemy on Malekula, since it was newly-arrived and so young? He admitted there wasn't a kastom explanation for this attack.

Some time ago, while researching these attacks, I did a Google search on shark attacks in Vanuatu to see if I could verify any of them from news media. I sure could—a site on world shark attacks had found and dutifully repeated all of these attacks from my Rural Vanuatu web site. Take this as a caution on Internet research. Except for information from my web site, of course.

Sexual Assault

Sexual assault is one of the dark sides of Vanuatu, which was ridiculously labeled "The Happiest Place on Earth" several years ago, and any woman on her own is considered to be sexually available. Village women never go anywhere except in the company of a number of other women, their husband, or an adult male relative. They especially do not leave their sleeping houses at night. Newcomer expat women, including tourists, learn this in an unpleasant manner: as a female English friend told us from personal experience, if they go to a beach alone or with their kids, a man appears making crude sexual invitations and/or masturbating. I once told this to a lady here in Canada who had visited Vanuatu. She said, "Yeah, I hired a taxi to drive me around the capital's island, and the driver pulled off into the bush and suggested we get down to it; which I declined". My response: "Yep".

Where do ni-Vanuatu get the idea that Western women are promiscuous? The same place they learn that the West is an extremely violent place where no-one works for a living—movies from the West. Videos were a popular entertainment in Vanuatu, and most people thought they were documentaries in which actual events were filmed.

I knew two CUSO women who woke up with a ni-Vanuatu man on top of them, one in a hammock on her veranda, the other while in bed with her husband. The former stopped taking naps outside; the latter started locking their door at night.

A family of CUSOs based in Luganville thought their house was private because it was surrounded by forest. So the parents didn't close their curtains while having sex. In fact, in Vanuatu the presence of the bush means a site is less private because people hide there to spy. It wasn't long before this family was subject to continual peeking through their windows and screen doors, sometimes by masturbating men, even though no sex was taking place at the time.

Before we became cooperants, CUSO had negligently omitted proper briefings in their Ottawa orientations about sexual assault in Vanuatu. In-country cooperants, after learning from experience the truth about this, wrote CUSO head office to protest, with no reply. We received a briefing in Ottawa from the lady who was attacked in her hammock. We didn't have any sexual assault problems in Vanuatu, but pre-warned, always drew our curtains and locked our door at night. Holly never went anywhere without me or a group of women. Friends who didn't take these precautions told us of the consequences of all three behaviors.

Vanuatu Inter-Island Flights

Air Melanesiæ, known locally as Air Mel, provided pretty good service between Vanuatu's islands using Twin Otters, a Bandeirante, Britten-Normand Islanders, and a Trilander.[1]

Air Mel, as it was known, did not use co-pilots, selling the seat next to the pilot to an extra passenger. In November, 1989, the Vanuatu Government forced the owner of Air Melanesiæ to sell his airline to them and renamed it Vanair.

Air Melanesiæ Twin Otter and Islander at Norsup Airport

Vanair came under a different regulatory regime and had to use co-pilots. One of the regular lone Air Mel pilots was an obese guy with a florid complexion who hopped out at every stop to suck desperately on a cigarette. Hardly confidence-inspiring, but the third world is a risky place compared to Canada. In any event, he never suffered a stroke while piloting... to my knowledge.

One day in Vila, I boarded a Normand Islander to fly back to Malekula. The islander is a small plane that boards four rows of two passengers from doors on its side, like a car, plus in this instance me in the co-pilot's seat. The pilot fiddled around with the controls for a few minutes, and then called over a ground crewman. He showed the pilot how to start the engine, and off we went! I gather that the pilot was a new hire and had never flown an Islander before.

Once, when living in Vila, we drove out to a friend's plantation for a barbecue. On the way to his house from the road, we were passed by another expat leaving. Jean-Michel explained that his friend had to get back to town to pilot a Vanair flight.

---

[1] An extended Islander with a third engine mounted in front of the tail.

A couple of hours later, we were all eating and drinking away when a Twin Otter flew over us just higher than the palm trees; the friend opened his window, turned off the engine, and yelled, "Hello!" down to us. He then started up the engine, swung around, and did it again!

Even in the South Pacific, there must be some regulations about this kind of thing on scheduled commercial flights.

Finally, an interesting although safe Air Mel flying experience I wrote about in an April 20, 1988 letter:

> Cyclone Dovi didn't really come very close, but I got stuck in Tanna for an extra day because the planes didn't fly. I almost got sick on the first half of the rough flight back to Vila. At the halfway stop at Erromango Island, the pilot asked if I wanted to sit in the cockpit—I was the only passenger in a Twin Otter. I was worried I would throw up all over his territory, but went up anyway. Luckily, he flew the rest of the way over the clouds, rather than under them as before, and the rest of the flight was smooth. Of course, I got a good view of our landing in a stiff crosswind. We flew at an angle to the end of the runway and then straightened out at the last second to bounce our way down. Do you ever get to fly on the first plane to fly after a hurricane? This was my second time this year—also after Cyclone Anne had kept us all in Santo an extra day in early January.

I relate the weirdest thing that happened to me on an Air Mel flight in the section of this memoir about leaving Malekula at the end of my CUSO contract.

Port Vila's Bus System
From a July 18, 1987 letter home:

They have a great bus system in Vila, which much of Canada could learn from. It is cheap and very convenient. There is a semi-defined route through town, with what seems like scores of guys driving 15-seater minibuses through. If you want one, you flag it down (stops are only observed some of the time and only in town) and tell the driver where you want to go. He takes you and all the other passengers right to their doors, or close anyway. Every trip is a different route, and you get a free tour of town every time! It's only 50vt [1](20vt for pikininis),

---

[1] My role in establishing this price is related in another section of this memoir

with an extra 10vt if you really want to go somewhere out-of-the-way. Even out at the airport, we never had to wait more than 10 minutes or so, but the system doesn't operate after about 1900. Every small city in Canada should have one like it.

Except possibly in large cities like Vancouver, Canadian bus systems are a costly weight on the public purse. When we lived in Kelowna, I read in the paper that the average ridership on each bus was 2.5 passengers.

It would be cheaper to hire taxis for everyone. I often suggested that a system like Vila's be set up, except with private automobiles, properly insured and with properly licensed drivers. These cars could flood the streets in rush hour and go home during the day. Oh! Did I just describe an Uber that carried more than one passenger per vehicle? Aside from the taxi drivers and bus drivers' union, who could object? In any case, Kelowna politicians never showed any interest.

The Port Vila Riot, May 16, 1988

From a June 29, 1988 letter:

> We had a central government cabinet shuffle here last month, also. Unfortunately, it was preceded by a two-hour riot that trashed downtown Port Vila, the capitol. This was all inspired by Minister Barak Sope, who coveted the PM's job but had been removed from Cabinet. The official excuse for dumping this guy was that the Minister of Tourism shouldn't encourage people to trash travel agent and airline offices. The Australian press played it up as an invasion by Libya (it's a long story, you have to be here), so it will be a long time before tourists return.

The true reason for removing Barak Sope from Cabinet was that an audit by Australian accountants brought in by the PM, Walter Lini, had confirmed that Sope was diverting to himself most of the rent paid by lessees in Port Vila, which is on his village's land. As these leases encompassed the entire town, this was a substantial amount of money.

Barak Sope later spent time in prison for forging government bonds and even later became Prime Minister from '99 to '01. Fason blong Vanuatu politics. Barak had visited Libya in 1987, probably to be seen distancing himself from white Australia, which reacted with alarm. It was then rumored around the country that Libya had sent him a shipping container of weapons. With Vanuatu's history of civil war seven years previous, this was a cause of concern among local people.

Two Years on Malekula

Vanuatu's piece of the South Pacific tourism market was tenuous. Its main source of tourists was Australia, but Bali offered warm beaches at a lower cost. To make matters worse, potential Australian tourists do not differentiate between the security situations of different places in the South Pacific—if there is a coup in Fiji or unrest in the Solomons, they stop coming to Vanuatu. Of course, the riot in Vila put a stop to Vanuatu tourism, hurting the incomes of the tenants of the rioters for some time.

The riot mostly followed the pattern of breaking into a store, drinking all the liquor, and moving on to the next store. All of the property destroyed belonged to tenants of the rioters' village.

A curfew was ordered and a few machine-gun bullets were put through a boat coming from the rioters' island in Port Vila's bay. Australia sent tear gas and other riot-control gear. They don't usually provide arms, etc. but, due to this cabinet minister's visit to Libya last year, there is a lot of nonsense on Radio Australia International about Vanuatu's "Libyan Connection", and Australian PM Bob Hawk pledging to keep the South Pacific safe for democracy. During the riot the police fired tear gas at the rioters, neglecting the fact that the police were themselves downwind. Reversing their trucks, they ran over a mentally disabled ni-Vanuatu; discovering this, they lurched forward and ran over him again, producing the riot's only fatality.

From the same letter:

> Then, our local MP joined this ex-Minister and a few other Vanua'aku Pati MPs and the opposition in signing a notice of no-confidence motion that the VP Speaker of Parliament tossed out on a pretty thin technicality (like the one used last year to exclude the leader of the opposition from parliament for the entire session). Of course, our local MP is now kicked out of the party and in danger of losing his seat (they have a technicality for every occasion). How dull Canadian politics are.

PART 3—WORKING ON MALEKULA

The Reality of International Development Where the Rubber Hits the Road

Underdevelopment in Vanuatu

I believe that "development" is the process of a community of people with common interests gaining control of its circumstances and future. This means, of course, that development must come from the bottom up, the process starting with a community defining its own goals.

From a 26 May, 1987 letter home:

> I've done a couple of economic analyses of aid projects recently, and in my naiveté, was shocked to find that the projects, instead of fostering economic independence, make the aid recipients dependent on the equipment and machinery donated. Since the projects can't make enough money to buy new equipment once it wears out (i.e. they lose money if depreciation is included), the aid recipients rely on continued donations.

Some Westerners will insist that development begins with basics like, for example, clean water. But, if the community being assisted doesn't accept the Western germ theory of disease and doesn't care if its water is clean of pathological organisms, the new water system will break down because nobody thinks it is worth fixing. I saw this very thing happen many times in Vanuatu.

Of course, to learn what the goals of a community are and what projects it considers worth-while, aid organizations have to actually go out into the community and assist it in articulating this in a form recognizable to aid donors. This takes time and money, and is all too often left out of the process to attain false economies. In any case, many aid donors prefer large infrastructure projects that offer large ribbon-cutting ceremonies with associated photo opportunities. Also, the large corporations that implement these projects prefer capital-intensive contracts that do not require complex social research. They are paid a percentage of gross costs, so the bigger the better.

Aid donors, of course, will usually have cultural or ethical objections to some of what communities want, so I believe aid projects should fall in the intersection of the two sets of what communities want and donors are willing to provide.

One of the first useful things I learned as a development advisor was that Vanuatu was getting a lot of technical, monetary, and in-kind assistance for the stated purpose of helping it adjust to its new universe. I also learned that most of this assistance was not really helping the vast majority of ni-Vanuatu grasp control of their circumstances or improve their lifestyles. Besides, very little of the progress attained was sustainable without continued aid. I concluded that aid donors,[1] ni-Vanuatu politicians, and Vanuatu's people had conspired to form a "cargo cult" dependency. I characterize "underdevelopment" in Vanuatu as a clash of the Melanesian and Western cultures, with "bewilderment" being the operative word on both sides.

Two Years on Malekula

I had the opportunity to see a lot of Vanuatu; I lived on an outer island and in the capital, and I traveled throughout the archipelago. I had dealings with all the regional governments, most of the central government departments, and most of the foreign aid donors. I worked with ni-Vanuatu and foreign aid advisers. I socialized with expatriate plantation mangers and businessmen. So, I got some idea of what was going on in Vanuatu.

I thought it was wasteful and a shame that many of Vanuatu's development decisions were made by ni-Vanuatu who did not understand the West and Westerners who did not understand Vanuatu.

"Development" is commonly defined as attaining a Western level of material wealth. We Westerners have obtained our material goods from our economic system. After thinking about it for a time, I concluded our economic system is intertwined with, and dependent on, our culture.

I also concluded Vanuatu's culture is not compatible with the Western economic system, and it is not realistic to expect that Vanuatu will reach our level of material wealth any time soon. Specifically, I found the following factors prevent Vanuatu from succeeding in our economic system:

1. For ni-Vanuatu, form usually trumps function. It is more important to be seen to be doing something than to do something that actually has a desired effect. For example, ni-Vanuatu who want to emulate Western wealth generation often make things to sell, but price them at less than the cost of materials. Or, supported by Western aid advisors who should have known better, set up fishing businesses that cost the fishermen for every kilo of fish they sell. Or, also supported by Westerners, enclose family chickens and buy feed for them instead of just letting them forage around the yard and produce meat at no cost.

2. In Vanuatu, "fair" means everyone ends up the same, rather than everyone starts out the same. If someone gets ahead, his neighbours are much more likely to bring him back down to their level rather than aspire to advance to his.

3. Ni-Vanuatu loyalty groups are very small and confined to family and clan. This is opposed to the West, where we tend to perceive at least our countrymen, and often the entire world population, as important to us.

4. In Vanuatu, if "you are not 100% with me, I perceive you as being 100% against me". Because very few people are likely to be 100% with anyone, the country is fragmented into hundreds of factions that do not work well together.

---

[1] In the late 1980s, Western politicians loved announcing that they were helping the third world. Their electorates that supported this knew nothing about doing it successfully, and most aid was "tied"; i.e. it had to be spent in the donor country. As a result, a lot of supposed international aid was actually subsidies to domestic industry.

5.   Ni-Vanuatu do not deal with the concept of chance well. Almost all occurrences are perceived to be the result of outside forces, often supernatural. Unwanted events are very often blamed on the actions of rivals or enemies. Therefore, because they don't think they can control the course of events, ni-Vanuatu often do not plan or take action to mitigate unwanted events. The exception is to attempt to use sorcery, which is not effective in the Western sense.

6.   Most ni-Vanuatu who start businesses do not differentiate between gross and net income or inventory vs. equity. Their relatives certainly don't, and demand a share of inventory or gross income, forcing the business to fail. For example:

(a) I once attended a conference on ni-Vanuatu business, at which four or five successful ni-Vanuatu businessmen and women were present. The British chair asked them why they succeeded where so many ni-Vanuatu didn't. They held a quick conference, then reported, "We pay our social obligations from our profits." Note that this would require that they be high in the social order, in order to resist demands on their gross incomes or inventories.

(b) When Westerners hire ni-Vanuatu, there frequently is a cycle: The employee learns his job and is good at it. Then, he just can't resist making things more "fair" in the Melanesian sense (i.e. we all must end up the same) and helps himself to cash or inventory. He gets caught and fired, receiving the government-mandated generous severance pay to boot. The cycle continues as he goes to work elsewhere while his former employer hires another ni-Vanuatu.

7.   Prior to contact, in the absence of markets for excess production, ni-Vanuatu sensibly only worked in their gardens until they had enough food, or in the forest to gather just enough bush materials to build a house. This attitude carries over into the present, and if possible, many ni-Vanuatu will work until they earn enough to make a planned purchase, and then quit. This drove the early planters crazy, so Tonkinese indentured labourers were imported from North Vietnam to plant all of Vanuatu's coconut plantations. There is some irony here, as many New Hebrideans were hired as indentured labourers in the 19th century to work in the sugar cane plantations of Queensland, Fiji, and Hawaii. There, of course, they had to work full-time. This was the controversial "blackbird" trade.

8.   The basic assumptions of my first university economics course, that man's needs are insatiable and can be expressed in monetary terms, don't apply here. Therefore, the rest of our economic theory built on these assumptions is a questionable basis for Western attempts to "develop" Vanuatu.

Of course, we have people in the West who have these characteristics, but they are a far smaller proportion of the population, and they usually don't run things.

So, Vanuatu is trying to play our economic and social game, with no chance of succeeding. I felt Vanuatu would be better off preserving the social and psychological benefits of village life, while providing some of what the West had to offer to people in the villages, rather than in the towns.

From an April 21, 1987 letter:

> Except for its inability to provide such imported services as modern health care and education, though, the economic system here does offer some advantages. Because the constitution decrees that all land belongs to the "custom" or original indigenous owners, every extended family owns land that is suitable for subsistence agriculture. When worse comes to worst, or if he tires of working for wages, every ni-Vanuatu just goes home to his family village and lives off the land. If all Europeans and their aid just up and went, life would go on with relatively minor adjustments. For example, nutrition would probably improve somewhat (tinned fish and white rice are big prestige foods here) and alcohol problems would disappear.

Unfortunately, as generations of ni-Vanuatu are raised in the urban areas of Port Vila and Luganville, some are losing their connection to their ancestral villages, land, and languages. People are becoming trapped in town and in the money economy.

The first two National Development Plans produced by the NPSO were laughable in their expectation that infrastructural and institutional development would result in an industrial economy. The Third National Vanuatu Development Plan that my compatriots and I wrote was focused on improving life in the rural villages rather than building up the two towns. Not that any attempt was made by those following us to implement it. In accordance with Vanuatu politics and government administrative principles, all of the ni-Vanuatu that we had trained to take over from us expatriates were dismissed and the NPSO shut down. Frankly, as Prime Minister Lini once stated on national radio, Vanuatu politicians saw us as obstacles to the receipt of aid from donors. He said we were "blocking development and building our own empires". In fact, we were unsuccessfully attempting to promote aid projects that did the most good for the entire country, rather than improve the lifestyle of the urban ni-Vanuatu elite, which was largely made up of politicians and senior civil servants. Fason blong Vanuatu and international aid in general.

I sometimes felt that the best development project for Vanuatu would be to bulldoze Port Vila, removing the incentive for politicians to push for and accept new government buildings, airport terminal, the parliament building (that replaced a perfectly good meeting room for the 50 MPs governing the population of a small city), national airline (a classic third-world money loser), and TV station (that served only the 20,000 people of Port Vila). The last three were considered top priorities by the government, and were not referred to the NPSO. When the French government donated Port Vila's TV station, national politicians started strutting around like they had accomplished the greatest feat of development ever.

As mentioned earlier, urban comforts were also an incentive for political corruption. Politicians who did not amass wealth during their terms had to return to their villages, a far cry from the fleshpots of Vila. This was a powerful incentive to do anything to squirrel away money while in power.

But, we Westerners feel we must at least try to help our fellow man, although it is not always successful or appreciated. As British colonialist Rudyard Kipling warned President Theodor Roosevelt, in what is today considered a non-Politically Correct poem, when the United States invaded and colonized the Philippines in 1899:

The White Man's Burden
- Rudyard Kipling

Take up the White Man's burden—
Send forth the best you breed—
Go bind your sons to exile
To serve your captive's need;
To wait in heavy harness,
On fluttered folk and wild—
Your new-caught, sullen peoples,
Half-devil and half-child.

Take up the White Man's burden—
In patience to abide,
To veil the threat of terror,
And check the show of pride;
By open speech and simple,
A hundred times made plain
To seek another's profit,
And work another's gain.

Two Years on Malekula

Take up the White Man's burden—
The savage wars of peace—
Fill full the mouth of Famine
And bid the sickness cease;
And when your goal is nearest
The end for others sought,
Watch sloth and heathen Folly
Bring all your hopes to nought.

Take up the White Man's burden—
No tawdry rule of kings,
But toil of serf and sweeper—
The tale of common things.
The ports ye shall not enter,
The roads ye shall not tread,
Go mark them with your living,
And mark them with your dead.

Take up the White Man's burden—
And reap his old reward;
The blame of those ye better,
The hate of those ye guard—
The cry of hosts ye humour
(Ah, slowly!) toward the light—
"Why brought he us from bondage,
Our loved Egyptian night?"

Take up the White Man's burden—
Ye dare not stoop to less—
Nor call too loud on Freedom
To cloak your weariness;
By all ye cry or whisper,
By all ye leave or do,
The silent, sullen peoples
Shall weigh your gods and you.

Take up the White Man's burden—
Have done with childish days—
The lightly proffered laurel,
The easy, ungrudged praise.
Comes now, to search your manhood
Through all the thankless years
Cold, edged with dear-bought wisdom,
The judgment of your peers!

Regional Development Planner Work

I'm not going to claim that my presence on Malekula had an extraordinary effect on the island. But, as an Australian co-worker in Vila, who really did know what he was doing, said about our office a few years later, I may have done less damage than someone else would have. Perhaps the most valuable thing I did in two years on Malekula was to learn about Vanuatu, so that in the future I did less damage as Vanuatu's first Regional Development Planning Advisor.

My job title was "Regional Development Planner", one of several CUSOs plus one weird Australian[1] who were assigned to Vanuatu's Local Government Councils. The job description CUSO gave me was a little sketchy, and CUSO hadn't bothered sending my CV to the Malekula LGC, so my first meeting with the LGC executive was a process of both sides feeling each other out.

They knew nothing about me except my name. I gave them a condensed version of my résumé, and they seemed pleased.

Mind you, I hadn't yet learned to read ni-Vanuatu body language. How could they be pleased with a guy whose professional experience consisted of managing livestock and agricultural lending? I then asked them what they wanted me to do for them.

CUSO had told me I'd be going out and communing with "the people"—helping them realize their hopes and dreams. Well, my compatriots did mention that, but it came through loud and clear that my first priority was to organize enterprises that would make the LGC a profit.

The LGC was desperate for funds. The central government had given it the right to collect head tax (1000 vatu/year/person) and sell business licenses. Most people wouldn't pay tax because they didn't think the LGC did anything for them and before independence the colonial powers provided everything free, or because they aren't in the money economy and had no source of funds. Also, because the Vanuatu constitution guarantees that the traditional land tenure system will prevail, there is no way to put a lien on a person's land, and no way to take it in lieu of unpaid taxes or loans. Nobody in Vanuatu has to pay anything they don't want to. This has had the unforeseen consequence of depriving ni-Vanuatu businesses and individuals of access to commercial credit,

---

[1] A "Breatharian" who believed that he could eventually obtain all his nutrition from the air. He refused to cooperate with CUSOs, persuaded the island on which he worked to buy a bunch of telephone equipment that never got working, and fled home with his wife after the May 16, 1988 Port Vila Riot. Months later, he phoned requesting my support for another business deal. I declined.

perhaps not altogether a bad thing given the propensity of ni-Vanuatu businesses to lose money and collapse.

The central government has told the LGCs to get into business to earn income. Easier said than done in a subsistence economy.

From a 9 March, 1987 letter:

> Every CUSO who had been to Vanuatu told me that T-shirt, shorts, and thongs were standard dress at all levels here, so that's all I brought. Hogwash! Every LGC office employee (except me) wears a shirt and trousers, and almost all wear shoes. I did bring a few Aloha shirts, so I've been wearing them with my shorts and thongs. Actually, I do have some pants, socks, and leather sandals, but this is more comfortable.

I also found some inexpensive white short-sleeved shorts at an After-Uma-Going-Out-of-Business sale on my first trip to Vila, and wore them frequently.

Working Relationships
From an April 12, 1987 letter:

> I am having a bit of trouble getting plugged in here. On Friday, I had started walking up the hill with my counterpart when he casually mentioned that a World Bank consultant was meeting with Keith Mala, the Malekula Local Government Council Secretary[1] When I expressed an interest in sitting in, he told me that he had considered it, but after all, we were going to speak with the assistant works foreman about the cost of manufacturing concrete bricks for sale. I managed to get us turned around and into the meeting. It turned out to be an Asian Development Bank team looking into vocational training in Vanuatu. I think that comes under "Regional Development Planning". In the meeting, during which the team leader constantly looked to me for input but I had the sense to remain silent, I learned that there were three vocational institutes on this island and I got a run-down on their strengths and weaknesses (all from the team). At least it has been decided to move my office

---

[1] Brit-speak for top civil servant.

down to next to Keith's. There won't be too many teams like that that get into his office without me then! They aren't big on sharing information here. We had a staff meeting this week (staff consisting mostly of blue-collar workers), in which a long time was spent telling us not to uncrumple stuff out of other peoples' wastebaskets to read(?) and not to read stuff on other peoples' desks.

Financial Analyses and Pricing of Services and Goods
The LGC Minibus

The first LGC business I tackled was the minibus. Impressively, since governments in Vanuatu almost always rely on foreign aid to obtain anything, shortly before I arrived the LGC had bought a 15-seat minibus which was servicing the mid- and north-east shores of Malekula.

This minibus was an important part of development because before it came along transportation on the island was very expensive by motorized vehicle or time-consuming on foot. Although it was true that nearly every vehicle (all pickups) on Malekula was a taxi, and several "speedboats" (small motorboats) also operated as taxis, these were inaccessible to almost everyone due to their cash fares. A typical fare was 5,000vt[1], which was far beyond the reach of most people. Now, the minibus was, at a small fraction of that cost, transporting people and their goods to the hospital, the government offices, the weekly Norsup market, and the Norsup airstrip.

I started off by asking for the LGC Minibus file, and received a thick folder of all the back correspondence with the central government. There were no cost or ridership estimates—I was still pretty green regarding ni-Vanuatu ways, but learning. So, I asked Lambert Maltock, my counterpart at the time, what fare was being charged. He replied 30vt. I then asked how that amount had been arrived at, and he told me that they had felt that was what people could afford.

Properly pricing goods for sale, i.e. hitting that "sweet spot" between covering all costs and what people were willing to pay, was a serious problem in Vanuatu. Most people, including men and women selling things, had little idea of how to do this.

Identical goods in adjacent stores could be offered at widely different prices, and comparison shopping or bargaining was rare.

This applied to western material goods; calculations of the cost of traditional purchases could be quite sophisticated. Lakatoro's Australian Livestock Officer

---

[1] Close enough to CAN$50.

told me his workers made complex calculations, of a net present value nature, comparing the costs of brides from different islands: "Brides are more expensive on Malekula, but if I buy a less expensive bride from another island, I'll have to pay in the future for her to periodically visit her family."

Complex economic arrangements were also made to accumulate the number of tusked pigs (at least 7 years old to have full-circle tusks) needed for killing in ceremonies that advanced men in the traditional nimangki grade-taking system. It would take years of planning, raising pigs, trading younger pigs for older, and calling in obligations to obtain the number of pigs required to advance a grade.

I researched the bus finances by quizzing the bus driver and LGC mechanics on the number of passengers, amount of gasoline used, price of gasoline, maintenance needed, and cost of that maintenance. Putting it all together, I discovered that the Minibus was losing money on each passenger. I was to later learn that this was not an unusual feature of ni-Vanuatu business, and was the cause of many frustrating failures to emulate Whiteman wealth generation.

Lambert Maltok, Assistant LGC Secretary and my first counterpart, on right with large yam he bought at a World Food Day market.

Sitting down with Lambert, I suggested that, as in Fiji where my family had laid over on the way to Vanuatu, we divide the island into zones. Then, we should charge 50vt per zone to make a reasonable return on the LGC's investment. Lambert thought that sounded OK, and Keith agreed, so the new pricing scheme was implemented.

A few days later, I heard on the radio that all the minibuses in Port Vila had raised their fares to 50vt. I had a pretty good idea where that notion had come from, and hoped nobody else in the country also knew.

Within the next year, three more minibuses started up on Malekula. They all lost money because, unlike the LGC bus, they only serviced their home villages. Other villages, especially remote ones, had no bus service at all, since the LGC minibus couldn't be everywhere at once. I suggested to one village minibus driver/owner that he provide service to some of these villages.

Rack of pigs' lower jaws with tusks on Vao Island displaying
one man's namangki progress.

He told me he went to one once, but nobody got on. I told him this was because they didn't know he was coming, and if he went there regularly, he would build up a clientele. No interest. I also learned, and maybe that driver knew better than me, that only people from the home village of a minibus would use it, because due to inter-village, -clan, -family, and -anything else rivalry, people would not give their money to minibuses or any other business that wasn't from their village. This is where the LGC minibus had the advantage, as it was owned by the neutral LGC rather than a rival ni-Vanuatu.

The LGC minibus ran successfully until my second Christmas on Malekula, when the driver over-indulged on holiday cheer and ran the bus into a coconut tree. Rough repairs were made, but the business seemed to be going downhill when I left.

Public Phones

After I priced the minibus, I took on pricing the public phones. There were only 7 telephones on Malekula, population 20,000: two in the LGC office, one LGC public phone in Lakatoro, one up island that had been taken over by an aggressive family with political connections, another run by the LGC in a different village, one on Metenesel Estates (a cocoa plantation run by the Commonwealth Development Corporation on Malekula's east coast), and presumably one on the privately-owned PRV plantation at Norsup. The LGC wanted me to organize things so that profit from the LGC's public phones paid for the two office phones. I soon learned all of the phone bills had been sent to the central government in Vila, which maintained tight control of LGC spending. After days going over all the information I could find in Lakatoro, I gave up hope of analysing the enterprise, and left the existing system in place.

The public phone system in Lakatoro was a lady in a room with a line-up of customers outside on the covered veranda. She used a wristwatch to time calls and charged a rate per minute. After an international call, she would phone the operator in Vila to learn what the charges were and add them to the normal cost. I had no idea if the system was even breaking even; what information I could find was incomprehensible.

One unique Vanuatu issue relating to telephone service on Malekula arose twice while we lived there. The connection between Port Vila and Luganville was about half-a-dozen circuits transmitted via microwave. One of the microwave towers was a bit north of Lakatoro. Whenever the owner of the land on which the tower was situated wanted to draw attention to a dispute over the ownership of an adjoining parcel of land, he would block access to the tower. He did this by fastening a nemele (tree fern) leaf to the gate of the chain link fence surrounding the tower. This signified a kastom tabu against entrance, punishable by death. The tower's relay electronics had to be periodically maintained to keep them operational, and when maintenance personnel couldn't get to it, it would eventually cease operating. Then, all telephone service between Vanuatu's two towns Luganville and Port Vila would be cut off, as well as service between Malekula and Luganville. Eventually the land owner would feel that honour had been served and remove the nemele leaf so telephone service could be resumed. One time, though, an especially adventurous serviceman climbed the fence to repair the electronics.

This land owner was at the time the national Commissioner of Police and later served as Prime Minister for a time. Fason blong Vanuatu Bigman.

Corrugated Iron Roofing Sheets and Concrete Blocks

The LGC also sold corrugated roofing iron and concrete blocks. I suggested prices for them after determining costs and adding a mark-up. The concrete blocks were interesting because the objective seemed to be to mix as little cement as possible with the sand in order to result in a block that kind-of held together. LGC staff no doubt knew their market well and kept prices as low as possible.

We sold concrete blocks to the company contracted by the Japanese to build a commercial centre, but the Japanese engineers were much more particular about their quality, bouncing a hammer off blocks made from different mixes until a recipe was found that provided blocks of suitable strength.

Resthouses

Another of the LGC's business was a resthouse (travellers' hostel) in Norsup, about 8km north of Lakatoro. The difficulty with this was that guests, who often flew into the Norsup airstrip, had to come to Lakatoro during business hours to pay and obtain the key.

There was also an LGC resthouse building in Lakatoro, but it had been abandoned after damage from various cyclones. The Fijian construction company building a Japanese-funded wharf and commercial centre needed a place for their workers to live, so I negotiated a deal with them to repair the resthouse in return for using it for a few months. The resthouse then returned to its intended use at a profit to the LGC.

While I was at it, I negotiated with the Japanese engineers on their rental of a couple of LGC rooms for offices in order to transfer as much money as possible from the wharf project to the Local Government Council.

Village Fisheries Project

Almost all fishing by ni-Vanuatu was done with hand lines off the coral reefs surrounding most of the islands' coasts or by spearing fish in shallow waters. Due to the steepness of the mountains that make up most of Vanuatu's islands, pelagic fish offshore are found at depths of 200 metres or more and are not accessible by traditional Vanuatu technology.

The Village Fisheries Project was designed to allow village men to access deep-water fish and sell them in towns. It was a collaborative effort by several aid agencies. Japan furnished several shipping containers of equipment, including pickups, motorcycles, outboard engines, generators, ice-making plants, and fishing equipment. In fact, they provided so much cargo that after a couple of years, they sent a volunteer whose job consisted solely of counting and cataloguing the tonnes of stuff that hadn't been used yet.

CUSO provided experienced Canadian commercial fishermen to act as Fisheries Officers in villages near airstrips around the archipelago. One of these Fisheries Centres was at Lakatoro.

A ni-Vanuatu boat-building enterprise was set up in Luganville to provide—wait for it—fishing boats.

Several Fish Aggregating Devices were put out in the sea near islands to encourage fish to congregate where they could be more easily harvested. The FADs were buoys with, to use the technical term, "stuff" extending down from them where things fish eat would grow and attract the fish. (It was this technical expertise that qualified me to handle the Fisheries aspect of the National Planning Office later on.)

Basically, ni-Vanuatu village men applied for positions in the programme. Successful applicants were lent money to purchase a package comprising a 15-ft plywood boat, 25hp and 15hp (for backup) outboard motors, a couple of large downrigger reels, and various lines, lures, and other fishing gear. The central government Fisheries Department sold them subsidized gasoline for their outboards.

The plan was for the fishermen to go offshore, repeatedly reel out a couple hundred metres of line, and pull in their catch. They would then sell the fish to their local Fisheries Centre, which would pack it in ice and take it to the nearby airstrip, from where it would be flown to the urban centres of Vila and Luganville to be sold in Fisheries Department retail shops.

One day early in my contract when I was otherwise unoccupied, I grabbed a cheap pupil's notebook and a pencil and headed down to the Lakatoro Fisheries Centre to gather data for another financial analysis. From fellow CUSO Ross Combdon (late of Joe Batt's Arm, Newfoundland), I learned how much the fishermens' loan payments were, their gasoline cost, their average catch, and how often they went out. Ross also gave me other information about the programme.

This is the reality I learned about the programme on Malekula:

- The fishermen were also subsistence farmers and were not available to go fishing more than two or three times per week.
- Reeling in fish from the deep takes a long time, and sharks often ate them on the way up.
- In the wet cyclone season, the sea was often too rough on both the east and west sides of Malekula for fishing.
- In the dry trade-wind season, the sea was often too rough on the east side of the island for fishing.
- The government dictated a low airfreight rate for the fish, so Air

Melanesiæ gave them a lower priority than other cargo. Fish were sometimes left behind to spoil.

- The Fisheries Department was always after the fishermen because they illegally, but sensibly, used their subsidized gasoline to run more-profitable boat taxi services rather than fishing.
- The generator and ice machine at the Lakatoro Fisheries Centre was greatly oversized and much more expensive to operate than necessary.

The bottom line was that the fishermen lost money on every kilo of fish they caught. In essence, cash-poor outer islanders were laboriously cutting copra, their only source of money, to subsidize protein consumption in the urban centres. I forwarded my findings to CUSO in Vila to no effect. Nobody wants to hear that a programme they invested heavily in, without doing due diligence up-front, is contributing to the problem, not the solution. Fason blong development agency.

The Lakatoro Bakery

From a November 20, 1987 letter to my father, who had worked on development projects around the world:

They don't have coffee cans[1] here, but I have discovered some new units of measure. Last week, I went down to the bakery down by the co-op store to calculate the cost of production of bread baking. The local measure of flour is the "Dribarm tin" (Australian brand of yeast), yeast and sugar are measured in soupspoons, and the correct amount of water is "about up to here in this bucket". I thought I had a chance at some hard information when I spotted a balance and the baker confirmed that yes, he did weigh the dough for each loaf. How much weight did he put on the balance per loaf? "Well, for the French loaf, I use these three rocks, I add this rock here for a small English loaf, and this other one for a big English loaf."

I borrowed his rocks and weighed them on a scale in the co-op store next door (300 gm per French loaf), and headed home to measure the volume of Holly's Dribarm tin (3.75 cups) and soupspoon (two teaspoons). Then to my reference, "The Joy of Cooking", for weight per volume of flour, sugar, and salt. I'm enclosing my rough copy of my advice to the people of Mbonvor Village on pricing their bread.

---

[1] Reported by my father to be the universal unit of measurement for livestock rations during his youth.

Maybe it's the same where you've been, but asking people how much or how many of something they've got is an interesting experience here. Anything over about three is just "a bunch". If you ask a farmer how many cattle he has, and there are, say, 12, he has to verbally count them up by name. Same with asking a village chief how many families are in the village he has lived in all of his life[1].

I have had to point out to expatriates that villagers who have told them the amount of time a task takes aren't wearing any watches, and probably have never owned one. Distance is the other one. I've come to the conclusion that "klosap" means, for example, if you are going to a klosap village, it is the next one on the road, no matter how far it is. I think "longwe litelbit" means it is the second or third. To confuse matters, "longwe" also just means "over there".

Women's Business Workshop

Holly assisted some women from the Vanuatu Women's Centre, both expat and ni-Vanuatu, with a one-month Business Workshop in Lakatoro. Most of the time was spent learning how to make things to sell, like quilts, jam[2], etc. I took it upon myself to appropriate an afternoon to speak on my favoured topic of pricing merchandise. As an example, I used the Island Dress, the ubiquitous rural female ni-Vanuatu garb. I guess the London Missionary Society preachers who came to the New Hebrides were less strict than the ones who went to Hawaii, because the ni-Vanuatu version of the muumuu only comes down to below the knee, rather than the ground. Island dresses are lovely, being made of colourful tropical prints, gathered at the waist, with wide lace on the shoulders and around the neck, and ribbons flying from the short sleeves. The necks are deep-cut for handy breast-feeding.

---

[1] A CUSO doctor later told me it was the same when asking a man how many children he had.

[2] An unintended consequence of Holly demonstrating her jam-making prowess was our neighbour's wife bringing up a bucket of guavas and announcing that she'd be back later for her jam. If you couldn't laugh at this stuff you'd go crazy, or go home as an "early return".

Women, some in island dresses, quilting at the
Women's Business Workshop.

These women were not stupid, and, as usual, I probably learned more from them than they did from me. I wrote on the blackboard as they told me what materials went into a dress, how much of each one was needed, and how much each cost. So far, so good. Then, the Whiteman added a line for labour. The women were adamant that their labour was worth nothing; they just made these things while they were sitting around chatting with other women.

I finally realized that it was true; there is so much excess female labour in villages, where cash is hard to get, that one woman can't ask another to pay scarce cash for labour they already have in abundance.

Sadly, though, I wasn't too surprised when I asked what they could sell a dress for, it was less than the cost of materials. Ni-Vanuatu saw Whitemen accumulating what to them was vast amounts of material goods by making or even just selling things, but were frustrated when they went through the motions but received no gain. Form over function.

Litzlitz Wharf

The biggest aid project implemented on Malekula during my two years there was the construction of a wharf south of Litzlitz, which was itself a bit south of Lakatoro. It was a Japanese aid project that had been selected and planned before I arrived and without, as far as I could tell, input from anyone on Malekula.

Two Years on Malekula

The wharf project was headed by two Japanese engineers, with a Fijian company contracted for the construction. All were pleasant to work with.

The site chosen for the wharf had apparently been the scene of executions of wrongdoers by drowning in the old days. So the "ground-breaking" ceremony did not feature the traditional sacrifice of a pig by clubbing it on the head. No, blood must be spilled. So the chief of Litzlitz village placed the apparently dull tip of his bushknife between two ribs of the chosen pig and hammered away on it with the palm of his hand, accompanied by the shrill protests of the recipient of this attention, until the bushknife finally found a vital spot.

Litzlitz chief killing pig with bushknife.

During the wharf's construction, I made it my business to attempt to:

1. Influence the project so that it provided more "development" for Malekula,

2. Limit any collateral damage from the project, and

3. Extract as much benefit as possible for the LGC.

To mis-quote Meatloaf, "One-and-a-half out of three ain't bad." I claim full points for Number 3, and half points for Number 2.

Two Years on Malekula

Litzlitz wharf under construction, with Heather flying a kite from it.

The wharf wasn't a bad thing for Malekula; perhaps it was the best infrastructure project possible. Malekula is one of the few Vanuatu islands with a rudimentary road network, but it did not have a wharf where the major exports—copra and cacao—could be loaded on coastal freighters to go to the international copra wharf at Luganville, Espiritu Santo Island. Cargo could only be loaded on freighters using small lighter boats, or it could be loaded on landing craft that pulled up onto beaches. The new wharf would be the hub of Malekula's transportation system.

Nevertheless, it would have been better if some consultation had taken place.

From a January 31, 1988 letter home:

> Speaking of development, I have had another coup regarding the Commercial Centre soon to be built by the Japanese. As you will recall, a wharf will be built in the bush a couple of kilometres south of Litzlitz, a few kilometres south of here. The plan was to erect a building with copra and cocoa storage, wholesale space, retail space, and bank offices near the wharf. Copra and cocoa storage makes sense, but who is going to relocate retail/banking to a spot in the bush? Not wanting to disrupt the PM's pet project, I didn't make an official fuss, but I did mention my feelings to all Ministers, Ministerial Assistants, MPs, LGC administrators, Japanese Engineers, etc. that came within range. With the head Japanese Engineer, I hit pay dirt. He told the Director of the Co-operative

Department (who I think is the governmental authority in charge of the project; it isn't really clear who is) that the existing plan wasn't logical and offered to split the building in two for no extra cost. I was copied in on a letter from the Director stating that they weren't going to repeat previous mistakes (two of these centres are presently sitting empty in the middle of nowhere), and the building was to be split with the commodity storage staying at the wharf and the wholesale/retail/banking part going to Lakatoro, where we have a site ready just across from the existing Co-op store. The saga continues.

In the event, the Japanese Government vetoed any changes to the project.

The Japanese government funded one infrastructure project in Vanuatu each year. A few years later, when my central government responsibilities included energy development, they planned to build a small hydroelectric project outside of Luganville, Espiritu Santo Island. Politicians started going on like this was going to be the Grand Coulee Dam, with free power for the town and the basis for an industrial park. I checked with Vanuatu's existing power company and learned that the Japanese hydro generator would produce less power than Vila's smallest backup diesel generator, i.e. a negligible amount. A team of New Zealand hydro experts took a quick look at the Japanese plans and determined that if it was built slightly differently, enough money would be saved to install a second generator at the site and double the project's electricity production. The Japanese government vetoed any changes. Once the Japanese Government decided how a project would be implemented, there was no room for adaptation to local conditions. Perhaps if someone on the spot like me had been involved with the initial planning, things would have turned out differently. So goes international development.

I turned my attention to mitigating negative consequences of the Malekula wharf project. A large quantity of sand was going to be needed for concrete. The easiest place to get it was from Aop Beach a couple of kilometres north of Lakatoro. Now, contrary to popular belief, not every south Pacific island is ringed with sand beaches. Most of the coasts of Vanuatu's islands are dead coral reefs that have risen out of the sea due to regular tectonic uplifts as Australia's plate pushes under Vanuatu's. Aop Beach was the only nice sandy beach on this part of the island. Not only did it protect the main road behind it from sea erosion, it might be the setting for a resort someday. I actually persuaded the Fijian construction company to use sand from the much less attractive south end of the beach. As an unforeseen positive consequence of my success, the ni-Vanuatu whose land included Aop Beach decided it had value to him and stopped letting other people take sand from it. Saving Aop Beach was perhaps my greatest achievement as a CUSO in Lakatoro, and not just because Aop Beach was our favourite Sunday picnic spot. Not much of a boast, but you take what you can get.

Me on Aop Beach, which I take personal credit for having saved.

Further in my letter:

> Last week, a subcontractor on the wharf project told me of his plan to put a bulk diesel storage tank on the beach I saved from the concrete mixer. Now, I just have to get him to use drums instead (hang the cost, the Japanese are paying!). He'll just have to confine his oil spills to the wharf area and kill the reef there.

Despite my protests, a large diesel tank was deposited there by a landing craft-type vessel to provide fuel for construction machinery. In the end, though, there was no noticeable pollution. One can't always be right.

The commercial centre associated with the wharf was constructed with concrete blocks manufactured and sold by the LGC The entire project was built by men housed in the LGC's future Lakatoro guest house and managed by Japanese engineers living in the LGC's Norsup guest house and using offices in rented LGC rooms. It was useful infrastructure, so things could have been worse.

Emergency Food Relief

In early 1988, I organized food relief for parts of Malekula. I had better preface this account with an explanation of my attitude towards relief aid in Vanuatu. It can be necessary on occasion, of course. Nevertheless, Vanuatu has a well-deserved reputation as being "the land of waving palms"; the Pacific as a whole up to this time having received many more times foreign aid per capita than places that could better use it, such as truly poor places like Bangladesh and many African countries. Part of ni-Vanuatu culture is that getting stuff for free brings social prestige, and as I later learned working in Vila in the National Planning Office, the nation will claim that any type of aid is essential. I had no intention of becoming perceived as a conduit for free stuff, or as it is known in Vanuatu, "cargo". I was determined to refuse to support unnecessary aid requests when appropriate[1]. I had seen unnecessary aid doled out on Efate after Cyclone Uma and later learned that there is extensive literature about inappropriate aid responses to natural disasters. Western governments often send aid that isn't useful instead of aid that is. This looks good to electorates who are demanding immediate action but have little idea of what is truly needed in disaster situations. (Spoiler Alert—it is tarps and plastic sheeting for shelter and water purification equipment, not food and clothing.)

The vast majority of Malekula's population,[2] like the rest of the country, were subsistence gardeners operating outside the money economy. They all grew their own food; they had little money to buy food, and outside of Lakatoro/Norsup there was no retail system where it could be purchased. CUSO cooperants who were posted anywhere but Vila, Santo, Lakatoro, or Tanna had to arrange for local gardeners to sell them food until their own gardens matured. They also had urban shops air-freight food to them.

The crops that provided almost all calories fell into two main categories. Root crops such as kumala (sweet potato), yams, cassava (tapioca), and cooking bananas were included in one of Vanuatu's official food groups: "Kakae blong givem paoa" or "Food for giving energy". The second food group was "Kakae blong bildimap bodi", or "Food for building bodies": i.e. protein such as seafood and meat. The main source of protein in rural Vanuatu was small snails picked up on coastal reefs at low tide, with the odd chicken and fruit bat thrown in. Cattle and pigs were too "lumpy" to serve as regular food; in the absence of refrigeration each one had to be eaten immediately, which made them suitable only for large feasts.

---

[1] When I applied later for the position of Regional Planning Advisor with the central government, the Malekula LGC did not support my application. Surprised, the National Planning Office aid advisors asked an Australian volunteer in Lakatoro why this was so. His response was that they didn't think I'd brought them enough cargo. I got the NPO job.

[2] 98% according to the then latest-available 1979 census.

Finally, there was "Kakae blong blockem mo daonem sik", or "Food for preventing and fighting illness": i.e., fruits and vegetables such as papayas, eating bananas, pineapples, oranges, grapefruit, and a leaf known as "island cabbage". Many fruits were seasonal and only available in the hot wet season.

I have been known to joke that Vanuatu, as a developing nation, could only afford three food groups, rather than Canada's then-five[1]: Veggies, Fruit, Cereals, Meat, and Milk. Of course, one of Canada's food groups, Milk products, was only included separately from other protein foods as a marketing tool for the dairy industry.

"Eat Some Food From Every Group Every Day to Remain in Good Health"

---

[1] Canada has since caught up with the Third World and now has the same three food groups as Vanuatu. Its heavily-protected dairy industry is not amused.

Two Years on Malekula

The dry season (May to October) of 1987 was much drier than usual, which my second counterpart, Kalosak Masing, attributed to the sun having moved 20km closer to the earth—he said he'd garnered this information from "The National Enquirer[1] " and wasn't interested in my input that with the sun averaging 150 million kilometres from earth, 20km wouldn't make any difference. Large numbers were not the average ni-Vanuatu's forte.

Root crops suffered from lack of rain, and yields were low that year. The normal response to this would be to simply eat more cooking bananas, which were preferred over root crops in any case. Unfortunately, this severe dry season was followed on January 11, 1988 by Cyclone Anne, which blew down most cooking banana plants[2]. It would take 3 months for new root crops to grow, and a year for new cooking bananas. Northwest Malekula, in the rain shadow of Malekula's mountains from the dry season's south-easterly Trade Winds, was affected more than northeast Malekula, while the south half of the island was relatively unscathed.

A few days after Cyclone Anne, the LGC started to get requests for food from Malekula villages. The point was made that places on Efate had received rice food aid last year after Cyclone Uma, even if they weren't damaged very much. This had been perceived by all as a real coup, as white rice was a luxury prestige convenience food in Vanuatu villages. It had to be purchased with money, was associated with Whitemen, and could be cooked in fifteen minutes. I just ignored the requests, but Lambert, the Assistant Secretary, called a meeting of the Disaster Response Committee, and it was decided, with my input, to request enough food to give the affected area (NW coast of Malekula) quarter-rations for a month.

Lambert, the LGC Assistant Secretary, didn't want to waste any time sending a few people over in a truck to verify the situation. The disaster relief people in Vila had other ideas, so I spent two days touring the area with two members of the Self-Defence Force (i.e., the military) and giving out a few tarps to people whose houses had been destroyed.

I finally accepted that some aid was required in this situation. Banana plants were about the only cyclone damage, though. Five houses on the East side of the island were washed away because they had been built right on the beach, an old rotten nurses' house up north was blown over, and a mango tree fell on a house in one village, injuring an elderly woman who was inside alone. Her considerate

---

[1] Yes, two copies weekly made their way to Vanuatu, and those pre-internet days I frequently bought one of them when we lived in Vila to supplement the BBC World Service News I got on my short-wave receiver. The main thing I learned was who Vanna White was.

[2] Contrary to popular belief in the northern hemisphere, bananas do not grow on trees. They grow on tall non-woody plants that are cut down in order to harvest the fruit. Years later, I chortled while watching contestants on the TV program "Survivor—Vanuatu" lift each other up so they could reach bananas and cut them down.

fellow villagers left her in bed for a week-and-a-half before a Rural Health truck came and took her to hospital. The bus fare would have been 100 vatu. In Vanuatu, if you don't have family to look after you, including providing food while you are in hospital, things can get rough.

Saturday January 23, a helicopter was supposed to come help us check out some places behind blocked roads, so I waited for an hour by the local soccer field, the usual local landing spot. The clouds were pretty low, though, so they didn't come. Later the two ni-Vanuatu soldiers who had come to do the damage survey asked me for a ride to the Norsup airstrip to be picked up by a New Zealand Air Force transport plane, so I told Holly I'd be half an hour and took them.

After the soldiers boarded, a plane crewman came over and told me that the helicopter was in Santo standing by waiting for me to assist in damage assessment of Malekula from the air. So, after extracting a promise from him to get me home that evening, I rolled up the windows on the LGC truck and hopped in the plane. Upon arrival in Santo, I learned that the helicopter first had to go up to the north of the island and would leave to inspect Malekula at 1500. I went off with another guy and visited some friends, had lunch, and bought some passion fruit (vt100/large basket) and chocolate bars for the family. This was a trip to the big city—a rare opportunity! I couldn't find peanut butter, as many of the stores were closed Saturday afternoon. At the Chinese café where I lunched, I ran into Mark Stafford, a Brit I'd met before. He told me he was in charge of distributing cyclone relief rice, so I took the opportunity to convince him to allot 25 tons for Malekula, whose request had been previously denied. Sometimes this disaster relief business can be a bit arbitrary.

Back at the airfield, we learned that the estimated time of departure was 1630, and that the helicopter had to be back in Vila (1-1/2 hour flight) by dark at 1900 so it could be washed in preparation for dismantling for shipping back to Australia in a Hercules the next morning.

We were just boarding at 1620, when along came the Minister of Finance. He just had to have a ride back to his village one-half hour flight away on the north of the island. The helicopter had picked him up there that morning, because he had to be in Vila the next morning to accept the acting Prime Ministership, the PM being in New Zealand for physiotherapy for stroke injuries suffered one year before. The Finance Minister's village airstrip was soggy from the hurricane rain, hence the special helicopter pickup. It was explained to him that the helicopter was needed for hurricane relief work. No matter, he hadn't brought his Vila house keys or family with him that morning. Claimed he hadn't known why the helicopter had come to pick him up. So, off went the helicopter for an hour.

At 1730, with the crew anxious to get the one-and-a-half hour flight to Vila over before 1900, we boarded. I had received the pre-flight passenger briefing during the first boarding attempt: "Put on this RFD (Rescue Flotation Device?—a type of inflatable life jacket). If we go down in water, don't exit the aircraft before it sinks; the spinning rotor blades will cut you in half. Wait for the helicopter to sink and fill with water before opening a door and exiting. Here, practice sliding the door open, but don't worry, it's a great machine." I lost brownie points by opining that I had never heard of anyone surviving a helicopter crash to the wait-for-it-to-sink stage.

There were a pilot and co-pilot up front and, in the back, a crewman at each window with me and Mark Stafford sitting between them. Everyone wore headsets for communication because of the engine noise, but because they were short one headset, I got to wear a helmet, just like Steve Canyon[1] ! We had two tarpaulins with us to deliver to a village cut off from Lakatoro by a high river, plus my personal family relief supplies of two baskets of passion fruit and a plastic bag of chocolate bars.

About ten minutes into the flight, a crewman spotted someone signalling us from the ground with a mirror. He reported that it was deliberate—the flash had followed us through 120 degrees. We circled back, swooped down, and I wasn't surprised to hear the report that a group of children were gaily waving at us, as I had witnessed the old mirror trick before. I switched on my intercom and reminded them that our primary mission here was to provide entertainment for the locals, but I got the impression that the crew didn't like my attitude. All-in-all, I found them pretty uptight.

Off we went down the west coast of Malekula. Of course, absolutely no damage was visible from the air. Their map showed Malekula as about one inch long, so I volunteered to guide us to Leviamp, where the tarps were to be dropped off. Leviamp is south of a cliff on the coast, so I guided them to a collection of bush houses south of a big cliff and told them to land at the soccer field. The pilot said something about not seeing the field, but since they were in a hurry, they would just plunk down on the beach. A crewman jumped out, dumped the tarps in front of some astounded villagers, who no doubt perceived this as manna from heaven, or at least consistent with the cargo cult philosophy. As we took off, I could see that this *wasn't* Leviamp, but a place next to the second cliff north of Leviamp. Everyone was in a big hurry, and I look at these tarps as political relief aid anyway, as everyone has zillions of friends and relatives to stay with for the few days it takes to build a new house. Therefore, I kept my peace, and off we went.

I requested we fly over the interior, so I could check out reports of landslides in gardens, but since they were in such a hurry, they took the most direct route to Norsup airport. This route, of course, went north of the area I wanted to inspect, so we landed in Norsup after I had wasted my entire afternoon. Such is development. At least I got some passion fruit and chocolate out of the deal,

---

[1] Heroic US Air Force character in an old comic strip.

which went some way to assuage Holly's displeasure with me disappearing without explanation for the afternoon. Of course, I had also secured rice food relief for Malekula from Mark.

So went my big day in Santo. I told all the CUSO's I had shared a beer with not to tell the CUSO Field Staff Officers in Vila that I had come up, or they might count it as one of my bush leaves.

The relief rice that Mark Stafford had promised showed up by ship in two batches. I had started planning its distribution by performing a rough census of the island so I would know how many people needed to be fed in each village. The word was sent out, and most villages responded quickly with a head count. I estimated the population of the few non-respondents by using the numbers I had received from responding villages to estimate the population growth since the 1979 official census and applying that rate to the '79 numbers of the non-respondent villages. Then, I recommended that with the first rice shipment we provide enough rice to the northwest villages to feed them twice a week for a few weeks and enough to the northeast villages to feed them once a week for the same period.

Moving these few tonnes of rice for this relatively small number of food-days educated me in the realities of food aid logistics. Malekula did not have a proper wharf, so the 25kg bags of rice were moved by lighter (small boat) from a coastal freighter lying off the Lakatoro landing stage. Men then carried them to a Public Works Department dump truck, which moved the rice to the LGC offices, where the men carried them into the meeting room where it was stored. Man; this was like moving hay bales in Alberta, except I was supervising rather than lugging.

The first quantity of rice was distributed over two days in a PWD dump truck, again loaded by men. We started with the northwest villages. At each village, everyone gathered and I explained that enough rice was being given for two day's food per week for a few weeks. This was readily understood by most, but I did get a couple of interesting responses. A man at one village wanted to know if this is how they would get all their food from now on—instant aid dependence! I responded, "No, this is only enough for…" At another village, a man asked the equivalent of the old Wendy's commercial, "Where's the Beef?", or in this case, "Why aren't you giving us any meat?" My response was, "Did the cyclone kill all the sea creatures you normally eat? Your cattle? Your pigs and chickens?" He had to admit not, and the rest of the village seemed satisfied with my response. A smaller ration of rice was distributed the next day to the northeast villages.

Several weeks later, another shipment of relief rice arrived. I was ready to repeat the original process, but the reality of Vanuatu politics and psychology, in which everyone fought to keep anyone getting ahead of them, interceded. Southern villages had expressed their dismay at not receiving any free food, and it was decreed that every village on Malekula would receive the same relative ration.

This time, we required each village to provide its own transport.
One area was excluded from this second tranche of rice, the Maskelyne Islands [1] off of Malekula's southeast corner. I had heard on Radio Vanuatu that this area that was relatively un-affected by Cyclone Anne had gone directly to a contact in the capital and received not only rice, but tinned fish and meat, building materials, and tools. So, I left them out of the LGC food aid distribution.

One day soon, I was called to the open-channel two-way radio that served as Vanuatu's communication link with remote communities. The Maskelynes were on the horn. In response to their enquiry as to where their rice from the LGC was, I had the pleasure of replying, with many other remote locations listening in, that they didn't need any of the LGC rice because they had received all that other stuff directly from Vila.

I finished this aid programme a few months later, after everyone who lost a home had had the opportunity to rebuild, by returning to everywhere I'd given emergency tarpaulins and asking for them back so they could be put into storage at the LGC for use in the next emergency. This probably did not make me a very popular expat. The next time I saw these distinctive yellow tarps, they were in use as a shelter over a reception for local and central government politicians. Fason blong ples, where anything stored for future use, e.g. bamboo poles behind my house, was appropriated by anyone having an immediate need for it.

Staff Education

A scheme we Regional Development Planners in various LGCs came up with was correspondence courses leading to an official qualification from the University of the South Pacific. I taught English and math courses to my counterpart, other LGC staff, and some staff from the Metenesel Estates cacao plantation across the island.

Rural Water Supplies

The 1980s were declared by the United Nations to be the "International Drinking Water Decade" in which everyone in the world was to be provided with clean, safe water. On the surface, this makes sense to Westerners, but in fact it was the most "top-down" (least likely to succeed at the village level) development project I encountered in Vanuatu. Ni-Vanuatu villagers do not accept the germ theory of disease. Although they acknowledge that there are "Waetman" diseases that respond to Western medical treatments—e.g. malaria, they know that most sicknesses are caused by sorcery.
Villagers do not generally distinguish between the quality of water from different sources, except that if they allow some Whitemen to build a village water supply

[1] Named after the British Astronomer Royal, Nevil Maskelyne, by Captain Cook when he traveled along Malekula's east coast in 1774.

system they will benefit by:

1. Receiving something for free that the next village didn't get, a strong motivation in Vanuatu's exceptionally competitive society.

2. Getting a more convenient source of water located right in the village.

3. Having a good excuse for a party to celebrate the system's completion.

It wasn't that clean water would not have improved health in rural Vanuatu; see the Rural Sanitation section below for details. It's just that clean water was not perceived as desirable by most ni-Vanuatu, so they had no motivation to keep clean water systems working. Sooner or later, many new water supply systems failed.

Donors such as the United Kingdom, Australia, France, and the Australian Seventh Day Adventist (SDA) Church rushed in to provide rural water supplies. The French, in their way, built their systems with materials from France that were entirely incompatible with the Australian materials used by the other donors. This made future maintenance very difficult; repair people were reduced to melting new plastic pipe to the old in order to connect repairs. Only the SDA required the villagers to provide free labour, but because they only worked with SDA villages, their projects weren't coordinated with any others. Other donors provided the labour or paid for it; their projects were perceived as "cargo", or free stuff.

Three types of systems were built in Vanuatu. In order of Whiteman preference due to water purity and cost, they were:

1. Gravity-Fed, with water from a source uphill piped down to the village.

2. Wells, where a gravity-fed source wasn't available and the rock to be drilled was coral—at the time, Vanuatu did not have a drill that could go through harder rock. A diesel pump and one 200-litre drum of fuel were provided to each completed project. These projects were most likely to fail when the diesel engine or pump broke down or the initial drum of diesel ran out because people considered repairs and fuel to be the responsibility of government.

3. Rainwater catchment from a corrugated iron roof, which was the least preferred by donors because of water contamination by dust, bird droppings, etc., but was the most preferred by ni-Vanuatu because they liked the taste of rainwater that had been collected on and stored in galvanized iron.

Nine months into my Lakatoro contract, I had an instructive experience with a team of "international small project specialists". Sitting in my office one day, I noticed the LGC Land Cruiser pull up and disgorge several Whitemen who went into the LGC Secretary's office. "Looks like something that might concern a

Two Years on Malekula

Regional Development Planner", methinks, and I invited myself into the meeting. Here's how I described the experience in a letter to my father, an international development consultant whose integrity and focus on positive results for communities I greatly admired:

November 20, 1987:

> I'm reconsidering my career choice as a professional international aid consultant after spending Tuesday afternoon and Wednesday morning with a team of four from Australia. One was from the Australian International Development Assistance Bureau (AIDAB, which funds lots of stuff here), one was from some "appropriate technology" institute in Darwin, one was with Vanuatu's National Statistics and Planning Office (which evaluates all aid projects) in Vila, and there was a woman who had spent three years with NPSO before going home this year. The team leader from AIDAB was a Charles Emerson Winchester III [1] clone, except Chuck had a better sense of humour. They had come to study all the Rural Water Supply Systems that Australia has funded here in the last four years. They were not amused to learn that many of the 85 systems (about 40 funded by Australia) on Malekula are in poor repair because the people using them refuse to pay for repairs, preferring to just go back to the river or traditional well, or drink green coconut juice and bathe in the ocean if their water system breaks down. I outlined my plans to set up a fee-for-service system to provide maintenance for those villages that seriously want it, and abandon the rest. This was not enthusiastically received, either. They desperately wanted some system of just forcing everyone to pay. "Good luck", I thought.
>
> So, I announced to the meeting that we were going on a tour to see some actual rural water systems in place, both aid-funded and traditional, and I pretty well forced everyone back into the Land Cruiser.
>
> What griped me was that these guys had absolutely no interest in local conditions or the cultural and psychological factors that were leading to the non-maintenance issue. The guy from NPSO, who you would think would want to get out and see the country for which he was making all of these development decisions, told me that he "didn't need to go" see the villages and water systems. The three men all sat, set-faced, in the back of the truck as we drove to a few villages.

I tried pointing out a few items of developmental interest along the road, for example a large rainwater storage tank with no roof in sight for rain collection. This was not unusual, as water tanks were a common "pork barrel" gift from politicians without regard for the existence of a rain-collecting surface. The

---

[1] For my younger readers, a pretentious MASH TV series character.

Two Years on Malekula

Australians, on the other hand, always provided the framework of a building with a corrugated roof of suitable size adjacent to the water tanks they built. This made their projects doubly appreciated, as the villagers could just add woven bamboo walls to obtain a new community centre.

> In any case you couldn't tell this team anything, so I gave up after receiving a stony silence.
> Neither the woman, who had presumably been hired because of her local knowledge, nor the NPSO guy, who had been here for a year and in the Solomons two years, spoke Bislama (also spoken in the Solomons). I mean, we're not talking about some exotic, impossible-to-learn language here. Nobody seemed too impressed with the local habit of answering English questions, always perfectly understood, with Bislama answers. The two NPSO types, with four years in Vanuatu between them, had never been on Malekula before.
>
> I asked them how water-tax collection was going on the other two islands they had visited. They told me that everyone on Ambae paid their water taxes, which is possible, but I think I'll check up on that when we visit in January. The team leader told me that on Tanna they had just started charging water taxes, and they were going to make everyone pay. I didn't make myself too popular by opining that I would like to check that one out after a year, because I thought it would be the same as here. Perhaps, despite him being an expert, nobody told him that the Tanna Local Government Council doesn't even collect regular taxes, because they are ideologically opposed to taxes, and tax non-collection was the main plank in their platform when the new councilors recently beat the party that used to form the LGC majority.

And, as explained earlier, taxes are impossible to collect, anyway.

Back to my letter:

> Actually, the woman was OK. It's only 50% her fault that she doesn't know anything about Vanuatu; NPSO doesn't encourage their expat employees to travel [1], and living in Vila is not living in Vanuatu. At least she was interested in what she was seeing, even though she asked questions, like "Who carries the water for an hour from the river when the system doesn't work", and seemed to believe the villager when he assured her that men and women shared the work evenly. Funny, all I've ever seen doing this has been women and children. Also, at least the guy from Darwin came with us, all of 25 metres, when I asked a villager to show us their alternate water source: two hand-dug wells about 5 metres deep (just holes in the ground, right next to the path. As always, I was

---

[1] A policy that changed immediately when I started working in NPSO the next year. Of course, we chose other expat aid workers to join us who were eager to learn about actual conditions in rural, i.e. most of, Vanuatu.

assured that children, cats, dogs, rats, land crabs, etc. never fell in.). The other two men couldn't be bothered, although the team leader did later come half-way and tell us to hurry up.

I had read about this kind of consultant team before, but never really appreciated the problem.

Upon reflection, aside from my lack of social skills, much of the problem with my interactions with this team probably stemmed from their perception of me. These were highly-paid development "professionals", and to them I was just a naïve volunteer "do-gooder" wearing shorts and flip-flops as opposed to their long pants and shoes. Holly was once asked by a woman at a Vila cocktail party what she did in Vanuatu, and when Holly responded that she was a development volunteer, the woman just turned on her heel and wordlessly walked away.

These team members had no idea that CUSO only sent experienced professionals out to the field and that my background included an MSc. in Agricultural Economics, agricultural lending for one of Canada's major banks, and running British Columbia's farm loan guarantee programme. These were jobs that required accurate judgements of project risk.

I thought we were all on the same team, but they must have felt annoyed that I behaved as if my skills were on the same plane as theirs. Fason blong fully-funded aid technical advisors.

I ended my letter by asking my father to please, please assure me that this wasn't his style. Actually, I knew it wasn't. Years of conversations around the dinner table at home had taught me a lot about the realities of effective development work. Unlike the consultants I met that seemed to just "find and replace" all the country names in the one report they had written before submitting it on the next assignment, Dad always exhaustively researched every community he worked in, often quoting Mao's axiom that the first step in solving a problem was to describe it.

Later, with NPSO in Vila, my desk handled Rural Water Supplies, and I learned a lot about their realities in Vanuatu. If a water pipe ran through a man's land and he became angry with one person of the hundreds being served by the pipe downstream, it was not uncommon for him to just cut it. If a village's standpipe was located where it was most convenient for most villagers, but the chief thought it should be outside his house, he might prohibit anyone from using it. When, inevitably, a faucet washer wore out, even though villagers could easily fashion a new washer from an old inner tube, nobody had a wrench to take the faucet apart. So people would try to stop the faucet dripping by turning the handle harder and harder until the faucet just broke. The Australian Army Engineers running the programme, to their credit, learned from experience. Rather than designing systems that were most financially efficient; i.e.

theoretically provided the most people with water for the least cost; they started designing systems that were the most socially efficient—one per village, standpipe outside chief's house if demanded, etc. When I started at NPSO, I was horrified to learn that someone had designed a system for Tanna that served many villages by pumping water with power from a hydroelectric generator. I believed that this project was too technically complicated and socially inappropriate. Before construction started, a landslide buried the hydro site— evidence that there is a God! The project was abandoned.

Rural Sanitation

Associated with the Rural Water Supply Project was the Rural Sanitation (read toilets) Project. The VIP, or "Ventilated Improved Pit" latrine had been chosen as the project's mainstay, and it was well designed. Basically, it was a concrete slab with a hole in the centre, meant to be placed over a pit in the ground, with privacy walls around it. The VIP's important features kept germ-carrying flies out of the hole and from escaping from it if they got in: first, a cover that closely fit the slab's hole kept most flies out. Second, the slab was well sealed to the ground except for a pipe that ran up above the roof and, most importantly, whose top end was tightly covered with fly-proof mesh. A feature of fly behavior is that they are attracted towards light, so that any fly that managed to get into the toilet pit would fly up to the top of the pipe, where it would remain trapped until it died.

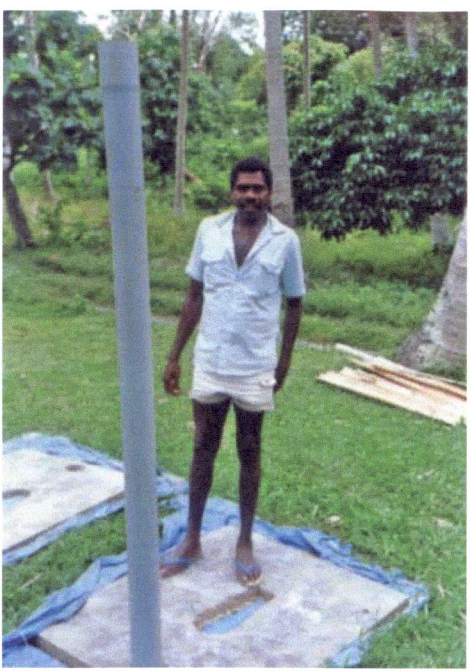

Newly-made VIP Toilet slab.

Two Years on Malekula

So, why are Malekula villages littered with VIP latrine slabs leaning against trees and stacked here and there? Indeed, why when I once inquired in a village where the toilet was, was I directed to an outhouse that had obviously never been used, as my foot went right through the floor? I knew the pieces of information, but didn't put them together until all was explained a couple of years later by a UN team providing VIP latrines to villages. In Vanuatu, it is known that an enemy or rival (i.e. pretty well everyone else, perhaps, excluding one's close family) who obtains a piece of you—for example nail clippings, hair, or excreta— can use it to harm you with black magic. Vanuatu villagers have absolutely no interest in depositing their faeces where it is conveniently available for anyone to get a sample. They defecate at night on the reef at low tide, or out in the bush in secret. Besides, who wants to do their business in a small smelly room, when the wide-open bush is available?

Unused Water Seal toilet slab from a previous
World Health Organization sanitation project.

A couple of years later, as the NPSO officer handling water and sanitation issues, I gave a report in Bislama explaining these sanitation project impediments to a meeting of central government First Secretaries (Deputy Ministers). The Chair, a priest serving as First Secretary to the Prime Minister, said in Bislama, "Well, that's true, isn't it?", and the other First Secretaries kind of looked down at their shoes and nodded assent. The missionaries had done a good job of making ni-Vanuatu ashamed of their traditional beliefs, or at least at hiding them from waetmen.

Two Years on Malekula

Of course, during the wet season, everything on the bush floor, including human and other faeces, is washed downhill into traditional wells, which are dug near the shore to access the freshwater lens a few feet underground. Hence, Vanuatu has a very high rate of several types of Hepatitis, and the need for clean water and proper sanitation projects. But ni-Vanuatu do not ascribe to the germ theory of disease, rather attributing many illnesses to sorcery by enemies. So, there is no motivation to build or use proper toilets.

Once, I mentioned to Kalosak Masing, my second counterpart who had been previously trained and worked as a public health officer, that Whitemen felt guilty about what happened to Vanuatu after contact. Puzzled, he asked me what I meant. After I explained about the devastation of Western diseases, he said I was mistaken. He knew about the post-contact depopulation, but told me it was caused by sorcerers who went on hills overlooking rival villages and massacred them with black magic.

Community Relations
From a 26 May, 1987 letter home:

> Michael, the CUSO RDP on Espiritu Santo, had a good development story. I guess he was alone in the office the other day, when a delegation from a local village came in and demanded that he do something to force a group of men from Ambrym island to return home. The complaint was that these men, who were on Santo to work, had been using magic to put the local men to sleep and seduce their women (who were also put into a trance so they wouldn't remember the experience). There was no doubt as to the truth of the charges—they had some of the smooth stones used to work the magic with. I told Michael he should have insisted on keeping a stone or two, as "evidence", of course. Keith and Lambert often meet with delegations about vague "problems" that I suspect are similar.

July 18, 1987:

> ...and I headed up to Ambae Island (Michener's "Bali Hai" in "Tales of the South Pacific"). There is a CUSO-sponsored mechanical workshop at Lolopuepue (lo-lo-POY-poy) there that the local MP (Minister of Education) is interfering with. One interpretation of his activities is that he is attempting to take it over as a family business, as he has forced his son in as counterpart (actually, he is a good candidate), and seems to be trying to get CUSO out. The workshop just got going in March, and it is much too early for the counterpart to run it. He has taken a basic mechanics course, but has no workshop or business experience. My assignment was to write a constitution for the workshop, making clear that it was owned and run by the community. I did my duty by advising

CUSO and Don and Doreen Lehman (the CUSO's) that I had never even read a community project constitution, and plunged right in. I'm sure that I missed a few angles, but I think it's a pretty fair first draft. I translated it into Bislama, and then went over it with the local priest, Pere Molini, who has really been the mover and shaker of the project over the years.

From an October 21, 1987 letter home:

I met a new RDP from Ghana while I was in Vila. They probably think that people from the developing world will be more sensitive to problems in places like this. He told me that he hadn't seen any oil palms yet and intended to have some seeds sent over. Then he said he had heard that people didn't dry their manioc and make porridge like back home. I didn't remind him that the climate here isn't suitable for oil palms or that they already produce and export a pile of copra for coconut oil that nobody wants. I did keep telling him that when they want to eat manioc, they just dig one up and boil it. Talk about encouraging inappropriate technology!

I later spent some time with this RDP on Ambae, where he was posted. He was an OK guy, and probably at least as, or perhaps more, effective as I was.

He was a big badminton fan and had a court set up outside his bamboo and thatch house[1] .

Roads

This was really the responsibility of the Public Works Department, but bears mention. All roads on Malekula were made of fossil coral that had turned into a powder. When it was watered and rolled, it made a hard surface. After it had been rutted and pot-holed from wet seasons, it was plowed up, graded, watered, and rolled smooth and hard again. There was never a high enough maintenance budget, though, which was exacerbated by politicians forcing the use of the maintenance budget for the construction of even more ever-popular roads.

Regional Development Planner Work—The Reality

From a 29 June, 1988 letter to a friend with international experience:

I've decided that regional development planning is not my first choice of careers. This may be because the professional experience here hasn't been all that hot. I'm a bit of a slow learner, but I've finally figured out this is

---

[1] We were very fortunate to have a concrete-block house. Although bamboo houses were cooler because of airflow through the walls, they also let malarial mosquitos in freely.

one of those programmes CUSO pushed on Vanuatu because CIDA is pressing for more bodies in the field to justify CUSO's funding. We are ignored both by the Central Government's planners (white contract workers) and our nominal Central Government overlords (ni-Vanuatu civil servants). Our Minister for the past few months wants us out of here. Aren't you glad to hear how your tax dollars are being well-spent?

CUSO's problem is that it has absolutely no guts. Here they are, providing a bunch of expensive (for Vanuatu, anyway) skilled people for free, and they won't insist that Vanuatu contribute anything in the way of political will or auxiliary funding[1] . I wouldn't even start such a programme without being sure that it was wanted and fit into a structure that would get some benefit from it. The basic problem is that we are supposed to be part of a big decentralization effort the ruling politicians make a lot of noise about. Reality, however, is that they have no intention of losing any tightly held central power. This is a closely controlled democratically elected one-party state. The Vanua'aku Pati controls every organization here, except the Seventh Day Adventist church. The only newspaper and radio station are owned by the government.
If that's what they want here, fine; but why should CUSO try to ram a decentralization programme down their throat? The CUSO Field Staff here are pretty naive and not at all professional. CUSO's headquarters is staffed top to bottom with starry-eyed ex-volunteers. CUPE[2] has been invited into the CUSO administration, so all positions are filled by internal competitions—even the Field Staff Officers and Regional Officers. Sounds like a great organization to the great unwashed, but I wonder how big a bang the Canadian Taxpayer gets for his buck.

Final Word on Technical Assistance to Vanuatu
"Our primary function here is to provide entertainment for the locals."

Prospective advisers who aren't comfortable with this should stay home to avoid supreme frustration.

---

[1] Three years in the Central Government planning department taught me that this was common to most of Vanuatu's international aid donors who were primarily concerned with meeting aid distribution targets.

[2] A Canadian public service union.

A Trip to the Southeast Corner of Malekula

From a 16 March, 1987 letter early in my contract:

My other big trip was for three days last week to Lamap, on the SE corner of the island. The Malekula Sports Council, of which my boss is President and my counterpart Secretary, held a soccer and volleyball tournament Tuesday to Saturday. I went to see the country and to spend a day with my boss meeting with people on a nearby island (one of the Maskelynes). We went down, together with a bunch of the teams, on an old wooden boat maybe 50-60 feet long. We were to meet at 7:30 and get going. Well, the boat showed at about 11:00, so we went down to the "wharf"[1] . The ship couldn't' get anywhere near, of course, so we all ferried out there in a 14' dinghy loaded each time with about 20 people and their stuff, so there was about 3" freeboard. My butt got wet when the tops of a couple of waves came over the side (you sit on the gunwale, just like they all do on the back of pickups around here). The big (?) boat was pitching up and down in the waves, so I took another half Gravol[2] while I was waiting in line on the wharf. There were 2 more trips of the lighter after mine, so we got started about 12:30, but had to pick up a guy on a nearby island, so we really got going about 13:00. I saw my first flying fish on the trip.

It took 4 hours to get there, during which time everyone slept, ate, read one old soccer magazine (French) and one old black and white "Phantom" comic (English), played cards, and picked nits out of each other's hair (popular local entertainment). I fried my legs and face in the sun. Upon arrival at Lamap, we unloaded into the small boat again and then waded ashore. I counted 80 passengers. (Lifejackets for crew only, of course.)

Lamap was Malekula's French Administrative Centre before it was moved to Norsup. There are semi-deserted administrative buildings, a school, and a hospital, which was ransacked by rioters during the civil war at independence. We bigwigs slept on beds in the "rest house" (portion of decaying administrative building). No electricity (the big generator had been taken to Norsup; no diesel for small one left behind), but running water in some taps—toilet tank broken; bring water in bucket to flush. The lighthouse there wasn't working. I commented on this to some local authorities, but they hadn't noticed.

The teams all slept on pandanus-leaf mats on concrete classroom floors. Suppers were white rice and meat stew (although one night, no one

---

[1] A landing stage, but the Bislama word "wof" means anything that a boat of any size can land at, from a rock sticking out from the shore to a huge commercial wharf.

[2] I am susceptible to seasickness.

would eat the meat—they told me it was spoiled, so we just had rice). One night, for a treat, my boss took me to a stall near the playing field for supper—we had rice and chicken stew (cold, because we went late). I had one breakfast with the teams—a large hunk of white bread and a mug of a hot drink. It was mostly sugar water, but had a weak brown colour and taste I can't place. It was boiled up in galvanized garbage cans over an open fire, so perhaps it won't do to speculate on the origin of the colour and flavour. Everyone seemed to thrive on it.

Later experience taught me that this was Milo, a malt and sugar drink manufactured by Nestlé Australia. Milo and sugar with hot water is a popular drink amongst ni-Vanuatu. The label proclaims it to be "Nutritious", but the small print tells you that it has to be mixed with milk to be so. Tragically, it is sometimes used by ni-Vanuatu as baby formula because it is cheaper than Lactogen, a baby formula manufactured by the same company. Fortunately, breast-feeding is pretty well universal in Vanuatu. I should mention that I administered an anti-Nestlé boycott at the University of Guelph, and conducted a survey of CUSOs in the field on breastfeeding incidence and formula marketing practices where they were posted. Holly was a member of La Leche League in Victoria, BC before we went to Vanuatu.

My counterpart, Lambert, when inviting me had mentioned that we would be eating island food, which would be a "good experience" for me, as he grinned slightly. Lucky for me, a local store sold juice and cream-centred cookies—I noticed a lot of team members there also. There were also a bunch of temporary stalls set up selling rice and stew, sweetened juice, donuts (formed in a figure eight here and not very sweet), and green coconuts. Green coconuts are a big deal here. Instead of buying a coke, you buy a green coconut and the lady husks it and cuts the top off. You walk around drinking the water, which is clear and sweet, but has something in it that makes my stomach rebel[1] .

The first day, we started with the opening ceremonies. Lambert had told all the team managers that we would go strictly by the timetable, which meant starting at 8:30. Of course, everyone (including Lambert) started wandering down about 9:00, and we got started about 9:30. The field is cut into a hill, and everyone uses the cliff for a grandstand. About twenty women and children with nothing else to do that morning gathered up on top to watch (they were the only people there except the teams and dignitaries), so Lambert got on his loud hailer and told them to all come down where they could hear the speeches. They did.

---

[1] I eventually learned to appreciate it. The past few years in Canada, I've seen canned coconut water for sale everywhere; I am a coconut water purist (or snob) and don't buy it.

Laurel drinking real coconut water from the source.

Once again, I was an "honoured guest" and sat with the bigwigs in a reviewing stand that had been built for the occasion. The athletes all paraded around the field while we clapped the whole time, and assembled in front for about one hour in the sun, while every local politician from local chief to MP and the Sports Federation President and Secretary gave speeches (my boss, Keith, gave a barnburner—sports is a big part of development, being the only real unifying factor on the island), the local priest prayed, and both the national and sports federation flags were hoisted (someone sent their kid up the poles prior to the ceremony to attach the ropes). Festivities included me and other honoured guests receiving leis from the local women's volleyball team (no kiss). Of course, mine didn't fit over my head, and I was afraid I was flubbing it until I asked Keith, who advised that sometimes they made headbands, and it was supposed to fit on my head. He may have been being diplomatic.

As the first game started, someone hauled out a portable generator, set up a big stereo, and proceeded to blast loud reggae music over the field. Apparently, this is standard procedure and actually was quite pleasant for me as a spectator. I watched soccer all day (wearing jeans and shoes to give my legs and feet a rest from sun—first time since Fiji). Lambert had hauled along a TV and VCR, which he couldn't get going the first night. I think the generator only had one outlet, and he couldn't find an octopus so he could run both appliances at the same time. The second night, he got them going and put on "Rocky IV". The person who used the tape before hadn't rewound it, and the credits came on in black and white. We fiddled with all the controls, but couldn't change it, so he declared the tape dead and switched to Plan B—part four of a TV miniseries called "Jesus of Nazareth". You can imagine how a crowd of 100 young men who were set for Rocky IV would react to that in Canada, but these guys really thought it was OK. When it started, I thought, "Oh no, some low-budget movie made by some obscure American TV evangelist like Rex Humbard, but it was real high quality with an all-star cast and good writing. The audience really got into it (it started the afternoon before the Last Supper)—when the Romans started whipping Jesus, the audience all clicked their tongues in disapproval, they all gasped when the crown of thorns was put on and He was nailed up, and Pilate got a big hiss. Nobody seemed to mind Caiaphas, though—maybe Anthony Quinn is a big favourite here.

You may have gathered that this country is heavily into Christianity. Unfortunately, depending on which missionary got there first and avoided being eaten (no joke), every island or part of island is a different denomination, and they really take their religious differences seriously. After that video, Lambert gave the crowd the choice between Rocky IV— he emphasized it was broken and in B&W—and a tape of a 1986 World Cup soccer game (his preference). The crowd went for Rocky, and it came on in colour (I suggested the next day that we had witnessed a miracle, which surprisingly didn't seem to offend anyone). The generator ran out of gas just after Apollo Creed was killed, so we all went to bed. We finished it off the next night, and it turned out that the credits were supposed to be black-and-white. Oh. I went to bed as they got into the soccer game video.

From a later April 2, 1987 letter:

I've decided that my mission here is to convince everyone that Sylvester Stallone didn't really have a boxing match with a Russian. I don't think they believe me. They really think that movies are for real, and they are their sole source of information about North America. On our trip yesterday, I told everyone that we'd been to Hollywood and seen the sets and whatnot, and this was news to some of them. When I told them Rocky IV was filmed in Southern Alberta and Vancouver, everyone was amazed—they thought it was really Russia.

Back to the original letter:

On the second day, I went to a Maskelynes Island with Keith and three influential chiefs to mediate a peace accord between warring factions. A truck had been hired to pick us up at 7:30, and when it didn't show, we found another one and got off for the southern beach at 8:30. Keith was concerned that our boat (a small outboard) would have been kept waiting, but no; he was just arriving when we got there. Keith had told me it was a five-minute ride. Actual time was 1 hour 20 minutes—they have a refreshingly informal notion of time here, although everyone wears a big wristwatch. We told the truck we'd definitely be back by 15:00.

We got to the island and shook hands with everyone, which is normal protocol when visiting a village—everyone lines up in order of social standing and shakes the hand of each visitor. Handshakes are limp and two-fingered. After a while, we headed into the village community centre (frame with concrete floor here) with 70-80 men. We "honoured guests" all sat at a table in the centre of one wall and everyone else sat against the wall on benches or the floor around the room. Keith told everyone we had to leave by 14:00 to catch our 15:00 truck.

The big issue was that the island, with a population of 2,000, was solidly Presbyterian, but three men and their families (total twenty people) had converted to Seventh Day Adventism. Last year, the SDA families had accumulated some building materials for a church, but the Presbyterians had taken the materials away. The police were called in, and eventually the SDA got their stuff back, but they still weren't allowed to build the church. Now, everyone wanted peace, and Keith was supposed to provide the solution. I told him he needed Solomon.

Of course, the community's sole idea of peace is for the SDAs to move off the island and that's that, even though the SDAs couldn't move even if they wanted to, because they only own land on this island. Land, by the Constitution, cannot be sold here and belongs to the "custom owner", although after 150 years of colonization, there is a big fight to determine whom many of the custom owners are. I've met one CUSO who works on it full time, and an entire separate system of land courts has been set up. Lots of land sits unused because it is under dispute.

Besides this, the Constitution also guarantees "Freedom of Worship". The people at the meeting argued back and forth in Bislama, and I didn't understand much besides a few general choruses of "Giaman! Giaman!" (Liar! Liar!). I did understand one guy who got up and argued that the Constitution also guaranteed "Public Safety", and how could you have public safety with another church in town? At 13:00 everyone just got up in disgust and walked out.

Two Years on Malekula

We went to the chief's for lunch (rice with tinned fish and greens stew) and, after, Keith went out and engaged in a little "Spirit Out!" style of faith healing.

Keith was a convert to the evangelical "Holiness Fellowship" sect. What he was doing was called "holem bel"—holding the belly—and involved Keith placing his hand on a person's stomach and loudly commanding a tevil (spirit) to vacate.

By 14:30, we all met again, and Keith announced that we had to go in 15 minutes to catch our truck. Keith and the chiefs all gave speeches, and the populace argued, and we quit about 15:30. We outsiders all came to the conclusion, of course, that these people had to work out a solution themselves, but they are absolutely unwilling to compromise, as in Vanuatu if you aren't 100% with me you are 100% against me. Keith told them that this type of dissension would doom any type of economic development they attempted. I wouldn't recommend a project for them on a bet if they can't come to an agreement on a little issue[1] like this. A typical development problem, I guess. I'm reading a book on Community Development now that states that social development must precede economic development, and I agree. Lots of time is needed, I guess.[2]

It was high tide on the way back, so we took a shortcut over the reef and met the truck at 16:40. One of the chiefs tried to get me worried by asking me what if the truck wasn't there? I called his bluff by saying we'd just walk (it's only about 6 km)—what else would we do, anyway? In the event, the truck driver told us no problem, he had just arrived. It's hard to tell—"just arrived" could mean he'd been waiting 2 hours. Of course, I could easily spend 2 hours at that beach. A bunch of soccer players were there swimming and spear fishing, cooking their catch, and weaving hats from palm fronds. It was a beautiful ride back on the boat between lush islands ringed with sandy beaches and coral reefs. I thought that most Canadians would have to pay big bucks to get into that situation—eat your hearts out!

I flew back to Lakatoro on Friday and got a good view of the south part of the island, as we first made a stop on the South West corner and then flew up the west coast of Malekula, crossing back to Norsup at the "dog's neck". (People claim that Malekula looks like a sitting dog. Norsup and Lakatoro are on the back of his neck.)

---

[1] I was to learn that religion was a big issue in Vanuatu. For example, SDA, or "seven dei" converts who hadn't mentioned their church when being hired, would on the first weekend announce that they wouldn't work on Saturdays, which caused all kinds of disruption.

[2] Yeah, well; Whitemen had been working at this in Vanuatu for 150 years; I didn't imagine my two years was going to transform things.

Two Years on Malekula

On Tour With the Acting Prime Minister
From a May 8, 1987 letter home:

Last week I drank kava with the Bishop; today it was the Acting Prime Minister (The PM had a stroke while in Washington in February; I'm sure it was in all the British Columbia papers). I guess all that is left is the Queen.

Sethy Reganvanu, the Acting PM, is the local MP and Minister of Home Affairs (i.e. my ultimate boss), and has been in the area for the past three days inspecting "development" projects that were funded with his MP discretionary development fund[1]. They range from boats to rainwater tanks to video machines. Did I mention that an election is scheduled soon? Maybe I shouldn't be so judgmental—the mechanics instructor at a vocational institute (bush materials shed) that we visited today told me he sometimes used the video machine's generator to power the electric welder. I was supposed to go on tour with the Minister on Wednesday, and then yesterday, but they kept leaving without me. I guess I should spend more time storianing with the bigwigs and less working in my office. He told me that yesterday I missed a ride in a big sailing canoe and later mentioned the kava drinking. Of course, I also missed getting home at 20:00, but if the cause was partying, it would have been worth it. In actuality, if today was an indication, I missed two valuable opportunities to learn the wants of various villages, and to see and be seen (I was one of the Minister's prime exhibits of what the Government is doing for the people).
At Leviamp, after inspecting the Vocational Institute and video machine w/ TV and generator, we were served lunch (ham spaghetti with purple yam on white rice—not bad, actually). After eating, we were discussing cash crops and I brought up kava. The conversation turned to kava drinking, the national sport—soccer runs a close second—and the Minister's Third Secretary[2] started in on how these days you could hardly get into a nakamal in Vila because of all the white men in them. He went on to say that all the embassy people rush to the nakamals every day right at 4:30. A few tongue-clicks issued forth from the group. Not only that, but they brought their wives! The clicks intensified. Sometimes, they even brought ni-Vanuatu women. A roar of clicks ensued, and "They break our customs!" was interjected. I felt that the time just wasn't ripe to mention that I had promised to take Holly to a nakamal on our

---
[1] Each MP was allotted 1,000,000vt (roughly CAN$10,000) annually to disperse as they felt suitable. Most of it seemed to go for generator/video machine/TV packages or rainwater collection tanks that stood by themselves with no roof to collect water in sight.
[2] Each of Vanuatu's Cabinet Ministers had three Secretaries: the First Secretary was the head of the Department, like a Canadian Deputy Minister. The Second Secretary was in charge of political matters. The Third Secretary was an aide to the Minister.

next trip to Vila or that on my last trip to Vila, I had gone to a nakamal with a group of CUSO's and a ni-Vanuatu girlfriend. I ascribe their openness to one of three possible explanations: (a) I was accepted as an honorary Blackman[1] , a great complement, or (b) as a Whiteman I didn't exist at the table, or (c)after hearing me speak for the past couple of days, they didn't think my Bislama was good enough to understand what they were saying, both not so complementary and more probable[2].

Tuesday, I was at a meeting with the Minister, where I was Keith's big exhibit. Keith kept asking me to tell everyone all about the great things I was doing and all the great ideas I have (?). At least two of the local participants have never let on that they understand any English, so I started off in Bislama. The Minister asked me to speak English[3] And it was the first time that I'd felt confident speaking Bislama in front of a group!

I was also asked to come along on this afternoon's trip to a village a couple of kilometres south of here. The request was made after a fruitless search for a camera, and I was asked to bring mine to take a picture of the local soccer team (surely the fame of the Litzlitz Swallow Birds has reached Victoria) in their new uniforms (you guessed it—another development project) that the Minister was going to give them, so pardon me if I feel that my economic expertise wasn't the only basis of the invite.

Litzlitz greeted us with a large banner assuring us that the village supported the Minister's party, and during the ceremony he was presented with an envelope to help the Vanua'aku Pati in the forthcoming election. No different from home, I guess, just more honest. The main event, actually, was the dedication of a rainwater collection tank—never mind you can tell by the patches that the thing is several years old. The ceremony was preceded by a welcome to everyone (the Minister's bodyguard received equal billing—so did I, so I guess I shouldn't have had so much trouble keeping my face straight). I snapped pictures through the whole thing, including a couple of the Minister with the team. I'd seen on the programme (handwritten) that a kava ceremony was to follow, so when we all took our places inside the half-finished community hall (at least it was half-roofed because they had installed all the roofing iron that they possessed since I had last visited), I got ready to get some good pictures. Then a guy came down the bench handing out plastic cups, immediately followed by a guy with a tea kettle pouring

---

[1] Oh, Pul-eese—the hubris of inexperience. I blush with embarrassment reading this.

[2] Most likely, they just didn't care.

[3] I had the impression that Minister Reganvanu did not like waetmen all that much. His wife was a New Zealander who, it was said had once made a break for home, but the Minister had her stopped at the Vila airport. She never acknowledged my presence the few times I saw her. His son, Ralph, who at the time of this writing is the Minister of Foreign Affairs, has also been quite reserved during our few interactions.

kava, everyone guzzled it down, and that was the ceremony. Only the bodyguard sat between me and the Minister, so I guess I got the place of second-honour. Just to make you cringe, I'll describe the meal that followed, which I quite enjoyed. The entire village had, as per the usual custom here, lined up to shake our hands after we were all presented with leis upon our arrival. We all sat on mats around communal batches of laplap, ripped off pieces, dipped them in the central pool of cream, and ate them by hand. (I had a good picture of a woman making coconut cream in the traditional manner—squeezing it out of grated coconut in her hands[1].)

There were also communal chicken halves that we ripped apart and ate. This meal occurs at any ceremony here, and I must have been here too long, because I've grown to like laplap (when served on the odd occasion—the locals eat it morning, noon, and night). It is grated carbohydrate (yam, banana, taro, kumala, etc.) mixed with coconut cream and maybe meat, wrapped in big leaves, and cooked on hot rocks. It's the bane of most expats' lives.

Afterwards, gifts to dignitaries were presented. In order of presentation (and attractiveness of gift), the Minister was given a carved and painted model outrigger canoe (kanu witem pikinini), the bodyguard got a woven tea tray with handles, the Third Secretary got a large floor mat, a Local Government Councillor got a fancy woven bag, I got a woven fan tastefully fringed with blue plastic baler twine, and the LGC Senior Executive Officer got a fan ringed with chicken feathers (I should have offered to trade). Then everyone lined up again to shake hands, and we departed.

About the entourage: the Third Secretary is the Minister's executive assistant. The bodyguard is a BIG, ugly, mean-looking guy who really gave me the geological survey[2] when I first walked up on Tuesday morning to say hello, but by today, I actually saw him smile and heard him say a few words. Having him along kind of gave me pause. I found him intimidating, but I got the impression that he wouldn't delay a professional or determined amateur (I never could detect that "tell-tale bulge" under his arm). If one assumed that there was some reason besides prestige for his presence, and given my lack of confidence in his abilities, could I count myself among the victims of any attack? Actually, I was probably in more danger from our mode of transport—the infamous LGC "green truck"—speeding along dirt roads at 50 kph behind our

---

[1] I shouldn't have been so flippant; village festivities with communal meals were frequently followed by communal bouts of dysentery or typhoid fever.

[2] A stony stare.

police escort—a blue crew cab Toyota pickup with a flashing red strobe light on top that blinded me every time I glanced through the windshield; I don't know how the driver could see anything. We shared the road with a grand total of about 5 vehicles during the day. The LGC uses the Green Truck with glee to transport VIP's around—they figure it lends credence to their pleas for a new truck. It should, but I don't think the message gets through. At least the VIP always gets to sit in the "death seat" next to the driver. The rest of us get to toss around in the back in case of an accident. Our seats are benches along the sides of the back. Seatbelts?—let's get serious.

Actually, for a politician, Sethy Regenvanu[1] is an OK guy. After the usual speech about how the LGC would have to pull up its own bootstraps and if we wanted something, why didn't we just ask, he seemed to listen to my ideas. The trouble with these guys is, just as at home, they don't want to admit that politicians come and go, but civil servants are forever. I expected the usual ministerial glad-handing, but he seemed genuinely friendly, to a reasonable point. A little more political sophistication here will take care of that.

Just for fun, I asked him if the report I heard on BBC last night that Vanuatu had unceremoniously expelled two Libyans who showed up unannounced to start up an embassy was true, since it was identified as a "report from Vanuatu" and wasn't repeated this morning. (Vanuatu's relations with Libya are a real sensitive issue in this region. This week the Australian Foreign Minister flew to New Zealand for consultations after hearing that Libya was going to set up an embassy here. Vanuatu is walking a tightrope between showing everyone how independent their foreign policy is and actually letting the Libyan maniacs in. (The local government-owned press and radio rarely report any substantial news like this.) Instead of inviting me to mind my own business or to leave the country, he actually gave what sounded like an honest answer—from a politician, yet! He told me that these two guys had turned up without credentials and Vanuatu had contacted their offices in Canberra and Tripoli to find out just whom they were. He didn't think that they had been expelled, because he would have made the decision. I was amazed to deduce that he apparently wasn't in daily telephone contact with Vila. All this was in English (my attempt at subtlety). Then he gave a statement in Bislama to the rest of the people around to the effect that foreign policy was of no importance to people at the village level. There

---

[1] Sethy's son, Ralph Reganvanu, has become a prominent politician in his own right since we left Vanuatu. I had heard good things about Ralph, so I asked for a short meeting in a coffee shop when Holly and I visited Vila in 2009. After he asked point blank what I wanted from him and got the reply, "Nothing", he cautiously thawed. He is one of the few Vanuatu politicians who are genuinely concerned for the entire nation, rather than himself. I think Ralph and the few others like him are the future hope of Vanuatu.

was general agreement, and to be honest, he's probably not too far off the mark, although only an aspiring suicide would express support for French nuclear testing in the same setting.

We were sitting on a bench in Leviamp's equivalent of a village square. It's a scene right out of South Pacific mythology—just behind us, a blacksand beach curved around for a couple of miles, interrupted only by stretches of rough lava with holes through which the surf spouted. Running down to the beach is green forest, and the water is blue. Of course, reality is slightly tarnished; nobody sets toe in the water because of the sharks[1], and Cyclone Uma broke the water pipe into town, so now all drinking water comes from springs along the river, which passes another village upstream. I knew we were getting the VIP treatment, because our water was served in glasses that still had the "Duralex" stickers on them.

Metenesel Estates Limited

One of Vanuatu's less well-thought-out development projects was Metenesel Estates Limited (MEL), a cacao (the source of chocolate) plantation on the west side of Malekula Island managed by the Commonwealth Development Corporation, which was owned by the UK Government and tasked with making beneficial investments in developing countries. The site had been chosen on the basis of rainfall records from the island's east side without consideration of the rain shadow effect caused by prevailing winds from the east and the mountains running north-south down Malekula's spine. The poor choice of site was compounded by the decision to start with a full-fledged plantation rather than a small test planting, which would have allowed the project to learn the realities of growing cacao on that site at a much lower cost.

Worse, the plantation was financed by a loan to the Vanuatu Government, which may have had technical assistance available to evaluate the project, but definitely lacked the aptitude to evaluate its risk. The Government also lacked the financial ability to bear the project's risk.

Quite a bit of violence was done to five hundred hectares of forest, with trees bulldozed over, roots torn from the ground, and much of the mess burned before cocoa seedlings were planted. Cacao trees are normally grown under shade, and three types of plantings were made here. One portion of the plantation was planted under the shade of existing trees, one portion was completely cleared with plantings under planted shade trees, and one portion was planted without

---

[1] Thought to be attracted to the shallows above black (volcanic) sand. For all I knew, this was true; I don't recall ever swimming at a black sand beach.

shade. Besides the foreseeable insufficient rainfall on the site, an unanticipated problem arose from a fungus that grew in the dead roots of cleared trees and spread to the roots of the plantings. Crops were poor.

On the positive side, a village with good quality houses and health, recreational, and market facilities was built to house 300 workers and their families. As well, there were Western-style executive offices, a clubhouse with swimming pool, and housing for the expatriate management, who were in general pretty good people doing their best with a poor site chosen by others.

Angry Ground at MEL

In March 1987, while I was at a meeting on the Maskelyne Islands off Malekula's SE coast, a woman suddenly started wailing in the distance and continued until after we left. Upon inquiring, I learned that someone on our boat had brought word of the death of her son at MEL. Back home a few days later, I learned some of the details of the death and subsequent events.

A week previous to the death of the young man from the Maskelynes, a woman worker at MEL had died from cerebral malaria, in which hordes of malarial parasites lodge in brain blood vessels, cutting off the blood supply. When the young man suddenly collapsed and died in the fields from what management felt was the same cause, his fellow workers came to a different conclusion. Overnight, they abandoned the MEL village and fled to their home villages, fearing that the "ground was angry" because it had been disturbed.
Work stopped completely, and management took direct action to prevent the project slipping even further behind schedule. A local "kleva", or sorcerer/healer, was hired for 3,000vt (about CAN$30) to make the ground happy again. The kleva came with a potion of kastom leaves and water in a large bottle and had himself driven over the fields. When he sensed that they were at a hot spot, he got out, performed a short ceremony, and poured some potion out. Upon returning to project headquarters, though, he declared that the ground was most angry in the Director's office and, to the consternation of the Director and amusement of everyone else, proceeded to placate the ground by emptying the bottle on the carpet.

Satisfied that the ground had been mollified, the employees returned and work carried on.

That wasn't the end of the affair though. When word got out that a kleva had performed heathen ceremonies at the project, one of the local Christian pastors insisted that he be allowed to bless the ground. Not to be outdone, pastors from each of Malekula's other denominations then demanded their turns, and Metenesel Estates Limited became the most blessed place on Malekula.

Carl Edwards, the Project Director whose carpet was soiled, left Malekula shortly before we did to become the manager of an Oil Palm plantation in Papua New Guinea. Three years later, we got word that he had been at the funeral of a worker who had died in an accident at a neighbouring plantation, when a relative of the dead man stepped forward and fatally stabbed him. This would be on the principle that, because the dead man had died on a White-owned plantation, a Whiteman should die as per the PNG "payback" revenge doctrine. The developing world lost a caring, competent, and good man.

Again, we met several people who had worked and lived in PNG, and it is not a place I would visit. Many CUSOs we knew who worked there returned early due to threats of violence.

Visiting a Small Nambas Kastom Village

The Small Nambas of Malekula are people of mid- and south-Malekula whose men traditionally wore small nambas (penis wrappers) made of banana leaves. While this is typical of all areas of Vanuatu, the people of south Malekula are specified as Small Nambas to differentiate them from the Big Nambas of north Malekula, whose nambas are made of a relatively large mass of pandanus fibres. A Kastom Village is one in which the people deliberately continue living in pre-contact ways.

From two letters home:
September 4, 1987:

> In a week and a half, I am heading up into Malekula's southern mountains to spend a couple of nights with the Small Nambas. Keith and I are going up with the area's Area Council Secretary to respond to a request for a road and a community building. We will have to walk one day in, but they will still have to walk down to meet us half-way.

> This request for a building is really something. These people deliberately live in the Stone Age way up in the hills. They got someone to type a letter directly to the Australian High Commission complaining that the Government is ignoring them and asking for a building. It should have an office, an aid post, a classroom, and (?) a recreation room! You have to walk two days to get up there. I wonder if they think someone is going to pack all the cement and roofing iron in? The crazy thing is, besides the fact that they are all up there to get away from civilization, they could easily build any sized building they want for free from bush materials. And what do they plan to do in the recreation room? Play Ping-Pong? Watch videos? Every village also already has a big nakamal, or men's club building, and this request came from men only. Actually, this isn't

the first community building request I've had. A delegation from a village had come to me with a request to rebuild all their bamboo houses with concrete blocks and roofing iron. A reasonable desire, as horizontal cyclonic winds blow rain through woven bamboo walls and soak everything. Plus, thatch roofs house multitudes of rats and termites, with an associated constant rain of rat excreta and sawdust. I said, "Great. I'll find some plans and a donor to provide tools, and you can raise money for materials and provide the labour." "Oh, no", they said. "We've already done our share by deciding what we want and asking for it." Fason blong Vanuatu. I didn't support this one.

People who wouldn't dream of spending a cent on a house won't get together to build a free community hall. Everyone thinks that because they pay the princely sum of 1000vt ($12.50) per year total taxes, the government should build these buildings for them. I don't think I'm quite plugged into the local psyche yet.

October 13, 1987:

Now, since I last wrote to you a month ago, my life has been full of all sorts of exciting happenings. First, I trekked into deepest darkest southern Malekula to the land of the Small Nambas. It is a 3-hour flat walk from the road to Melken, where there are a few sheets of roofing iron as evidence of Western influence (they roll them up and pack them in). Another hour's flat walk, and then it's straight up the mountain on a muddy trail. They don't believe in switchbacks here. It's real take-off-your-thongs-and-dig-your-toes-in country.

After 3 hours of this, we got to Imarao, our destination. Here, they wear clothes[1], but all have holes in their nasal septa (only one woman had anything stuck in there, though: a silver metal tube). They have a custom house that only initiated males[2] are allowed in. It contains the heads of departed male ancestors. When a man dies, they put his body up in the rafters of his house. After it gets a bit soft, holes are poked in it with thorns to let the juices out. Because they don't have chimneys[3] for their cooking fires, the bodies get smoke-cured. The heads are removed at this stage and dried over a fire and mud used to reform the facial features.

---

[1] Donned because a Whiteman was there; the missionaries did a good job of shaming ni-Vanuatu about nudity. The Bislama word for "naked" is "malmal", from the French "badbad".

[2] Circumcised at age 12 or 13 and taught the basic village cultural and kastom secrets. A man on Atchin Island once told me in their village, they circumcised boys by nicking the foreskin and ripping it off. "It's difficult (for the boys)", he said, repeating it to be sure I understood. I got it.

[3] I only saw one chimney in a Vanuatu village; a man had tried out the Whiteman way as an experiment. Nobody emulated him. Constant exposure to wood smoke causes a lot of eye problems in Vanuatu.

Imarao chief blowing Triton-shell trumpet to call villagers to meeting.

Anyone who complains about the smell during all of this is heavily fined (vatu and tusked pigs) by the chief. After one hundred days, the body is laid out and funeral dances take place. The bodies of bigwigs are then also put into the custom house, and in times of war arrowheads are made from their bones. These arrowheads are believed to be poisonous[1]. Of course, they also have a Presbyterian pastor up there with a chapel and small school. The men and women sleep and eat separately. I think they have their, uh-hem, marital relations out in their gardens.

---

[1] Holly and I once ran into Viene, a Vanuatu Cultural Centre fieldworker from Vao Island off of Malekula's north-west coast, at the Norsup airstrip. He had several human bone arrowheads in his hand. He warned the ni-Vanuatu bystanders away from them, and they backed off. He let Holly handle one, though, explaining that because she was a Whiteman, the black magic wouldn't affect her. Presumably, Viene had some kind of kastom protection himself.

If you walk another half-day up and down mountains, you get to Lendamboi, which is real kastom country. No pastors, schools, or clothes up there. You could see the lumps of the Imarao men's nambas under their shorts, but the men from Lendamboi were wearing their nambas uncovered, right along with their T-shirts.

Imarao Women and Girls.

Anyway, we had our big community meeting in the school—us with the men in one room and the women listening through the wall in the other room. We discussed the road to Imarao they were requesting, warned them that with a road comes civilization, and asked them to think about it a bit. We spoke Bislama and a young man translated into the local language. The next topic of discussion was where to have the polling station in November's general election, and it was decided to pack the ballot boxes into Imarao, rather than all the way up to Lendamboi. The guys in their nambas from Lendamboi had one other request: they want barbed wire to pack in on their backs, since one guy has already done it! I told them that John Kamphorst[1] had the idea that they could use the placement of salt to control cattle, and maybe we should all sit down and consider the alternatives before a final cattle-control strategy was decided upon. After all, it is pretty well a free-range situation, with miles of bush before the next guy's property is reached I thought at the time; upon reflection, perhaps there were some local land dispute issues involved.

[1] Australian volunteer Livestock Officer based at Lakatoro, who had previously visited Imarao.

Two Years on Malekula

I told them that in these situations in Canada, we just rounded up cattle with horses, but they weren't too interested. Resistant to change I guess[1].

John told me yesterday that right now they are chasing the cattle with dogs, spearing the cows, and tying up the calves with vines. We[2] dropped off some rope for them during our circumnavigation of Malekula last month. We got an offer from the New Zealand Air Force yesterday to drop off anything anywhere that can be reached by a helicopter, but John has decided not to assist them with barbed wire on the theory that if you have to helicopter it in, proper marketing channels for the cattle don't really exist yet. The concept of the present system is that they will lead rope-trained calves down to the coast to sell.

I discussed the Imarao villagers with Kirk Huffman (an Anglo-American anthropologist), the curator of the museum in Vila, last week, and he says they use money to buy tusked pigs from the coast to use in their various ceremonies and exchanges. He gives them a hand by buying stuff for the museum from them. He lived with these people for a couple of years in the Seventies, and was disappointed to see most of them were wearing clothes in my pictures. He is very anti-Christian as it applies to these people. Apparently the first conversions were in 1980, and he says they are just playing with it to see what material goods it gives them. It is now possible for them to experiment with Christianity because most mainstream denominations allow custom practices to coexist with the Christian ones.

---

[1] I was a ranch hand during my misspent youth in Canada. I was just messing with them, in my culturally sensitive Whiteman way.
[2] John, CUSO Fisheries Officer Ross Combdon, and I.

115

You don't see too many waetman wearing a nambas. Kirk Huffman in kastom dress at his 2004 kastom wedding to his wife Yvonne. He is holding a nalnal (club) in his right hand and bonara in his left. Photo by Ralph Regenvanu, used by permission.

Although they have firearms, the Small Nambas like to hunt birds and pigs with bow and arrow, presumably because there is no cash cost involved. Military technology is at a low level—the arrows are not fletched (fitted with feathers). It probably isn't a disadvantage in the dense forest, where you can't shoot very far anyway. Bows and arrows are lying around Imarao everywhere.

Anyway, after the meeting, we had the traditional awards ceremony. All the women were sent off the other side of the village, and someone went off to the custom men's house and returned with a Nambugi ("against sorcery" in Small Nambas Language), a stick with a stylized head on the end. It has bug eyes and big nose and pig's tusks embedded in the cheeks. Kirk told me that men achieve or buy the right to make certain styles of these things, and at their 100-day-after-death ceremony, the types that the deceased used to make are all made and stuck in the ground around the body. Real powerful ones have a skull in them, but this one is made of leaves covered with spider webs (these are very strong here) and mud, then painted with vegetable pastes. The nambugi was presented to Keith, and then spirited off before the women came back, as women are only allowed to see these things during the public funeral ceremonies. When we left that afternoon, a guy gave the nambugi, wrapped in leaves, back to us a few metres down the trail.

Presentation of Nambugi to Keith Mala, Local Government Secretary and my boss. Note nambas lump under shorts of man in centre of photo.

Guide carrying nambugi covered with banana leaves down the trail. The rest of us all required walking sticks to keep our balance down the steep slope.

Returning to the coast.

I must admit I really coveted the nambugi, but kept my mouth shut. Lucky for me, Keith's evangelical Holiness Fellowship Sect is really against custom, and Keith doesn't allow custom objects in his house—he gave it to me! My first artifact! I really feel like a third-world volunteer now; I hung it right up on my living room wall in the approved fashion. Kirk checked out a picture of it I showed him and pronounced it a garden variety one (i.e. he would give the required permission to export it), but a real museum piece. You can buy them, but being presented with one only second-hand from the actual users is much more satisfying.

Laurel, Me, and Heather with the nambugi.

Circumnavigating Malekula

From a September 4,1987 letter:

Last week, I circumnavigated the island with Ross Combdon, the CUSO fisheries officer from Newfoundland, and John Kamphorst, the Australian Livestock Officer. We took this big 10 metre fishing boat, one of four that the Japanese Gov't gave to Vanuatu. It's useless for fishing, of course, but it has two bunks, so Ross uses it for trips like this. John slept on deck. I was told I had to bring a case (24 tins) of beer as admission. I didn't drink much, but they finished off all 72 cans by Saturday, besides kava every night (any clues towards why I am off kava now?). We left Monday the 24th, and returned a week later on the 31st. John visited cattle projects, Ross visited fishing projects, and I took a roll of barbed wire to Hokai so they can keep the cattle out of their water supply.

Unfortunately, we ran out of beer the evening that we anchored in a wonderfully beautiful cove in the Maskelynes I had scouted out on my previous trips through the islands on the south coast. John and I went snorkeling that night, but he (who had the torch[1]) saw a 6-ft. shark, so we got back on the boat. John had a dream of catching a big shark, and had brought some special shark hooks and some rotting pig guts along for the job. Ross and I had insisted on tossing the guts a few days previous after we found we could easily find the boat in the dark without a flashlight.[2] Anyway, that was the only night we caught one. It was about 2 ft. and, as the world should be, man ate shark. I finally saw my first shark in the water the next day. It was also 2 ft. and swam away.

Ruin of plantation house on Sakao Island in the Maskelynes.
The most beautiful place I found on Malekula.

We got a laugh out of this shark business. At every village, the same conversation took place with the locals. We always asked (I'll translate into English for those who don't speak Bislama) "I gat sak lo ples ia?"

[1] British for "flashlight".
[2] Canadian for "torch".

("Got any sharks here?") "O, fulap." ("Oh, yeah, zillions.") "Oli kaekae man?" ("Do they bite people?") "No, oli pleple nomo." ("Oh no, they just mess around.") When we got to Hokai, where I knew a guy had been chewed on, I had my chance to continue the conversation, which had gone true to form to that point: "Be mi bin harem se wan sak i kaekae John Miller." ("Yeah, but what about John Miller?") "Hem nomo." ("Oh, just him.") I'm sure glad I've been relying on local knowledge to choose swimming sites so far.

Delivering roll of barbed wire and box of staples to Hokai village.

Actually, when we got to Lamap, we did get a different answer: Two years ago, an American tourist on a yacht put her small child in a swim ring or something in the ocean, and a shark came and ate it. That would kind of put a damper on your vacation, wouldn't it?

Whenever we pulled up at a village, a crowd of varying size would show up on the beach to watch us. As it seemed evident that everyone had shown up in hopes that the Whitemen would entertain them by sinking their boat, I formulated a theory that the size of the crowd was directly proportional to the number of hidden rocks on the approach to the beach. I fell down in the surf a couple of times when we landed our dinghy, which everyone thought was great. John figures that our main function here is to provide entertainment for the locals[1].

---

[1] And he was right.

Two Years on Malekula

Custom owners of the west of Sakao Island. When Holly and I came through on another occasion, the guy in red paid somewhat more attention to her than I was happy with.

We got two reactions from children. At some places, a zillion would come out in outrigger canoes and swarm over the boat. As we looked back from the dinghy on our way ashore, the boat would be black with them. On the other hand, one day we were walking around a small island with a ni-Vanuatu, and every time we approached a village kids would start howling and run away. The noise would keep up for several minutes. We asked our guide if we were the cause of all this, and he said, "Yes". I've always wanted to have that effect on children. I think we can all guess whom parents tell their pikininis will eat them if they don't eat their island cabbage[1] .

Speaking of eating, John asked a coworker how people used to eat the missionaries, and Willie told him that, as opposed to the cartoon images of missionaries boiling in big pots on a fire, New Hebridans made them into laplap in earth ovens heated by hot stones. Whenever we pulled up to a beach, John would claim that he could see the women hurrying off to heat up their laplap stones.

John and I had hard times on the trip; he kept losing things, and I spent all my time dripping blood on the deck. The first day, half his pipe dropped overboard when he was landing a fish. He had to roll cigarettes

[1] A large-leafed member of the hibiscus family. When boiled in water, it exudes a large amount of slime that strings from your fork to your plate when you eat it. To avoid the slime, you cook it in coconut milk or re-fry it.

the rest of the time. Then a pair of shorts and a T-shirt disappeared, probably overboard. One of his special shark hooks got caught on the bottom and was lost. On the last day, he hooked his gaff into a maemae (dolphin fish), and it got off the hook and swam away with the gaff.

I stubbed both big toes and scraped the end off another toe while we were on shore. My biggest problem, however, was with these three bolts sticking up from the deck of the boat. You wouldn't think that anyone would leave them there after they had removed a piece of equipment (the life raft, of course)—but they lack safety awareness in underdeveloped parts of the world—Newfoundland, in this case. First, I tore a chunk out of my thigh sliding off into the dinghy. Worst of all, when the boat was rolling one morning, I kicked a bolt and split the skin right through from the top of the space between my right big toe and the next toe, and my sole. Right where my thong strap goes. It seems to be healing, but I fear I will be permanently disfigured with a scar. Anyway, Dad will be gratified by my description of what happens when you don't wear shoes in LDCs[1] To top it all off, my hand slipped when I was trying to pull a Horse Mussel shell out of the sand, and my finger hit some coral, flaying the skin off its tip. That really bled for a long time. It's almost healed over now, so perhaps I'll be able to play the guitar again.[2] I don't know how it happened—after all, I had a pair of gloves purchased especially for diving right in my bag back on the boat.

One of the reasons that this boat is useless for fishing is that it rolls a lot. A couple of nights, we just about had to hang onto our bunks by our fingernails, and when we got up, the sea was smooth. I was afraid of getting seasick, so I put one of those Scopolamine patches behind my ear before we left. It worked pretty well, and I didn't get sick; but after we got back, it took two days for the ground to stop moving. You just can't win.

---

[1] Dad did a lot of work in Less Developed Countries, and was always stubbing his toe on uneven sidewalks. He often warned me to always wear shoes in the third world. We didn't have sidewalks on Malekula, just dirt paths. In fact, on our first bush leave to Vila, the girls asked what were these hard things we were walking on. And, what was that big thing flying high above through the sky? They became "man bush" pretty quickly.
[2] Tip of left middle finger; it let me know it was there for some years when I played.

The New Patrol Boat

Australia gave Vanuatu a patrol boat, and one of several ceremonies performed during a tour of the archipelago was held down at the Lakatoro landing stage.

From a September 13, 1987 letter:

> The Patrol Boat anchored out a ways, which was too bad, because like all the people who watched us come into beaches on southern Malekula[1], I hoped to be entertained by watching it sink on a hidden rock. We all lined up on the beach to shake hands when the time came, and three canoes were sent out to bring in the officers plus assorted bureaucrats and politician (the Minister of Local Government, the local MP) who had come to bask in the limelight. We were specially honoured because this was the boat's first stop after the capital on its show-it-to-everyone tour. We were lined up on the side of the landing stage where canoes usually don't come in, and as I foresaw, all the canoes headed to the wrong side, and a guy had to run out on the wharf and wave them in on the other side (I got a photo). Men in semi-custom dress (i.e. leaves over shorts) went out and carried all the bigwigs to shore, where they lined up opposite us. Then the local chief strode out in true custom dress waving a big club and asking these guys just who they thought they were coming onto his ground without first asking permission. After a few minutes of threats and club-waving, another chief in custom dress came out with a kava leaf and explained that these people had meant no harm, and they should all make peace with the kastom lif[2]. This satisfied the custom owner, and the two chiefs exited, stage left. This is the first time I had seen this ceremony. I think it signifies that the people here really see this patrol boat as being a big deal. It symbolizes them taking control of their as-yet-theoretical 200-mile exclusive economic zone.
>
> American tuna boats have always just come in and fished without paying a license fee, although the Americans finally signed an agreement and paid up early this year (to keep up with the Russians, who did it last year).

---

[1] Referring to the tour Ross Combdon, John Kamphorst, and I had made around the island in a Fisheries boat.

[2] Of the kava plant, the traditional leaf of peace.

Local chief formally challenging patrol boat officers and politicians.
Patrol boat not in frame.

Mind you, the Australians, who donated the boat (31.5 metres, top speed 23 knots) refused to put a gun on it. I suppose they can tote along a "numba 12" (shotgun) to shoot over the bows of any renegade fishing boat. (which will no doubt reply with something like a .50 cal. machine-gun.)

Then we had speeches, in which Keith thanked the Minister for all of his hard work in getting the boat. You would have thought the Minister had built it himself—not a mention was made of the Australians. Afterwards, a light breakfast of grapefruit pieces, whole roasted steer and pig, and roasted yam, banana, and taro was served. The expected custom dancing never materialized, although a few men beat on slit drums and sang a bit.

Two Years on Malekula

Regional Development Planners Conference

From an October 13, 1987 letter to my father:

> I was off directly to Efate for the week-long RDP conference. It was
> CUSO-funded and, as our Field Staff Officer Sydne told me, held on the
> far side of the island from Vila so we couldn't get into town at night. Let
> it never be said that someone had fun while at a CUSO-sponsored event.
> I think a big part of the thinking was to get the Department of Local
> Government bigwigs to stay for all of the meetings and not just spend a
> few moments and then go back to their offices. Well, Sydne was really
> put out when they came out for the first day and headed right back to
> Vila for the rest of the week, leaving her with several empty prepaid
> rooms. There really is justice in this world.

To quote Rudyard Kipling again:

Now it is not good for the Christian's health to hustle the Aryan brown,
For the Christian riles, and the Aryan smiles and he weareth the Christian
down;
And the end of the fight is a tombstone white with the name of the late
deceased,
And the epitaph drear: "A Fool lies here who tried to hustle the East."
                    - THE NAULAHKA

Back to the letter to my father:

> Actually, Sydne and I are getting along OK now, since I had it out
> with her about our bush leaves.
>
> We CUSO RDPs had a real split with the only non-CUSO RDP, an
> Australian volunteer. I got a bad feeling at breakfast Monday, when
> he filled us all in on his nutritional theories—it is proven that
> everything you need is present in the air, and those with
> presumably the right karma are "breathairians", existing only on
> air. Also, nobody needs to eat the three food groups that are on the
> posters here—kaekae blong givem paoa (carbohydrates and fats),
> kakae blong bildemap bodi (protein), and kakae blong blokem sik
> (fruit and vegetables). Finally, everybody eats too much, and

Ethiopians only starve because they are afraid of starving.
My opinion of the Australian volunteer agency, the Overseas Service Bureau, and their screening process dropped a few notches.

The main problem, though, is that this guy has an entirely different
philosophy and approach to development than that of the CUSO
RDPs. His is the "Lone Ranger" approach. He doesn't want to be
responsible to local government or work under their authority, he
wants to work towards his own preset objectives only, and he has a
list of specific technologies that he wants to put in place. When we
rejected his attempt to write all of this in stone, he decided that we
were all against him (especially since we had previously met
without him; I had foreseen that this could cause problems),
withdrew from most discussions, and made a speech on the last day
in which he rejected most of what had gone on.

After we forced this Australian to withdraw his proposal, the ni-
Vanuatu officials present told us we had "too much conflict". Their
approach to this type of situation is to talk around the issue for the
rest of the allotted time, look at their watches, put off continued
discussion until tomorrow, and not bring it up again. Sydne and I
showed great cultural sensitivity by replying that we had only two
years here to get something done, and besides, we had learned the
confrontational approach with our mother's milk. One of the CUSO
RDPs made a Vanuatu-style public admission that we had
unfortunately had strong words, complete with the traditional gift
(a Black Swan beer instead of a chicken, because Peter is a
vegetarian), but Peter would have none of it; consensus or majority
rule isn't his style.

Anyway, we got a job description, a counterpart training
programme, and proposed small project funding scheme out of the
meetings, which is what I wanted.

A guy from the Labour Department came on the last day and tried
to get the Secretaries to publicly oppose new draft minimum wage
legislation (election coming up), but got the talk it over all
afternoon and bring it up tomorrow treatment. These guys are all,

in effect, political appointees, and aren't about to oppose the ruling party in public. I can't say I blame them, although I gave my negative opinion on the proposal. It sets up detailed job descriptions with associated minimum wages for each job. I say let the unions do their own work.

The official line is that the mean Whitemen are ripping off all their underpaid workers, but the Labour Dept. guy advised that all expat companies pay at least 50% more than the existing minimum wage. All prosecutions are of ni-Vanuatu employers, and most politically embarrassing is that the worst offenders are the cooperatives (controlled by the ruling Vanua'aku Pati). Of course, the ni-Vanuatu businesses can't afford to pay the minimum wage, and they provide entry-level jobs for inexperienced ni-Vanuatu who later move on to higher-paid jobs with expat employers. Anyway, I followed my philosophy of providing the politicians with my opinion of the consequences of their proposals and leaving them to make the final decisions. A couple of years ago, a private member's bill was introduced to increase the minimum wage by over 100% and no politician dared speak against it. After it passed, the large plantations all shut down, throwing a big chunk of those employed out of work, and waited until the bill was rescinded before resuming production.

After the meetings, I stayed over in Vila to do our Christmas shopping. Unfortunately, I got there Friday afternoon, shops are closed Saturday PM, and Monday the 5th was a national holiday, Constitution Day (do they have a constitution in Indonesia?)[1] I had to spend a week there to get in three days shopping. I started off Friday afternoon by going up to the Doctor's. Then I went out for pizza with my most valuable contact in Vila—a recently ex-CUSO woman with a video machine. The French don't really have pizza-making down right. I ordered salami and black olives and got a pizza with five whole unpitted olives stuck on it. At least it wasn't green olives, like in Ontario. Although, the slices of garlic on this French pizza tasted very good.

[1] My Dad was working in Indonesia, and I frequently pulled his chain about how even Vanuatu was more democratic.

The New Aid Post

From an October 21, 1987 letter:

> Yesterday I went to the grand opening of a new clinic south of here. Actually, they had just added one room to the existing aid post and hired a nurse. The Ministers of Health and Home Affairs were there. The Minister of Health told everyone about AIDS, which is now recognized as a potential problem here. They really are defenceless and really won't even be able to know when it hits them, as there is little hope of getting diagnostic facilities. Not that they could do anything about it anyway. The Minister answered a question about where AIDS had come from pretty well. Of course, he talked like homosexuality was unknown in Vanuatu. Not according to my Bislama dictionary. Someone else wanted to know about another new disease—breast cancer. The Minister had to explain that it wasn't new.

Vanuatu had a high incidence and wide variety of STDs, including some unusual ones. Besides ni-Vanuatu fishing crews bringing them home from Thailand, Western cruise ship crews would compete over who could get laid first in port. As well, the general population was promiscuous. For some reason, though, the first case of AIDS wasn't found until years after we left.

Later, when we were living in Vila, Holly became a CUSO again and worked at the Central Hospital laboratory. One of her responsibilities was overseeing AIDS testing. First, she found that visibly suspicious tests were being classified as negative without being sent to Australia for definitive testing. After she corrected that, the guy doing the tests wouldn't write any identities on the tubes. He just didn't want to find any positives or be able to identify anyone with AIDS.

Besides Vanuatu's presumably normal incidence of homosexuality and lesbianism, Tom Harrison in his book "Savage Civilization" wrote that each Big Nambas man had a young boy assigned to him for sexual purposes, and at the traditional initiation and circumcision ceremony, these boys "changed sex" and thereafter had sex with females and presumably eventually their own young boy. Traditional Big Nambas homosexuality is also reported by anthropologists; e.g. Michael R. Allen in his book "Ritualized Homosexuality in Melanesia".

Back to my letter:

> One guy asked Sethy Reganvanu, the Minister of Home Affairs, if the New Zealand soldiers he had heard about being here had invaded us

(they are on maneuvers training the local armed forces in transportation and communication techniques). I rescued Sethy on one toughie, being, as he put it, his "technical expert". A man had said he had heard that a new gold mine was extracting minerals from the island's soil, and since minerals were necessary for crop growth (at least the Ag. Dept.'s messages have been getting through), would the presence of this mine in the centre of the island ruin the coconut crops on the coast? I reassured everyone that the mine would only affect the place where the hole was dug and the place where they put the dirt. A guy asked for the road, which has been recently extended to about 20 miles N of there, to be further extended to his village. Sethy, laughing, said he promised it would, but only if he got every single vote in the region in November. He did promise them a two-way radio before the election.

The Proposed Brenwe Falls Hydroelectricity Project

The Brenwe River runs south through northern Malekula, emptying into the sea at the "dog's chin" of the island. There is a road parallel to its deep canyon that the French built for some reason, perhaps to give the Church access to the interior it crosses on the upper plateau on its way to Amok. Amok is a small Big Nambas village where at the time kastom ways were followed. One can park where the road fords the river and either walk a bit upstream to a wonderful swimming pool, or find one's way downstream a few score metres to the top of a tall waterfall. For some reason, the river bed here isn't slippery, and I've stood in the flowing water looking over the edge.

Brenwe River pools.

One day, a team of New Zealander hydroelectricity consultants came to check out the Brenwe for its power generation potential. I accompanied them to see it for myself. We drove up the road with a guide and parked. Then, we scrambled down about 100m of very steep canyon wall hanging on to bushes and vines, some of which I learned had thorns and biting ants. At the bottom, we found a beautiful series of limestone pools with blue water flowing over the lip of one into another. The water, like that from glaciers in the Canadian Rockies, was that colour because of the limestone it contained, in this case from the coral rock substrate through which it passed.

We didn't hike upstream to the falls, but clawed our way up the canyon wall to our truck. On the way back to Lakatoro, the conversation was about the hydro possibilities of the site. They said that the power could be used to dry cacao beans at the nearby Metenesel Estates Ltd. plantation. I told them this was a possibility, but other markets presented difficulties. First, ni-Vanuatu villagers were in the non-cash subsistence economy. Those few who did have access to diesel-powered electricity may have had one 40-watt light bulb in their bamboo houses, but could not afford any other appliances or the power to run them. Second, the largest markets on Malekula, the PRV coconut plantation and the Lakatoro government station, were nicely served by one diesel generator each and were on the other side of the island. Very expensive transmission infrastructure would be required to get power over to their limited demand. In the event, the team did not recommend that the project proceed.

I heard that after we left Vanuatu the second time, a Chinese company came in and started building a hydro project, later abandoned. I don't know how that turned out, but I hope they didn't ruin the falls and pools.

Relations with the National Planning and Statistics Office

The National Planning and Statistics Office in Vila was staffed by several expatriate aid workers with little knowledge of Vanuatu outside the expatriate playground of Port Vila. A town of 20,000 with about 2,000 expatriates, Port Vila had a couple of French cafes where one could breakfast on pain chocolat, two French bakeries where one could get fresh croissants at 6AM 7 days-a-week, a total of 30 restaurants including a couple of top-grade French eateries, a tennis club, squash courts, three golf courses, and two riding clubs. Life there, as we learned later living there for three years, was hard (not). But it wasn't Vanuatu.

So, it wasn't unusual for aid to be planned in a top-down manner, especially since Vanuatu's unspoken official objective was to obtain as much aid as possible of whatever kind. The Council of Ministers (Cabinet) was incapable of prioritizing aid projects, abdicating the responsibility of project choice to the aid donors. Not exactly analogous with the notion of "development" being the

131

process of communities gaining control over their situation and future, but such is the reality of international aid.

From a November 20, 1987 letter:

> I must admit that I am prejudiced against NPSO. I have discussed with them my proposed Community Small Grants Programme, where the LGCs would disburse a bunch of aid money in $500-$1000 chunks to community projects. Such piddling amounts, you'd think they would be glad to see us take the burden off them. Well, all I've gotten from them has been a zillion reasons why it won't work, because all the money will be wasted and they would have to scrutinize and monitor each project, so the programme could be quickly ended if they spotted any abuses. They also want to hire a guy to monitor us RDPs and give us advice. I wrote a letter telling them to stick to their own Ministry. They have just no trust or willingness to delegate even the smallest bit of authority.
>
> I was ready for these problems from ni-Vanuatu, but it's funny—the ex-pats are the obstruction. The real problem is that the Government as a whole didn't get its act together regarding our role in the system. I'm sending off my draft project proposal to NPSO and the other RDPs next week, after it has sat on my Local Gov't Dept. contact's desk for a month without him reading it (inactivity of local staff can be a problem—actually, he's catatonic because he is intimidated by the job). I've already set up, administered, and had complete signing authority on a similar programme in BC (except I was handing out $1.5 million in $40,000 chunks, a fact I'm going to have to mention one of these days), so I think the first draft is presentable. It will be interesting to get their objections on paper, unless they just ignore it. (In case you are wondering, I got my DLG contact's permission to send out the draft; he seemed relieved that I would take some of this off his hands, although eventually it will have to go through him.) This proposal was given unanimous approval by all of the LGC Secretaries, all the RDPs, and the Director of the DLG at the meeting we had last month, so it's not just some lonely crusade of mine, although I may find myself alone when resistance is encountered. Oh, well, I'm heading home when I'm done; I don't have to live in any mess they make with their mistakes (or mine either, I guess).

The British man on NPSO's desk handling local government matters was a nice enough guy, but told me that when the Regional Development Planner programme that I was part of had been initiated, the NPSO had decided not to cooperate with it at all because we volunteer RDPs were just a bunch of amateurs seeking cargo for the outer regions. I couldn't believe it. Two years later, I was sitting in his desk with the other expat staffers with rural third-world experience we recruited from Australia, Britain, Denmark, and Germany; there was a definite change of attitude.

Effectiveness may not have changed though. The fact was the only reason the Government of Vanuatu had a National Planning and Statistics Office was because the British made it a condition of further development aid. The politicians had no interest in prioritizing development efforts nor the ability to do so. Basically, they just wanted more free stuff from aid donors, abdicating Vanuatu's development project decisions to the aid donors. Donors did not coordinate their individual programmes, which they ran in their own interests, so there really wasn't any coordinated development.

The Game

One afternoon, I returned to the office after lunch, and there was a line of men extending out the main office door, down the steps, and out into the yard. I asked Kalosak, my counterpart, why they were all there, and he said, "The Game". "What game?" I countered, and upon further enquiry learned that the men were all lined up to use the office photocopy machine in order to get in on an elaborate chain letter scheme. The deal was that they sent US$10 or so, along with the names of 6 people, to somewhere in Europe. Then, the European connection sent letters to the six nominees, each of which was to give the guy at the top of the list $10. This was obviously a scheme in which the European outfit made money from everyone who participated. I tried to give Kalosak a quick rundown on geometric progressions and how this chain would, at best, reach every adult male in Vanuatu in about 4 iterations. Only the first few people in Vanuatu who got in on it would make any money; everyone else would lose.

For many rural ni-Vanuatu, every amount above three is "a bunch", and very large numbers are nobody's strength. Kalosak's eyes glazed over, and I gave it up, leaving all the game players to their fates. Later, I learned that the game had come to Malekula via a Fijian woman who was the PRV Plantation accountant; I'm sure she cleaned up. Another expat draining very hard-earned money from rural Vanuatu.

At about the same time, letters started circulating advertising a Canadian company that, for a fee, would guarantee the applicant would get a credit card. Sure. This appealed to ni-Vanuatu, since nobody pays back loans from anyone but family, and credit in rural Vanuatu is considered free money. Most villages had a retail store that had failed because they gave credit that was never repaid.

Logging on Malekula

The Taiwanese

One day, David Wood showed up in my Lakatoro office. David is one of the good guys of international aid technical assistance. An Australian, he was with the Forestry Department. When we flew into Port Vila from Brisbane in 2009, he and his wife, Bronwyn, were in the First Class section of the plane; evidently, they've done well.

On this occasion, David showed me a logging proposal from the Taiwanese Tien Su logging company. On the title page, he'd penciled in "Rape and Pillage", which gave me an idea of the contents. Representatives from this company had visited a few southern Malekula villages, showing proper respect to the chiefs by gifting them a few cases of beer. The proposal was familiar to many Canadians; the company would build roads into the blocks they wanted to log, clear-cut large areas, and leave.

The ni-Vanuatu chiefs heard this: We are going to get roads into our villages, and garden land will be cleared without the normal large amounts of our labour, for free! In fact, they will pay us for this! Hold my beer while I sign up.

What the Australian logging expert and the Canadian Regional Development Planner heard was this: These rapacious foreigners, who don't give a good God-damn about Vanuatu, are planning to build the cheapest roads they can. Soon after they leave, and certainly by the first wet season, the roads will deteriorate and collapse, leaving an eroding mess. Using these roads, they will strip the cut blocks of the nutrients that in the tropics are stored in vegetation rather than the soil. They will cherry-pick the most valuable timber and leave the place a shambles. Erosion will occur, stripping the land of its thin layer of soil and depositing it on the reefs, killing all the sea life that comprise the villagers' major source of protein. The logs they chose would be exported to Taiwanese lumber mills, where all the value-added would accumulate.

The Vanuatu Customs Department got involved in the Tien Su logging episode. In the words of Norman Shackley, the British expatriate Director of Customs & Taxes at the time :

> "It was a senior Ni-Vanuatu Customs officer who brought an envelope containing bank notes in local currency into my office, saying 'I think someone just tried to bribe me!'

> "Following further investigations I then laid information before the local magistrate and applied for search warrants on the Tien Su bank account and, later, also sought and obtained warrants to access a number of other accounts suspected of receiving corrupt payments.

> "The case caused considerable problems at the time (the senior Taiwanese national arrested turned out to be the brother-in-law of the President of Taiwan) with the British and Australian governments favouring a back-off in the investigations, with only New Zealand among the local High Commissions wanting to see them continue. In the end, the two Taiwanese were imprisoned and a number of ni-Vanuatu were dismissed

from government service and one, the main offender, who received the largest corrupt payments and acted as the middleman with the Malekulan chiefs was charged, went to trial and was given a suspended sentence."

I left Malekula before the Taiwanese episode played out, but understand some logging by other companies has taken place; I have no idea what the final effects were.

Small Scale and Local Logging

When I was with the NPSO in Vila, I got to know the American woman running the local office of the South Pacific People's Federation, a bottom-up non-government aid organization. She told me they were working on a logging project, which given my experience with the Taiwanese proposal, got my hackles up. "No, no", she said, "It's like this…" and explained the SPPF's idea. They would bring in small mills that could be moved to each tree to be cut and processed. Technical and business training and mentorship would be provided to each ni-Vanuatu village logger who bought a mill. The idea was not to export lumber, but to provide dimensional lumber to villagers at a price they could afford. This was important, because it is impossible to fasten the corrugated iron roofs that people wanted to irregular branches from the bush.

Well, it wasn't long before Australian Greenies showed up in Vila to stop this project, including threatening to pressure Australian politicians to cut aid to Vanuatu. They were absolutely opposed to any logging in the tropics. "Where were they when the Taiwanese came?" I wondered. I could see their point regarding what was happening in southeast Asia, but we were talking about local people cutting a small number of trees with little environmental effect—the logs would even be milled right where they were felled, avoiding the damage of roads into the forest. Also, due to frequent cyclones, Vanuatu had no tertiary forests taking centuries to regenerate that needed protecting.

The only conclusion I could come to was that these people were afraid to tackle the big corporations doing real damage to tropical rainforests, so they had chosen a soft target, Vanuatu, on whose back to ineffectually fight their battles.

I heard that the small-scale logging project finally got off the ground after we left Vanuatu for good, and enjoyed some success after suffering local political interference.

Personnel Issues

Dealing with Fully-Funded (Well-Paid) Consultants.

One problem we all had, and which CUSO had warned us about, was the attitude of fully-funded technical advisors towards volunteers. Some of the fully-funded guys were pretty good, especially if they had once been volunteers. Others didn't know their ass from a hole in the ground. They had the attitude that, because they made big bucks and we didn't, they knew everything and we didn't. Note that the average age of CUSO cooperants at that time was 35, and all had experience in their field before they were given an assignment.

This wasn't so much a problem with the British, because they had a system that took in new graduates and put them through an international career with increasing responsibilities. Other countries, such as Canada, took professionals in mid-career and put them out in the field to transfer the latest Western technology to places where it was not appropriate.

Many development projects were contracted out to consulting, often engineering, companies that had three main objectives: Find the next contract, make every project as expensive as possible because they netted a percentage of money spent, and do the job as inexpensively as possible. This led to big centralized projects that were inappropriate and/or didn't do anything for the rural majorities of undeveloped countries. I sometimes thought that maybe some consultants had one report on their computers' world processors in which they made minor amendments when they moved on to a new contract in another country. When I was in the NPSO in Vila, they would come into my office and pick my brains because they didn't know anything about Vanuatu. I'd cooperate in an effort to lessen the damage.

During my time in Vanuatu, I only saw one report that didn't leave out the final required work or end with "work beyond the scope of this contract is required". The exception was from a New Zealand team of energy experts; they did their job completely, and even gave me some free consulting because they saw they had the skills to help.

Victor Cumming, perhaps our most capable Regional Development Planner, just about foamed at the mouth when he talked about advisors funded by the Canadian International Development Agency. I guess he spent 2 years with CUSO in Botswana, and later joined up with a couple of other Botswana hands to get a CIDA contract there. They were obliged to go to Ottawa for a three-day CIDA briefing on Botswana. Upon arrival, they were shown into a conference room with two guys from the Southern Africa desk. Then a woman, who was an old beer-drinking buddy of Victor's from Botswana, came in and they shot the bull for an hour or so about the old days. All this time, the two CIDAs just looked down at their ties. The woman finally said she had a meeting, and left. After a moment of silence, the one CIDA said to the other, "Gee, I guess these guys already know about Botswana." Then to Victor and his compatriots, "Well, if you need us, we'll be in our offices." and they ran off.

A Unique Consultant

After leaving Malekula, when we were living and working in Port Vila, an American nobody knew and without any evident qualifications suddenly appeared as a special consultant to one of the Central Government Ministers. Some of the technical advisors whose work he was interfering with wrote off to the US to get some background on this guy, and the reply letter was circulated amongst the rest of us: He had spent time in a California prison for smuggling illegal immigrants into the state, and the FBI was interested in chatting with him about another matter.

It wasn't long before he was popularly known as "Rick the Dick". Rick had turned up on a sailing yacht, walked into this Minister's office, and talked himself into his very senior position. A CUSO told me that he had met Rick while waiting outside the Minister's office and asked him what it was that he did. The reply was, "The same as you: I smile, pat 'em on the ass, and tell them what they want to hear." Sorry, Rick; that was not at all what we were all doing. Often, we were telling the politicians what they did not want to hear.

One day, Rick wasn't there anymore; who knows why he left or where he went.

CUSO Cooperant Issues

Most of the CUSOs in Vanuatu were competent and dedicated. They did their jobs well. As in any organization, especially one sending people to live and work in a foreign culture, however, there were a few hiccups.

CUSO didn't know that the very competent Quebecois couple we travelled out with didn't speak English. In a CUSOesque effort to be politically correct, they had asked the couple at their French-language interview, "Parlez-vous Anglais?", and the reply, "Oui" was taken at face value. When we met them after several months in-country, we always communicated in Bislama, much to the amusement of any ni-Vanuatu present.

Another cooperant did a good job, but broke his contract four months early so he could get back to his previous job at the Canadian International Development Agency in September when the plum positions are handed out. Our Field Staff Officer was not amused; CUSO had spent a lot of money getting him out there and supporting him while he became effective in Vanuatu. I always suspected he was only with CUSO so he could get some international experience on his CV. It also hadn't endeared him to the FSO when his family first arrived and his wife came off the plane carrying an oxygen bottle for her respiratory problems; she had got her physician to falsify her CUSO medical form.

Another RDP was an OK guy, but I think CUSO made a mistake sending him to Vanuatu. He was from Toronto, and had spent some time working with native communities in Ontario. His girlfriend was a physician, who was supposed to

The Quebecois couple, Daniel and Simone (in dark shirts), that we travelled to Vanuatu with, and who shared our Cyclone Uma experience upon arrival.

join him after a separation of one year. We first met him when he arrived, and he was already painfully lonely after one week.[1] He was posted to a remote island, but CUSO brought him to Vila for long stretches because of the isolation hardship of his post in the Banks Islands.

For want of an alternative, he was forced to live in the LGC Secretary's house up in Sola. Living in a ni-Vanuatu household is very difficult for most Westerners, and the inevitable cultural and personal conflicts arose. Also, Sola was very isolated compared to Lakatoro, where we lived. For example, I imagine the diet in Sola was large helpings of white rice, three times per day. In Lakatoro we could readily purchase meat, fruit, and vegetables, which are not for sale in most of Vanuatu. As a family, we also provided our own same-culture companionship. Rather than bringing him into the capital regularly, CUSO would have done better to insist that a house be built for him, even if CUSO had to provide funding. Then, like other isolated CUSOs, he would have had privacy and could

---

[1] I recently learned that his brother had committed suicide shortly before he came to Vanuatu; this must have contributed to his mood.

have cooked groceries that were flown in from Luganville on the regular air service.

His physician girlfriend eventually came for a couple of months. She told Holly that she just didn't see any role for her up on her partner's island, this being an entire region of the country with several thousand people who didn't have any doctor at all. She thought she might want to organize a primary health care system, which the government has already done using nurses and paramedics. She also said that they didn't have any labs up there, so how could she diagnose anyone? After meeting her (nice enough person), I thought she was just firmly attached to the bright lights of Toronto. How CUSO fell for this line about her coming after a year, I don't know. Maybe they didn't; they did get a good potential RDP, but as I say, he was in Vila, rather than at his post, much of the time.

One CUSO couple brought the man's son with them to get him away from his druggie friends and learn some responsibility working with his father on a Fisheries Project. I must say, the son fit right into Vanuatu. It wasn't long before he was spending all his time drinking kava with his new friends on Ambae Island. His father sent him home.

Three cooperants I know of got into legal troubles growing Marijuana. The thing is, there are no secrets in Vanuatu, and if you think you have found a place unknown to all for growing weed, you are seriously mistaken. Inevitably, someone develops a grudge against you and makes a report to the authorities. This is what happened to the first CUSO to have this legal problem, before we were in Vanuatu. He had been posted on Tanna, but happened to be in Vila when the police started looking for him. Somehow he got word, and CUSO got him on a plane out of the country before he could be arrested.

In another case, our FSO wasn't so helpful; from a March, 19, 1987 letter:

> An example of FSO support: a CUSO was arrested for marijuana posses-
> sion last year, and not only did the FSOs immediately presume him
> guilty (wouldn't lend him money for a lawyer or even visit him in jail),
> they acted as if all the CUSOs were operating a drug ring and asked the
> government to close the borders to all CUSOs!

In general, I thought that the FSOs we had while in Lakatoro were much too concerned with not damaging their relations with the Vanuatu government than protecting their cooperants. They did not stand up for cooperants in other instances, such as ensuring proper housing was provided. By the time we returned to Vanuatu to work in Vila, an excellent FSO, Simon Swale, had taken over the position. All of his cooperants were bitching about their conditions when we arrived, so I volunteered to give a talk about how things had been only one year earlier—lower pay, fighting for bush leaves, cold water only out in Lakatoro, etc. The complaints ceased.

The third marijuana case was more complex, but may well have eventually resulted in an arrest in any case. A Swiss couple visited Vanuatu and made friends with a CUSO on Ambae before spending some time with us on Malekula. After they left Vanuatu, they went to Southeast Asia, from where they mailed some Marijuana seeds to their friend on Ambae. Unfortunately for him, at the same time the Australian police were onto a Chinese businessman smuggling heroin to Australia through Vanuatu. The Australians were going through mail to Vanuatu very thoroughly and found the seeds. The CUSO spent several months in prison before being deported. Some time after, the Swiss wrote me asking why their letters to the Ambae CUSO weren't being answered.

I told them I hated to be the bearer of bad news, but gave them the word. I kind of think that friendship died.

One CUSO brought her teenaged daughter along to her post in Vila. The girl got bored and started making the rounds of the expat men, some married, in Vila— her mother affectionately referred to her as "quite the social butterfly". That's one way to put it, I guess. This wasn't illegal or even immoral, but it didn't exactly put CUSO in a good light.

A CUSO working with the National Women's Centre had the bright idea to tackle Vanuatu's national rape problem, which is very real, by having the Centre print up a bunch of posters in all three of Vanuatu's main languages and put them up around Vila. The posters had a picture of a man attacking a woman and read, "The Fear of Rape is the Same as the Fear of Castration". That same day, all the posters were ripped down and the CUSO's ni-Vanuatu counterpart was beaten so badly by her husband that she was admitted to the hospital.

We met a couple of expatriate black women who were careful to dress in a very Western manner so people didn't think they were ni-Vanuatu. One was a CUSO who brought her son and put him in a ni-Vanuatu boarding school. He found the conditions unbearable, and I don't blame him. Food was poor, and the dormitory, which I once visited, was primitive and not screened properly against mosquitoes. I don't imagine the schooling was up to Canadian standards, either. He left early.

One CUSO, Gudrun Leys, managed a cooperatively-run furniture factory in Vila. When her CUSO contract ended, the workers voted to hire her to continue. I thought this was a successful conclusion, but the CUSO Field Staff Officer was angered that the ex-cooperant, rather than one of the ni-Vanuatu workers, became the permanent manager. As far as I was concerned, the workers had recognized that their strength was manufacturing rather than management and had taken appropriate action. I dropped in on the factory when we visited Vila two decades later in 2009 and was offered the empty management job on the spot; I declined.

One recurring issue was families who brought children and then felt guilty because "the kids didn't ask to come". One family that told me they felt that way completed their contract; another one, after trying vainly to make things as much like Canada as possible for their sons, was an early return. On the other hand, we knew families, including ours, which did just fine.

At one point, the woman who had recruited me in Victoria, Carol Sherwood, visited us for five days. The visit went better than I had feared, and there were a few bright points. One was the look on her face when I explained how the prices at Norsup's expat plantation company store were lower than those at Lakatoro's government-owned co-op. That was worth going over there for.

CUSO ideology held that co-operatives were the only proper ownership and management structure in the third world. In fact, I was unaware of any village co-operative venture in Vanuatu that survived — only family consortiums were successful. The Lakatoro Co-op store was part of a nation-wide co-op programme that had been launched soon after independence. It included a nation-wide shipping programme to serve remote locations previously left out of the colonial private transportation system. This programme soon ran up a huge debt; there was a business reason that private ships did not call at very remote islands. The government paid this debt by selling import monopolies on sugar, rice, tobacco, and cement to powerful local businessmen of Vietnamese origin. Ten years later when we were there, the population was still paying higher-than-necessary prices for all of these commodities. A few of the co-op retail stores, like the one in Lakatoro, survived.

The other high point of Carol's visit was, after spending a few days telling her what a great time we were having and showing her the sailboat, etc., hearing her tell us that "You should suffer a little bit, you know!" Forget it; we were having the times of our lives. I didn't believe we had to suffer for other's lives to become better.

While we were in Vanuatu, my father was working on a contract at an English-as-a-second-language programme in Irian Jaya, Indonesia. He wrote me about CUSO cooperants being assigned to his project, being concerned, needlessly as it turned out, that he would get an ideologue rather than a good teacher. Fason blong fully-funded technical expert. I replied:

January 15, 1988:

> I understand your concern about being assigned a CUSO to work with. It's a bit hit-or-miss. My feeling is that the ideological problem is centred in the bureaucracy in Ottawa and the Field Staff Offices, and to a lesser extent in the field. The "it's all the fault of the rich countries" slant is

> widely present to a small degree, though. Most CUSO's are pretty reasonable, but there are exceptions. The biggest problem, as far as I am concerned, is with the increasing number of yuppies that are finding their way out here. We have two of them here in Vanuatu, both fellow RDPs, although one has shown a certain ability to adapt and is an OK guy.

And:

> Once again, don't sweat the CUSO angle until you meet the people you will be working with. There was a small rebellion at our Ottawa orientation when we had the third session on "nuclear-free Pacific". The Ottawa CUSO "elite" tend to be more interested in the ideology than most of the cooperants.

As it turned out, Dad's CUSO was great.

Volunteers Suffering in Vanuatu

At CAN$800 per month for Holly and I, our family made more than anyone else in Lakatoro, including my boss the LGC Secretary, a fact I kept under my hat. In fact, counting the quarterly stipend CUSO gave us for such things as storage of furniture at home, our resettlement allowance in lieu of qualifying for unemployment insurance in Canada, and because we got housing and utilities free, my take-home pay was about the same as it would have been in Canada.

We used to get together with other volunteers and chortle about what a comfortable posting Vanuatu was—good weather (except the odd cyclone), nice beaches and snorkeling/diving, non-violent society, no dangerous land animals (although sharks in the sea), and only one dangerous disease, malaria, that was easily avoided. Dengue Fever came to Vanuatu a few years later, when we lived in Vila; Holly may have had it; she had the symptoms; but there were no diagnostic facilities in-country.

A few years ago, Holly and I attended a CUSO event in Vancouver and were told by an old Africa cooperant, partially tongue-in-cheek, that Vanuatu cooperants weren't true CUSOs. Well, sori long yu (Tough Luck!), fella!

South Pacific Travel-Not What the Brochures Promised!

When I was working in the National Planning Office, and we were in the throes of writing Vanuatu's latest Development Plan, three of us set off to seek input from a remote village. Jimmy was there to provide a ni-Vanuatu focus, Irishman Garvin was along to experience some real Vanuatu, and I was the Canadian instigator. Our destination was Vetumboso on Vanua Lava Island in the north of the archipelago. Inter-island freighters rarely venture to this region; without access to the international copra market or merchandise, few benefits of "development" come here. The money economy is distant, and subsistence gardening is the major economic activity.

That afternoon, our Vanair Twin Otter overflew stretches of the Coral Sea and several islands of vertical greenery ringed with necklaces of white foam crescents on turquoise shallows. Our most spectacular view was of the semicircular lake high in the ancient crater of the island of Gaua (also known as Santa Maria) volcano. At our destination we bumped to earth and retrieved our packs from the agent unloading the cargo bay.

I planted my foot on the rear tire of the waiting half-ton taxi truck, swung over the side, and took my place next to Jimmy. We stood hanging to the bar above the rear cab window, the better to absorb the shock of potholes with our knees. Giving the cab roof a slap (the national code for "we probably won't fall off if you start now"—twice means "stop here"), we bumped down the coral road, keeping an eye out for fast-approaching branches. A short ride brought us to the Island Government resthouse, a large woven bamboo building with corrugated roof. Inside, we each claimed an iron cot, hung a mosquito net by the nails protruding from the walls and ceiling, and cooked our evening meal. Tonight's entree was made of rice and tinned meat we had brought on the expectation that local shop shelves would be bare. I read a bit by the Coleman kerosene lantern, caught the BBC World Service news on my pocket shortwave radio, and hit the hay.

The next morning was gray and windy. After a hearty breakfast of cabin crackers and peanut butter (don't leave home without it), we ambled down to the Sola wharf for our 5-metre open "speedboat" taxi. The two risk-adverse Westerners located life jackets, and I noticed with relief that the 15-HP back-up had not yet replaced the standard-issue 25-HP outboard motor on the aid-subsidized plywood ex-fishing boat.

Soon out of the bay, we wallowed through rain and 1.5-metre seas on our two-hour voyage up the coast to the point from where we would walk. In the absence of two-way communication, Plan "A" was that someone in the village would have heard our previous week's service message over Radio Vanuatu. We further hoped the village would have seen fit to send someone to guide us through the maze of trails and, indeed, that the villagers considered it worth their time to meet with us. Meanwhile, after an hour the sea's motion overcame me and I employed my well-worn strategy of finding a spot where I would least inconvenience my fellow sailors (on a 5-metre boat?), laying my head on the gunwale, and dozing between bouts of illness.

Finally our captain pointed out our landing, a small rocky beach at the mouth of a small river. I asked if he could drop us on the north side, where the path to the village began, but he pointed out the beach on the south was the only spot where waves were not pounding the sharp reef. Well, a swim across the river wouldn't dampen us much more, but I found we were in luck. Not only was a young man from Vetumboso awaiting us, an old one-man dugout canoe was on the river bank. Swallowing my misgivings about "playing Bwana", I accepted the guide's offer to push us across, and we crossed the river in turns.

Vanuatu's frequent cyclones prevent the development of tertiary rainforest and undergrowth chokes the lower bush, but our path was well traveled and clear. The rain made our way especially dark, and from under my poncho hood I had the sensation of traveling down a tunnel along the forest floor. Usually a morning's bush walk found my face collecting swatches of the previous night's spider webs, but this time the weather had discouraged their construction or another tall person had already swept the way clear. Rainwater funnelled down the path however; it was like wading up a small stream in a tepid shower. I was well served by my rain outfit of thongs, shorts, and poncho, which sacrificed my bare lower legs and feet to the rain while keeping my upper body reasonably dry. The running water kept the mud from forming a slippery layer between my feet and thongs, allowing me to remain shod.

An hour and a half's walk, and the trail discharged us into the village clearing. We were ushered into the bamboo and Sago-thatched Community Hall. The weather deepened the interior gloom, but I could soon make out forty or so men and women and several shy children who had come to talk with us. Dress was post-missionary Vanuatu—men in second-hand shorts and T-shirts collected by Western charities and sold to the Third World to raise funds, and women in their beautiful island dresses of hibiscus prints embellished with lace and festooned with flowing ribbons. We gently shook hands[1] with all and were seated on

---

[1] The normal ni-Vanuatu handshake was limp; meeting someone with Whiteman

wooden benches. Things got underway with a welcome from the Chief, introductions, and a prayer by the village Pastor capped by the usual round of applause.

In Bislama, I explained why I wanted to know their development priorities. I then used the example of a short journey to convey the concepts, quickly grasped, of "Objective" (Where do I want to go?), "Strategy" (How am I going to try to get there?), "Monitoring Progress" (Am I still on course, or on the right path?), and "Making Adjustments" (Changing my heading to remain on-course). There was some discussion, and we were told what I eventually heard from all regions of Vanuatu: both men and women wanted opportunities to make money, preferably by selling agricultural products to the export market. The women also wanted better child-birthing facilities, and as their family's primary food producers, instruction on cultivating foreign vegetables.

With that the meeting concluded, and we were shown the courtesy of a mid-day meal—the villagers were well aware that Europeans eat three meals a day rather than their customary two. A special lap-lap had been prepared by grating yams, adding coconut milk and pieces of pork, wrapping the mixture in large leaves, and baking it for several hours on hot stones in a pit oven. Lap-lap is an acquired taste, but after the morning's exertions it was very good.

The rain continued, and our wade back to the river's mouth was uneventful. We shouldn't have been as surprised as we were, however, to find that after a day's rain, the river had by now risen a half-metre and doubled its breadth. Jimmy and Garvin had had enough of the old canoe and opted to swim across. I chose the high tech option and led the crossing by balancing myself in the tiny craft and starting the 20-metre paddle. Almost within arm's reach of the opposite shore, SNAP!; the outrigger broke, rolling me into the water. Blinded by my shifting poncho and struggling to disentangle my arms to avoid drowning, I became aware of small beasties scrambling over my shoulders, along with pinpricks of pain. Floating down the river on some bit of flotsam, a colony of biting ants had climbed on the first solid object they bumped into, attacking when they discovered it was alive. I busied myself dealing with the poncho, scrambling ashore, and scraping off the ants. Then, trying not to drown by inhaling water in their laughter, my companions swam across without incident.

Our taxi boat came in from offshore, we launched it, and clambered in. The return voyage was a repeat of the morning's except I was sick the entire way. Back in Sola, I gave supper a miss and collapsed into my bed, while Garvin and Jimmy struck out for the evening, hoping to find a kava bar in which to boost the local economy.

After another night's rain, we faced one of Vanuatu's rainy-season travel uncertainties: would the grass airstrip be too soggy for our flight to land, forcing us to stay the weekend? As always, though, Vanair came through, and we were back in Port Vila that evening.

---

experience and a firm grip could be a painful experience.

Two Years on Malekula

At the next National Planning Office meeting, my report drew a good laugh from all. I sobered things a bit by reminding my fellow expats of what the ni-Vanuatu planners were well aware: for most of the nation's populace, the trip's difficulties were everyday experiences.

Part 4—The CUSO Cooperant Life on Malekula

Or

"Little House on the Prairie" Meets "South Pacific"

Two Years on Malekula

Lakatoro: Home, Sweet Home

To set the scene, Lakatoro is set back a hundred metres or so of bush plateau from the sea and across the road that runs up Malekula's east coast. Then, going uphill towards the central mountains, there was a soccer field and English-language government school.[1]

In front of the government offices and then about 50 concrete block houses for LGC employees. [2] It had many trees, with the grass mowed under them and various well-trimmed bushes.

View from road over soccer field to Lakatoro.
Most of the buildings are hidden in the trees.

I came to believe that mowed lawns were a curse foisted on Vanuatu by colonization. Scarce money had to be spent on push power mowers designed for Western home lawns, so they wore out quickly being used on large expanses. Their fuel also consumed cash. And, a multitude of LGC employee man-hours were spent pushing these mowers back and forth. Lawnmowers were also thought essential for soccer fields; I wondered if a few dozen fit young men with bushknives might be able to cut the grass short before each game.

---

[1] When we were in Vanuatu, all of the government primary schools were either English- or French-language.

[2] Except for that of Ross Combden, the CUSO Fisheries Advisor. CUSO had promised him that they would provide suitable housing for him, his wife, and young daughter, but when he arrived, it consisted of a pile of building materials on the beach; only enough to build a house with primarily woven-bamboo walls.

Two Years on Malekula

The bushes and trees were trimmed with bushknives and axes by inhabitants of the Lakatoro prison. An Australian friend once caught a ride in the front seat of a police pickup carrying a prison work party with their tools in the truck bed. He said he suddenly realized that he and the policeman driving were the only unarmed people in the truck.

Lakatoro, with neighbouring Norsup 8km north, was Vanuatu's third largest urban concentration, so there were the luxuries of a co-op store and bakery. Norsup had two other stores, one with a butchery, as well as a twice-weekly villagers' market. Lakatoro was one of the few places in Vanuatu where food could be purchased; most ni-Vanuatu grew their own.

Our house was at 80 metres elevation up the hill, on the upper edge of Lakatoro, where the bush began. It was the former housegirl house and garage for British District Agent Darvall Wilkins, whose family had lived just below us in the large house now inhabited by my boss, Keith Mala, the LGC Secretary. About 7 x 9 metres, our house was made of concrete blocks with a corrugated iron roof. The master bedroom floor had oil stains from the vehicles parked there before it was walled in for us, the living room had formerly been the open hand-laundry area, and there were a second bedroom and a kitchen. The bathroom, with shower and flush toilet, was accessed from a door leading from the veranda[1], which was soon half-walled and insect-screened for us. We had running cold water, as well as central generator power from 0530 to 2245 to start, and mornings and evenings later on. We used a Canadian-made Coleman kerosene single-mantle pressure lantern for light in the mornings before the power came on.

---

[1] Standard in Vanuatu; people did not want toilets accessed from kitchens or other rooms.

Two Years on Malekula

The Combs/Morgan residence before the veranda was screened in.

Each room was well ventilated by glass louvered windows, which were well screened against mosquitoes. At first, we used towels for curtains, but Holly later made bright tropical-print[1] cloth curtains to foil the night-time "peepers" common in Vanuatu. Rather than being drawn to the side during the day, the curtains were always tied in a knot, Vanuatu-style, to let light in. We had been advised by experienced Vanuatu CUSOs in Ottawa to, while in Fiji, buy rectangular mosquito nets with a hexagonal weave that would allow better air circulation than the traditional conical regular weave nets, and we installed them over the two beds in the girls' room and our bed. It didn't turn out to be necessary to tuck them in at night; mosquitos never tried to fly up them from the bottom edges, which hung 20cm or so below the mattresses.

The living room had a simple couch and chair, coffee table, and shelves on the walls. We bought a large pandanus mat for the floor. The kitchen had a butane stove/oven with burners that had to be manually lit. We kept some plastic bottles of water in the freezer, which kept things cold when Lakatoro's generators were turned off at night and (later on) mid-day. CUSOs living without electricity used kerosene refrigerators, but reported that they required a lot of maintenance, especially in regard to keeping the wick trimmed and clean, so we lived in relative luxury.

---

[1] All cloth in Vanuatu seemed to have some variation of a hibiscus pattern.

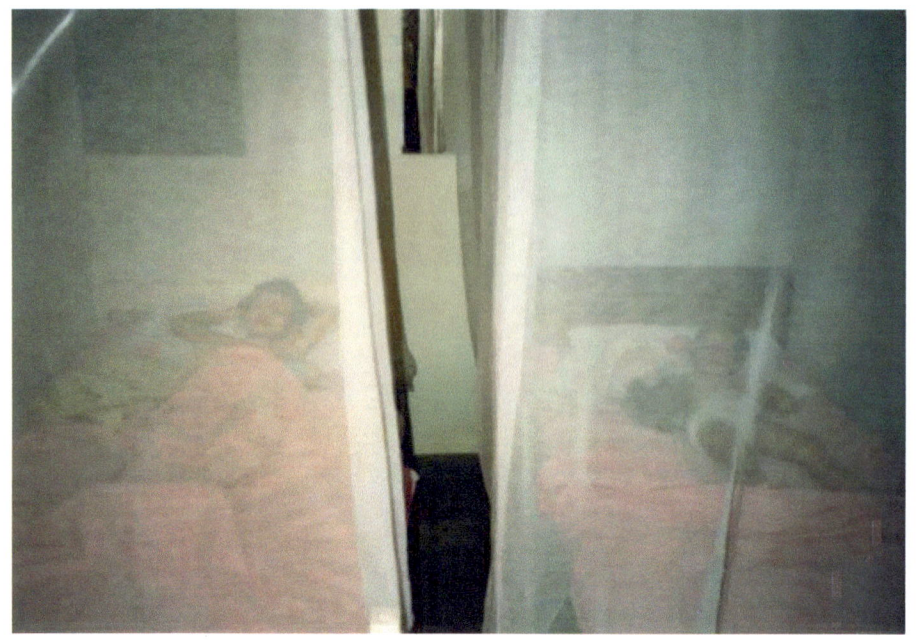

Heather and Laurel with Rose the Teddy Bear in their netted beds.

The Kitchen

Two Years on Malekula

Breakfast. Laurel sporting her Mullet after asking Heather to style her hair.

Aside from two years of cold showers as the only Vanuatu CUSOs without hot water (Geez, we were tough!), we were quite comfortable.

Frangipani (plumeria) trees grew outside the kitchen and girls' bedroom windows. It soon became evident that the frangipani branches were just the right size for the neighbourhood chickens to roost on. We didn't mind the hens, but the roosters started crowing at 0400, not dawn as in the old Merry Melodies cartoons, and continuing thereafter. I trained the roosters not to roost in those trees by going out each evening just after they'd flown up there and pushing them down with a length of bamboo. After two or three nights, they were trained—except one persistent one who just wouldn't get the message. At my request, his owner, my neighbour, ate him.

There were several coconut palms surrounding the house, and we occasionally heard a loud crash as a coconut or frond fell to earth. About one ni-Vanuatu, often a child or baby, was killed each year by a falling coconut, although one of my counterparts told me jokingly that the reason ni-Vanuatu had woolly hair was for falling coconut protection. In any case, the stereotype of natives resting under palm trees is false; nobody spends any unnecessary time in the danger zone.

Rare branched coconut palm on Malekula. In 2008, the BBC World Service reported that the Côte d'Ivoire's Marc Delorme coconut research station claimed they had the only one in Africa and were selling it for one million dollars.

Holly hired the local Woman's Club to clear an old kumala patch behind our house. She put a small garden there, with garlic, cucumbers, lettuce, and (unsuccessfully) corn. The cucumber vines fell victim to orange beetles that seemed to thoroughly enjoy taking dust baths in the rotenone I powdered them with. We could buy large cucumbers at the local market; I didn't want to think what had been put on them to kill the little beasties—the only measure between none and all in Vanuatu is "half", and what is called "white man's medicine", including pesticides, is thought to be good stuff, with more always being better than less.

Two Years on Malekula

One serious garden pest was the Giant African Snail. Imported in a failed scheme to raise them for the French restaurant trade, they escaped and caused great damage to agricultural crops in Vanuatu. They were eventually brought under control by the importation of a parasitic snail that feeds on them. Plus, Holly on her daily personal mission zig-zagging down the hill from our house in her thongs stomping on as many as she could find.

Together with slugs, these snails were voracious. I bought snail bait at the local Agriculture Department office and ringed the garden with it. After only a few days, there was a rotting pile of dead snails and slugs encircling our garden. The neighbourhood chickens also took their toll of the garden, despite my efforts to fence them out with bamboo.

From a letter home February 20, 1987:

Well, here we are in Lakatoro! After spending a week studying Bislama (Mi toktok smolsmol Bislama[1]), we were originally scheduled to spend some time on the island of Tanna with a Regional Development Planner who's been here six months, but Tanna was hit hard by Cyclone Uma, and I still haven't heard from him.

I was told that a house was ready for us in Lakatoro, but there was no furniture yet. It was in a warehouse in Vila under the control of the Public Works Department. So, we went to Luganville on Espiritu Santo (both island and town known locally as just "Santo") last Sunday the 15th to visit a Regional Development Planner (RDP) who's been here three months. I didn't learn a lot about the job from him, but we spent four days buying household food, guitar, and ukulele (we got a ghetto-blaster in Vila). I also spent the time phoning Lakatoro to let them know I was coming and put a bit of pressure on re: scrounging up temporary furniture. It was finally agreed that we would come on Thursday.

We got here yesterday and were met at the airport by the President, Secretary, Assistant Secretary of the Lakatoro Local Government Council, a CUSO Fisheries Officer who lives here, and a Council member.

We are as high up the hill as any of the houses, with the bush starting behind the house (the LGC Secretary has a garden on the edge of it). We have a mango and mandarin tree out front, and there are papaya and banana plants off to one side (I'm not sure to whom they belong). There is a small store with everything behind the counter in town, and 2 more stores in Norsup (8km North).

---

[1] I speak a bit of Bislama

Heather in mango tree near our house. The bamboo leaning against the tree is for knocking down mangos. We never got any mangos from our trees to eat because, before they were ripe, local kids would knock down each one, take one bite of the green mango, and drop it on the ground. The ground under these trees would be littered with green mangos with one bite out of them; the kids never seemed to learn to just wait another week or so. We had to buy eating mangos at the market.

Anyway, I think we'll be quite comfortable. We have our share of ants, but no geckos or lizards so far—nowhere to hide yet. A couple of big cockroaches last night. Rat droppings this AM, so I got a trap today; I'll probably just catch one of the girls. The rats are small here. The house was recently renovated, but a few holes were left in the ceiling.

The rats come through a hole under the door, I think. (From the smell, they live under the sink—job #1.)

Lakatoro was a purpose-built government station, rather than an existing village. It was built by Malekula's former British District Agent, Darvall Wilkins, in the 1960s. We eventually met Darvall and became good friends with his son and daughter-in-law when they visited Lakatoro.

From a letter home July 19, 1987:

All Malekula has been ecstatic this week because "Mr. Wilkins" (pronounced "Mee'sta Weel'keen") is visiting. He is the former British District Agent (1957-77) who built Lakatoro. I didn't even see Keith upon my return until yesterday, because he has been running around from one welcoming ceremony to another with Mr. Wilkins. The only reason he came up yesterday was so Mr. Wilkins could take a look at the changes to his former servant's quarters, where we live. Holly and I took the opportunity to have Darvall in for a chat, since we figured he would be a good source of information. He's a pretty good guy, and of course, really knows the score around here. He is actually Australian, and didn't bring his wife because his last visit was a disappointment due to the physical changes here (remember my wish to be here when the former administrators saw the bush kitchens behind their fancy houses?). Now he is used to it and really glad he came back. He is thinking of putting up a shack on a piece of ground he was given and vacationing here in the future.

"Mista Wilkin" was loved and respected; When he arrived, Lakatoro rang with joyous shouts of "Mista Wilkin i kam!", and everyone forgot to come get me when I flew into the airstrip that morning. A plaque below his former house announced that he was a "man ples", or true local, a rare honour for a Whiteman. The Wilkins family wanted to build a vacation home on Malekula, and a ni-Vanuatu landowner was willing to lease them land. But, in Vila, former colonial administrators were not being granted special favours. I tried to convince the Land Committee which approved all land leases, and on which I sat a few years later, to approve the lease. The application was refused because the policy was that only agricultural leases would be granted in rural areas.

Darvall Keppel Wilkins lived his last years in Port Vila, where he died on July 14, 2018. He was buried with great ceremony in Lakatoro at a funeral attended by hundreds of ni-Vanuatu.

Two Years on Malekula

16 March, 1987:

We are well settled in. We would eat more coconuts, but I haven't bought a coconut scraper yet (a serrated crescent-shaped blade attached to a board. You sit on the board with the scraper sticking out in front and scrape out the meat from half a shell.) To get coconuts, we just pick them off our lawn. Holly has developed a mean arm with a busnaef (bushknife, or machete) and just whacks off the husk. A bushknife is a necessity of life here. Everyone has one and uses it for an all-purpose axe, jack-knife, hedge-trimmer, pruning saw, shovel, etc., etc. They keep them razor-sharp and just whack away at coconuts, etc. held in their hands—I've shaken hands with several men who seem to have cut the tendons to their fingers like Dad did that time[1].

Heather scraping a coconut.

Once you have skrasem coconut, you put one hand with its back facing you and its thumb down, and other hand interlocking it with the thumb up. Put the coconut meal in-between the hands and squeeze, letting the milk run down the lower thumb into a container or onto the food being prepared. This is also the technique used for squeezing ground kava roots.

---

[1] While castrating an uncooperative (go figure) boar.

Domestic Life

Holly had come without a specific job; she was expected to find or make one for herself after arrival, which was a generous policy of the CUSO of that day—it was later changed to only spouses with pre-arranged jobs being sent overseas. The first six months she was busy with domestic chores, as we had initial expenses and our pay didn't immediately catch up with us. A lot of time was spent washing clothes, which in Vanuatu means scrubbing at them with a brush on a wooden plank. Keeping the house clean was also time consuming, especially with constant ash falling from the volcanoes on neighbouring Ambrym Island. Eventually we did hire a housegirl—every Vanuatu household, Melanesian or expatriate, has one, if only a younger relative. In fact, when we needed a babysitter in Vila, our housegirl sent her housegirl to do the job. Our Lakatoro housegirl freed up Holly's time to work with the local Women's Club. Then, in January, 1988 Holly started using her Medical Laboratory Technologist professional qualification part-time at the Norsup Hospital Laboratory.

Heather and Laurel washing dishes in our kitchen; perhaps
the last time in their lives. Good thing I caught the moment on film.

Heather, five, and Laurel, three, soon fit into Malekula society. Ni-Vanuatu love children—if all of a couple's kids have left home, they may borrow and adopt a baby from an extended family member. The Bislama word for "mother" includes all extended family females of one's biological mother's generation. The same wide definition applies to "father", "sister", and "brother". In Canada, Heather and Laurel's paranoid parents kept them under constant surveillance; on Malekula, they ran free. Every woman just looked after any child within eyesight. For example, on Heather's first day at school, the LGC minibus didn't show up to collect her for hours after school let out. When she finally got home, we asked Heather what she had done. "Oh, I played in the sea with some kids, and their mother gave me some food". Laurel hung out with the prisoners who were on landscape maintenance duty, although I felt she went too far when she lent them my bushknife and sharpening file. I later found them leaning against a tree near the house.

More about Laurel and her new friends -
in a letter of November 5, 1987:

> Laurel has been busy making friends with all the prisoners that are swarming around here these days trimming bushes—all armed with bushnaefs and axes and with no supervision in sight. I guess they had an overdue court session in Santo a few weeks ago. Since the Santo prison couldn't handle the resultant batch of convicts, a planeload or so were shipped here. Laurel sits around storianing (chatting) with them—conditions on the chain gang aren't too severe here—and shuttling water and goodies to them. Today, she didn't want to go to Kinder, because she had made arrangements to chat with a prisoner this morning.
> While they aren't chatting up my daughter, the prisoners clean up the grounds of palm fronds, rotten mangoes, etc. Despite it being the end of dry season, everything is burned. Holly and the Mala's housegirl put out our front lawn with hose and bucket this morning.
>
> For my peace of mind, I haven't inquired too closely into just why the prisoners are in the kalabus (prison). Time is not a commodity with a great value attached here, and general opinion seems to be that these guys are pretty well off sitting around in jail being fed and not working very hard.

One evening, we all attended a Women's Club potluck dinner:

April 12, 1987:

> I enjoyed the affair and Holly's Jamaica Baked Bananas were a hit. All the men sat on benches on one side, of course, with women and children on mats on the other side of the food, which was laid out on benches. I tried to storian or chew the fat, literally a national institution, a bit with a

couple of guys, and then the programme began. Following the obligatory prayer, after which everyone clapped as per usual (?), a couple of women got up and told funny stories, of which I missed everything. The first one seemed to be about some Whitemen from Australia who didn't speak Bislama on a visit to Tanna. It had the audience rolling in the aisles. The second one was about a couple of guys who competed with each other to prepare the worst laplap, the national dish of grated root or banana with or without meat cooked in leaves on hot stones. I caught something about someone breaking a tooth, and I was later told that the story culminated in one of the guys making laplap with a live pig that got up and ran away when the other tried to eat it. I guess you had to be there. Then a group of women got up and sang a few hymns, one with motions. This is pretty standard fare at any gathering.

The programme ended with a couple of relay races run by two teams of women. One race involved one woman from each team, when their number was called, running to two 150cm sticks, picking them up, and competing for a piece of cloth with the sticks. The winner was the one who put it into a cardboard box. As with anything that requires hand-eye coordination, most of them were pretty good. One would swoop it up first try, just about stick it in the box, and the other would just swoop it away. They all played scrupulously fair, with no body contact or edging the stick or box around for the next bout.

April 23, 1987:

Last week, Keith's wife, Aslika, invited us to a "children's picnic" on Friday. I instructed Holly to grill her about who was putting it on, but Aslika remained vague, so I assumed correctly that it was their church. We went anyway, and the only indication that it was a Sunday-School picnic was the absence of beer and the fact that everyone called each other "brother". We all went in shifts in the LGC minibus to a long blacksand beach south of here. The kids all played on the beach and swam in the river—nobody went deeper than ankle-deep in the ocean, because blacksand beaches have the worst reputation for shark attacks.

We adults played volleyball, which along with soccer is the rage here[1], on the beach. There is no segregation along age lines—even small children play with adults. I have noticed, though, that although women play with men, men won't play on teams that have a majority of women.

A massive amount of boneless and fatless meat was cooked, and everyone brought food. Holly's banana bread was popular. We saw some

---

[1] Every village had a dirt volleyball court, even if the net was just a vine stretched between two sticks stuck into the ground.

160

hapless land crab (one of zillions around here) that was pinned with a rock upside-down in the crotch of a tree awaiting the traditional fate— legs ripped off (to prevent escape) and tossed on the fire to cook.

Mail delivery on Malekula was somewhat tenuous. In the first place, there was only one post office, at Norsup, and I think from there mail was just sent to each village with whomever from there happened to stop in at the post office. Then, there was just plain inefficiency. Most mail would come in a bag flown in daily to the Norsup airstrip. The Postmaster was supposed to pick it up daily with a motorcycle supplied by his employer for this purpose, but frequently didn't. Once a bag of mail got to the Post Office, the Postmaster was supposed to sort it, but this sometimes didn't get done. Finally, mail to Lakatoro was supposed to be picked up daily by an LGC employee, which sometimes didn't happen.

As a Westerner far from home who really wanted his mail, I developed the habit, whenever possible, of driving an LGC truck to the airstrip and checking if a bag was still there. If so, I'd deliver it to the Post Office and wait to watch the Postmaster sort it (occasionally ignoring his comments that it was quitting time), and then take Lakatoro's mail back to the office. Even if the Postmaster had picked up the mail, I'd get Lakatoro's mail from the post office.

After a while, I discovered that if registered mail had arrived for me at the Post Office, the Postmaster wouldn't tell me; I guess I was a pain in the butt for him. So, I learned to ask every week if there was registered mail for me.

Surface mail was the most unreliable. The coastal freighters that carried surface mail to the islands weren't paid to carry it, so mail was a low priority for them. It often took a long time for bags of surface mail to leave the Central Post Office in Vila and then find its way to the Norsup Post Office. In Norsup, it had no priority at all.

One day, the nuns at Walarano told me that they were expecting some surface mail, and they had seen the surface mailbag sit on the Norsup Post Office floor for five weeks. They found this quite frustrating, of course. Not being as charitable or patient as the nuns, and on the principle that the Lord helps those who help themselves, the next time I was in the Post Office, I asked the Postmaster for some scissors, cut the twine sealing that surface mailbag, and dumped it on the floor. I could immediately see why it was given such low priority; almost all of it was the late Herbert W. Armstrong's Worldwide Church of God's publication, "The World Today". In any case, the nuns got their mail that day.

Thereafter, whenever I saw a surface mailbag in the Post Office, I repeated the procedure. It took the Postmaster all of 15 minutes to sort the bag of mail. Of course, one time I cut open and dumped a bag that was supposed to have gone to another island. Oh.

Two Years on Malekula

The Postmaster and I never actually had words, but I was probably his least-favourite client. Of course, things got off to a rocky start when I first arrived at Lakatoro. I had some irreplaceable slides of Cyclone Uma damage, and foolishly believed returned CUSOs in Canada who told me the Vanuatu mail service was safe enough to send cash by. I mailed the slides to be made into prints with cash payment in an envelope, and never saw them again. I always suspected the Postmaster stole the money and tossed the slides.

I discussed the issue in a letter home April, 23 1987:

> I guess it's being driven home that it's millions of these little things, not big problems, that slow down development. For example, a fishing boat could sit idle for a week while an order or payment for an engine part sat in the local mailbag. The connection obviously hasn't been made yet. I thought CUSO at our Ottawa orientation was being racist by saying any Canadian could help organize things in the Third World. In fact, we just have experience living and working in a money economy.

From letters:

April 23, 1987:

> Laurel is really into singing the hymns that everyone sings here. She sings the English ones with a Bislama accent, just like she learns at Kinder. Everyone around here thinks it's great and gets a special kick out of her rendition of "Jesus said, 'I am the whale, the truth, and the light'". She even sings when she is washing her hair in the shower now—I think she and Heather have forgotten what hot water is, at last.

And:

> So, here I am at home again. It's quite the domestic scene—I'm writing at the table while the yams cook, and Holly is scraping coconuts out on the veranda. After two-and-a-half months, we've finally husked some co-conuts the easy way—Aslika (neighbour's wife) showed Holly, and she showed me. I even had the guts to hold the coconut in my hand and whack at it with our bushnaef until it cracked. A coconut scraper is a round, serrated blade that is attached to wan pis timba that you sit on and scrape out the coconut meat. Then you squeeze the milk out of the pulp and use it to cook everything (my arteries clog as I write).

May 26, 1987:

Just to twist the knife, Mary, I've been busy eating papayas every morning for breakfast for the past couple of weeks, as our trees finally started ripening. This morning, that little ingrate, Heather, said she was tired of papaya and demanded an orange!

Papaya ready to be picked; if left, flying foxes would eat
the ripe yellow portion that night.

June 24, 1987:

Holly's been storianing with a local woman who's been telling her about a bird that comes flying down from the tree every time it hears her stirring sugar in her tea, so it can have a sip. Sara also used to have a pet flying fox, which she raised from a baby by hanging it from a stick and letting it lap milk from a saucer. It had a little cage to sleep in during the day, and even brought a mate back home for a while until some neighbour's kid saw it hanging from the mango tree and (tears come to her eyes) killed it with a stick.

July 1, 1987:

I caught a tuna on Saturday, after towing a lure for three hours. I didn't even see it get caught, as I was concentrating unsuccessfully on taking a leak at the time—ever try peeing from a small moving boat? Impossible to relax enough. Anyway, when I looked up, there it was, dragging along. It was very small, and I was going to throw it back, but because I had told everyone that I had never caught a fish from a boat before, they made me keep it. It made one meal of curry.

July 16, 1987:

I see out the window that the kids are playing in the plumeria tree outside the kitchen window. They've been out there all day. At first, they were playing Chinese Acrobats like the ones we'd seen on bush leave in Vila—swinging from branch to branch (about 5 ft. up) with the other one on the ground holding onto loops of string from their ankles. Lord knows what they are playing now. It involves finding comfortable places to lounge in the branches. Heather just took off her t-shirt and made a pillow out of it. Laurel's teddy bear was swinging from a strip of cloth, but it just fell out. This morning, I came out the door and hollered at them to get the scrap of mosquito screen out of the veranda and into the garbage. They dutifully started to comply, and Holly informed me that it was one of their toys—they had been using it as a mosquito net for their baby.

They don't play much with Keith's kids Margret and Jerry anymore, who have been treating us like we have the plague. I think that they figure that we're going to hell and they don't want any to rub off on them. Keith and Aslika have been friendly, though. The kids used to come home telling us that everything was poison or full of the devil, which was what Margret was telling them. Heather and Laurel now play a lot with the neighbours on our other side, Kristal and her little brother. As Kristal is more their age, I am happier anyway. Jerry likes to play this game where he sticks his tongue out at Heather when Holly's back is turned and then, after Heather complains, look all innocent when Holly looks at him. I get a good laugh out of Holly's description of all this.

Two Years on Malekula

Laurel and Heather with our neighbours, the Rory Family

The other local sensation has been a snake that has been spending his days on tree branches near my office. I would never have noticed him, but the eagle-eyed ni-Vanuatu pick him out every day, even after he changes trees. Despite not having any poisonous land snakes in Vanuatu, everyone is desperately afraid of them. I told them that I used to have a pet snake, which is related with wonder to everyone, who give me looks like I am either crazy or in league with the devil. I think my comment that they eat rats was news to everyone; one neighbour asked me if I had fed my snake papaya (considered food for all pets, I guess).

I discussed this snake with my counterpart, who informed me that snakes with short tails were "kastom" snakes with malevolent powers. He wasn't too interested in my comment that snakes with short tails are female. And yes, you can tell; their underside scales are different on their tails.

One day when visiting Vao island with Vieni, he warned us not to look up into a certain tree because a kastom sinek[1] lived up there. If we made eye contact with it, it would take control of our minds. I didn't look up there to test the theory.

---

[1] Snake. A grammatical rule of Bislama is that no two consonants can be adjacent to form a diphthong. An "i" is usually inserted between the consonants; i.e. "milik" is Bislama for "milk".

Two Years on Malekula

From a letter August 8, 1987:

I have sworn off making requests from home since the great thong hunt, but since you asked, there is something that we need and you can afford to buy and send: a good, old-fashioned fly swatter [1] with a wire handle . You wouldn't believe how smart the flies are here! And quick, too [2]. Rolled newspaper just won't do the job.

And:

November 1, 1987 (three months later):

> I don't want you to feel guilty about us surviving fly season armed only with a shredded, fly-juice-stained newspaper. Don't even think about the time and gasoline wasted in hopeful daily trips to the Post Office, or the crushed, downcast faces of two little girls learning that once again, Mommy and Daddy have returned home empty-handed. Instead, let's look at the positive side: I am thankful for the opportunity offered to rid myself of my former prejudice against several flies at a time crawling over my lower legs or in my food. Why, we hardly even sneeze anymore when they fly up our noses! Sadly, wet season is due to begin any day now, and our friends the flies will soon be gone, their places taken by mosquitoes.

Asking for things to be sent from Canada was an exercise in frustration. After multiple requests, we got five flyswatters from three different correspondents.

And thongs. My size 12-1/2 thongs soon wore out, having been permeated with glass shards from the cyclone-shattered glass in our original hotel in Vila; I removed each one as it worked its way up through the thick sole to my foot. The largest thong sold in Vanuatu was size 11-1/2. I made fruitless appeals home; finally, a friend sent a properly-sized rainbow pair from Hawaii with little palm trees on their straps. I wore them for the rest of my contract.
Holly's parents sent us a stove-top toaster—months after we requested it; they thought it would make a nice Christmas present.

The worst was tax forms. I repeatedly begged for them from my family for four months, asking for at least acknowledgement that they had received my request. They finally came.

---

[1] Surprisingly, we couldn't find a fly swatter anywhere in Vanuatu. I tried making one out of re-folded mosquito netting and a thin bamboo stem, but it didn't last. Oh, if I'd only had some duct tape.
[2] Vanuatu mosquitos were as fast as Canadian flies, and Vanuatu flies one order of magnitude above that.

Two Years on Malekula

Regarding our finances:
October 11, 1987:

Because there isn't anything to spend money on on Malekula, we easily save 30,000vt every month. We cheerfully spend it all during marathon bush-leave shopping in Vila and Santo. To top it all off, we eat better than in Canada because we can afford beef here. And, a beautiful beach is a short bike-ride down the road. Life as a volunteer in the third world is heck. But, as they say, somebody has to do it.

And: August 17, 1988:

> I guess I should admit that as a poor, suffering "volunteer", I am making about the same take-home pay after housing and utilities that I did in Canada. We're just always broke because: (a) our dear old Land Cruiser, which is working better than ever after a major carburettor overhaul (I can hardly wait to find out what breaks next!), (b) some expat necessities of life (like peanut butter—650vt or about $CAN8.00 per Kraft 780g jar) are a bit expensive, and (c) huge chunks of my money is put into our account in Canada and will be given to us at the end of my contract, like $12,000 altogether [1]. Now, we could invest that sensibly for our old age or the girls' education, or just blow it on an Australian tour. Which do you think we will do? Heh, heh. I've never had that much money all in one chunk of cash. I think I smell my pockets burning.

More snippets from letters home:

September 5, 1987:

> There was just a huge explosion outside, followed by loud screaming. I thought someone had been injured by a shotgun, but it turned out to just be someone shooting a wild pig 50 metres from our house, followed by the usual whooping it up at any excuse. I must say that ni-Vanuatu have no concept of firearms safety. Hunting this close to houses is not unusual. Rifles and shotguns are carried any which-way and pointed at all and sundry. They are just seen as glorified bows and arrows with no recognition that they are more dangerous to those using them. Kids are always running through here with air rifles.

---

[1] This would include our last month's pay and vacation pay owing because we didn't take our month's vacation during the last year of our contract.

Two Years on Malekula

January 19, 1988

Sunday, we went up to Champagne Beach (on north-west Espiritu Santo Island) for the first time. Holly found a nice, big helmet shell and was discussing methods of separating the animal from the shell on the beach, when a female French homeopathic doctor came up with a sick look on her face and rescued the snail, saying she had just put it in a visible place under the sea so people could enjoy looking at and photographing it. I had to laugh when I got back in from snorkelling and heard the story—my guess is that after she gently placed it back in the water, it ended up in a ni-Vanuatu supper pot that evening. She must have been a charter member of the Royal Society for the Prevention of Cruelty to Shellfish.

Holly and the girls frolicking with fellow CUSO Daniel Vigneault on Champagne Beach, so-named for the iridescent effect of its fine white sand under the clear sapphire water.

April 20, 1988:

After supper, I tried to dissuade the girls from eating any of the brownies I made last night by telling them there were bugs and larvae in them, which is true. They ignored me and wolfed them down. When I bought the flour, you could see a couple of weevils crawling around inside the plastic bag, and I asked the ni-Vanuatu saleslady if they were included at no extra charge. No response. I put the flour through a strainer, but everything but a big fly maggot and some web stuff (Holly claims this contains the eggs) went right through. Are you still with me? Obviously, this stuff is just right for brownies. I wouldn't use it for a white cake, but Holly says she just picks out the black bugs when she's kneading bread dough.

The only way you can get flour without baking soda already in it[1] is to buy this stuff that's been sitting around in an open bag at the bakery. You see, if you want chewy brownies, you can't have baking soda in the recipe, so that is why I bought plain flour. I put the rest of the flour in the freezer to slow things down a bit.

June 23, 1988:

Why are you messing around with Laundromats? Just do like us, and hire a fifteen-year-old for 70 vatu per hour to wear out all your clothes scrubbing them on a board with a brush. When she's done, she can wash your entire house's floor with a mop and about one inch of water in a bucket—you should see the nice brown stripe around the bottom of our white walls [2]. You should be glad you don't live over here—all of our neighbours hire an aunt or niece or sister to be full-time twenty-four-hour housegirls for 4,000 vatu or CAN$50 per month.

August 1, 1988:

Since when is long hair necessary for headbands? Heather and Laurel wear them off to school. Standard headgear around here includes three-quarters of old soccer balls, silver Christmas tree garland, plastic Newfie sou'wester rain hats, two-metre-wide woven palm leaf hats, etc.

August 10, 1988:

A delegation of co-workers came into my office today and wanted to put claims on various items of ours for when we go in six months; they want time to save up. Holly's sewing machine (hand-crank Singer Zig Zag) has been spoken for since she bought it.

---

[1] An Australian must-have, apparently. "Self-Raising" flour from Australia was all that the local stores stocked.

[2] The ni-Vanuatu objective of washing floors is to get them wet (Form over function). Properly designed houses in Vanuatu have a row of dark tiles around the bottom of walls.

Two Years on Malekula

January 1, 1989:

Surely, you got all the details of the President's attempt a couple of weeks ago to illegally dissolve Parliament and set up a new government? I've never lived anywhere before where the President spent Christmas and New Year's in jail. His court hearing is this week. They arrested about 50 people so far over all this, but have had to let most of them out on bail because there was no room in the jail (little Christmas biblical allusion there). Some have been shipped to the Norsup prison, which always happens when the Vila and Santo jails are full. There was going to be a demonstration in Lakatoro on the 16th, but it didn't get any farther than a Barbecue at our local beach, where the police went down and told them to go home. They all did, but there have been a bunch of arrests here, because they weren't even supposed to do that. Everybody is real proud of having been arrested. Now they are all martyrs, and besides, going to jail here is not considered a negative experience. It's thought of a bit of a vacation, where you get to eat free white rice and sit around pretending to work on the work crews—They actually sit around talking with Laurel.

Life for Heather and Laurel

The kids may have gotten a bit too much into the local culture. I don't think they found anything—this time. Our neighbours would crack lice between their teeth.

Two Years on Malekula

Heather was five and Laurel three when we moved to Lakatoro. They adapted quite quickly to life there, especially since their parents didn't indicate that moving across the world was anything unusual. Years later back in Canada, they tried, as a teenaged bargaining ploy, to argue that they had been deprived in Vanuatu—unsuccessfully. Nevertheless, as adults they admit that it was a valuable experience.

From Letters:
March 16, 1987:

> Yesterday, in a fit of guilt, I asked the girls if they liked it here, and they both agreed it was better than Canada. Heather liked her school and the fact that we could go on long bike rides (??). Our previous two trips had been ordeals of crying, falls, and threats. Laurel likes all the kids to play with. There are lots of kids, and we can just let the girls run around, rather than keeping them locked in the backyard like at home.

Holly, Laurel, and Heather suffering on Aop Beach.

April 2, 1987:

> What Laurel really hates is cold showers, especially washing her hair. She yells and howls and drums her feet on the floor during the entire process. One night, I put Laurel in the shower and then went back to the house.

When I came back 15 minutes later, she was in the corner of the shower, bone dry, a situation that was immediately rectified.

April 12, 1987:

> Poor Heather: Holly buys a brand of French laundry soap that includes a small plastic gift in each box. So far, we have a soap bar holder and a dishrag holder. Heather desperately longs for the yo-yo she sees on the front of the box. Last night, I made the mistake of reading out-loud off the side of the box that you can send for a list of the available gifts and, if you desire, send in the one in your box for the one you want. I'm not sure how many tens of thousands of kilometres this offer extends to, as the company offers to pay postage both ways. I told her I'd look in Vila next time and, in the meantime, put the word in this letter.

> For all the good it did. For some reason, in most cases people just didn't send us what we requested. Or, they waited until Christmas in one case. Hey; when we ask for a stove-top toaster, we need it now, not in several months. A friend finally brought yo-yos from Vila, but the girls didn't really show a lot of interest.

April 12, 1987:

> I have announced my intention to buy a fledgling parrot (300vt at the market, when they are available) once the veranda is screened in. Laurel reminded me that if we got one, we would have to take it home with us (a reason I've given for not taking in one of Keith's cat's new kittens). When I told her we couldn't, she asked why, and I gave her the whole run-down about how the Canadian government was afraid that a parrot might bring in a disease and then farmers' chickens would get sick and the farmers would lose money. "Will the farmers lose their money because the chickens puke on it?", she asked.

Two Years on Malekula

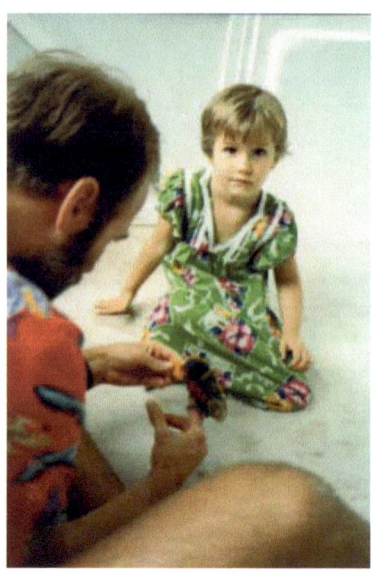

Laurel supervising the Lorikeet's feeding

May 14, 1988:

> Heather wants hot dogs for her birthday, so we got some Chinese canned
> sausages that expired in March (manufactured 1985) for the big day;
> yum, yum. Laurel asked plaintively for "a pretty dress"—NOT a hand-
> me-down. So, when I was in Vila before their birthdays, I spent my last
> 1100 vatu on a nice island dress. When she opened it on her birthday, it
> was way too big. She wanted to wear it anyway, but we gave it to
> Heather, and promised her another one. Last week, I searched Santo and
> finally found one that was not too bad. She is convinced it's OK.

After Christmas, Laurel had requested more toys next time and offered to show
me a store in Santo where I could buy some. So, I got them each a toy in Vila —
Chinese Checkers for Heather and a tool set for Laurel. It's really hard to find
anything but Barbie and Transformers. The Vila toyshop had three different M16
rifles, though.

May 25, 1988:

> Laurel is going to have to undergo some adjustment if we ever get back
> to Canada—like she is going to have to learn to speak English. Her
> speech is full of Bislama-isms, like her food "hears" good (the verb
> "harem" covers all five senses here) and a wasp "ate" her ("kakae" means
> eat, bite, sting, erode, use up, wear on, etc.). She just translates them

directly into English. Good luck to her Canadian teacher. Tonight, we had a ni-Vanuatu dinner guest and so spoke Bislama, and she started throwing in French expressions—she can't even keep her Bislama straight. Of course, she and Heather are fluent in Bislama—even speak common English-Bislama words like "yes" with different accents when speaking the different languages, and the little so-and-sos have taken to correcting me. If Holly and I sing an English song she's learned here, Laurel gets mad and insists we sing it "in Bislama", and then out it comes in a ni-Vanuatu English accent, just like a recording of whoever taught it to her.

Norsup French Elementary School — the "Groupe Scolaire Edmond Caillard" and the Lakatoro Kinder

From letters home soon after we arrived in Lakatoro:

February 20, 1987:

We registered Heather in the French elementary school in Norsup this afternoon. Grade One started 2 weeks ago. None of the kids here speak French or English until they start school, so she should be OK. She'll take a bus from here and return for lunch. The school isn't open Friday afternoon, so we had to wait some time for the Headmaster, and the girls played with a bunch of kids while we conversed (?) with their mothers in Bislama. I think Heather is looking forward to starting. The Headmaster didn't look too enthused about us—he had been shooting the breeze down by the store. We did our business with him in fractured French (I'm starting to feel quite the linguist). I don't know how much it costs— we have to sort that out with the Norsup Regional Council[1] .

---

[1] It turned out to be free.

Two Years on Malekula

Groupe Scolaire Edmond Caillard.

March 16, 1987:

The girls do get lots of attention. After the first couple of days at school, Heather started staying in her classroom during recess because all the kids just formed a circle around her and stared. In fact, the first time she stayed in, the teacher had to shoo them all away from the windows. After a week or so (at first we bugged her about it, then laid off), she ventured out again. I think she has a couple of friends that she plays with. According to other CUSOs we'd spoken with, Heather's experience is typical, except older boys sometimes get picked on. Despite what everyone told us about children learning languages instantly, neither Heather nor Laurel has picked up more than two phrases of Bislama. Since the kids at Heather's school don't speak any English, I don't know how she communicates. She is ahead of most of her fellow students, though, because she has four months of Canadian French-Immersion kindergarten. The ni-Vanuatu kids are getting their first exposure to French.

Heather's teacher still doesn't know her name, although we registered her in writing and have written a couple of notes on the subject. Her stuff comes back labelled "Hedrada". Laurel brought home from Kinder a painting of a red fish labelled "ORONG", which we assumed was the local name of the fish. It turned out that her teacher thought that was Laurel's name!

175

Two Years on Malekula

Laurel's class paints with their fingers because they don't have any brushes. Laurel's complaint is that some boys in her class keep touching her hair. She now wants to stay home, but Holly won't let her. Laurel goes 08:00-11:30 weekdays here in Lakatoro in a semi-open bamboo building with attached corrugated iron outhouse ("smolhaus" here). It costs 2500vt every 4 months. They play and paint on the back of scrap paper.

Heather goes to the French School in Norsup 5 mi. north of here (There is an English school here in Lakatoro). She takes the minibus back and forth, and goes 7:30-11:30 and 13:30-15:30 Monday-Thursday and 7:30-11:30 Friday. (English school goes all day Friday.) It took her a week to find the bathroom at school—and only after we'd written a note to the teacher asking her to show it to her. The teacher is a bit weird—in contrast to everyone else here, who grins and says hello even if they've never seen you before—she ignores us when I meet her every Saturday at market. I went up and said "Hi" once and spoke a bit with her, but it didn't help. I suppose someday we'll find out that we committed some horrible gaffe [1].

Heather thinks her school is great because it's across the road from the ocean—no beach, just a coral shelf—and she can play there picking up shells and stuff before and after school—the bus service is irregular, to say the least. She got home at 17:00 the other night because a previous passenger wanted to go way up island—you don't get that kind of service in Canada!

April 2, 1987:

Heather is just starting to utter the odd word of Bislama and is getting picked on a bit at school because she is unable to communicate. She does learn from them. She wants to learn how to skip rope, but when I told her I would teach her, she said we don't have the right kind of rope—at school the kids "tie wriggly branches together"—I think she means vines. It's true—nobody buys string or rope here—they tie up everything from crabs to houses with vines and grass. I saw a lady buying beef from a guy in the back of a pickup tell him to make it easy to carry, so he punctured it with a knife and tied a strip of bark through the hole as a handle.

Eventually, Heather and Laurel had three languages: Bislama while playing with friends, although not at the French school where pupils were disciplined (read "spanked") for speaking anything other than French; French at school, and English at home.
Universal education was available in Vanuatu up to Grade Six, although often school fees were collected. Many children were from small remote villages with no road access, so many of the schools had boarding facilities. I always thought it

---

[1] It turned out she was just shy.

was sad, in a culture where children were so valued, to walk into a village devoid of school-aged children. Equipment and facilities were limited. Although the Norsup school buildings were good, there were only a few textbooks that had to be shared, and the backs of government payroll computer printouts were used for written exercises. Teachers were poorly trained and used the methods they had experienced at school: rote memorization with corporal punishment for incorrect answers. Heather did better under this system than Laurel; Heather told us she "listened real good the first time." (See, it works!) She once expressed sympathy for her teacher: "We took something new today. Nobody knew the answers, and she got a sore arm from spanking the entire class." And then there was the first day of Grade Two, when Vanuatu students learn to read—nobody could read what was on the board except the pupils who had been held back from the last year, and all the kids new to the grade got spanked. One of their teachers prepared for each class by having her students collect sticks on their way to class; she broke them over kids' heads after wrong answers. And, there were the two boys who misbehaved, so the teacher made them walk on their bare knees on the concrete floor until they bled. Then, she sent them to the adjoining hospital clinic to be bandaged.

After a couple of weeks of being the strange white kid, Heather became just one of the gang. Eventually, the school population included Heather and Laurel, a black kid from Martinique, and an albino ni-Vanuatu, known respectively as "the white kids", "the white kid who is black", and "the black kid who is white"—culture first, then skin colour.

The "white kid who is black" with Heather.

Two Years on Malekula

There seemed to be an inordinate number of albino ni-Vanuatu. There must be a genetic advantage to the heterozygous state of this (one recessive gene that doesn't express itself), because the albinos suffered greatly from the sun's strong UV rays on their skin, and the bright sunlight in their eyes. Perhaps it is akin to carriers of the sickle-cell anaemia gene who are resistant to malaria.

Heather's playground activities included "skipping over wiggly branches", making balls from the sap of a rubber tree in the schoolyard, and doing a kind of cloth origami with handkerchiefs. Heather made a favourite for us, "titis", which she gleefully demonstrated sucking from. Various cat's cradle games were also played with loops of bark.

Eventually, Heather was invited to have her lunch each day at the home of a fellow student whose mother was the housegirl of one of the administrators of Norsup's Plantation Reunion de Vanuatu coconut plantation. When this woman's nearby village was preparing a traditional ceremony, Heather learned the dances along with her friend and performed with a group of children on the big day.

"One of these things is not like the others."

Two Years on Malekula

Laurel's Kinder class performing.

Laurel spent her first year in the Lakatoro pre-school, or "Kinder". There were a lot of private pre-schools on Malekula; they were thought to give children a good foundation for later education. Ni-Vanuatu do recognize that a good education has benefits, but I'm not sure for the same reason as in the West. I came to regard Vanuatu's education system as a lottery. At the end of Grade Six, there are national exams, which only allow 10% of the pupils into junior secondary school. Then, after Grade 10, another set of exams allowed 10% of those students into residential high schools. Those who graduate from high school can be sponsored by an aid donor to attend university overseas and return to a relatively well-paying government job in Vila, where there are diversions that are not present back in the village. It is not easy, socially or psychologically, for the students who do well and graduate from university. First, they have to abandon the support of their village environment while at high school and especially at a foreign university. Then, with no Western job experience, they are expected to jump into a Western governmental environment. Many of them find this bewildering and do not do what would be considered a good job in the West. If they return to their village, they are faced with the attitude of, "So, Mr. Big Shot with your fancy-dancy education, just what practical things are you going to do for us?"

Laurel was a bit of what in Bislama is called a "strong-head", and probably had a few more run-ins with her teacher's flip-flop than Heather did. She had a strong desire to learn to read, though, and constantly pestered me to let her read to me a series of basic readers that we were given by another expatriate family.

Reading with the girls.

Unfortunately, both Heather and Laurel were undeservedly placed at the head of their graduating classes because they were Whitemen. Fason blong Vanuatu. I believe, though, that being the racial and cultural minority at school was a good experience for them

July 18, 1987:

> Heather has been filling us in on discipline at her school. If the kids can't repeat a French word, they get smacked on the leg with a stick, or for serious infractions (two wrong words in a row?), the teacher pulls down their pants and spanks them! Heather reports that she has been swatted on the leg a couple of times. It doesn't seem to bother her, so I guess I'll let it go. Complaining would just cause more problems than it would solve. Heather tells us that on the playground you don't dare speak Bislama around the Doctor's kid from Martinique, who speaks only French, because he rats on you and you get in big trouble.

Two Years on Malekula

Back to school, our second year in Lakatoro March 2, 1988 letter:

Heather and Laurel started school again last month. We put Laurel into Grade One a year early, after Heather just brought home colouring all last year[1]. Laurel is having a much easier time of it, as Heather already broke the colour barrier last year, and Laurel speaks Bislama well. She does have a bit different character than Heather, though (in Bislama, "Hemi gat stronghed" —Him he got strong-head), so while Heather never got disciplined, Laurel reports that she gets whacked daily. She really does seem to be learning French, though. Maybe with her second Combs child, the First Grade teacher will learn her name. Madam Christian started out calling Heather "Hedrada", by which all the kids still know her, but switched to "Hewther" (it's written on all Heather's schoolwork) after I sent a printed message to her.

Heather, in Grade Two, is busy learning French phonetics and writing "Voici papa". Instead of being one-half year ahead upon returning to Canada, as we had hoped, I fear she will be one-half year behind[2] (but not so much that we didn't miss half the Canadian school year by travelling through Australia, Indonesia, and Hawaii on our way home). In her perverse way, she refuses to speak French in my presence, but I've caught her at it at the home of French friends.

Education is a dangerous thing. Heather has finally figured out that my French is lousy, and she insists on correcting my Bislama.

To my sister, an elementary school teacher in Lethbridge, Alberta: April 25, 1988:

I can write about teaching in the Third World, though. It can be richly rewarding, but you have to develop a new skill: beating the little beggers at the drop of a hat. Heather and Laurel report that kids in their classes get spanked continuously, usually for not knowing the right answer. Sounds great, eh? You'd better get into training!

---

[1] When she attended Grade One, where we later learned that ni-Vanuatu children learn to speak English or French; it is more like the French version of kindergarten. In Grade Two, they start learning what Canadian kids learn in Grade One.

[2] In the event, we put both the girls into a very good private French school for three years while we lived in Port Vila. Later in Canada, we put them into the school system set up for Francophone Quebecois children in Anglophone British Columbia. There, they were ahead of the other children. As an adult, Heather became a French Immersion teacher in Canada.

Two Years on Malekula

June 21, 1988:

> I, too, used to think that I'd fly off the handle if a teacher struck my child, but:
>
> 1. After living with them for a few years, I can understand the need for occasional negative reinforcement (remember Dad's story about the origin of the "Klobber Method of Child Psychology"?)[1].
>
> 2. Laurel can be a pain in the butt at times.
>
> 3. Last time I asked Laurel, she hadn't been hit for some time.
>
> Laurel has settled nicely into Grade One by now. She had several disciplinary run-ins with her teacher as her stubborn disposition ran into the fairly old-style school system here. I think she bent. She came home today barefoot again—gave her thongs to another girl to wear, who wore them home. Do you have this problem?
>
> Last night, Heather told me she was fed up with hearing me telling everyone she wasn't learning to read or write at school, and she produced a sentence written in French.
>
> Our kids have to take stuff like pandanus leaves (long and fibrous) and coconut palm brooms (the veins of the leaves) to school to weave mats and stuff. Heather came home with a fan last week—pretty intricate two-tone job. They sell all this stuff to buy paper and paint and stuff for the classes—a bit different from Canada, huh? Schools here also save on grounds keeping—the principle mows the lawn, and the kids pick up all the leaves, paper, branches, etc. every week.

One day, Heather came home with an assignment to bring some pandanus leaves to school the next day. I thought, "Surely, we non-villager types aren't expected to come up with pandanus leaves." Heather got spanked the next day, and we went out and found pandanus leaves.

---

[1] The renowned Child Psychologist Dr. Klobber insisted that children not be disciplined. Of course, his kids ran roughshod over him, causing a nervous breakdown. As the ambulance attendants carried his stretcher away, his arm twitched and hit one of the kids. After that, they all behaved like angels and the Doctor's life was happy ever after.

Health Issues

In January 1988, Holly, a Professional Laboratory Technologist with a B.Sc. in Medical Laboratory Technology, started working part-time at the Norsup Hospital Lab. There, Holly personally brought Norsup's official malaria rate down from the highest in Vanuatu to one of the lowest; later while in the NPSO, I saw this in the national health statistics.

She achieved this by cleaning the microscopes and politely asking her co-workers to show her the malarial parasites on the blood smear slides they had been reporting as positive. They couldn't, and reported positives became much fewer. Lord knows how much malaria medication was wasted on false positives before this. Of course, it may not have been a waste, because everyone in Vanuatu harbours malaria parasites. Newly arrived Western physicians on Malekula were always alarmed by the swollen spleen of the first child they examined. Then, the next one was the same, and the one after that; all caused by malaria. Whenever a ni-Vanuatu's system was stressed by another illness, malaria, or "fiva", would flare up. Malaria was known as a "Whiteman's disease" that responded to Western medicine, as opposed to most other illnesses that were ascribed to supernatural causes. Brendan Hanley, a CUSO friend who was the physician at the Norsup Hospital in 1988, was once puzzled because a urinary infection he was treating just wasn't responding. Then, he learned that when he wasn't on the ward, a "kleva", or sorcerer, was coming in daily and pushing a bamboo shoot up the patient's urethra.

Holly at work in the Norsup Hospital Laboratory with a colleague.

Of course, Holly had to adapt to local conditions. For example, she couldn't leave blood smear slides out overnight like she had in Canada. The slides would be clean in the morning because cockroaches had eaten all the blood.

Two Years on Malekula

During our first year in Lakatoro, a doctor at the hospital ran into some issues;

From a letter home June 27, 1987:

The French Doctor has dug his own grave by behaving as Whiteman Doctors are wont to do—demanding and arrogant. He has let hospital workers know that their work isn't up to European standards and told Holly that, in order to keep his workload manageable, he is rude to patients who insist on seeing him instead of the Dresser (a ni-Vanuatu with minimal diagnostic skills).

To make matters worse, his wife, a paediatric nurse, has been working closely with him in a role somewhat broader than her official job as pharmacy worker. Head Nurses here don't like this type of treatment any more than at home, but here they can do something about it[1]. At the last LGC Executive meeting, it came out that a semi-official complaint has been made that he sends too many people to Santo for treatment, including a broken arm with no sling, and four people have died because of improper prescriptions[2]. Later, I was told that "his wife also follows him around too closely". It's evident to me that the local nurses aren't qualified to second-guess him, although he has told us that he sends everything that isn't simple to Santo (just as if he is a G.P. in a western city). The council executive decided to ask the Health Dept. in Vila to replace him.

After the meeting, I told Keith that I thought the decision was a little hasty, since the doctor does have a heavy workload and if he goes, we have no doctor, but the subject wasn't open to discussion. The Doctor has been a fool, but I guess he just can't go with the flow. Unfortunately, that kind of arrogance and inflexibility is a product of western medical schools. I have also heard that the island used to have another Doctor in the south, who was forced out after he publicized the names of people who hadn't paid their bills. The LGC Executive has this fantasy that another Doctor will be immediately forthcoming.

Unfortunately, all Doctors here for the past few years have been in the shadow of a previous CUSO Doctor that everyone still raves about. He was a legend in his own time, admired as a crazy man for, among other things, SCUBA diving everywhere everyone else is afraid to set flipper, and his general disregard for convention. There's a lesson in all of this somewhere.

---

[1] It wasn't long before she was banned from the hospital for the rest of her husband's one-year contract. Like many French physicians and teachers in Vanuatu, he was there in lieu of military service.

[2] He was also accused of experimenting on patients, perhaps because his lack of experience caused him to be less confident and somewhat hesitant. All of these accusations were unfounded, but typical, ni-Vanuatu statements about a person they did not like.

Two Years on Malekula

On to my health issues. From a letter April 23, 1987:

Holly made me go outside and bring in the laundry. I stepped on a nail that was really meant for her, and now I am in agony. It's all her fault. When I die of tetanus, you can have the ukulele with the string tied together, even though Holly is yelling that it is hers. (I am reading this aloud in a dramatic fashion even as I write.) I asked Mom and Dad to send a new set of ukulele strings. That bottom string just doesn't sound too good with a knot in it.

I just finished an hour's drudgery washing dishes, while standing in pain on a hard concrete floor. I was interrupted by Heather, who convinced me, after I spent three nights telling her it was a pimple, that the thing on her knee is a boil. Holly informs me that five-year-olds don't get pimples. I thought girls matured faster.

And, a few weeks later:
May 8 ,1987:

I've been telling Holly (loudly) for the past few weeks that I must have an abscess in my foot where, when performing the unmanly duty of hanging out washing, I stepped on the nail that was really meant for her. She claimed it was just the normal healing process. Yesterday, I finally got a piece of the scar tissue off the hole, squeezed, and out popped (just like a warble[1]) a little piece of my thong sole with associated guck. I guess the nail cut a bit of the sole out and rammed it up into my foot. I cut all the skin off above the hole, so now it can heal properly from the bottom up—or top down, as this case may be.

For the first time since I injured it, my foot didn't hurt today. If we had a scalpel in that useless CUSO medical kit instead of prophylactics and throat lozenges, I could have got the darn thing drained last week. My trusty Swiss Army knife, although it had no trouble slicing through that wire and my thumb at Sharon's, wasn't sharp enough to cut through a little sole-of-foot skin. I thought that the kit would be full of things like penicillin and good stuff. Ha- we've already used up the piddling containers of the only useful stuff in them- OFF and Elastoplast bandages. There isn't a prescription drug or antibiotic in the thing. I've got more useful stuff (like more Band-Aids and a pair of artery forceps) in my 4x3x2 in. first-aid kit that I take backpacking, and here, thank goodness.

---

[1] For those non-livestock people amongst my readers, a Warble Fly's pupa develops under the skin on the back of cattle. After the fly eats its way out through the skin, a popular rural Alberta sport is squeezing out the empty pupa and associated pus. Don't lean your face over too close, though; it squirts.

Two Years on Malekula

May 26, 1987:

Something that you'll no doubt think is funny did happen to me last week. I saw a ripe papaya on a tree sticking out of the bush behind our house, so I slashed my way into deepest, darkest Vanuatu to get it. I had knocked the papaya down and was slashing my way out again by a shortcut, when I was attacked by a wasp that stung me four times. Of course, while I was thrashing around (sorry for the writing; I'm laughing now — maybe it's the vermouth), I cut my knee with my bushknife. Good thing I had just sharpened it. Holly heard the commotion and thought I had cut off my arm or something — she doesn't trust me with sharp objects. I guess Vanuatu wasps aren't too venomous — the stings never swelled up much and stopped hurting after an hour or two. The wasp started stinging just in front of my left ear and worked its way down my left shoulder and elbow before crossing over to my right wrist as I swatted at him. I suppose next time I hear loud bussing around my ears, I won't ignore it for five minutes. The worst of it was that I dropped my papaya and had to go back for it after I'd washed all the blood off my leg.

July 1, 1987:

I went out with a Maternal and Child Health Team a few weeks back and learned that all children here are vaccinated against TB at birth, 5 yr and 10 yr. CUSO had told us that it wasn't necessary, but both the French Doctor and Kate[1]. (paediatric nurse) strongly advised it. So, I lined up the family a couple of weeks ago and had the local health unit givim olgeta stik[2] It was Number Two for Holly and I, as we were vaccinated years ago[3]. We took our own syringes, but tuberculin[4] ones were required. They use fresh disposable needles here, but we were only able to get first crack at the syringe by being first in line in the morning. I wanted to get it done quickly because they were scheduled to line up Heather's class later that week to do the whole bunch.

---

[1] John Kamphorst's wife had simply inserted herself into the local Team as a true volunteer.

[2] "Give all of us an injection". One night, John was at the local nakamal and cutting some stick tobacco for his pipe. The other guys there, who had heard the warnings on the radio about AIDS spreading by sharing needles, asked him if he wasn't afraid of getting AIDS from his "stik tobako".

[3] TB vaccinations (BCGs) are the worst, resulting in a boil-like sore that takes weeks to heal. And, after all that, they only provide 50% protection from the disease! After our first one, Holly and I didn't even react to a TB skin test, although we did after the second.

[4] Long, narrow 1ml syringes with finely graduated volume markers.

Kate, who vaccinated and inspected Heather's class, advised us that 90% of the class was infested by lice. Not unexpected, but upon inspection, none of CUSO's health information mentions delousing, which I would think is probably one of the most common health issues faced in the field. Last time I was in Vila, I bought some delousing solution. If (or when) it is needed, I hope it works—the preferred one was Lindane, which I didn't buy because it has been banned in Canada as a carcinogen (after I sprayed 400 sheep twice with it!). I also have good old rotenone as a backup. It didn't slow down the bugs in the garden, though.

July 16, 1987:

I'm going to close with the diseases of the week[1]. Lice don't count, because they are a parasite. I went to the doctor when we were in Vila for spots-on-skin day. I have one on my forearm that he said might-someday-in-the-far-future-turn-into-the-precursor-of-something-that-might-turn-into-something-malignant (and Holly said it was only a liver spot)[2]. Both of us have tinea versicolour, which is a horrible yeast that manifests itself in little white spots on your tanned back that grow until they join up and turn you into an albino. Holly had told me that they were a side effect of Maloprim antimalarials[3]. We have to rub Selsun shampoo on our backs every night for 2 weeks. The CUSO health book has no information on lice or tinea versicolour, which are 2 things everyone gets.

Both Heather and Laurel got malaria at Lakatoro, because they were too young to take Maloprim, a stronger anti-malarial than the chloroquine they took. Years later, when they gave blood in Canada, they were informed that, aside from their history of malaria, they had "community acquired" antibodies to Hepatitis B[4], and invited not to return. Holly and I had three-monthly injections of gamma globulin to protect us from Hepatitis A. At the time, CUSO used gamma globulin from the United States, where blood donations are paid for and often come from drug addicts. This was before AIDS was known well and taken seriously; I think

---

[1] A phrase I teased my mother with. She and my father lived for decades in various tropical places, and she started each letter by relating a new illness.

[2] I had it removed years later, just to be safe, you know.

[3] To be fair, she'd heard this nonsense from our CUSO Field Staff Officer. You wouldn't believe the garbage that circulated among expatriates about malaria, like antimalarials "just mask the symptoms". Well, yeah—like death. About one person in Vanuatu, some expatriates, per year died from cerebral malaria. Everyone else who got malaria without seeking treatment spent a miserable week-and-a-half with headache, fever, chills, and puking. Then, there was the message we got from CUSO after returning to Canada that they would be testing a homeopathic malaria treatment—I blasted them and was in turn accused of being close-minded to alternatives.

[4] I think this means they were exposed, but not infected. Vanuatu has every type of Hepatitis in the alphabet due to poor village water supplies and inadequate sanitation.

Two Years on Malekula

we dodged the bullet of AIDS only because gamma globulin undergoes an alcohol wash that kills all viruses.

To my sister, the elementary teacher, September 4, 1987:

> You better not come over here if that kid who used your harmonica bothered you. All the local pikininis run around with big green "Number Elevens" running down from their nostrils to their mouths. Holly makes them blow before they are allowed in the house. I had one of our toilet paper wrappers saved from the bathroom garbage to send you, but I think Holly threw it away when I was gone last week. I'll find you another one and a sample. It's great stuff—better than Canadian. You only need two squares at a time. Those Chinese really know their toilet paper!

From a letter September 13, 1987:

> You will be glad to hear that we discovered little white worms crawling in and out of the girls a week ago and treated the whole family with this awful stuff that they give to all the ni-Vanuatu in the villages here. Kate, who works for Rural Health, gave them to us. Yesterday, we learned that if we hadn't been too lazy to go to the hospital, wait in line, and pay our Whiteman fee (refundable from CUSO), we would have gotten some other stuff that kills more kinds of worms and doesn't have side effects like making you sick for a day or killing all your white blood cells.

And:
September 8, 1987:

> We took our worm medicine[1] last night. I think I'd rather tolerate a few worms. Now I have some sympathy with the cattle I've treated for warbles by pouring a liquid pesticide on their backs. Our medicine must have been a systemic insecticide, because Holly and I spent the night feeling sick and with the taste of insecticide in our mouths. It finally wore off this afternoon. We have to do it again next Monday night. Umm...umm, good! Kills five different species of worms, they claim, and it isn't the one with side effects, like vomiting, or the big 30 cm roundworms climbing up your throat to get away from it, so they say. I'm sure glad we brought "Where There Is No Doctor", so we could read up on all of this. To give you the specific dope, the only type of worms we've really seen are pinworms crawling in and out of the girls' various nether orifices.

---

[1] We pitied the ni-Vanuatu for whom they were the only remedy available, but after this experience, when we needed it we had more pleasant worm medicine sent from a Vila pharmacy.

Two Years on Malekula

May 14, 1988:

> Holly now works part-time at the Norsup Hospital lab. From what she
> tells me, if I get sick, I'm going to Vila.

May 24, 1988:

> I have an ear infection that isn't going away fast. My guess is that
> Heather has malaria again. The girls both had lice over the weekend. Ho,
> Hum.

January 1, 1989:

> I will go get my AIDS public service message T-shirt like the one I sent to
> Cindy and translate it for her. The front says:
>
> LUKAUT AIDS O SIDA.
> Beware of AIDS, or SIDA ("syndrome immunodéficitaire acquis", French
> for AIDS; this is a trilingual country. People laugh when I tell them
> whom I interviewed for in Indonesia—CIDA, the Canadian International
> Development Agency).
>
> EMI KILIM MAN.
> It strikes people.
>
> The back says:
>
> STAP KWAET WAN MAN O WOMAN NOMO; WAN BOEFREN
> Stay (with) one husband or wife only; one boyfriend or
>
> GELFREN NOMO.
> girlfriend only.
>
> *YU YU GAT WAN LAEF NOMO*
> You have one life only
>
> Yu save nau? (Got it?)
>
> These t-shirts are the latest fashion accessory here now (as are all new
> public service message t-shirts), so I'm sure you will want to wear yours
> to work. It's kind of interesting here. Because there aren't any billboards
> and nobody reads anything but "The Plain Truth", whenever a
> government department wants to get a message out, they have a bunch of
> t-shirts printed up and sell them around the country at cost. People line
> up to buy them because they are cheap, considered stylish, and make
> people feel good about spreading useful messages. There are all kinds

189

around, like "support women and agriculture", "plant peanuts", "vaccinate your cattle", "eat nutritious food", "don't eat junk food", "conserve Vanuatu's forests", etc.

This morning, we had our regular Sunday morning pancakes (still with the Mapleline syrup you sent, thank you) and chloroquine tablets. Holly says she'll never again be able to eat pancakes without tasting quinine.

Heather and Laurel avoided pancakes for some years after.

Relations With Other Malekula Expatriates

We got along very well with all of the Malekula expatriates, including PRV plantation management, the New Zealand nuns at Walarano, the Metenesel Estates management, the Education Advisor couple in Norsup, and the other two volunteer families at Lakatoro. Holly did get the "witch with a capital B" treatment once, though:

One day, the LGC held a big reception for local political bigwigs; the local MP/Cabinet Minister was there, as well as the Local Government Council President and others. Expats like Holly and I and management from Metenesel Estates were also invited. Holly took the opportunity to wear a beautiful island dress that I had bought for her in Vila. This manner of dress was unknown among expatriate women save volunteers and missionaries. When she entered the LGC office, all the women there started clapping. When we got to the reception, a British woman from Metenesel Estates said, "Oh, I see you've gone native." Fason blong misis.

Holly goes (sniff) "native"

Two Years on Malekula

> A little expatriate humour, which I expect is common to all of the tropics: During your first six months, when a fly gets in your drink, you toss out the drink; during the second six months, you flick out the fly and drink the drink; and in the third six months, you just swallow the fly. Back in Canada, I continue to adhere to this convention.

Interactions with Other CUSO Cooperants

We also got along well with our fellow cooperants, some of whom remain friends today. Here's a sample from a letter written after visiting Don and Doreen Lehman on Ambae Island:
July 18, 1987:

I had never met Don or Doreen, who are fiftyish and are from Cardston. He has 30 years of mechanical and service manager experience. They assumed I was a Mormon when I declined coffee and tea, and I really never did find out if they are Mormons. We drank a fair bit of beer and kava as they smoked and drank coffee, anyway. My reputation had preceded me—I had no warning that Doreen is Robert Service's number one fan in the South Pacific. She waxed enthusiastic about my Bislama "Cremation of Sam McGee" I had submitted to the Vanuatu cooperant newsletter and was convinced that she had at long last found a fellow enthusiast. She is really nice, and I couldn't let on that, in truth, I had only done the translation because I'm such a wild and crazy guy. I had really let myself in for it. I had to spend an evening reading selections from her "Collected Works of Robert Service" out loud, tape record "The Cremation of Sam McGee" in Bislama, and think of noncommittal replies to repeated suggestions that I next translate "Bessie's Boil" (Darn, I see it's not included in my copy of "The Best of Robert Service"). I did find out the title to one of his poems that I had been trying to find—"The Ballad of Blasphemous Bill" — my kind of poem; I recommend you find it.

TAEM MI BONEM SAM MCGEE

Man we i digim gol i mekem krangke samting taem i aninit san blong medel naet;
Rod blong Arctic i got secret store we mekem blad blong yu i go kol.
Laet blong not bin luk hafkrangke samting, be samting moa hafkrangke we i luk;
I bin naet ya we mi stap long saed blong Lugun Lebarge mo mi bonem Sam McGee.

The first stanza of "The Night I Cremated Sam McGee"; I'll spare my readers the rest of it.

192

Two Years on Malekula

Père Molini, the priest at the local Catholic Church, is a pretty good guy, and has been in Vanuatu for 24 years. He is from south of Milan, Italy, and is heading back for his parent's golden wedding anniversary in August. He is really into kava—drinks it with the men in the nakamal every night before supper. He prays over it like a meal. He has a huge kava plant next to his house that he planted 3 1/2 years ago and plans to dig it up for a big party before he leaves for Italy. Even women are to be allowed one shell.

Don and I went with him to the local nakamal (kastom, not commercial) every night except one, when he took us to what was described as a "kava fight" in a village up the mountain. You can imagine what images that name brought up. Men throwing kava at each other? Men fighting over their share of the Kava? A drinking contest? It turned out to be a "sori" (memorial service), which is a ceremonial kava drinking function held in Ambae villages every 5 days for 100 days after someone, in this case an elderly woman, dies. This was day 10. You can imagine that a lot of kava is required quite often for these affairs, so to ensure that it is forthcoming, two groups of men prepare kava and exchange it. (Presumably there is a lot of social pressure to exchange one's share.) Hence the name. Gifts are also exchanged between the groups, but each time you must give a better gift. For example, this time there were two small birds impaled on a stick and roasted (I really mean small. One was about 8cm long and they were on a 2cm diameter stick.) At 5 days, 1 bird had been received. Bread was also exchanged. At 100 days, all is settled up, including the deceased's social debts, with the exchange of dyed straw mats.

These mats are made from pandanus leaves with purple designs stencilled on them, the stencils being made from banana leaves. They are also used by the hundreds to purchase wives and for the husband's family to buy the children of the couple when they are born, because they belong to the wife's family at birth. Get it? They are also used to separate tourists and temporary residents from small amounts of their savings; I bought one while I was on Ambae.

The last night I was there, I found out that those gaudy sunsets on loud aloha shirts are no exaggeration. The sky was orange, the clouds were purple, and the palm trees were black silhouettes. As we are on the east side of Malekula's mountains, we only see sunrises in Lakatoro. Now I really want one of those shirts, but I can only find them in polyester, which I refuse to wear.

Interactions With Animals
Goat

From a September 5, 1987 letter:

> We now have a nanny for our kids. Actually, she's John's, but he doesn't have enough grass for her down at his place, so I told him we'd keep her up here if we could have one of the kids to eat. She has triplets, which frolic around and harass her anytime she stands still. Amazingly, the kids have only eaten a couple of corn plants in the garden so far. The mother is tied up in various places as she clears bush for me around our back yard.

The Combs' livestock.

In early September, '87, John Kamphorst, Lakatoro's volunteer Australian Livestock Advisor, told me he had been thinking about managing the mimosa, or sensitive plant (leaves closed when touched) that covers much of the plantations here. He had observed that the cattle used to eat down plant growth, so fallen coconuts could be found and picked up, were not eating it. Goats might keep it down, he figured, so he'd obtained a nanny with three newborn kids to see if they would do the job. His immediate problem was that he didn't have anywhere suitable to keep them in the short term.

Two Years on Malekula

I offered a solution, and we agreed that I'd keep the goats until the kids were weaned in exchange for one of the kids, objective—an eventual barbecue. Before I brought the goats home, I gave the girls a lecture on the theory of goat-keeping; i.e. you only keep them in order to eat their babies, which they claimed to understand. I tied the nanny to a sapling and, as a demonstration of modern livestock husbandry, did something unheard of here—I provided water for her. Most livestock in Vanuatu is left to roam free, sometimes in fenced pastures with no water source (where of course a number die of thirst each dry season), but some cattle and pigs are tied up and left to obtain moisture from their feed. A surprising number survive this, but production has got to be hampered.

I once told Keith, my boss, that if one tied up an animal without water in Canada, they could be prosecuted. He replied that, in Vanuatu, livestock were not pets.

Over the days, I moved the nanny around to areas I wanted cleared, and the kids frolicked about as goat kids will. By four weeks of age, though, they were starting to wander further afield and eat from our and Keith's garden. I was tempted to show our neighbours just whose livestock could do the most damage to whose garden, as ours had been feeding their chickens for months. Nevertheless, I forbore and tied up the kids. After 24 hours of protesting the loss of their freedom and calling for mom, they lost their voices and/or resigned themselves to their new situation, like weaned calves do in Canada. I started letting them loose to suck morning, noon, and night, with the intention of restricting them to twice daily in a week or two.

Laurel and her pastry interact with the nanny.

I quickly became a very popular person with the goat set, the kids developing a keen sense of time. It wasn't long until I was in tune with the rhythms of nature, and my life began to revolve around their nutritional desires. When I turned them loose, they would bound off through the grass, dragging their little ropes behind them, directly to the last spot where their mother had last been. They had to be shown her new location, and then off they went. I let the skinny one get a head start before all three had to fight it out for the nanny's two teats. Once the skinny one started to catch up with the others, I began rotating the one that got to strip her of the most nutritious milk at the end of each feeding session.

I attempted to introduce the girls to the concept of chores, which is, after all, good for the soul, but had no better luck than later in their lives. I tried telling Heather that she could learn to milk the nanny, just like Shirley Temple in the movie "Heidi" we had watched, but no interest was shown.

After a couple of months, the kids were old enough to be weaned, so I selected the larger male to keep and John took back the nanny and her remaining two kids.

One day, as I left the office for noon hour, I was met by Laurel out for a walk with the goat on the end of his rope. Just a girl and her goat. Mi talem long hem se, "Yu save wanem mbae yumi mekem witem hem?". Laurel i talem se, "Kakae hem". (I asked "Do you know what we are going to do with him?". Laurel replied, "Eat him".) As long as we all have that straight.

Come to think of it, we never did name the goat.

Those who are familiar with goats will know that mature males exude a very strong odor. Not wishing to experience that 24/7, and not intending to breed him anyway, when our goat was about six months old, I decided to castrate him. As all of the cattle, sheep, and pigs I had managed in my youth were sold as breeding stock, I had never actually castrated anything, but had covered the subject in one of my Animal Science lectures. In the event, all went according to plan: I tied up the goat, slit the bottom of both sides of his scrotum[1], pulled out each testicle, and scraped each attaching cord[2] with my knife until it parted. The goat wasn't especially happy with the procedure, but survived without complications. Heather watched with interest, exclaiming at one point, "But, he's bleeding!" Maybe I should have gone into a bit more detail about what was about to happen. The excess testicles were thrown into the bush, from where the neighbour's dog quickly retrieved and ate them.

The time eventually came, near the end of January '88, when we were preparing to leave Lakatoro. Ross Combdon, the CUSO Fisheries Advisor, and his family were also nearing the end of their term, so a combined farewell barbecue, starring our goat, was held by the Local Government Council staff. They came up the hill to our house with the small Toyota pickup to collect the goat, and the

---

[1] To allow for post-procedural drainage.

[2] To leave ragged edges on the blood vessels so they would clot up quickly with minimal loss of blood.

next time we saw him, he had been processed through an earth oven. He was delicious, and the entire family dug in. Of course now, 20+ years later, the girls claim they had no idea they were eating our goat, and all of their troubles can be ascribed to this episode of extreme child abuse trauma. I tell them, "Life is tough."

Goat in pickup on way to party.

Goat in earth oven at the party.

Two Years on Malekula

As for John and his mimosa control project, it turned out that cattle willingly eat mimosa in the dry season after the more palatable forage is gone, and his goats were probably given to his ni-Vanuatu co-workers.

Cattle
I went out one day with John and wrote home about it:

April 12, 1987:

> The reason we were out in the field was to help one guy build a corral and chute, so John could bleed his cattle for TB and Brucellosis tests. He had 15 cattle on 5 ha and their numbers were increasing because nobody from the local village would buy them. This was because, in the dry season, some of them always died from a mysterious disease. The "disease", of course, is thirst and starvation. The plan is to make a production of testing them, declare them disease-free, sell a bunch, and bring the herd numbers down to the pasture's carrying capacity. Whether the owner will be able to bring himself to decrease his herd when the time comes is open to question.

Crabs[1]
Land Crab (Cardisoma carnifex)
Pretty well all of Malekula's non-rock flat land near the sea is inhabited by land crabs, which are reddish and about 15cm across. There are hundreds of thousands, if not millions, of them which live in holes they dig in the sandy soil. I presume that the bottoms of their holes are under the water table, where they can periodically wet their gills when they are not foraging for food above ground. There were always many for sale at the market, tied with pandanus leaves in stacks of five for 100 vatu (roughly $CAN1.00).

We, along with John and Kate Kamphorst and his visiting sister and her partner, declared one Sunday in October to be "Crab Day". We all piled into an Agriculture Department pickup and drove a few kilometres south to the appropriately named Crab Bay. The event commenced with snorkeling in the bay, where we were joined by a Public Works Department employee filling a sack with giant clam meat; you know, the ones that are endangered. Another fason blong Vanuatu.

After lunch, John, whom I dubbed the "Great White Hunter" due to his activities in Australia, South Asia, and Africa, made his day by shooting a fish with a

---

[1] Crustaceans, not the insect.

198

bonara (bow and arrow) that he had purchased locally. Seated in a mangrove tree, he succeeded with his third try. I photographed him and his (small) quarry for posterity.

John and his fish.

The day's highlight, however, was the Great Crab Hunt. The area was crawling (so to speak) with zillions of medium-sized land crabs. So, here we were, six adults running around the bush flushing out crabs from under logs and roots, trying to grab them without getting pinched, and stuffing them in a gunny sack. It was great fun, especially listening to Kate squeal as she ran to the sack with crabs attached to her fingers. I used a stick to get them out from under logs (allowed, although John claimed that clubbing them before capture was unsporting). I must say, it beats Palolo worm hunting in both sport and taste. When our blood lust was sated, we returned in the pickup to John and Kate's house to barbecue our catch. I observed that only half the crab-handling had been completed, and a good portion of the fun was yet to come.

It was pitch dark before we got our bed of coals going well. The chosen cooking technique consisted of tearing off the front claws and tossing them on the fire, with the rest of the crab going to ni-Vanuatu neighbours. Needless to say, the crabs were somewhat uncooperative. So, we had this sack of about thirty or forty unhappy crabs, each of which had to be manhandled in the dark. There were a few mass escapes, with associated panic, as it is hard to tell which end of the crab to grab in the dark. A couple of John and Kate's ni-Vanuatu neighbours came over, attracted by the screams, no doubt, and got the door prize of a bag of eight-legged crabs. The neighbours showed us how to kill the little devils by sticking the vein of a palm leaf through a chink in their shell into the brain, how to link up a bunch of small legs to roast as one unit, and other useful land-crab culinary skills. Then we all sat around cracking claws with chunks of coral and stuffing on the meat. Life was tough there in Lakatoro, but someone had to do it.

Coconut Crab (Birgus latro, family Paguridae)

Two Coconut crabs. From English Wikipedia, author Brocken Inaglory.
I can't believe I never took a photo of one.

Two Years on Malekula

Coconut Crabs are the world's largest land crabs. Actually a hermit crab sans shell, they live in holes in the ground near coconut palms and get their name from their practice of opening cracked or sprouted coconuts with their powerful front claws to get at the meat within. Sometimes a restaurant will have one tied up that, for the entertainment of patrons, they persuade to break a broomstick with those claws. You don't want one to get hold of a finger; fortunately, they are slow-moving.

Due to their ground habitat and lack of speed, coconut crabs are easily captured to satisfy the high demand from expatriate restaurants. Their life cycle, which begins in the ocean, is not well understood, but it is known that they are slow-growing and don't breed until several years of age. Unable to replace those harvested quickly enough, at the time they were growing shorter in supply.

Everyone in Vanuatu has heard the tale of the expat who buys a coconut crab at the market and takes it home, where it gets loose, climbs up into the rafters, and generally terrorizes everyone while they all play Annie Hall. Or even better, the coconut crab that gets loose in an inter-island Twin Otter plane with similar effect, except there are a few dozen panicked people confined in a small space. I don't doubt that it's happened, and that a ni-Vanuatu calmly captured the crab and tied it up securely again. Coconut crabs move pretty slowly, so they're pretty easy to handle if you are careful.

From a May 2, 1987 letter:

It's the first payday we've had here that we got our entire pay (Holly got a big advance when we arrived so it would be out of CUSO's 1986 budget), so we celebrated by spending it all so that we're just as poor today as we usually are. One of the things we bought today (to go with the one bottle of wine that's left from Thursday's splurge) was a coconut crab. I just measured this one, and if his tail was uncurled from under him, he would be 45cm from end of big front claws to tail. From tip of side leg to the tip of the other side leg would be 80cm across. He cost 400vt and came all tied up with old red nylon rope. When I picked him up, he latched onto a basket of something else the lady was selling, so I pulled hard on him, and the lady pulled hard on the basket, which provided great entertainment to everyone in the vicinity, until the bit of palm leaf in his claw ripped off and I triumphantly toted him off to his doom.

I put him in a big bucket, and of course, after we got home he got his rope loose. I was trying to round him up by remote control when Holly suggested I just do what she always does in these situations—ask Aslika. So, I hauled my bucket over to the neighbours, where I learned that the ropes that these things come wrapped up in are tied to the thorax, and the proper way to store them until dinner is hanging from the nearest tree to your house. Or you put them in the broken-down freezer on your back porch and feed them coconuts until they are eating size. Or you put them in that big pot over there with a heavy rock on top. Anyway, Keith just grabbed him by the front claws and untangled the ropes and the crab is now dangling from our mandarin orange tree. Luckily, Keith also showed me the pinchers on his rear legs that I didn't know about. Later, Keith is going to give us a lesson on how to kill them by cutting off various parts of their heads or whatever. Good thing—I was wondering how I was going to force him into our 29cm pot full of boiling water.

After a while:

It's getting near suppertime, and I see that Keith isn't home. It's beginning to look like I'll have to tackle that crab on my own. Maybe his previous owner trained him to jump through a hoop into a pot of boiling water on command. To tell you the truth, he looks a little... well, crabby, hanging out there. Maybe I should have started with a little one. Perhaps if I just hack at him with a bushknife a bit. Or, I could put him in the fridge for a while to slow him down. I wonder if the "Joy of Cooking" has any helpful hints for these situations? If I only had a microwave, I could just stuff him in and switch it on like in the movie "Gremlins". "Joy of Cooking" has instructions for killing soft-shell crabs, which I hope are transferable to giant killer coconut crabs. Here I go. Ah, is that Keith's car I hear coming up the hill? Maybe I'll get lucky.

Later that same half-hour:

It wasn't Keith's car, but he was home anyway, so I was lucky. In retrospect, I don't think the "Joy of Cooking" method would have done the job. Keith pried the crab's entire head off with my bushknife, and the crab is safely in the pot boiling now (I did that part!). I suppose that now, I'll have to help eat the thing. I'm not all that keen on seafood, especially that with 10 legs. The coconut crab is kind of the national animal here—is on all the coins and stuff, but they are very pragmatic here and would probably eat a Bald Eagle if they were in the States. Anyway, all the tourist literature goes on at length about the delicious coconut crabs and their coconut-flavoured flesh, so I'd better try one. Keith said something about eating soft stuff from the tail with a spoon, so I think I'll give the tail to the kids. I'll sign this off after supper—I think I'd better give the bottle of wine mouth-to-mouth resuscitation.

And, still later that same evening:

I guess I've recovered enough to finish this. The crab tasted just like any other crab or lobster I've ever eaten, but was much easier to eat. When you cracked a leg (good thing I brought my Canadian Tire water pump pliers), you got some meat. I'd never had to use a knife to cut crabmeat into mouth-sized bits before. When we broke the tail off, we could see some kind of goop in there. Holly wanted to cut it open, but I wouldn't let her before we ate. Now I know where the screenwriter of "Aliens" got all of his ideas.

Caledonie Crab (Scylla serrate)

Caledonie Crabs are large crabs that live underwater in mangrove swamps. They are shaped like Dungeness Crabs, but the shells are about 30cm wide. We occasionally bought one at the market, and just plopped them in our 30cm aluminum cooking pot to cook. Like for the Coconut Crab, we used water pump pliers to crack their claws and a knife and fork to carve the meat into suitable pieces.

Spiny Lobster (Panulirus longipes bispinosus)

I occasionally bought one at the market and served it up to the family.

About to introduce a lobster to my cooking pot.

Broadclub Cuttlefish (Sepia latimanus)

Cuttlefish waiting for a cuddle.

Occasionally, I ran into one of these while SCUBA diving. Just for fun, I would maneuver them into a standstill by, as when cutting out cattle from a herd on horseback and corralling them, watching their eyes and in this instance using my hands to position them in front of me. Then, I would stroke them. Of course, the first time I had no idea if it would shoot out its two long tentacles, pull my hand in, and bite me or whatever, but it didn't. As my hand passed down their body from head to tip of body, a wave of colour change would follow my touch. Eventually, the cuttlefish would get tired of the attention and swim off.

Giant Clam (Tridacna gigas)

This is the largest clam species; it wasn't unusual for us to see ones that were 60cm or more across. Sometimes, I would also stroke the mantle of these clams.

Unlike in cartoons and legend, they do not clamp down on your limb and hold you down. Unfortunately, they are easy to kill and extract meat from, so they are endangered.

Fruit Bat or Vanuatu Flying Fox (Pteropus anetianus)

I have a compulsion to touch pretty well any animal I come across, although I gave a miss to a cassowary that wandered through my campsite in Queensland in 1970—fortuitously, as they attack and kill people. The last time I was in Vanuatu (2009), I was invited by a guide at an exhibit to stroke a caged Fruit Bat, and the damned thing bit my finger. I'd never heard of anyone getting sick from a Fruit Bat bite in Vanuatu, where people handle them all the time to eat. Nevertheless, I did some investigation when I later reached Australia because Australian Fruit Bats have been known to carry a variant of the rabies lyssavirus lethal to humans. An Australian public health nurse advised me to get an expensive series of rabies vaccinations, so I phoned a ni-Vanuatu physician in Port Vila who told me not to worry. I didn't, and I'm still here. So far.

Dugong, or "Kaufis" (Dugong dugon, family Dugongidae)

One day I was exploring Tanna Island with two CUSOs based there, when we came to Port Resolution, named by Captain James Cook after his ship when he anchored there in 1774 on his second south Pacific voyage. At the time, most tourists visiting Tanna confined themselves to a one-day trip from Vila to drive and walk up to the lip of Yasur volcano and look down into one of the world's most accessible active volcanoes. Then, they'd take a swing through Sulfur Bay village, where the Jon Frum cargo cult is centred, before returning to the airstrip for the flight back to Vila. Port Resolution, especially since earthquakes of 1878-1888 that raised it 20m and made it inaccessible to large boats, was off the beaten track. I've heard that since I was there it has become more of a tourist destination.

We checked out the local Protestant missionary graveyards, one of many throughout Vanuatu. As usual, it housed a collection of young wives and small children. Nineteenth-century South Pacific missionaries did not lead easy lives.

Two Years on Malekula

One wonders why British women signed on for a short life far away from home marred by the tragic loss of babies; maybe it wasn't too different from conditions in Great Britain. Despite the efforts and sacrifices of these Presbyterians, this village now belongs to the Seventh Day Adventist denomination.

Grave of Minnie Watt, daughter of missionary on Aneityum Island.

Then, we wandered down to the shore, and found a number of young boys in the water playing with a Dugong (similar to the Florida Manatee), known in Bislama as a "kaufis"[1]. I am a fan of inter-species interaction, and this was too good an opportunity to miss. I stripped down to my underwear and jumped in. The dugong was somewhat shy, but I could make a dash from a metre away and touch its side towards the rear. I climbed out and thanked the boys, who told me the dugong came when they splashed the water.

Some say that sailors took dugongs to be mermaids; all I can say is that they must have been at sea a long, long time, because presumably aside to other dugongs, they are pretty ugly. Their closest relative is the elephant; like them and apes (including us), their mammary glands are between their front limbs.

My friends were impressed by this, and a few months later when they were there again, Avril went in to commune with the dugong. Unfortunately, the dugong gave her a much different reception. Avril was pushed out from shore, butted,

---

[1] Literally "Cow Fish", which is interesting, because the Bislama term for "cow" is "mama buluk", or "mother bovine".

and tossed out of the water. Finally, Avril was able to make her way back to shore with bruises and scratches. Sometime after this, Holly and I were back on Tanna visiting with our CUSO friends. One of the places we visited was Port Resolution, and we had brought along our masks and snorkels. I went into the sea with the dugong, with our elder daughter, Heather, behind me. Sure enough, the dugong exhibited its friendliness by coming right up to me[1] but I held it off by straight-arming its head.

A ni-Vanuatu and I hold off dugong.

I commune with killer dugong after persuading it to be nice.

---

[1] An old Montana cowboy joke, arr, arr…

I heard later that, after a period of charging tourists to swim with the dugong, the local boys would no longer get in the water with it. There was a mother/calf pair for a while, but someone killed and ate the mother. Dugongs are rare in Vanuatu, but conservation is not a ni-Vanuatu strong suit. Our neighbour in Lakatoro once told us that it was known that certain species were disappearing, but they would probably keep killing them anyway. Or, as an Australian friend once put it: "The Vanuatu Conservation Ethic—If it moves, kill it!" Not far off the mark; many practices that may have been appropriate, and even essential for survival, prior to contact are not suitable in the new universe in which Vanuatu finds itself. Archeologists in Vanuatu find bones of species that were exterminated by the first Melanesians to arrive on the islands.

Palolo Worm (Palolo viridis)

Palolo worms live in coral and every year, on the fifth night after the first full moon in October, they release their sexual organs into the sea to mix sperm with eggs. Pre-contact, this was the beginning of Vanuatu's new year. The LGC typist told me they come out and go into the earth to help the newly planted yams to grow.

The day preceding "Worm Night" was a time of great excitement in Lakatoro. People busied themselves making scoops out of loops of branches covered with mosquito netting. I've read that, pre-contact, people scooped up the worms with baskets. The idea is to scoop up as many worms as possible and then put them into laplap.

The Great Worm Hunt.

Two Years on Malekula

We just had to "share the experience", so at 2100, there we were wading around in worm sperm on the reef with our plastic bucket and Coleman lantern scooping up hordes of disgusting, slimy, wiggly worms. Our neighbour Aslika kept telling us to throw out the shrimp because they would ruin the taste. Um, Um, Good! Several types came out in turn, one after another. I caught a baby sea snake, but Aslika tossed it too. I hadn't realized you could have so much fun on a weeknight. And nutritious, too! Fit right in with World Food Day that Friday, to say nothing of Canadian Thanksgiving on the second Monday in October.

John Kamphorst examining our catch.

We gave all of our worms to our neighbour, but:

October 13, 1987:

> Aslika sent over some nice worms fried up with flour. I divvied them up and had a great time telling the kids to "Eat your worms, now". They wouldn't touch them, but I ate my share. Yum, yum! They tasted like

fried baby squid. Fortunately, everything from the ocean tastes basically the same—like scummy seawater. To paraphrase Jed Clampett's assurance to the oilmen about 'possum innards on the first episode of "The Beverly Hillbillies", "That's the thing about palolo worms—they're just as good the second day!"

I had the girls take them out to the goat, who refused them. Of course, the neighbour's girl Margret found them out there and ran home shouting that the Whitemen had discarded the worms they had cooked just special for us. There are no secrets in Vanuatu.

Pigs' Tusks (Sus Scrofa domesticus)

Pigs' tusks in a complete circle are important objects of societal exchange in Vanuatu. They are used to buy men's rank in the custom system, as part of bride prices, to pay fines if custom rules are broken, to wear as pendants or bracelets as a sign of status, and to sell to tourists.

Tusks forming a double circle are especially rare; there is one in the Vanuatu National Museum that was gifted by Queen Elizabeth II after she was presented it during her 1974 visit to the New Hebrides.

From a November 12, 1987 letter:

A couple of weeks ago, a woman Holly met at the Women's Business Management Workshop she helped at in September dropped in to copy a shorts pattern to make for her teen-aged daughter. (?-I've never seen a ni-Vanuatu female outside Vila wearing pants, let alone shorts. Holly informs me that they wear shorts to "swim", i.e. bathe or shower.) Her husband, who was pretty shy, was along. Lina advised that Matthew had a "tut blong pig" for sale for 5,000vt (about CAN $62 or 63), just like the one he had just sold in Vila for 10,000vt. Along about here, I realized we were discussing, in true ambiguous Bislama fashion, an entire lower jaw with two tusks. The going price in town to tourists is 10-13,000vt. We're pretty strapped this month, so we looked pretty doubtful while they conferred in village language. She bid 4,000, while he didn't look too happy about it, and we agreed that once we had seen the jaw, if it was satisfactory, we'd take it. A good pig tusk has been on my list of things to pick up here when the opportunity cropped up, while unbeknownst to me, Holly has had her eye on them as potential bangle bracelets.

To digress, which readers may have noticed is my wont; they didn't have gold here before white men arrived, so they had to invent something else that was useless and scarce enough to be valuable. The commodity agreed upon was live pigs with lower tusks that are in a complete circle.

To get one, you take a partially-grown male pig (maybe 40-50 kilos), and pry out his upper tusks with a file tang (the part that sticks into a handle). Like beavers' front teeth, pig's tusks grow continuously, wearing against each other to keep the proper length. With the upper ones missing, the lower tusks grow around in curves while the owner feeds it nice soft cooked food, so it doesn't break the tusks. After a mere seven years or so, the tusks curve back around and grow through the pig's cheeks. With patience and lots of luck (it helps to remove any molars in the way), they will even grow through the jaws and emerge up front again. Because the roots of these tusks start way back in the jaw, where there is a bump on the side, a full circle is reached when they just start to re-enter the jaw the first time. At this point, the pigs become very valuable, and the value increases as the ends overlap more. This is a classic risk situation, though, due to a key economic factor: after death, the pigs and tusks are worthless. (Except for the modern salvage value of selling the jaw or tusks to tourists. I think we're seen as crazy to waste money on anything so obviously without value, but they're happy to separate us from our money.) To get full value, you must use or sell the pig after the tusk reaches full circle, but before it dies. Here in Malekula, anyway. In Ambae, where they must be a bit more pragmatic, the pig isn't officially dead until its skull is broken. Tusked pig skulls there retain their value until they are ceremonially broken.

Pig with tusk growing back into its cheek. This is a traditional breed pig, as evidenced by its long cone-shaped snout.

So, what in the heck do they use these pigs for? In order to attain various ranks in the social systems here (it is always compared to the Masons), you have to demonstrate your social prowess by clubbing an increasing number of pigs with better and better tusks at each ranking ceremony. It takes years to accumulate both pigs and enough IOUs to call in other peoples' pigs to do this, especially as you get higher up. Pigs are also a part of every bride price, and are killed at all sorts of ceremonial occasions, like nakamal openings or visits of Cardinals. I've asked a few times just what a tusked pig is worth and never got a straight answer. I'm getting the impression that the price is paid in personal favours or other non-monetary means. These pigs are really important and valuable.

On to my story. On Sunday, we were up island with the LGC Land Cruiser, so we took the opportunity to drop in on Lina and Matthew. After several wasted trips on small truck trails off the main road, we found the village they had told us they were from (and a new leak in the truck's radiator, but that's another story). Silly us! Of course, they didn't really live there, just in the general vicinity. Actually, this type of fuzziness is the norm here, so we weren't really very surprised or dismayed (going "bush", I guess). We just poured a bucket of water into the radiator and set off again with a man and woman who decided to take the opportunity to use our transport to pay a social call and guide us in return.

Matthew with the tusked lower pig jaw.

We headed back down the road and then off on a trail that left about 2cm on each side of the truck between coconut trees, and reached our destination. Lina and Matthew were even home, or just coming back from bathing in the ocean, anyway. We checked out the jaw, and it really was a good one. After some discussion, during which Holly allowed as how she didn't want a half-cleaned pig jaw sitting on her living room table (I think she really had jewellery on her mind), we decided to take Matthew up on his offer to remove the tusks for us. He hauled out a metre-long bow saw and bush knife and gave us a demonstration of delicate dental surgery. I'll send the pictures when we have the money to develop and mail them.

Removing tusks from jaw with bow saw.

The tusks are very good. One is a classic; overlaps with a sharp end to the tooth. The other has had the tip broken off along the way. For 4,000vt, they were an "affaire formidable" as Daniel Cotourier told me when I showed them to him. I really should clean them some day; they still have an air about them. We also got the whole sad story (with an unfortunately not-uncommon Melanesian twist) behind these particular tusks. Matthew raises a few of these pigs to sell or whatever, but it is Lina's job to feed them. I guess the quality of care declined while she was at the month-long workshop here, because the pig died while she was gone (my guess is of starvation).

On Monday, I told Keith about my purchase, and he said that he had some jaws hanging around that I could have. I think it is all part of his tossing all custom symbols, which is due to his new church, and which has, as you know, been very profitable for me in the past. Sure enough, that evening he brought over three jaws: the pig he had killed at his marriage, the one Aslika had killed the same day, and the one Jerry, his 11-year old son had killed when he got his first rank (my guess is when he got his custom name). We told him he didn't really want to part with these things, but he was adamant. We said they were here any time he changed his mind, and have decided to leave them intact. Out of the six tusks, only one is in the league of the good one we bought. So now I have his nambugi[1] , two chief's clubs, a paddle used in a dance, and three pig jaws.

Chicken (Gallus gallus domesticus)

Every ni-Vanuatu village family kept chickens. They mostly ran around on their own, although people would sometimes throw them the coconut meal left after squeezing out the milk. As an Animal Science graduate, I always thought chickens are a great way to turn an uncultivated area into meat and eggs as the chickens eat bugs and weed seeds. For some unfathomable reason, though, the Vanuatu Department of Agriculture kept trying to get people to pen their chickens and buy feed for them. Maybe because Whitemen do that at home, so it must be the best way. Ni-Vanuatu kept notice of what their chickens were up to, and recognized their various calls. "Oh, your hen just laid an egg" they would occasionally tell Holly.

Our first hen was given as a birthday present to Heather from a friend. It was from a house not too far from ours and initially tried to return home. In ni-Vanuatu fashion, we tied her by the leg to the base of one of our frangipani trees for a week or two until she recognized her new territory. During this period, she would occasionally go up onto a branch and then try to come down on the other side of the branch. We'd come out, see her hanging upside down by a leg, and rescue her. One aspect of her former home she never let go of: Every morning she'd give a special call, and the rooster from over there would come over, mount her, and go back. The brazen hussy.

---

[1] "Against sorcery". A southern Malekula Small Nambas funerary object.

Heather with Doogie, our first hen, who is tethered by a length of plastic twine.

From an August 14, 1988 letter home:

Our chickens are finally starting to reproduce. Doogie has a horde of 3 chicks, and Blackie's nest has eight or nine eggs in it. After Holly found the nest the other day, the girls heard us discussing our usual trick of marking the eggs and taking some of the fresh ones as they appear over the days. They got upset and told us to leave the eggs so they would hatch. That evening, I held up one of the eggs and asked the girls if we should: (a) put it back into the nest, where it would turn into a nice fluffy yellow little chick, or (b) make cookies. Heather, a girl after my own heart, went for the cookies immediately. Laurel voted for putting it back in the nest. I told her she could abstain from the cookies out of respect for Blackie (there never really was any question of what was really going to happen to that egg), but she sold out pretty quickly when they came out of the oven (almond-chocolate with nuts).

Occasionally, I would let a hen hatch a brood. As the chicks grew, the girls taught them to eat rice from their hands. Then, when they got even larger, the males would start practicing their crowing. As soon as one started this, I'd have the girls put a handful of rice out and grab it for Sunday dinner.

Heather and Laurel training Blackie and her chicks.

I didn't grow up on a farm, so chicken slaughtering wasn't one of my known skills. I did work out a quick process after a messy first attempt with a not-sharp-enough jackknife. I pounded two nails into a plank about neck-width apart, protruding about 2cm. Now, don't get ahead of me here. Grasping dinner by the legs, I'd hook the head on the nails and remove it with a quick chop of my bushknife. Then, having no desire for the messy traditional running-around-with-its-head-chopped off, I'd hold the decapitated chicken out from my legs until it bled out.

From a 26 May, 1987 letter:

> Hey, we learned the Vanuatu method of chicken-killing the other day. It is, of course, a method without tools. I would have thought ni-Vanuatu would just wring chickens' necks, but Aslika showed us how to tuck a hen under your arm, pull out a big wing feather, and pith it like a frog.

It wasn't the ni-Vanuatu custom to bleed their chickens.

Plucking chickens was another learning experience for me. I just pulled the feathers from our first chicken dinner, a long messy process. Hordes of chicken lice crawled onto my arms and proceeded uphill to my head. Fortunately, chicken lice have evolved to hang onto feathers rather than hair, and are easily shampooed out.

Soon after, I was relating this experience to a more knowledgeable CUSO, and she told me you should first dip the dead chicken into scalding water. Oh. So, thereafter I did, the feathers came out easily, and no lice crawled onto me. We ended up having chicken on most Sundays and brownies fairly frequently. A British friend did sympathize with us once when I took a pan of brownies out of the oven—"Oh, your chocolate cake has fallen!" We did our best to educate such friends in the ways of the world out there.

Speaking of poultry products, during the 1988 Christmas season some British friends came over from Metenesel Estates with family that was visiting for the holidays. I had just made a batch of eggnog from store-bought eggs and offered some all around. Having just experienced England's salmonella scandal[1] they were horrified and emphatically refused.

Oh, well; more for me. And, I survived, as I have every Christmas before and since in both Vanuatu and Canada.

From an October 11, 1987 letter:

> The girls went out with Keith and Aslika last week to work on their garden on the other side of the island. In true ni-Vanuatu fashion, they took no food, and their son, Jerry, snared a wild hen for lunch. Heather and Laurel brought back one of her newly-hatched chicks and actually looked after it very well. It followed them around and they hauled it everywhere until Friday night, when Laurel stepped on it. Two heartbroken little girls. It wasn't quite dead, so I went to wring its neck, but the head popped off. I didn't show this to the girls, and we quickly buried it in one heap. Yesterday, the little dears exhumed it to show a friend, and finding only the body, came in to announce that their friend had proclaimed that Jesus had taken its head to Heaven. Yet another church will soon be born here, no doubt.

Coconut Lorikeet (Trichoglossus haematodus Massena)

These are green, yellow, and blue parrot-type birds that are somewhat larger than a budgie. The end of their tongues is fibrous to lap up their diet of soft fruit.

From letters home:
September 5, 1987:

> We also have a new Coconut Lori, whom we have named "Fang" (guess why). Aslika told Holly that we should really give him another name if

---

[1] Health Minister Edwina Currie was forced to resign after saying in an interview that "Most of the egg production in this country, sadly, is now affected with salmonella". BBC reported that in fact, although 30 million eggs were being consumed per day, there were only 26 cases of salmonellosis in all of the UK during the time in question.

we want to tame him. Actually, if you work with him, he isn't too bad. He only drew my blood once today and once yesterday. Heather takes him out every day and puts him in a tree, where he spends his time eating berries with the Mala's Lori, Willie. Heather is desperate for a pet to be her friend. The goats are pretty affectionate, but I guess she doesn't want to invest too much emotional capital in them, as she knows that the cute little blue one will soon be a rug in John's house and one of the others is going to be the guest of honour at a big barbecue.

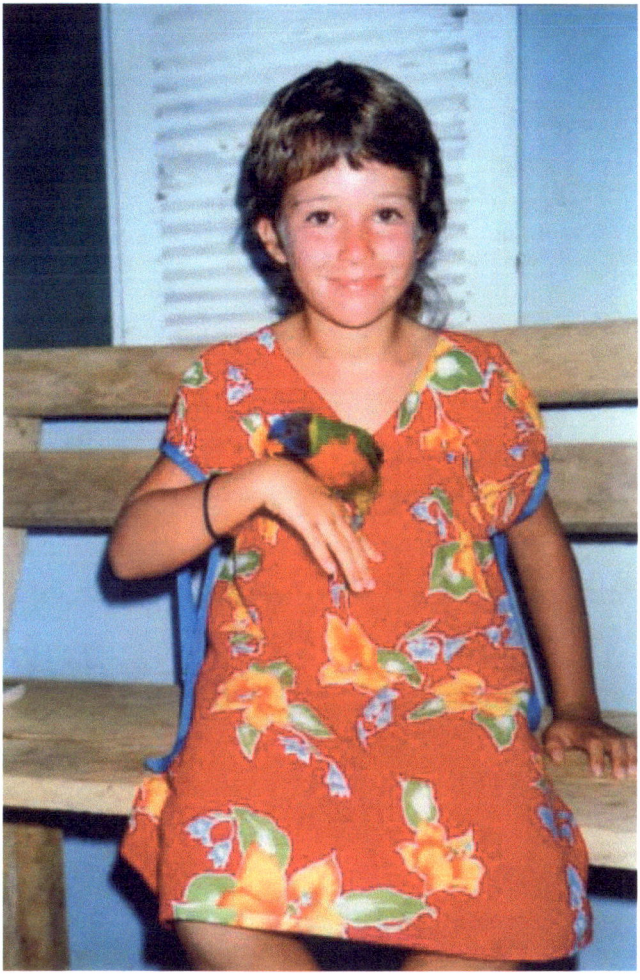

Heather with Coconut Lorikeet camouflaged against her colourful island dress.

Big emergency. I just had to go out and rescue Fang from a large spider's web. That will learn him to make unauthorized trips to the big outdoors. His wing and tail feathers have been cut so he can't fly very well. I don't know how he got way up there about 10 feet up in that web between the tree and the roof. He must have crawled up the tree and made a break for the wild blue yonder from there. Maybe he has found a hole between the veranda and house roof where he can get out on the roof. Those spiders (we got big 'uns here) have been working on their web for several months. I fixed them by getting a stick and ripping it down. We let Fang loose in the veranda, and I think he crawls out through the space under the screen door. It's pretty difficult for a parrot to waddle to freedom, though.

Rat (Rattus exulans)

When we first moved into our house in Lakatoro, there was a hole gnawed on the bottom of the front door that looked suspiciously like a rat access to me. From the smell, I also thought that there was rat activity under the kitchen sink cabinets. I asked the LGC mechanic and construction staff to put sheet metal over the hole in the floor, and removed the sink and cabinet to have a look down there. I found a rat skull and a few bones, but no droppings or suggestion of recent activity.

We had no evidence of rats in the house for two months, but one night we heard a rat in the attic, so noisy as to prevent sleep.

From a 16 March, 1987 letter:

I've got to tell you the saga of me vs. the rat. We had a rat in the attic running around and chewing all night. (I thought we also had one inside, but it turned out to be gecko droppings.) I got a trap and put it up there. I put bread on as bait, which disappeared, so the next night, I tried bread with peanut butter, which also vanished. The night after, I tried tying bread on the trigger with thread. That damn rat just ate it and took the thread. The next night, I filed down the triggering mechanism so I could hardly set the trap down without setting it off (only caught my hand once!) —bread vanished again. Finally, I had had it. I took a cabin biscuit (hard cracker) and put a wire through a hole in it and wired it to the trigger. About 21:00 that night, I heard a SNAP! and "thump, thump, thump". That will learn him to mess with me! I disposed of the carcass in the garbage can.

Two Years on Malekula

And five weeks later: 23 April, 1987:

> Two nights ago, we heard something gnawing at the box I use for a
> bedside table and then scamper off when Holly turned on her bedside
> flashlight. I told Holly it was a large gecko just moving the box, but she
> refused (if you can believe it!) to accept this and insisted it must be a rat
> and that we must exterminate it (especially after she found all the
> droppings on top of the fridge). So, last night, I had to get my trusty rat
> trap out of the attic where I left it set after my last kill. I had wondered
> why it hadn't caught the workmen who went up there last week (sans
> warning from me, of course), and I found out—apparently, I caught
> another rat a month or so ago. He was stuck pretty good to the trap, so I
> had to scrape him off with a stick. Things just don't keep well in the
> tropics! Something had eaten the bait, so I wired another piece of cabin
> cracker on the trigger and set the trap behind the stove where I wouldn't
> step on it during the night. It only took about five minutes after we
> turned out the lights to nab the little so-and-so. Of course, he was only
> pinned down, so I had to take him out and dispatch him with my rat
> rock. We don't have a fishpond here[1] . This time, I removed him from the
> trap while he was still fresh, which was much easier. Tonight the trap
> goes back up in the attic. I'll have to remember to check it more often.

With this sure-fire technique, it never took me more than one night to catch a rat
for the next six years, including half-a-dozen slow learners in half-an-hour in our
Vila house's storeroom.

Ants (Who Knows; there's a zillion species)

From letters: 24 February, 1987:

> Life has settled into a battle with millions of little black ants. It's the same as at
> home—if you keep the place clean, they stay away. Right now, for instance, the
> place is almost free of ants. Put one speck of food out though, and thousands of
> them show up instantly. They usually cover the table before we have finished our
> meals. Most of the time, there is a line of them coming out of their favourite hole
> in the ceiling and down the wall, with another line retracing their route back
> home. Once in a while, you look over, and a big black lump is moving up the
> wall—a pack of them carrying a bug, bread crumb, or a piece of food. I see one
> making a beeline, or antline, if you will, for that hole right now; probably going
> to get his friends.

---

[1] A reference to my parents' method of dispatching live-trapped rats in Indonesia.

Two Years on Malekula

23 April, 1987:

I just watched about thirty little ants carry a piece of hamburger up the wall and over the window ledge. Just imagine how boring life would get if I swept the floor. Sometimes, when the ants get to the crack that goes outside, whatever they are carrying won't fit, which causes quite a stir. Another piece of ant lore—you can always tell when your bananas are ripe, because they get covered with little ants. Also, if you haven't been sweeping your floor regularly, you have to eat quickly before hundreds of them invade the table top. Finally, when you wipe them off the table, you have to quickly rinse out the cloth in soapy water (under the tap won't do), or they run up all over your arms. There go another two with a little hunk of hamburger, just speeding up the wall.

Holly keeps spraying their favourite entrances with some deadly insecticide that's probably old stock banned in North America, but they just move to another crack or hole.

News Flash—There go another ten ants with a medium chunk—Holly is implying that my kitchen cleaning does not meet the standard she expects.

When a family of Australians from Metenesel Estates Ltd. came to visit:
May 10, 1987

I think their children lead sheltered lives—the six-year-old went out of her way to warn us that we had "ants in your bin". I managed to contain my shock. Our garbage can has, despite Holly's continued efforts, nourished several generations of a large colony somewhere outside the house since we got here. The MEL management houses are all built on stilts—maybe the ends are set in cans of kerosene or something.

In the absence of TV, ants were a constant source of entertainment.

Cockroaches (Again, Who Knows the species)

Cockroaches were a normal part of life, but once they got a bit out of hand. We came home one night from a social occasion, and when I opened the door of our screened-in veranda, it was full of flying cockroaches. Holly and the girls waited while I fought my way through the mass and into the house, from which I retrieved my spray can of Baygon insecticide. A thorough spraying later, there were at least 5cm of dead cockroaches on the veranda floor. I swept them all out into the yard, and the next morning they were all gone. Eaten by something, I presume. If it was the neighbourhood chickens, I'm not sure if Baygon is approved for meat chickens. The neighbours all used it to spray their own and their own kids' heads when they got lice, anyway.

The "White Man's Rat" (Cavia porcellus)

The annual week-long Malekula LGC Anniversary celebrations took place every August 18. In 1987, as usual, there was a collection of booths built by ni-Vanuatu around the circumference of a soccer field, where they earned a little cash by selling food to celebrants. There was one unique booth this year, though, with a sign that read in Bislama:

> I GAT WAN GUINEA PIG (RAT BLONG WAET MAN) ISTAP
> LONG STALL (BARAK) IA. YU WE YU NEVA GAT WAN
> CHANCE BLONG LUK WAN RAT OLSEM YET, YU SAVE
> KAM ASKEM STALL KEEPER BLONG LUK MO SEM TAEM
> PEM 20VT OSEM FEE BLONG LUK. SO NO MESTEM
> CHANCE BLONG YU.

Which translates into:

> There's a guinea pig (white man's rat) in this stall (behind). You who've never had the chance to see one rat like this yet, you can come ask the stall keeper to look and at the same time pay the 20vt fee to look. So don't miss your chance.

Marie-Pauline with Kwik-Kwik, carefully shielding her from the freeloader behind.

Heather and Holly, with Laurel in carrier, on the way from Lakatoro to Aop Beach

I couldn't resist stepping up and paying my fee to go around back to see and photograph this wonder, which belonged to a friendly local woman we knew named Marie-Pauline. Her story was that she had obtained Kwik-Kwik the Wonder White Man Rat, which by the way had only one eye, some years previously from a French woman for whom she had worked in Port Vila. Kwik-Kwik was, I'm sure, the only guinea pig on Malekula and perhaps in Vanuatu. Apparently, Kwik-Kwik was a female, so I'm sure it was a good thing there was only one of the species on Malekula, or the island would no doubt have become infested with them. Marie-Pauline told me she had made about 500vt (about CAN$5) so far towards her daughter's school fees.

Personal Transportation (aside from Shank's Mare)
Bicycles

We took four bicycles with us from Canada, including a child seat and training wheels for three-year-old Laurel, taking advantage of an Air Canada loophole that allowed a bicycle box as a piece of luggage. Of course, there is a lot of empty space in a box with a bike in it, and we filled it with tools, computer paper, and other stuff. An obscenity was written on the outside of one box by a disgruntled baggage handler, and one wheel was bent by something heavy being dropped on it; I had that straightened at a Port Vila motorcycle shop.

Once in Lakatoro, however, it soon became evident that the hot, humid climate and poor state of the roads was not going to allow for long bicycle trips[1]; we restricted ourselves to riding no further than the 8 kilometres to Norsup. In particular, there was no way Heather could ride her bike up the steep hill at Lakatoro up to our house.

Holly had a few incidents while riding to and from the Wednesday farmers' market at Norsup.

From an October 19, 1987 letter:

> Holly got run off the road while riding her bicycle home from Norsup market on Wednesday. Some jerk playing chicken who didn't stop. She couldn't identify him, but he later told people about the experience. I don't think we have enough to go to the police, and I don't want to start a feud, but Keith has said he will call the guy in for an informal chat with me and the police chief this week. Given the extreme aversion to personal confrontation here, unless you are trying to kill the guy, I'll believe it when it happens. Because of this quantum-jump type of personal interaction, I'm reluctant to just corner the guy and give him a piece of my mind. Holly badly sprained her foot when she fell off her bike and has been limping around.

This was a bad way to handle the situation. I should have gone to the police and had him fined in court. A more experienced colonist friend of ours took a local ni-Vanuatu to court for making a sexual comment to his wife. The offender's father asked my friend if there was another way this could be settled. My burly friend offered the option of spending 5 minutes with his "bull-dick" club in a locked room with the guy. A "bull-dick" is a length of bull's penis that has been split, twisted, and dried; a nasty piece of work. My friend's offer was refused. I still own a bull-dick that my friend gave me to keep in our bedroom for personal protection when we moved to Port Vila.

Holly was also bitten once by a dog belonging to the family of the Vanuatu Police Chief Inspector, later off-and-on Prime Minister. There was no rabies in Vanuatu, so that wasn't an issue, but she didn't like being nipped. CUSO had issued us with an air horn to blow if we were in personal danger, so she started carrying that with her on her bike and blasting the mutt with it; it worked.

Motorcycle
We had brought motorcycle helmets for all of us based on CUSO Ottawa telling

---

[1] Nevertheless, a CUSO doctor who came to Norsup after we had left made a name for himself by pedaling his bike all over this island. Tougher than us, I guess.

me I would be provided with a motorcycle[1], but promises in Ottawa did not hold in the field. Eventually, after six months, Lakatoro's CUSO Fishery Officer received one of the 4WD pickups sent by the Japanese, and I inherited his Yamaha 100 trail bike with new tires provided by CUSO.

Only two of us would fit on the motorcycle, so we didn't really use it much for family outings. I would mount our small outboard and paddles on it and take one kid down to the landing stage, while Holly and the other daughter walked the short distance. From there, we'd go on an outing in our canoe or sailboat.

Once, I found myself on the road next to the Norsup airstrip as a Twin Otter was taking off. I played "Top Gun" by racing it down the strip; it won.

The trail bike did come in handy later, like when I had to cross a river to get to Norsup after Cyclone Bola washed out the bridge, and also to scour the island to find used parts for the Land Cruiser we eventually bought.

Renting a Truck from the LGC

The LGC had a sub-compact white Toyota pickup, and since we eventually got bored of not being able to explore the island on my days off, I made a deal to rent it for a per kilometre charge. That got us out to beaches and parties held by other expats on this island.

Loading up the LGC Hilux to go see the Walarano Mission passion play.

---

[1] I had a motorcycle license thanks to Alberta's policy of including them on automobile drivers' licenses when I was 17, and actual riding experience due to adventures in Australia a year later. Peace Corps volunteers, however, would be dismissed and sent home if they were caught riding a motorcycle. This was due to a high number of Peace Corps motorcycle accident injuries in the field.

Attaching the outrigger to my canoe.

The paddles I bought for the canoe.

One such party was held at Metenesel Estates on Malekula's west coast. Holly and I dressed up, engaged our housegirl to babysit, took the white pickup, and started off. In the centre of the island was a deep ravine, and I made the mistake of slowing down at the bottom. The truck would not go up the other side, and I didn't expect any traffic until the morrow. Finally, I backed up the side we'd come down as far as I could, put the tailgate down, and had Holly in her nice dress sit on the tailgate and bounce as we attempted to go up the other side. Success—Alberta farm experience comes in handy again. We had a good time at Metenesel where we of course told everyone our story, and I hit the gas going through that ravine on the way home.

Canoe

After a few months, I decided to get some sea transport and ordered a dugout canoe to be made for us on Vao, the northernmost of three small islands off the northeast coast of Malekula. When the canoe was finally ready, it turned out not to be new. It was the canoe used to retrieve the remains of a boy who had been killed up there by a shark, and nobody wanted to use it any more. I made exhaustive inquiries around the office and determined that the canoe was not considered to bear bad luck, so I bought it. When it was ready, I went up to Vao with the LGC plumber, who was delivering cement to make water-seal toilets with, in an LGC Toyota pickup to get it. It had to be disassembled to fit on the truck, so I asked the vendor and his friend to come down and put it back together again for me. That was an interesting process that involved pounding stakes into the outrigger and tying them to the crossbars, which themselves were tied to holes in the canoe. Said holes were plugged up with coconut coir, fiber from the outer husk of a coconut.

I later installed an outboard motor mount and painted the canoe Rescue Orange, as that was the only colour available in any of the Malekula stores. I bought paddles from a local man, and lifejackets for the family in Vila—got the only two child-sized ones in town. These canoes always leak or water comes in over the side, so the traditional half coconut shell for bailing was brought along on all trips. I kept the canoe chained to a tree down by the landing stage so it wouldn't get borrowed by someone who felt they had an immediate need for it—that sort of thing often didn't quite make it back to where it came from.

We paid about CAN$60 for the canoe, and were constantly asked by ni-Vanuatu how much we paid for it. They always clicked their tongues and said that was a lot. I asked around if we had paid too much, but was told we hadn't. I think people were just expressing that they would rather get it for less if they bought it.

From an October 26, 1987 letter:

> We got our canoe going this weekend, after a slight delay caused by failure to turn on the gas cock on the outboard. I had cleaned the spark plug and was gathering my tools to disassemble the carburettor when I noticed the problem.

We ran around a bit in the canoe, but didn't really get a lot of use from it. I later sold it to one of my co-workers.

Fireball Racing Sailing Dinghy

When I was doing my Master's at the University of Guelph in the late '70s, Holly and I took an inexpensive students' dinghy sailing course. So we were interested when we heard that Daniel and Michelle Couturier (the French Education advisor in Norsup) had their 5m Fireball up for sale[1] .

The Fireball.

From letters home:
October 26, 1987:

> I want to start the Royal Lakatoro Yacht Club. People without boats can become social members, but they have to pay dues of a case of beer— every week.

---

[1] To recap one of my shark stories, Michelle declared she would not get in it again after a 6m Tiger Shark circled them for a while out in Aop Bay, while we were swimming and watching them out there.

And:
November 1, 1987:

> We took delivery on our sailboat yesterday. Daniel and I sailed it over from Norsup. There was a moderate wind, and we had to hike out the entire way, i.e. hook our feet in straps and hang out horizontally over the side, to balance the boat as the wind pushed it over. Some local guys were really impressed because we beat their truck, as well as a boat with a 15hp outboard, for part of the way. This is the root of the problem. It's a racing boat, not really a family daysailer. I may try to find a frustrated racer in the Vila Yacht Club[1] who has a tub and try to trade. You take what you can get in the third world.

At home, we could never afford a sailboat. I offered 90,000 vatu for it, but Daniel and Michelle bargained me down to 70,000 (CAN$900). It's a "Fireball", about 5 metres long, and Holly tells me I shouldn't be surprised at its handling characteristics[2] with that name.

Motoring to Uripiv Island. We had found and bought
the only two child's life jackets in Port Vila.

---

[1] I never did.

[2] Daniel had replaced its broken wooden centerboard with a heavy steel one, so it would not plane. But, having a huge sail area compared to its hull size, it really went.

A few days later:
January 15, 1988:

> A young Australian who runs a gold assay lab in Santo, and who is nuts about sailing, had come down to see us when he learned we had a Fireball. The first time we went out on it, he told me that beginners using the trapeze[1] (you hook your waist to a wire from the mast and hang over the side, standing on the gunwale) just have to learn to "trust the wire". No sweat; I swung out, saying "Yep, just trust the w...", and snap!, a shackle broke and I found myself in the ocean[2] . He came back and picked me up and off we went again. You always get wet in that boat anyway[3] .

And, two months after that:
January 15, 1988:

> After New Year's, we flew to Ambae. We spent three nights with Don and Doreen Lehman, during which we sat around and watched the rain fall. Once again, I read several selections of Robert Service for Doreen. She is really into silk-screening T-shirts, so I finally relented, designed (with major help from Holly), and printed a couple of "Royal Lakatoro Yacht Club" shirts. They have our sailboat on them with a shark's fin alongside the hull.

The Fireball was not suitable for sailing with the kids, and since we didn't have child care for them, Holly and I didn't ever sail it together. It came with a motor mount, though, and made a good family vessel for trips to Uripiv Island just south of Lakatoro.

---

[1] I hadn't told him that I'd crewed on one in Australia in 1969 and knew the drill.

[2] With numerous sharks, no doubt.

[3] Says Holly: "In the meantime your wife and kids were standing on the shore watching this, with wife muttering "don't kick and attract sharks.""

Land Cruiser

From letters home after ten months of scrounging for family transportation:
January 15, 1988:

> Holly has given me the choice between automobile ownership and divorce, so we are in the market. The challenge is to find something for under 200,000vt that runs and has a roof. The first two are merely difficult, the last perhaps impossible[1]. The money would have to be, of course, borrowed from CUSO against our end-of-contract bonus. I hate to spend the money, but then I don't want to sit around in Lakatoro all the time, either.

And later, in a January 27, 1988 letter:

> Speaking of spending money, I've got a line on a great truck. Remember how I've often written of that old junk-heap of a Land Cruiser that the LGC owns? Well, this one is even worse! But, it fits our budget and has four-wheel drive, so it will take us everywhere (if it works). It even has a roof—a ragtop in the true sense of the word. I've said I won't buy it until the brakes (a mere 5 pumps needed now) and lights (all signal and brake lights now missing) are working[2].
> Four new tires will cost a mere 50,000vt or CAN $630. Purchase price of this machine is 170,000vt ; I figure tires, repairs, road tax, and insurance (we'll probably have the only liability insurance in town), will bring it up to 250,000vt or CAN$3,000[3]. That was wildly optimistic, particularly the repairs aspect.
> We'll borrow the funds from CUSO, which will put one-third of our resettlement allowance at risk if the truck is totaled or a tree falls on it. The vendor, who works with me, wants to buy it back when we go, which I don't really understand. Mind you, he just bought the thing and got his mechanic brother to fix it up, so that doesn't make sense, either. He paid 150,000 for it. I think his family (extended) took it over, and he doesn't like that. His brothers, of course, aren't too excited about selling it, so this may all fall through.

And, five weeks later:
March 2, 1988:

> Our Land Cruiser's on blocks at present, waiting for a long list of spare parts to be air-freighted in from Australia (quicker and cheaper than

---

[1] Hah! All three turned out to be impossible.

[2] Well, I did buy it without any of that work being done.

[3] Didn't happen; surprise.

> buying from the local New-Zealander-owned monopoly, if you can believe it). I figure I can start driving it after replacing all brake cylinder seals, brake shoes, and tires next week. Frills like signal lights, muffler, front U-joints, and new clutch can come later.

Obviously, the co-worker who sold it to me had attended the North American School for Used Car Salesmen. Unfortunately, it was the only vehicle for sale on the island, or I wouldn't have accepted the condition it came in.

Seven weeks after that, from an April 20, 1988 letter home:

> You want to talk about old cars? I'll tell you about old cars. I bought my fun-truck two-and-a-half months ago, and it's still in bits. I could go on for pages about the problems I had with Australian morons, both in Vila and Australia, getting parts in. Today, I finally got the last brake cylinders on (one with the old cups, because I got fed up with not getting what I ordered). Now, I just have to put the drums on, adjust and bleed the brakes, put the new exhaust pipe and muffler on, and get the engine to start. It ran when I drove it into the shop; why the hell won't it start now? I spent about $600 on four new tires and then discovered I was in need of two hard-to-find fifteen-inch rims to have a spare tire and four rims that really fit well. I finally found them on Tanna Island last week (extension of a business trip), but only had 100 vatu, so I couldn't pay the 1,650 vatu demanded for overweight baggage. I hid my pack and got them to put one rim (weight fifteen kilos, equal to the baggage allowance) on the plane. Yesterday, I sent the money down to ship the other one up. It would have been easier to just buy sixteen-inch tires and four sixteen-inch rims—the spare that came with the truck is sixteen-inch. Holly and I have inspected every rubbish truck around here and bought bits and pieces off of all of them—door latches, door window, all four signal lights, etc. I finally got hold of a parts book and learned the truck is a '73 model, not late '60's, as I was told. Only one year older than Holly's Datsun; a mere fifteen years old. This truck's a beauty, I tell you.

When I got this 1973 Land Cruiser, license plate M-169, the brakes on only one wheel worked, and that was metal-on-metal. The slave cylinders on the other three wheels were rusted together. Two wheels weren't the proper size. The starter motor didn't work. The master clutch cylinder leaked and had to be refilled each morning. The gas tank leaked, fortunately only from the top half. There were no headlights or rear lights. No signal lights. One front window wouldn't roll up. You could see the road going by through the front floor, and the back was so full of holes I was afraid the kids would fall through. The seat covers were nonexistent. The rear had no roof, and the front only rags. There was no muffler. Some of the wiring under the dashboard was fried. The speedometer and fuel gauge didn't work.

It was three months before I got it on the road, with the help of Heather and Laurel emulating me with their toy tool set. Fortunately, the LGC had a parts manual for this year and model, which was a big help, especially when I ordered parts from Australia.

Laurel and Heather helping me repair the Land Cruiser.

There was a company in Brisbane that bought things for people living in remote places and shipped them out. I found out about them from the Metenesel Estates management and got to know them very well. Part-way through the process, my counterpart Kalosak wanted to know how I got all these parts in cheaper than ordering them from Vila. So, I explained that I phoned the company in Brisbane and ordered the parts. Then, I had my bank transfer the funds to it. Next, I phoned my shipping agent in Vila to alert her (a ni-Vanuatu woman) that the parts were coming in, and she should forward them to me. About half-way through my account, Kalosak's eyes glazed over, and I realized that the LGC wasn't going to go through this process, and this was why the Toyota dealership in Vila got away with its prices.

Ordering in parts from overseas wasn't trouble-free though. I did help the LGC order in an automatic transmission part for its Toyota pickup. The one that arrived, although it was listed as being proper for this model, make, and serial number, was not at all the same as the one that came out of the actual truck. It turns out that manufacturers sometimes change things like transmission assemblies without making note of it in their parts specifications. Fortunately, a guy from the Brisbane shipping company just happened to be on the island visiting Metenesel. We showed him the problem, he took note, and had the proper part sent out to us.

Two Years on Malekula

I'm not exactly a mechanic, but I had some experience that helped me with this project. I had rebuilt a motorcycle in Melbourne when I was there in 1969. I had also followed manuals to replace the drive belt on a Bobcat Loader tractor on a farm in Alberta; and to remove the engine head from our Datsun B-210 when I was at Guelph, and replace it after the valves had been repaired. I did all of my own tune-ups until electronic ignitions became universal.

The LGC let me use their automotive workshop and tools, and the mechanics did some paid work for me during their lunch hours.
There was a ruined truck of the same model behind the Public Works Department; I studied the routing of wires beneath its dashboard to learn how to replace some burned-out wires in my truck.

From a May 14, 1988 letter home:

> My truck, which has been my major preoccupation for the past three months and the reason I don't write anyone, as well as the subject with which I bore those to whom I do write, is coming right along. It sat on blocks until about three weeks ago, while I suffered comments from all the other Malekula expats ranging from, "Here's Stan, we'd better not discuss the truck" to "Maybe it will run in time to take him to the airport when he leaves." I always told everyone that it was going to work "next weekend".

Joseph Migoti, wonder mechanic.

Two Years on Malekula

I finally put the brakes all together again, but then the engine wouldn't run. I got Joseph Migoti, the Italian mechanic from a nearby big plantation, to get it running (he has relatives in Calgary, but only speaks Italian, French, and Bislama, so you can imagine me telling him what is wrong). Migoti came over to Lakatoro, and while running alongside the truck (he must have been in his 70s) as it idled downhill, tuned it by ear using a minimum of tools; he used a matchbook cover to measure and set the contact gap.

Then the battery wouldn't charge. Joseph assured me he would fix it in an hour if I brought the truck into the PRV plantation. The plantation doesn't do outside repairs due to government regulations that reserve commercial automobile repairs on outer islands for ni-Vanuatu. When Gabby de Fontaine, the plantation manager, found out I had bought an old truck, he had taken me aside in Migoti's presence and told me in so many words that he "didn't want to see my truck in the workshop". I reminded Joseph of this, and he replied in Bislama, "No sweat, just do what everyone else in the area does: wait until Gabby leaves town and bring it in." Gabby went to Fiji, and my truck sat at the PRV workshop for three days, while they did the "one-hour job". In the end, they decided I needed a new alternator, and one of the assistant mechanics just happened to have an old one—for 10,000 vatu, or US$100. Holly and I spent a day looking for one more reasonably priced, but I finally had to cough up. So, as of last Sunday, we can actually go places that don't have a hill to park on. Today, I put some old brake lights on (didn't quite fit, so I used baling wire) and got them hooked up. I also have one front parking light, but I can't get the signal lights to flash. I can't get the gas gauge to work, either, so I haul around a couple of gallons to put in so I can get home after running out. It took a fair bit of work to get the gas tank so it didn't leak when it was half full. A fine machine.

One of my ni-Vanuatu co-workers asked me why I carried around a couple of Jerry cans of gasoline in my truck. When I told him, he exclaimed, "You white men think of everything! We would just run out of gas and walk to the nearest store for more." Once it became known in the community that I had extra gasoline on hand, I had several people come up to the house to buy it during times that all stores were closed. I eventually started charging more than the store price, and people stopped bothering me on Sundays.

This morning, I also put in new clutch release cylinder seals, so I don't have to put in new clutch fluid and bleed the cylinder every morning.

The only part left of the US$1,000's-worth of spare parts we bought (not including $550 for tires) is a new clutch, which I'm bugging the LGC mechanic to help me with some Saturday. Of course, the water pump is starting to make noises, and a front wheel seal is leaking grease. I think I have a new hobby! It does run well, to everyone's surprise.

And, finally, four months after purchase:

May 25, 1988:

News Flash! My truck works! Actually, it ran well last week until the LGC Mechanic and I (he did all the skilled work) tore it apart to replace the clutch. Then it wouldn't work until he came back the next day and suggested I take the 4WD shift out of neutral. Oh. So, I gave him a ride into Norsup, where I noticed water was squirting out of a hole in the radiator. Pulled the radiator out Sunday, got hole soldered up Monday, and got it back in yesterday. Runs like a charm now.

All our money goes into gasoline—US$50 to fill her up; about CAN$1.06 per litre.

The finished product! I can see the wood bed lining and a spare gas jerry can, but apparently the spare tire hadn't been chained on yet.

Holly made seat covers from old woven plastic rice bags. Of course, when we drove through mud, the *inside* of the windshield got dirty from mud coming up through the floor, and when it rained, the girls in back got wet. But, it was warm rain, and toughened them up.

Two Years on Malekula

There was one regular weekly activity during our last month in Lakatoro:

December 31, 1988:

> I spent a good part of the morning soldering up another hole in this radiator of mine. Of course, a one-hour search for the Council employee who had taken the workshop key home for the long weekend was necessary first, so I could borrow a soldering iron. I struck gold on the fifth guy, who lived in the fourth village that I tried. Locks and keys are definitely inappropriate technology here. All keys for a lock except one are immediately lost, and the one remaining key is always with a guy who has gone into the bush to work on his garden, or he has gone to a wedding somewhere for a week, etc.
>
> Whenever possible, I scrounge radiator soldering off the workshop of a local plantation, but they were too busy today, so I had to do it myself. When they do it, the guy just daubs a bit of solder on and draws it smoothly over the hole. I have to spend a half-hour splotching on about three inches of the solder bar into a big puddle running down the radiator, uncovering the previous hole I soldered in the process. Once again, I finally got blobs of solder globbed onto all of the holes. I thought I had solved this problem several weeks ago, when I put a can of that gunk that plugs these holes into the coolant, but I guess that only works on small holes. I just hope I don't see that little spray of water squirting out from my grill before I get the truck sold. Of course, that was probably the thinking of the guy who sold it to me.

In the end, of course, I sold the truck only on the condition that I sent a new radiator back when I got to Australia. I should have bought one myself months earlier.

M-169 really changed our lives, and is perhaps the reason I have fewer letters from April 1988 on[1]. Now, we could easily get to the local beach, and without too much trouble to the nice beach at Espiegle Bay on the northwest of the island. When visitors came, we could take them to the custom cave and the Brenwe rapids. We could go to parties across the island without getting stuck at the bottom of that ravine, and to any party at night.

---

[1] There was also the matter of having to order in "sub-C" batteries and solder them together to make a new laptop (on which I wrote my letters) battery pack, and my printer giving up the ghost. I finally dumped the printer into a Vila trash bin and borrowed one from a generous Asian Development Bank engineer.

Loaded up with family, friends, and visitors for a day at Espiegle Bay.
Note elegant spare tire mounting system.

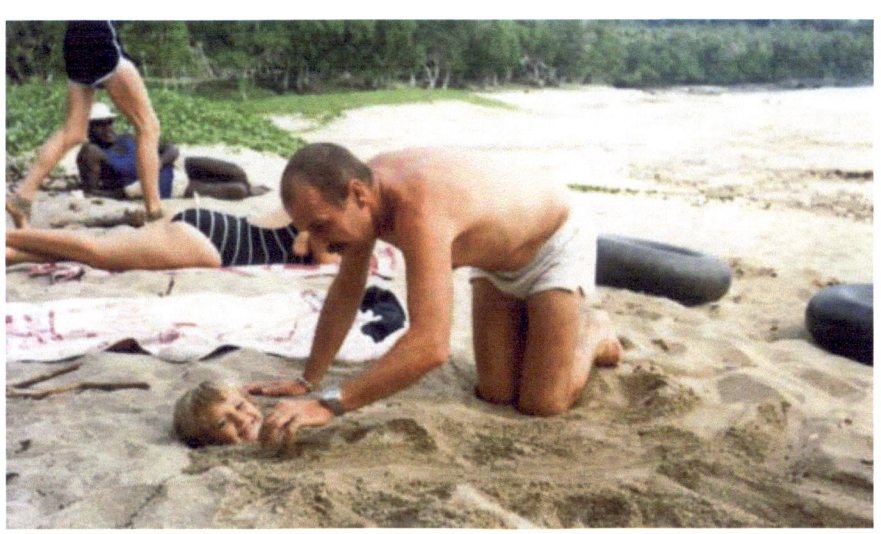

Friend Daniel Couturier burying Laurel at Espiegle Bay.

Daniel cooking lunch of steak and lobster at Espiegle Bay. Note clever use of old fridge shelves for grill; usual Malekula practice. Life on Malekula was hard.

Fellow CUSOs David and Nada Boote at Espiegle Bay. An editor made me crop out toddler daughter Sonia mooning the camera.

Mind you, on one trip up the Lakatoro hill to our house after a party, I managed to stop just before running over a man lying comatose across the road. He had a glass bowl with the remnants of kava in it, and after unsuccessful attempts to rouse him I dragged him off the road and continued to the house. He wasn't there in the morning.

The first time I drove the truck around to the other side of the island, people stared and pointed as I passed them; all of Malekula's few trucks are well known to everyone, and everyone was amazed that this one had been resurrected from the junk heap.

I mentioned some hazards of driving on Malekula in an August 1, 1988 letter home:

> Did I tell you about the time we were driving home from a day at the beach at Espiegle Bay, and we came (or actually, drove) across the Great Baby Frog Migration? Did you know that when you run over a baby frog, it pops just like those plastic packing bubbles do? Occasionally, we drive over huge[1] land crab congregations. They just crunch.

We should have bought a truck when we arrived; I recommend that all volunteers who can afford it do so.

When we left Malekula, I sold the Land Cruiser to a fellow CUSO, who also had a great time with it until his contract was finished a year later.

Charismatic Religion Next Door

Our neighbour and my boss, Keith Mala, had by all accounts including his own been quite a wild man in his youth. He had got things together, though, by joining the Holiness Fellowship, quitting drinking, and settling down. Living next to a large house that lent itself to church meetings could be comment-worthy, though.

We all got along OK, although there were periods of frostiness, the causes of which I suspected included me singing songs gently satirizing religion[2], putting out carved Hallowe'en pumpkins, and refusing our daughter permission to attend their Sunday school.

---

[1] The congregations, not the crabs.

[2] Like "We Need a Whole Lot More of Jesus, and a Lot Less Rock 'N Roll", "Away, Away With Rum, By Gum", and "I Saw the Light". Too bad I didn't know "Drop Kick Me Jesus Through the Goal Posts of Life" at the time.

Two Years on Malekula

From letters home:

April 23, 1987:

Things are really getting wild next door, where my boss lives. I mentioned in previous letters that he fancies himself a faith healer and an electric band and choir practiced there for a week. Well, this week all heaven has broken out every evening. "Brother Thomas", who works for the Health Department, has been coming over and leading some sort of service. He preaches hellfire and brimstone and everyone hoots and hollers, "Amen!", "Hallelujah!", etc. When they get warmed up, they really go! Are your church services like that?

Oh, I almost forgot the reason I wrote this letter. I'm enclosing some slides of our trip to Keith and Aslika's church's Sunday School Good Friday Picnic. I'm not sure if Brother Thomas was there—oh, Holly just told me he was the loudmouth on my volleyball team. Things are pretty quiet next-door tonight—I guess he's giving his vocal chords a rest.

May 2, 1987:

Tomorrow, there is another big "Malekula For Jesus Christ" rally, and the choir has got their electric guitars and sound system going at Keith and Aslika's next door again right now. At least they didn't go at it eight hours a day all week like they did last time. I had heard before we came that Vanuatu is a Christian country and that everyone took it very seriously, so I always thought that the goings-on next door were normal for here. I am now learning that most people around here consider it a little extreme. Holly, as per usual, has been storianing (chatting) around with the local women, and the scoop is that Keith used to be pretty wild, which I already knew. The interesting part is that he used to drink too much and he and Aslika would really go at it when he came home. One time she piled all of his clothes on the floor and set them on fire, which burned the whole house down. I haven't looked yet, but apparently Keith has a big scar on his upper arm where Aslika let him have it with a fork. When I heard all this, I remembered that I had heard some of it when I was in Victoria from a returned CUSO. It sounds like it isn't all bad that Keith has found a stabilizing influence. I think it is a pretty standard story—one is always meeting born-again people who think you would be surprised to hear how wild they used to be. I think they just never got out of the stage of kids who are searching for limits.

June 27, 1987:

Holly and I have noticed that the neighbours are a little cool these days and, having discussed possible causes at length, have compiled a long list, including having attended the opening of the nakamal built by Daniel Couturier, a French expat friend, or being seen with the nuns who give us rides to French lessons, speaking in defence of the only Doctor on the island (who is on the verge of being ousted), or being heard singing "We Need A Whole Lot More Of Jesus, and A Lot Less Rock And Roll". We have come to the conclusion that in a mixed community like this, in a society divided into small village groups and where if-you're-not-with-us-you're-against-us, it is inevitable that you are going to offend someone. We will remain our cheerful selves and wait for the problem to blow over, or until we receive the dreaded "Green Letter" (deportation order).

I got back this morning from an overnight visit to a village on the SW corner of the island. Keith and I went down to officiate at the grand opening of a new water supply project and my first look at the area. We flew down (15 min.) and took a boat across the bay, and brought the boat back (3.5 hr. with an 8 HP "speedboat"). I had been told by the Head of Water Supply here that it would be a big party, but I got my first clue of reality when I asked Keith what videos he had with him, and he said that religious ones had been requested. He had "Jesus of Nazareth, Parts. 1, 3, & 4", and his favourite Jimmy Swaggart Tape[1].

When we arrived and I saw the programme, at 1900, where it should have said "Party with free kava for honoured guests", it said "Church Service featuring Keith Mala". I heard them pounding kava at the nakamal near the building where we stayed and wandered over, but the door was closed and I was a little gun-shy of offending kastom again, so I gave it a miss.

Actually, I wanted to go to the service so (a) I could see what a ni-Vanuatu church service was like and (b) I could learn more about Keith. It was fairly standard stuff, although it's been at least 15 years since I've been to church (except Easter in Greece 10 years ago), and I may have forgotten. At one point, one of the Elders (this was a Presbyterian Village) read from a Bislama Bible and the old guy next to me shared his King James Version with me (I was supposed to go sit up front with Keith and the Elders, but I slipped into a back pew on the way up the aisle). The Bislama version very generally followed the King James Version , but was really loaded down with interpretation not identified as such[2]. I suspect that the translator really did a number on the people here by rewriting

---

[1] There was a Jimmy Swaggart office in Vila that sold such things. Either word of Jimmy's spiritual downfall hadn't reached Vanuatu, or true believers didn't care.

[2] I'm not exactly a Biblical scholar (could never get past Numbers), but did spend many a youthful hour at Sunday School and Vacation Bible Schools and Camps.

the Bible. It's bad enough that they foisted the Whiteman's religion on them, but this translation bit is a bit much. I'm going to have to buy a Bislama Bible and check this out further. We sang several hymns on the general principle that the louder, the more pious[1], and Keith did his number. Having heard him speak on development, I have commented that his true calling is television evangelism, but I was unaware of how close I was to the mark.

Keith started in on the standard "I was a sinner—smoked three packs a day, drank kava, and never went to bed sober" routine, and told us all the story of how on December 2, 1983, he was on a course in Australia. Everyone but him had gone to church, and bored, he switched on the TV. There he was—Jimmy Swaggart, preaching as if he was talking about Keith only. (Good thing I haven't discussed Jim and Tammy Bakker with him). Keith also has some weird and wonderful interpretations of Genesis (need I say that Evolution doesn't figure in) and Revelations, although the details have already slipped my mind.

Every few minutes, he'd give the "Praise the Master" cue, but not being his usual Charismatic congregation, no response was given. I'm not sure the definition of a sinner as someone who used tobacco, liquor, and kava struck a responsive chord, but people appreciated the call for interdenominational fellowship (quite easy, as everyone knew that he was leaving the next day—a proposition of a new denomination in the village would undoubtedly be a bit less well received) and increased faith. Anyway, I'm glad I went, and I'm also glad I wouldn't let the kids go to Keith's Sunday School. (That was worth a week's coolness.)

Stan vs. the BBC World Service

During our four-day layover in Fiji on the way to Vanuatu, I bought a tape deck with AM/FM/SW radio. I've always liked to keep up on world news, so I used it to listen to shortwave news broadcasts, especially from the BBC World Service.

My reception wasn't very good, so I wrote to the British Broadcasting Corporation in London requesting their how-to-make-a-short-wave-radio-antenna pamphlet. In my letter, I included a reception report as per their frequent requests and mentioned that I was choosing some of their broadcasts

---

[1] And, the quicker you get to heaven! Minibuses in Vila would drive around with their windshields, except for a small hole on the driver's side, covered with posters for the next revival, presumably on the same principle for the driver, and as a bonus, for his passengers.

beamed to other continents by referring to a map. There weren't any broadcasts beamed towards Vanuatu, so I used a Mercator projection map, on which area shapes are distorted but directions in a straight line are true. I used the BBC World Service schedule they had sent me and by checking out transmission sites and targets, found some targets that Vanuatu was behind on a straight line from the transmitter. For example, I can sometimes get BBC from the Antilles beamed at Central America and from Ascension Island beamed at Africa. It seemed to work.

Some weeks later, my letter found its way on to the Waveguide programme, on which the commentator announced my name and location and then ridiculed, to the entire world, my map and frequency guide method of locating audible broadcasts. He also announced in his veddy correct accent that (referring to me) "He doesn't seem to have anything very special in receivers; he refers to one as a... "Ghet'-to Blas'-ta".

I'm still[1] waiting for them to apologize for humiliating me [2] in front of the whole world. They didn't even send me a T-shirt for using my letter.

Other Short-Wave Radio Services and News Media

From an April 12, 1987 letter:

> Holly thinks that I'm going to hell in a hand-basket since I've sent away for and received a schedule from BBC. She says I'm on my way to becoming one of those expats who alienate themselves from the locals, but I caught her, schedule in hand, fiddling with the dial this morning. When I first read the BBC World Service magazine, I got all excited about all the drama and interesting programmes that they have. Since then, of course, I've discovered that none of the good stuff is scheduled for those listeners in the middle of the Pacific. A play that looks interesting is on tonight at 2300 (or 600 this AM), so I think I'll try setting the recording function on the tape deck with a 90-minute tape when we retire at 2230 tonight.

In the event, we lost the BBC signal before the programme started; we never were able to get any dramas. Life is hard in the South Pacific.

> Most of what we get is news and analysis, which is interesting, but wears a bit thin on the 3rd repetition during an evening. I also catch Australian World News once a day, but the rest of ABC is elevator music, prattling,

---

[1] Written in September, 1987; I continue to wait by the mailbox.
[2] Not.

and one long advertisement for Australian technology and know-how. They really try too hard to establish an Australian identity.

After we returned to Canada and I eventually started reading the Australian Broadcasting Corporation news on the Internet, the ABC twice announced it was shutting down its broadcasts to the Pacific. Both times I emailed them explaining that their shortwave news was the only regional international news, and even unbiased national news, that people on Vanuatu's outer islands could access. I don't know what influence that had, but at least the first time, the Pacific broadcast service continued.

Radio Canada International news broadcasts
September 5, 1987:

> You wouldn't believe how useless this news is. Nothing about what is happening in Canada is mentioned—only stuff that External Affairs is doing in Ottawa. That means only stories about Joe Clark and Brian Mulroney. Ho, Hum. I mean, does anyone really care about Joe Clark going to South Africa or the Francophone Summit? Somehow, all the other international news services that I listen to are missing these stories...

Other short-wave news services:

April 12, 1987:

> I am growing weary of trying to find the different frequencies on the dial—ABC, Radio Français, Radio Moscow, and VOA are the bane of my existence; the first two because they are everywhere and their signals overpowering, and the others because they are in English and mislead me. Moscow would use announcers with British Accents, so you would mistake them for the BBC. Only when they announce the latest tractor production statistics for the Ukraine will you know whom you are listening to. Sometimes, I listen to a bit of Radio Japan, which is in a continual mode of arguing their side of the trade dispute with the US. They sound so wounded while they explain the reasonableness of their position.

Two Years on Malekula

Local Vanuatu Media:

April 12, 1987:

> We also listen to the local Bislama news and subscribe to the local weekly newspaper. Both the paper and radio station are run by the government, so you can imagine how complete local coverage is, especially of political opposition activities. Anyway, the news in both media is trilingual, but with different degrees of completeness in each language. For example, the account of a recent shark attack was much more lurid on the Bislama radio news than the English. A recent story in the English section of the paper stated that a man had been found dead in his hotel room in Vila, full stop. Moving on to the Bislama version, I learned that he had been found by a man who worked for the hotel. In the French section, I finally found out that the cause of death was thought to be cardiac arrest.

> I read the paper in my order of language proficiency. This week's paper carried a story of a mugging in Bislama only. My Bislama has finally reached the stage where I can generally follow the radio news, slow speech, and staff meetings. I probably understand just enough to get into trouble.

The Custom Cave

Immediately prior to my first visit to the Custom Cave, I was on a side bench in the back of the Local Government Council's old extended-body dark green Land Cruiser with my counterpart and four elected Councilors, and the LGC driver and my boss in the front seat. We were returning from a visit to Malekula's northwest coast, from about as far as the road went. As we bounced along on the packed coral road, someone shouted, "Custard Apples![1]", and we immediately pulled up and piled out.

This was my first introduction to what soon became my favorite fruit. Shaped like a scaly egg from the film "Alien" (I would tell the girls to not let them get too close to their faces), the sweet—and, well, custardy—fruit is delicious, especially in the purple (most are green) variety. In custard apple season, I was always sure to get to the Saturday Norsup market by 6AM, before the wealthier expats from across the island arrived, and buy all of them. After, I'd chuckle inwardly while they asked each other why there were never any custard apples at the market— nice guy, aren't I?

---

[1] The "Joy of Cooking" calls them Cherimoya (Annona cherimola, family Annonaceae).

Custom Cave Entrance.

Anyway, my compatriots and I picked a number of them from a tree, feasted, licked off our fingers, got back in the truck, and continued on our way.

Shortly thereafter, somebody pointed out a dark cave entrance in the base of a coral cliff 100 metres inland through coconut palms and bush. We parked and all walked over to the large opening, which was ornamented with several dozen reverse hand shadows made by placing a hand on the rock and spraying pigment from one's mouth over and around it.

Custom Cave Hand silhouettes.

Here, I received instruction on the correct procedures for safely entering and exploring this cave. First, we had to be an even number of people, although we dispensed with the requirement for each pair to hold hands. This was to avoid a spirit holding your hand while you thought it was a friend, and taking over your mind. Fortunately, we were an octet.

Laurel and Heather keeping each other safe in the cave.

Then, a member of our party located one small hole of many in the honeycombed coral entrance, distinguished by the wear around it. He blew into it, making a trumpet sound, three times. This was to announce to the spirits living in the cave that we were coming, so they would have time to vacate the premises while we were there.

Preparing to blow a warning to the spirits within the cave.

As we entered the initial chamber, say 10 metres across, there was a low passage to the right leading to a smaller exit. If I went through there, I had to be very careful not to touch the roof with my back, or I would die a violent death that day. I was told that in the past, men on their way to battle would go through there, and any whose back touched would stay home that time. An Australian friend who had grown up on Malekula later told me that as a child his back had touched, and he was terrified of an auto accident all the way home.

A slew of baby boy stones.

Holly braves the low exit.

To our left was a wide, high passage floored with large boulders, with light filtering in from the far end. As we clambered along, a half-metre ledge on our right was pointed out to me. If I tossed a stone up there with my left hand, and it stayed, my next child would be a boy, and indeed the ledge was covered with small stones, with a pile of girl stones on the ground below. My family was complete, so I didn't try my luck.

As we neared the end of this passage, the source of illumination became evident. We entered the main chamber of the cave, which was a vault about 30 metres wide by 15 metres high. In the centre was a 3-metre hill of rock with a tree rooted in it, the bare trunk growing up through a 5-metre circular hole in the ceiling, where its branches and leaves spread out into the sunlight. This tree was, I was told, the means of entry and egress of the spirits of warriors who had died in battle,—the cave denizens. If you found footprints in the dust without toes, these were theirs. Later, when I took the family to this cave and told them these things, the kids ran around with their toes up to make spirit footprints. Of course, all the time they were tightly holding hands so the spirits wouldn't possess them.

Holly at base of tree in custom cave.

My counterpart later told me that soon after the first men came to Malek-ula, an old man planted his walking stick in the floor of the cave. It took root and grew up through the roof. He wasn't too interested in my theory that the roof had fallen in and the tree had grown from the resultant pile of debris.

251

Two Years on Malekula

The base of the chamber was ringed with petroglyphs that someone, perhaps a documentarian, had traced out with white chalk. Most were human-like, some with lines extending from their heads that I later told expat friends were obviously space suit helmets and proof of Erich von Däniken's theories in the book "Chariots of the Gods?". There was also a three-masted ship, perhaps inscribed soon after Western contact.

Obvious alien.

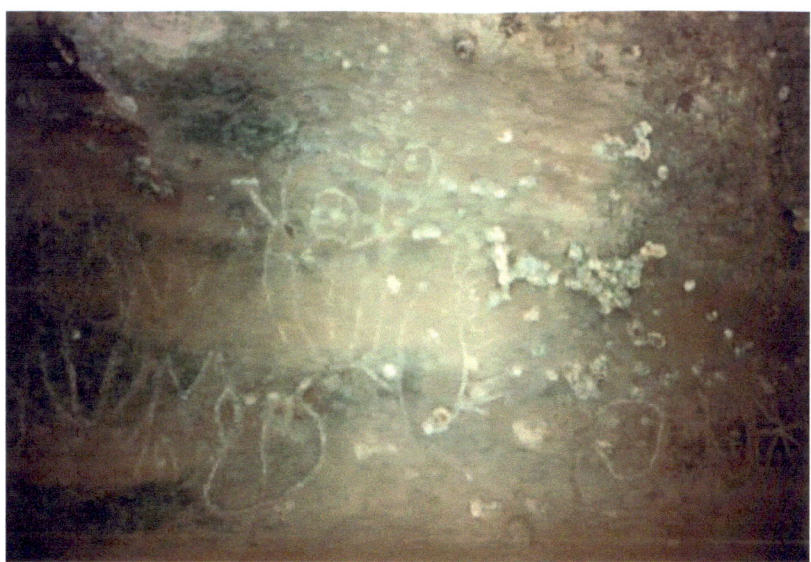

Turtle and Fish.

Man holding fish.

Exiting the cave, three more blasts were blown into the coral to advise the fallen warriors that we had left and they could climb back down the tree trunk. We all crossed to the road, folded ourselves into the truck, and were on our way home to Lakatoro.

Labour Day Festivities at the Norsup Catholic Church

From a letter written a few months after we arrived in Lakatoro. Everything was still new to us:

May 2, 1987:

> Yesterday was Labour Day here.[1] Last week Holly saw a sign advertising a bazaar at the Catholic Church at Norsup, so we went. It was supposed to start (like everything here does) with a church service at 0800, so we thought if we left on bicycles from here at that time, we would get there at 0900, late enough to miss the service but early enough to get the good buys. As it turned out, we didn't get started until 0900 and when we got there at 1000, the service was still going, as they always are. We went for a walk until we saw people walking by with Bibles and then went back.

Heather cycles past plantation worker housing in Norsup.

> It turns out that a church bazaar here is somewhat different from one in Canada. There weren't any crafts or second-hand items for sale, but several stalls selling fruit and food and a couple of the type of games where you put your money on a colour and they spin a big wheel [2]. At one stall the prize was money (200vt from 14 colours at 20vt each, or a 71.4% return to the gamblers), the other place gave 2 kg of sugar or flour,

---

[1] May 1st, as in much of the world.

[2] Prepare to be bored by my obsession with the mathematics of gambling.

or a carton of cigarettes (retail value approx. 200 vatu) on 15 colours at 20vt each (66.7% return). A third place had a real money machine. This guy sat at a table with 6 places marked with spots from the sides of a die. After 6 people had put 20vt each on the 6 places, he rolled the die. The winner got 100vt and he kept 20vt. The 83.3% return to players was the best of all, but the turnover was much faster than the other games. I timed him at about 5 throws every 2 minutes, which meant that he was taking in 5/2x60x20vt=3000vt per hour. Not bad in a place where a labourer makes 70vt per hour.

Norsup Catholic Church.

We went over and introduced ourselves to some people who we've been meaning to meet: the new French Doctor and wife (she's from Martinique) with a 6-yr. son and 5-month-old daughter; and a woman who's the government educational inspector and her husband, also French (they have a sailboat and I wanted to grill them[1]). Being the only Anglophones, we struggled along in fractured French and bastardized Bislama. The priest who had given the service, which turned out to be a confirmation ceremony, was also there. Occasionally, someone would say a few words of English and, as far as I was concerned, no one spoke it that well. Holly, however, thought the Priest must have learned his in North America because it didn't sound too British, so she asked him where he had learned English. He advised her that he had been born and brought up near Boston (no wonder I thought English was his second

---

[1] The one we later bought.

language). We also met three of the nuns from New Zealand who are based near here. I had seen them around and knew they were nuns, but it was still disappointing that they weren't dressed like penguins. Come to think of it, I haven't seen a nun in a habit for eons. What ever happened to the good old traditions? Especially here in the tropics—you'd think that they would welcome the opportunity to suffer a bit. (I once worked with a guy in Australia who followed a nun up a ladder in pre-WW II Papua New Guinea—he reported that she wasn't wearing underwear.) Since all of these people were going to the confirmation lunch, we went along with them.

After lunch, dancing was featured. We thought it was going to be real traditional stuff—you know, like they always have at the Tiki-Tiki Restaurant. It turned out to be a local talent show. The first skit was some women doing a custom dance after finishing off a bottle—some of them started twisting, etc. Then we had an air band (yes, the worst of western civilization has reached even here) and something about a cowardly soldier. Then some local dude with a Rastafarian hairdo and tight red pants who had seen too many rock videos led the first of 3 group dance numbers. The first was with about 30 girls and resembled an aerobics class. Then, the ever-popular (here) "We Are the World". Later he returned with about 10 young men, who looked like they were on their coffee break from loading copra, for 2 or 3 other numbers. Unfortunately, he was the only one who was really committed. When they got to the part where they were supposed to do the "bee's knees", most of them looked pretty embarrassed and just faked it.

The big hits, however, were skits put on by the young men, with humour that more than bordered on anal fixation (don't forget that this was a church function—no accounting for taste, I guess). It probably lost something in translation, but one popular number involved two guys who were hunting something at night with torches (which kept, in real life, burning their hands—I got a laugh out of that part), that went out. Some other guy was covered in burlap with eyeholes and was on all fours. A red hibiscus was pinned to his derriere, which he was waving around. Apparently one guy stumbling around in the dark took this hibiscus for a spark and tried, at length, to restart his torch by putting it next to the flower and blowing on it. The further he stuck his nose up there, the more the crowd howled. I have no idea what type of animal or monster or spirit being or whatever the burlap guy was supposed to be. The real big laughs were reserved for a delicate number about a guy who was fishing and suddenly had to move his bowels (no detail was spared—he had an extra pair of jockey shorts on with a piece of papaya shoved in the back). Just as he was wiping himself with a stick, he got a big strike, and needing both hands to play the fish, stuck the stick between his teeth. The crowd went wild.

Lighting the torch from the spirit's butt.

We finally got to some real live custom dancing. About 30 women did a couple of dances wearing a close approximation of custom dress—lavalava[1] skirts with brassieres (basket blong titi or titiklos in the vernacular), some modestly draped with handkerchiefs. Holly had seen a couple of them buying their lavalavas at a store in Norsup on Wednesday, and they had shown her how to properly tie them on. Unfortunately, the lavalavas they ship here for sale are rejects of ones made in Hong Kong or somewhere for the tourist trade—three of the women were wearing ones boldly emblazed with "LOOKING IS FREE, BUT TOUCHING WILL COST YOU"[2]. I hope it comes out in our pictures.

Women dancers from Pentecost Island.

[1] Sarong.
[2] Guess what I got the next Christmas.

Two Years on Malekula

I went over to the priest and told him that he would do them a kindness if he translated their lavalavas for them, but I don't think he had noticed. I started talking with him, and asked him how long he had been here, and he said 39 years. I had visions of a lonely martyr ministering to his flock in a forgotten corner of the world, and asked him if it had all been with this church, and he said yes, then hesitated and said it had been on several different islands. I thought I had found a vast source of local knowledge and during the conversation asked him some local questions, which he seemed a little vague on. He kept referring to Vila and told me that I should drop in some time if I was there. I finally started catching on, and asked him if he was based in Vila. I guess he caught on too, as he replied yes, he was from Vila and introduced himself as Bishop Lamont. How in the heck are you supposed to know these things these days—he wasn't even wearing a black shirt or white collar, so I thought I was doing well identifying him as a priest. You'd think they would wear a sign or something. I had noticed that he was wearing a big gold ring, and thought it was nice for the Catholic Church to buy nice jewelry like that for everybody out in the sticks[1]. Later, of course, I noticed that everyone he said "Hi" to was kissing it. He told me that his grandparents were from Quebec. Holly and the kids and I were all getting ready to leave, when he asked me if I'd go with him and a friend to the nakamal. I thought that it wasn't every-day that the Bishop of Vanuatu offers to shout you a shell of kava, so I said sure. It was a good move, because besides getting a guided explanation from him about how it was prepared, I met a couple of guys who work at Lakatoro that I should have met long ago, the heads of the Labour office and Public Works. I'm just going to have to spend more time drinking kava. The Bishop told me that the Church was, while not exactly pushing kava, encouraging its use as a substitute for alcohol.

Michelle, the education person, is giving Conversational French lessons in Norsup every Thursday evening, and we have a date with Sister Judith for rides there.

I got the girls to contribute their bits to the letter as follows:

Heather says, "I ride my bike all the way to Norsup, where there was something like a party, where I saw all the people doing shows. I also ride my bike to the beach, when we want to go to the beach and it's the day that we go to the beach. We are having our hair shampooed every day so we don't get bugs in our hair, which the people here do."

---

[1] I'm pretty ignorant about some things.

> Laurel says "I still have itchy hair (as she scratches—she gets heat rash or
> something on her scalp—the dandruff hasn't had legs yet). I'm buying
> gum with money that I won yesterday on the table." Laurel hit a lucky
> streak at the dice table and won 2 out of 4 tries.

From a letter about a dinner with the French couple:

May 8, 1987:

> They were quite amused to hear that I hadn't recognized the Bishop as
> such last weekend—hadn't I noticed him doing the first half of a garbage-
> man's handshake [1] while eating laplap when a woman came up to kiss
> his ring? They had gotten a large charge out of that.

Bush Leaves in Port Vila

At our CUSO orientation in Ottawa, we were told that rural cooperants such as
ourselves were given "bush leave" every six months, for which CUSO would pay
our transportation, in this case air fare, to town so we could see doctors and den-
tists, and shop for things that weren't available where we lived. This very soon
became a matter of contention between me and our Field Staff Officer, who maintained that we didn't need bush leave because there was a hospital on Malekula.
I finally got tired of the dance and wrote requesting (OK, demanding) a definitive ruling on the matter on the basis that:

1   We were the only CUSOs in Vanuatu who didn't live in town or whose
    work didn't take us to town regularly.

2   Although Lakatoro/Norsup was Vanuatu's third-largest urban area, it was
    pretty bush with a couple hundred people compared to 7,000 or so in Lu-
    ganville and triple that in Vila.

The FSO finally caved, but maintained that a visit to Luganville, rather than Vila,
was sufficient. Bro-ther. We always paid the difference in air fares to Vila rather
than Santo.

Visiting Port Vila wasn't as simple for a family as it was for single cooperants.
They could easily find a spare bed to sleep on; we had to find accommodations
for four. My work occasionally took me to Vila or Santo, but Holly didn't get off
Malekula as often as she would have liked.

---

[1] Wipe one's hand off on one's pants prior to shaking.

Two Years on Malekula

Our first bush leave in Vila:

July 16, 1987:

> We underwent culture shock upon entry to the big city. I felt like Crocodile Dundee in New York—wanted to say "Hello" to everyone on the street while they were ignoring me. The ni-Vanuatu sure treat you differently in Vila; they just ignore you unless you speak Bislama to them, and then they will often storian for a while, especially since lots of them are from Malekula. The place is full of overpaid (i.e. higher income than me) expats[1] who act like spoiled brats, and it crawls with (horrors...) tourists on cruise-ship day. Coming from Victoria, we felt right at home. The crowd we mix with are great people, and it's a nice place to visit, etc.
>
> The poor kids spent Monday–Friday trailing around after us shopping. We did spend a couple of half-days at the library, which we joined. If you write down all the titles you want, you can request that they send them to you three-at-a-time when you get home. The Library appears to be full of books that people bring with them and donate when they go home, so it has lots of good books. Someone has kept up Canada's image by donating such barnburners as "The History of Hansard"[2], "Canadian Fishes", "The Life of John A. McDonald"[3] and other popular volumes.

And July 18, 1987:

> Let's see; what else did we do on our spel (leave)? I got Holly out with some people for kava—she wasn't all that impressed.

> But, wait! There's more:

> The weather in Vila was cloudy and showery, but it started to get better as the weekend approached, and was pretty good for our big day on Saturday and perfect on Sunday. Saturday started out with Holly noticing some small scabs on Laurel's scalp. Fortunately, I am somewhat wiser in the ways of the world, and examined the scabs for legs, which of course they had. Lousy kids! Heather also had a few, and Laurel had lots of nits. We only had a half hour before our ride to the cruise, and everything closes for the weekend at noon Saturday. So, we warned the kids not to mention this little gem of information during the day and I whisked into town to get some louse shampoo (they have to keep their hair clean too, you know!) before we headed out.

---

[1] Foreshadowing our future, although of course our behavior in that situation was exemplary.

[2] The official record of the Canadian parliament. Who wouldn't want to read the history of that?

[3] Canada's first Prime Minister.

Excuse me while I take a break to scratch my head—power of suggestion, you know—admit it now, you're doing the same. We treated the entire family that night, and Holly picked up more shampoo and a nit comb Monday morning. It's been a week, and I think I'll give everyone the treatment again tonight. It's been a miracle that we haven't got them sooner. John and Kate have gone through 2 or 3 bouts so far.

Two lousy girls with Nicholas and David Gray on the Congoola. The boys' late father, Michael, was the only one working with me later at the NPSO who really knew what he was doing.

Anyway, we had a great day. We went out on a ketch (two–masted boat with steering wheel behind the second sail for you landlubbers) named the "Congoola", although we motored the whole way. I think the masts are just for the tourists, like at Disneyland. There was supposed to be just our group of 30, but the owners snuck on another 6 tourists to up their profit. First, we went to see a big cave on an island[1] . It was huge, and the walls had finger marks all around them in two rings, one for every man who had died on that island for the past thousand years or so. There were also paintings on the walls and the inevitable names and dates inscribed near the entrance, some reportedly dating back to the 1700's (I was busy looking at the paintings while the guide was talking about the dates). Then we went to another island and landed on a small isolated beach, where we snorkelled and drank beer and wine from the cooler

---

[1] Hat Island; guess what it looks like from Efate.

while the crew cooked up a big barbecue. All agreed that this was the South Pacific we had come to see.

Congoola Barbecue.

On the way home, Holly and I were up on the roof having a beer, while the kids were down on the deck playing around. Suddenly, everyone on the deck started making a fuss and rushed to the rail, pointing at the water. Holly jumped up and got pretty excited asking "Which child fell in?" (I was my usual relaxed shelf). It turned out to be a bunch of dolphins that swam along playing at the bow of the boat for quite a while. Every once in a while, a couple would go out to the side, jump a few times, and go back to the bow. I think the owners paid the dolphins for the show, or something. We also saw schools (or maybe flocks?) of flying fish in the morning.

While we were motoring along, we got fed croissants in the morning and fresh fruit and punch in the afternoon. I trust you're all green with envy. Fortunately, the sea was calm, so I wasn't green.

Two Years on Malekula

Our last bush leave:

August 10, 1988:

> Even though I bought her a truck and sweated blood to make it run, Holly is going bush because she hasn't been off Malekula for eight months. We've temporarily stopped buying spare parts and cut down on gas and food this month, so that by also getting a big advance on next month's pay, we can spend the last two weeks of this month in Vila. I persuaded CUSO that Holly and the kids had to see the dentist and that since we didn't go on our spring bush leave to Santo, CUSO should buy their tickets to Vila (double the price to Santo). In my opinion, a trip to Santo is a trip to the bush, rather than away. Picture one street lined with a dozen Chinese general stores, all selling the same stuff, the monotony broken only by the ruins of the old WW II whorehouse set up for the 250,000 American servicemen. Or, should that be "serviced men"?

> We've traded houses for our Vila trip with a guy who's building a wharf here and has a wife and child in Vila.

August 14, 1988:

> We are going to Vila on Friday for a 2 weeks' vacation. We planned ahead for this one and started a crash savings programme 2 weeks ago. We now have one-half month's pay in our account for this trip—pretty amazing, eh? That's about 4 times what we usually have at this point of the month. I figure we'll just do what we did last time—get a big advance on next month's salary and then succeeding smaller advances in the following months until we are back to living on our monthly pay. When you're a volunteer, you don't have to be responsible.

Walking Across Southern Malekula

From an August 7, 1987 letter to family:

> I took Holly on her dream vacation this week, and have warned her that its memory will be dredged up on any future occasion that she complains about her lot in life.

> Put on an appropriate record [1], and imagine, if you will... (Tiny bubbles, in the wine...) Strolling barefoot along volcanic sand beaches in the fabled South Pacific; Nights spent in romantic thatched beach bungalows;

---

[1] For my younger readers, these were vinyl disks on which sounds were stored as irregularities in a groove that spiraled from the edge towards the centre.

Two Years on Malekula

Authentic local cuisine; Live entertainment; Exotic drinks; Private nude swims; Leisurely cruises through mysterious tropical islands; Expensively-appointed yachts; Gazing over tropical seas at volcanoes spouting red fire... (...Make me happy, Make me feel fine...)

Yes, that once-in-a-lifetime tropical tour along the south coast of Malekula, in the Island Paradise of Vanuatu. Mind you, Holly alleges that a brisk walk for several hours a day behind Ni-Vanuatu guides, compounded by the difficulties of walking in ankle-deep soft sand, is not a stroll. She was barefoot because the blisters caused by her new thongs were infected, and walking was only possible with the assistance of 222s[1]. Our bush materials "rest house" at Hokai had a sand floor with only grass mats to sleep on—at least it didn't have a galvanized roof, from which our condensed breath dripped on us all night, like the one in Mbonvor. Our diet consisted of boiled taro with coconut cream or, when news of our impending arrival preceded us via pikinini, laplap prepared special for the honoured guests. Live entertainment consisted of me swapping songs with the local guys on a well-abused and un-tunable five-remaining-string guitar. One night, I overindulged on kava and had to lay about in a stupor, while Holly (having had only half as much) had a great time storianing with our host and wife. "Swim" in Bislama translates into "shower"[2], and it was only private because I held a cloth over the open doorway of the bamboo stall as Holly washed (I waited until dark). Our "speedboat" trip of the last day was leisurely because the number of people in and on the five-metre boat matched the number of horsepower of the outboard (fifteen). Yes, we did pass someone else's big yacht anchored by a beach. And, our view of the volcano was from Lamap, which even I describe as the "armpit of Malekula", as it is the largely abandoned and decaying former French administrative centre[3]. All I can say is some people don't know how to have a good time! I also harbour a conceit that I may have a career ahead of me as the author of travel brochures[4].

Holly and I spent Wednesday and Thursday composing the above, which is all true, depending on where you choose to place emphasis. It is all carefully crafted to continue my policy of twisting the knife, as the first section describes the vacation everyone wishes he could afford, and the second section the experience money can't buy. I trust you are either all drooling or hate my guts by now. "Love it; love it", as Dad likes to chortle.

---

[1] A Canadian over-the-counter concoction of acetaminophen and codeine.

[2] And any other activity that involves immersion in water, but "wasem" (wash) means to water them.

[3] Ransacked, for all I know "just because we can", by locals during the brief civil war at independence in 1980.

[4] Or a memoir.

Two Years on Malekula

Now for a more neutral description of our travels. I have been sitting around at work reading magazines and generally feeling kind of useless lately. I wanted to get out and see the Island, and Keith had been promising a tour of the South Coast sometime in the vague future, which never seemed to get any closer. John and Kate have been going off here and there to all sorts of interesting places. So Saturday I finally got off my duff and just decided to fly to Wintua, on the southwest corner of the island, on Monday; and make my way to Lamap on the southeast corner for the Friday flight home. I consulted a few people to ensure that a trail existed (there is no road) and got some approximate walking times from spot to spot. This doesn't really decrease the risk of a trip, since the Melanesian concept of time is a bit vague, as is the definition of "trail" (I'll just mention that the Bislama word is "rod", which covers everything from a superhighway to the spaces between lines of coconut trees). John and Kate offered to take the kids[1] , so Holly came along. We packed a daypack each with one blanket and a sheet between us, a change of clothes, and a bit of food (corned beef to supplement the exclusive local carbohydrate diet, crackers, and that essential—peanut butter.) Sorry, Dad, no shoes[2].

Monday, we flew the 15 minutes to Wintua. Lucky it was only a 15 minute flight, because it was rough and I, of course, felt sick. It was a good old Canadian Twin Otter though, so I knew I was safe. One of the joys of making sudden decisions like this is that no one knows you are coming, so we got the Area Council Secretary up from his nap (it was working hours, after all) and we spent the afternoon with him talking with the providers of various government services (education, health, etc.) in town—well, large collection of bamboo shacks, anyway. After a while, he stopped being crabby[3] , and we had a good session.

We didn't stay in the local rest house. You know, I always had this vision of the missionary in Vanuatu as some martyr who escaped being eaten on the beach and wasted away in an old shack suffering from various tropical diseases.

---

[1] Who had a great time, including getting rich filling coconut seedling bags with soil at 1 vatu per bag, and eating ice cream that we never bought them. Of course, stronghead Laurel had a little trouble one morning when she wouldn't get out of bed, even when John took away her Teddy bear. She finally capitulated when he poured water on her, which was good for her dark little soul.

[2] Dad was a strong believer in the necessity for sturdy footwear when working in developing countries. Standard volunteer footwear in Vanuatu was thongs along with shorts, but not t-shirts as I had been erroneously advised in Canada. Professionals in the NPSO also dressed this way. White-collar ni-Vanuatu always wear long pants and shoes, though.

[3] OK, I'm not a people person.

Two Years on Malekula

Not in Wintua. We stayed with the local Presbyterian Elder in the former missionary house—a large, well appointed western-style house, wired and plumbed (of course now you have to haul in a bucket of water from the standpipe in the yard to flush the toilet), with a magnificent view of the sunset from the expansive veranda.

The Secretary and a Chief asked if I drank kava, and off we went to make it. They asked me why I had ditched Holly, and I learned that Southwest Bay is the only area that I know of where women are free to drink kava. This is because kava is not traditional to all areas of Vanuatu, and the traditional non-drinking areas made up their own traditions when it was introduced to them. So, I got Holly, and we sat around and storianed as the kava was prepared. The Secretary came up with a bunch of roots that he had had around for a while and which had dried out. Everyone told me that this meant that it would be really strong, but I thought that it was the usual "our beer is stronger that the other country's" B.S.

Anyway, instead of shells for the kava, they had bowls, so I had just one, in accordance with my moderation policy, and Holly had a half-bowl. After a while of storian, I... started... to... talk... real... slow... and... figured... out... that... they... weren't... just... kidding... about... the... kava... being... strong. It didn't help that one bowl must be equal to about two shells. When dinner was announced, I staggered back to the house, but just didn't feel like eating for some reason. I sacked out in a stupor on the bed for an hour while Holly chatted away gaily with the Elder and his wife.

The next morning, Tuesday, we hopped into the local Agriculture Department "speedboat" (anything with an outboard motor—this 5.6-metre number was underpowered with 8 HP. I think anything with an inboard is classified as a "sip"). After 2 hours, we were deposited at Melip on the south coast. This place had a radio, and the Secretary had radioed ahead that we were on our way, so a guide[1] was ready. We had been warned that guides would be needed, and it was true. Although there was a trail the entire way, there is a whole network of trails going to gardens, copra patches, etc., and it would be real easy to get off on the wrong one. They need some Germans over here to get them organized with a system of little symbols at every trail junction, with corresponding markings on the maps[2].

---

[1] As a government official, I took it upon myself to appropriate a guide on each leg of the walk that week. Usually, it was someone who wanted to go where we were off to.

[2] I did some hiking in Baden-Württemberg in the summer of 1973. As per the stereotype of Germans, the trails were very well organized.

Two Years on Malekula

Southwest Bay. The small island is known locally as "Ten-Stick Island" because it was bought by the American armed forces in WWII for ten sticks of tobacco and used for a practice bombing target.

We wandered through Mbwat Bang (the first waetmen in months) and past this Grade One class and teacher. They were out with 1-metre sticks measuring things. One of my favourite Vanuatu photos.

Two Years on Malekula

We trotted off after our guide, Ambol, and after 2 3/4 hr. and 8-10 miles, came to Malfakhal (also named Mbenvat)[1]. I had heard about a vocational school here that had been set up solely by the community.

The Marven Training Centre was set up by the local Presbyterian Church to convert the local heathen (their word) as they moved down from the hills and to teach agriculture and management skills. We spent the afternoon looking around and talking with the manager. They offer a two-year course of instruction interspersed with the students living at home and applying their new knowledge. The current class started out with about 20, and is now down to 8 as the rest "made mistakes in life, wanted to go home", etc. The Australian Gov't just gave them a generator and a few electric hand tools and they want to set up a furniture factory. Why they need power tools and where their market is, I don't know. The LGC just gave them a few sheets of roofing iron so they can build a shed for the generator and collect water for their new rainwater tank (built by the national NGO aid agency—controlled by the governing party, as is everything—without any iron roof for catching rainwater in sight, as is often the case). Their fondest wish is now for a chainsaw. Their budget is about $1,200 per year, and I don't know where they intend to get gas for the generator, let alone a chainsaw. Chainsaws here have a life of about 1 year, which would kind of leave the training centre out in the cold when it breaks. Community-defined development is a great thing.

Late that afternoon, we continued on with a new set of guides for a half-hour to Mbonvor (silent M, so why bother?) Of course, we had earlier passed through Mbwat Bang, silent M and w, where our impending arrival had been announced by tell-a-pikinini [2], upon which the local women had busied themselves making a couple of special laplaps. Um, um, good! (Not my favourite dish) At least our visit gave the villagers an excuse for a (to them) special meal. I should mention that Whitemen, while not unknown, are a bit of a rarity in these parts. The occasional tourist comes around to intrude on the Small Nambas up in the hills, but that's another story. The odd aid worker also comes through—funny, all the ones I was told about were volunteers; no fully-funded types. A Yorkshireman is down there building water supplies for the villages and went through this area planning systems a while back, a CUSO with the Lands Dept. went through a few months ago; and an American working for a New Zealand agency spent 2 years as an Ag Rep in the area a year or two ago. In several places, I got the impression that this scarcity of

---

[1] I have no idea why some places had two local names.

[2] Take-off on old joke: "What are the three fastest means of communication? Telegraph, telephone, and tell-a-woman." "Pikinini" being Bislama for "child". My boss, Keith Mala, was mystified when I told him that calling a black child a pikinini in North America might result in a punch in the mouth. After puzzling it out a while, he suggested that perhaps if the "k" was changed into "g" as is commonly done in Vanuatu, it might be thought that you were calling the child a pig.

The friendly people of Mbonvor.

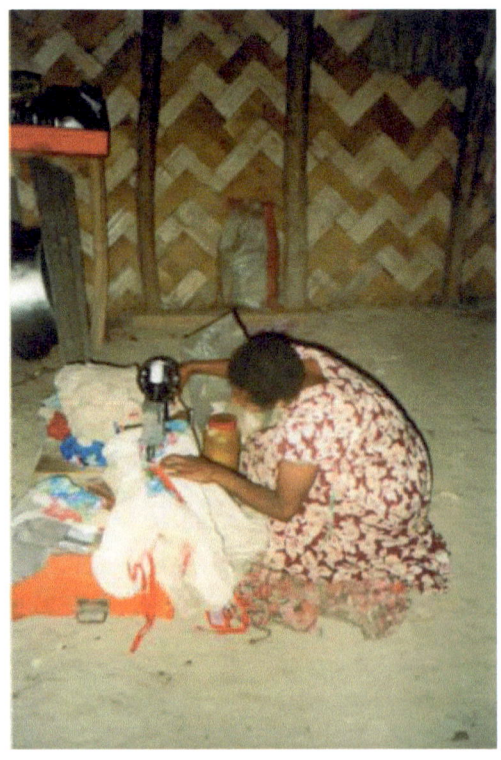

Mbonvor woman sewing island dress with hand-crank sewing machine.

Whitemen and government employees wasn't perceived to be all that undesirable. I think that the only time they regularly see a gov't employee is at head-tax time every June.

The Mbonvor women hauled a couple of bushels of trash out of the "haus blong ol woman"—ladies' clubhouse—and we were installed with a foam mattress and kerosene wick lamp. Dinner was duly laid on, during which a man asked me when I intended to hold the meeting. I gathered that a meeting was expected of all government reps, and since I was supposed to be there on work, I sort of had to hold one. Later that same evening, the head honcho blew his shell trumpet, and all the men gathered in the community hall (women and children outside, peering in through chinks in the woven bamboo walls; fason blong Vanuatu). So, here I am, half-a-year after insisting to CUSO that I can handle community development, no sweat—having to actually fake it. I told them who I am, what I think I do, and asked if they had any community projects that they want some help with. After about a half-hour of discussion in their village language, it was suggested that they could use a bread oven. Whew, I thought, I can handle that. At least it's not something useless and expensive like a shiny new truck. After learning that nobody there had any idea how to build an oven, discouraging the notion of buying a generator and electric oven, and being assured that somebody at least knew how to make bread, I announced I would find out how to build a wood-fired oven, what materials were needed, and how much it cost. They allowed as how they could sell the bread and repay a loan for construction costs. I have seen such an oven in use on Ambae and there's always someone selling bread at the market here (I bought a loaf today), so I think the idea is feasible. It seems a shame to encourage the consumption of imported flour, but they are buying white rice now, so I guess it wouldn't make any net difference. Besides, bottom-up development dictates that you give people what they want, right? The theory is that after they have, as it were, got sick on junk food, they will graduate to a nutritious diet (if they're still strong enough to eat).

Next, the guy who had insisted on the meeting stated, if I understood him correctly, that if I wasn't talking bullshit (his term), I would present them with a new truck. I asked for clarification, and the request was rephrased. After pointing out that there wasn't a road within at least a day's walk, I was assured that if I gave them a truck, they would build roads to all their copra patches and use the truck for a community-run taxi. You have to sympathize with the request. These guys haul 60kg bags of dried copra out of the bush on their backs to the nearest cove that a small boat can land at. This is after gathering up enough coconuts to make up a Tonne of dried copra, cutting them open, scooping out the meat, carrying the wet meat to a dryer, and carrying firewood to the dryer. An incredible amount of labour to get 23,000 vatu, about $300. No wonder cash is used as little as possible. We had seen men carrying chunks of smouldering wood impaled on the end of their bushknives along the trail that day, in lieu of matches. The men of Mbonvor had walked about 40 minutes that evening just to return from where they had been making copra. I can also see the bitterness against Whitemen that culminated in the cargo cults on Tanna and elsewhere. To them, our vatu come effortlessly and abundantly.

Back to the real world, where Whitemen have to sweat and lead regimented lives in temperate climates to get the tax dollars to send trucks to people in the third world who don't maintain them and who leave them to rust after being unable to decide who is in charge of them. I told them that the Gov't didn't have enough money to give out trucks and they should consider applying for a loan, building the roads, and then taking out the loan for the truck. I think that killed the idea. Frankly, I would just halter-train a few of the many cattle around and use them to pack out the copra. I didn't make the suggestion, though, as I fear polite derision (or starved cattle haltered permanently to trees) would be the only result. Maybe I should have, though.

Village life does have a few quirks. Toilet facilities are interesting. Every village has two or three privies—usually about 100 metres from the nearest house. I've never seen a ni-Vanuatu heading in one's direction. They don't drink water, and they don't urinate [1]. The rumour is that they defecate in the ocean at night only. Nobody wants to spend any time in a filthy place like a toilet, and the missionaries that introduced them neglected to give instructions on cleaning them [2], so they are filthy. I don't use them myself—good example, eh? Once, at a village, I finally asked some men, "Yu go wea long pis-pis?" (Where do you go to piss)", and was dutifully led to an outhouse. It had obviously not been used by one of them for years, if ever—my foot went through the floor upon entry. The big problem is that villages are surrounded by coconut or cocoa trees, which provide open areas, not bush, so you can't just duck out for a quick leak. All you can do in self-defense is join them by not drinking, despite all those CUSO health lectures about dehydration and urinary infections [3].

After a night under the dripping roof, we had orange leaf tea the next morning, since a ship[4] hadn't been around for a few months and the

---

[1] This falsehood is what my high school English teacher told us was a figure of speech known as "exaggeration".

[2] In reality, they probably spent countless fruitless hours pushing the concept that "cleanliness is next to godliness". Who wants to clean a smelly toilet when all that bush and ocean is readily available?

[3] Of which I had my share on Malekula.

[4] Coastal trading ship bringing in vatu and goods, and taking away copra.

stores were out of everything—a common situation. A somewhat reluctant guide was commandeered for the trip to the next village, and we were off again. Whenever possible, these trails just were a beach, which was nice unless, as mentioned above, the sand was soft. Most of the trip was flat, but because I had talked with others who had done some bushwalking, I knew what was coming when our guide removed his thongs. We were soon also digging our toes into the mud on an almost-vertical path up a hill. It was only a short hill, though, and at the top, the guide told us the trail was easy to follow from here, and turned back.

Guide grinning down at white lady climbing steep trail barefoot, flipflops in hand. My right knee brushed against a nangalak leaf on the way up, resulting in a burning rash for the next week-and-a-half.

Two Years on Malekula

View back towards Umbeb Bay, along which we had just walked. Our friend, Simon Wilkins, whose father had been the British District Agent during colonial times, told us that his family used to take the official boat down here to enjoy the beach and surf. This is one of the rare beaches in Vanuatu with surf.

After Mbonvor, nobody knew we were coming, which wasn't all bad (no more laplap). On our way to Farun, the next village, upon rounding a corner, we caught a glimpse of a woman coming our way on the trail. When we reached the spot, however, all we found were two bags of ocean snails and a bushknife hastily dropped on the trail—their owner had taken off into the bush and was undoubtedly peering out from behind a tree. Near to Farun, we sang out "Howdy" to a woman cutting cocoa, and she just about jumped out of her skin.

My intention had been to visit the government Agriculture Representative stationed at Farun and beg a tour of the area in his speedboat, but we had learned from people met on the trail that he had gone the previous week to Lamap for the July 30 Independence Celebrations and hadn't returned yet. We found his assistant (recognizable by his badge of office—rubber boots, one with large hole), and spent a couple of hours chewing the fat and resting up. The Ag. Assistant came up with a few kumala, and we had lunch. Only adolescents were around, as all adults spend the day out in their gardens or making copra (the gov't marketing agency price just went up—world price hasn't risen, but there's an upcoming election in November), and all children were at school on a nearby island. A girl from Farun recently came to Lakatoro to visit her brother, who works at the Agriculture Station here. This is the big smoke for her; she had never seen a motor vehicle before.

Everyone remaining for the day in Farun.

After some discussion, we decided to push on that afternoon to Hokai, and the Ag. Assistant agreed to go with us so he could visit relatives. This was a long day, I estimate 18-20 miles, and this segment was where Holly ran into trouble with her feet and legs. Even ni-Vanuatu are impressed when I tell them we walked from Mbonvor to Hokai in one day. It was really only 7 hour's walking, but as I have said, these guys don't waste any time on the trail. I didn't find it too bad, as we weren't carrying much weight, but for some reason Holly's thongs rubbed her toes and the quick long strides were hard on her knees. It was nothing for a triathlete from Alberta [1].

Hokai, like many of the villages here, was really quite nice, if you don't need a toilet. You wouldn't expect it, but many of the villages here are laid out on a grid, with streets between the bamboo and palm-thatch houses. The streets are often lined with decorative bushes and shrubs. All of the ground at Hokai is covered with a layer of white sand, which is

---

[1] I had done a few short triathlons in Victoria, British Columbia, and had grown up in Alberta, whose inhabitants can be considered a little obnoxious by other Canadians.

nice. They had a fairly new rest house with two rooms, one with table. It was very clean and had coconut leaf mats covering the bedroom floor. One of the chiefs got a couple of pandanus leaf mats and a pillow for us from his house. Don't ask me why, but lots of villages elect two chiefs, and there is often a custom chief too. We got boiled taro for supper, which like kumala is quite good with coconut cream.

Holly and Lesli Kalson, our guide for this section, crossing a river. I note that nobody ever offered to carry *my* pack.

Hokai Village. Village woman is next to one of the village water stand-pipes; Holly is in the doorway of the village rest house where we slept.

Two Years on Malekula

I guess I haven't mentioned that we were, of course, the main item of entertainment at these villages. The women of Hokai were quite shy, but Holly won them over with her witty conversation and by holding the chief's baby. Whenever we arrived at a village, it was always insisted that we go into the rest house or equivalent to "spel" (rest), and everyone around crowded in and stood around looking at us. All the kids peered in the windows and through the holes between the bamboo. If we announced that we thought we might take a nap, we were told to just go ahead—don't mind us. After we laid down and shut our eyes, everyone would steal away silently and go back to their business.

There was one sad thing about Hokai. All ni-Vanuatu really love children, and always asked us all the details about ours. Here, however, like many villages, there was a complete absence of children because they were off at school. The nearest school to Hokai is on Akhamb Island, off Farun, which, as we well knew, was a good 3 1/2 hour walk away. The children all board there and come back only every 4 months for school break. This is a common situation. The schools don't seem very healthy places to me—Heather's is right in mosquito territory and there are no screens. The diet is mostly white rice, I think. Nevertheless, even though education is not compulsory and it isn't likely that most students will leave the village, almost everyone sends their kids off to primary school. If their children's marks are high enough to qualify, many families really sacrifice to send their kids on to high school, which must be paid for.

That evening at Hokai, I cleverly staved off any meeting by remarking that I could hear a guitar being played and asking if anybody had a spare one. The vintage five-stringer was produced, and the village crowded into and around our hut. I wowed them all with "Hey, Hey, Good Lookin'", followed by "I Saw The Light"—to think they hadn't been introduced to Hank Williams before! Good thing the Canadian Taxpayer shelled out to get me down here before it was too late! We traded the instrument back and forth a while, but my problem is that, although I know lots of songs in my books, I haven't actually memorized very many of them. I managed to dredge up a few, though, and tried to explain what they were about. They all knew what a cowboy was, but I don't think I was able to get the "rodeo" concept over too well after "Someday Soon". Their songs were all very beautiful, even the one we've heard Laurel sing zillions of times—"Jesus Said I Am The Way" (or Whale, depending on whose [1] interpretation it is). Three other sources of distraction were, as always: 1. my underwater camera and its price, 2. my topographic map of South Malekula, and 3. my US Army-style can opener. My camera is

---

[1] I.e., Laurel's. She also managed to transform "Jesus took my burdens, and threw them in the sea" to "Jesus took my babies...". Why do we have children? To laugh at them while they're young, and embarrass them later on.

Hokai guitarist/singer. He was very good; apparently we caught him
on his way to "swim", or bathe in one of the community showers.

good, because I can lock the shutter and just hand it to the crowd to play
with. Because it has a thick plastic case, it is difficult to harm.

Of course, after playing "I Saw The Light" and "Michael Row The Boat
Ashore", everyone wanted to know what church we go to. Holly has
picked up an unfortunate habit of responding to this question by telling
people that we are "olsem man blong bus", which to them means
"heathen", to which they cluck their tongues and tell us no, we couldn't
be that bad. I just say I don't have a church, and when inevitably pressed
quiet them with the statement that my father is a Presbyterian [1] (you have
no idea how difficult it has been for me to learn to spell that).

One of the Hokai chiefs, John Miller, told us a good shark story. I guess
one day a big hammerhead shark came in close to the village, and people
were frightened that it might eat a child playing in the water. Well, I
would have just told the kids to keep out of the water until the shark
swam away after a while, but John hopped in his trusty outrigger canoe

[1] At least a 50% truth.

Canoes drawn up on Hokai beach.

with a spear and went after it. When he stabbed it, it attacked the canoe, breaking the outrigger and throwing John into the water, where it proceeded to take a chunk out of his butt. Rather than turning the other cheek, when it came in again, he grabbed it by the elongated head and managed to roll over it. After a couple rounds of this, the shark retreated with his spear. A draw, I guess. You have to be quick on your feet around here.

This is probably as good a place as any to go into this man blong bus business, and if it isn't, I'm going to anyway. Most of the people on the coast of Malekula have only come down from the hills since the late forties. When modern rifles became widely available up there, the inter-tribal rivalries became overly lethal, and people fled to the coast, which was controlled and policed by the colonial powers. There is a plaque at Mbonvor which says that the first Christian came there in 1949. A few hundred people up in the mountains of Southern Malekula still follow the custom way of life, although they send some of their kids down to the coast to stay with relatives and go to school. John Kamphorst went up there for a couple of days two weeks ago to look at their cattle. He was accompanied by a guy who came down to the coast with his father and family in the 60's. John reports that these people in the hills are the real thing—bones in noses, no clothes, hunt with bows, strictly follow custom, etc. At the first village he came to, the chief sat him down and told him in no uncertain terms that, unless he was there for work only, he could just turn around and go back. The week before, a couple of American tourists had had 1000 vatu extracted from them and been turned back at spear point after the woman had entered the village along a path that was tabu to women. John figures that they tolerated him because he had come by a difficult, circuitous route in order to see some other cattle projects on the way. What they wanted in a professional way from John was advice on how to trap wild cattle. This, of course, is right up John's alley, so he filled them in on using salt to lure cattle into corrals. There is also some thought of raising calves to lead down to the coast for sale. I am trying to convince John that an agricultural economist would be of use on his next trip up there, but I don't think I'm having much success [1].

Back to our walk along the south coast. On Thursday, the plan was to walk for a couple of hours to Avok Island and catch a speedboat to Lamap Point, and then walk to Lamap to speak with the South Malekula Area Council Secretary before flying back to Lakatoro on Friday morning. First, though, to justify my trip, I asked one chief if the village had any projects it wanted. He immediately said, yes, they wanted some improvements to the water system, which is seven public standpipes fed from a spring up the hill. The taps were only about 1/2 metre off the ground, so kids play with them (two are broken) and dogs lick them to get water. They want the pipes extended to 1 metre's height. So, all that is required is 7 pieces of 50 cm pipe with threaded connections and a couple feet of Teflon tape. One problem is that the nearest pipe is in Lakatoro, but that can be sent down. The real problem is that the nearest pipe wrenches are also in Lakatoro, and sending them down with a man is expensive. Not insurmountable; I could bring them down with the pipe on another trip. I have since checked with Rural Water Supply, though, and found that the village is due for a complete new water supply early next year, so the problem is solved. The new standard includes 1 metre standpipes and showers. This village had built showers by running hoses to nearby stalls, where the water sprayed from cans with holes in them. Crude, but effective [2].

The chief also wanted to show me a problem with the spring. With the feeling that I was glad I was inspecting the source of our drinking water after we had been drinking it, I followed him. My premonition was correct: I had been spared a lot of concern. The spring was full of the dainty footprints of cattle. I paced off the area and found that 500 metres of barbed wire would fence it. Water trickles below the dam all year, so

---

[1] I eventually made it there on LGC business.

[2] When followed by, "Neat, but not gaudy", a common saying of a man I once worked with in Australia after he had built something.

there is no incentive for the cattle to break the fence. I asked the chief if I found the wire, would the village build the fence[1] ? He seemed a little taken aback, but said they would. I later found that these guys all know that it is the village responsibility to fence the springs, but since they pay the princely sum of 1000 vatu per man (500vt per woman) head tax each year, they expect the gov't to do it. Meanwhile, everyone drinks water spiked with cow manure and urine[2]. I priced wire in Lamap at 3700 vatu for a 500 metre roll, which, with staples, means that if all 18 households in Hokai chipped in 300 vatu each, they could solve the problem the next time someone went to Lamap. I think I'll make the suggestion. Bottom-up development means weaning oneself from dependence on others [3].

The chief wasn't too willing to provide a guide to Avok Island, since everyone had just been there two days before for a wedding, but after I said we would then go on our own, said he would dragoon some poor kid for the job. Just when we were returning to the village, salvation (for him, and I'll admit it, for us, as Holly's feet had had it) turned up in the form of a speedboat coming into shore. It was on its way to Lamap Point, but when I tried to ascertain the price, I was puzzled by the captain's question as to my employer and his statement that he would work it out later with Andre Marshal, the Area Secretary.

We hopped in anyway. This was the 5 metre boat of the first page of this letter. At this point, we had seven on board (no life jackets, as per usual). We stopped in at Avok Island for another 4, then at the Maskelynes Islands for a further 4. Then I learned that we had lucked into a boat that was picking up all of the South Malekula Area Councilors and taking them to Lamap Point, were we would be met by a truck to take us to Lamap for an Area Council meeting. Not only did we get free transport, but I finally got to attend an Area Council Meeting.

When we hit Lamap, Holly and I celebrated our return to civilization by heading to the nearest store and each eating a chocolate bar (only slightly stale) immediately. All of our fellow travelers hit the same store and loaded up on cargo (aluminium[4] kettles and wash basins, thongs, big bags of flour, etc.) to take home that evening. It's not every day you get a free ride to the big city in that neck of the woods. Maybe I should mention that a store here is a single small room with maybe a thousand

---

[1] Of course, they could have just fenced it off with bamboo from the adjacent grove, but it was the principle that counted—the government was supposed to do these things.

[2] The chief allowed that he knew the contaminated water was making the village children ill. But, it was the principle…

3 I later caved and brought them some wire and staples. Fason blong CUSO cooperant.

4 Non-North American spelling and pronunciation.

dollars (make that a hundred in a small village) of merchandise scattered around the walls behind a counter.

I won't bore you with the meeting details, but our stay in Lamap was uneventful, except for me wearing a piece of the hide on my butt off while riding in a trailer behind a tractor back to the airport, and we flew home on Friday.

Now, instead of lacking work, I have a pile of it to follow up on — all the stuff I found out and was asked along the way.

The sight that greeted us upon our return to Lakatoro. John and Kate Kamphorst spoiling the girls rotten with ice cream cones. Note that the little traitors aren't exactly running to greet us. Laurel and Heather would ask us why they didn't get ice cream cones every day like all the other kids in Lakatoro. We pointed out that the other kids never got to eat meat because their parents spent their food budget on ice cream cones; I'm not sure they were impressed with the explanation.

White Ladies Make Wedding Cakes

From a September 4, 1987 letter:

> For some reason, there haven't been any eggs for sale here for the past month or so [1]. John and Kate were really sweating a few weeks ago, because she had promised a guy who works for John (the one who picked up the wife on Ambrym for 80,000vt) that she would bake him a wedding cake. He ordered a big white tiered cake with lots of fancy coloured trim. White people can do anything, you know.
>
> She finally told him that he would have to provide the eggs, so I guess the village of Litzlitz was scoured and 5 were produced. One exploded when she put it down on the counter, another was also rotten, and the other three had chickens in them. Finally, she hit up some expats at Lambubu[2] and got some from their chickens. She made two round cakes, frosted them white with blue trim, and stood the second layer on four toilet paper tubes covered with foil. I hear it went over real big. Willy was really proud that, of the three local weddings in August, his was the only one where the couple's children weren't in attendance—he told John that his was the only "Christian" one. The other weddings occurred because our bud Sister Judith has been having some success at working at these guys to get straight with the church. You know there is a family involved when it is a "wedding and a blessing". We haven't been invited to a wedding yet, but my ex-counterpart, Lambert, once said we could come to his. I may have told you that he was going to get married last year, but decided to buy a truck instead. His last payment was last month, so he's all set to go. I think woman blong hem is anxious to get on with it, since their one-year-old will be blessed at the same time. I asked him if he had to pay extra for a proven breeder, but I got the impression that this wasn't a joking matter. Maybe we won't get asked to the ceremony, after all [3].

One morning, a young ni-Vanuatu woman knocked on our door with an emerg-

---

[1] An annual event, as hens in Port Vila commercial egg farms stopped laying for a period, perhaps due to changes in daylength.

[2] Location of Metenesel Estates Ltd.

[3] We weren't.

ency. Her wedding was that afternoon, and a friend had sent her a wedding gift of a cake from Vila. Unfortunately, it had not survived the Twin Otter flight north. Someone had sent her to the missis [4] up the hill for assistance.

Holly agreed to help, and as the woman left, she turned and said that we were invited to the reception, too.

Holly hustled down the hill to the co-op store to buy eggs. We already had the other ingredients, including the vanilla extract we made from finely chopped vanilla beans [5] soaked in a half-full pop bottle of vodka. (Thank you, "The Joy of Cooking".)

Holly made a nice layer cake, frosted with white icing and decorated with frangipani flowers. It was gratefully received.

Holly and I put in a short appearance at the wedding reception that evening, where the bride and her police officer husband in dress uniform made a striking couple.

---

[4] Bislama for "white woman". A white man is "masta"; their children "smol missis" or "smol masta". A ni-Vanuatu labourer is "boi". A sentence one does not hear in Canada was once said by a shopkeeper, serving my visiting father, to a black staff member, "Boi, karem bia ia long trak blong masta." Or, "boy, carry this beer to the masta's car." The true translation is, "Employee, carry this beer to the white man's car."

[5] Readily available at a French-owned supermarket in Vila, although the only vanilla extract in the country was artificial. I have my standards.

The proud couple.

Two Years on Malekula

Stan Gets Blessed by a Cardinal [1]

From a September 13, 1987 letter to my family:

This week suddenly turned into wik blong lafet (party week) on Tuesday. Keith was told that Cardinal Gantin, who as the Pope's personal emissary has come for the Catholic Church's centenary in Vanuatu, had unexpectedly decided to tour Malekula on Thursday; and that the Government's new patrol boat (i.e. the navy) would be here this Sunday morning. One thing that ni-Vanuatu are good at organizing is a party. Quick as a flash, two days of lafet (i.e. PARTY TIME!) were set up. I think it's just a matter of interest. The legacy of several hundred years of traditional affluent subsistence and a century of western hand-outs is that the only thing lots of people genuinely think is worth working to organize is ceremonies and parties.

I spent the day tailing after the Cardinal since I wanted to see the custom dancing and visit the small island of Vao. When Sethy Reganvanu (local MP, my minister, and Deputy PM) tours Malekula, he receives the Royal Treatment and gets to sit in the front seat of the LGC's old green Land Cruiser station wagon. Caesar gets what is his, but God gets his due—the LGC gave the Cardinal the Imperial Treatment and pulled their minibus out of service for the day to ferry him around. I sat in the back, but because I was in the party, I was once again an Honoured Guest and seated front and centre at all functions (except Mass—you'd think they would be consistent).

Once again, these Catholics tripped me up. We were all lined up to greet the Cardinal on the airstrip, and the plane pulled up. I've seen parts of "The Thornbirds" and know what a Cardinal looks like, but out came this tall black guy who wasn't even wearing a white collar. I was still waiting for the Cardinal—you know, in red robes and everything. I still think they should wear signs or something. He didn't even kiss the ground. Anyway, all the custom dancers did their thing, all the speeches were given (in French—the official language of the Vanuatu Catholic Church) and the Cardinal came down the reception line making polite comments to everyone. I was the first Whiteman that he hit, and midway through his sentence, I realized that he was speaking French! Fortunately, I was able to understand "Est que vous residez ici?", and answer "Oui" before he moved on to Ross Combden at my side. He asked Ross "Vous aussi?", and Ross got away with a nod[2].

---

[1] And, I don't mean shat upon by a bird.

[2] In turn, for those without the benefit of Canadian high school French, which is apparently not part of the Newfoundland curriculum: "Do you live here?", "Yes", and, "You too?".

His Eminence, Bernardin Cardinal Gantin, Archbishop
of Cotonou. I should have recognized him because he
was the one wearing shoes.

We all hopped in the bus and drove off very carefully to Unmet on the
west side of Malekula, where we were entertained by custom dancers,
this time Big Nambas. These guys were the first custom dancers I had
seen to actually wear their nambas.[1] Lakatoro's side of the island is
relatively civilized and custom dancers all wear shorts. There were also
women wearing their long red wigs[2] made of long pandanus fibres dyed
red, as were the men's nambas, but some wore basket blong titi and
others had draped towels over their shoulders, perhaps in deference to
His Eminence. I'll send the pictures after I have them developed. Then off
to the priest's house for half a soft drink (have you ever clinked glasses
with a Cardinal?), and off again.

---

[1] Penis wrappers, large bundles of red fibres in the case of Big Nambas people.

[2] Made of long pandanus fibres dyed red, as were the men's nambas.

Two Years on Malekula

Unmet Big Nambas people dance for the Cardinal. The pig to the left was killed with a club to the head soon after, a traditional way of marking an important occasion. I took this photo from my usual spot seated with olgeta bigman.

We went off to the Mission at Walarano (where our buds Sisters Judith, Danielle, and Patricia live), a village opposite the small islands of Wala and Rano. After speeches and songs of welcome, we went into the church for mass (my second one in a month; I'm becoming a Catholic by osmosis). As Honoured Guests, all us non-priests from the bus were seated just inside the door in real chairs. The great unwashed all sat on benches.

Just as the first people started coming in after us, some guy just happened to be shaking our hands. You have to live here to appreciate what next happened. Receiving lines are a national institution, and upon entering and leaving a village, you often shake hands with the entire population, who are lined up for the purpose. Well, when the first guy who came in saw me (next to door) shaking this guy's hand, he put his out, and the chain reaction started. We shook hands with every man (we were on the men's side of the church) who entered the church, and it is a big one. Also all their kids. Luckily, handshakes here are limp-wristed, milquetoast single shakes, except when you run into some guy who wants to demonstrate that he knows fason blong Whiteman and crushes your hand.

Then things started happening the way they are supposed to. In paraded the priests in their white robes and the Cardinal (also in white, darn it) with a big gold miter hat on and a big staff with a gold crook on the end. When he took off his hat—at last, a red beanie. Then we had a long mass in which the police inspector and Keith, who are not Catholics and were sitting to my right, only reluctantly stood up when everyone else did during the prayers. Ecumenicalism isn't real big here in Vanuatu. The Sisters later told me that they were disappointed that the Mass was so short. Before communion, the custom dancers all danced down the aisle with gifts for the Cardinal.

Cardinal Gantin in traditional dress.

Afta, as they say here, ol bigman olgeta retired to the Sisters' house for drinks and snacks. Knowing that this would be the only can we would hit during the day, I headed off for it. Unfortunately, I glanced back down the hall, and here came Sister Patricia with the Cardinal (now in a white robe with red sash) after me. I felt I should stand aside and let him go first, so I had to wait. Maybe I should have stayed true to the family's

Congregationalist roots and demonstrated that all men are equal before God by making him wait. I managed to get the Imperial Treatment on his coattails, though. The Sisters haven't had piped water for months, but hauled in water to fill the toilet tank, and I got to use the flush toilet too, rather than the outhouse.

There was a big spread of food out, which everyone but me was ignoring. I thought it was lunch, but it turned out to just be appetizers. We all headed out for lunch of Whiteman-style food at a table (other ranks got laplap while sitting on the ground) while being entertained by more custom dancing. One dance had a guy shooting fish (in the form of other men wearing masks with big carved fish on top of their heads) with a bonara (figured out what that is yet?), but his bow broke when he drew it, and he had to throw the arrows like spears instead—he didn't miss a beat. Ni-Vanuatu are nothing if not adaptable.

Back into the bus, and off to Vao Island. At Vao mainland, mats (strewn with frangipani blossoms, as was the ground everywhere we went) had been put down from the bus to the beach for us to walk on. (We had walked on a special kind of palm fronds at Walarano). All the boys on the bus also collected leis at each stop. You hide them under the seat before you get to the next place, so you can be greeted with new ones.

Cardinal Gantin carried in canoe on Vao Island.

From the beach, the welcoming committee carried the Cardinal through the water to the open boat, and everyone else had to get their shoes wet. Except me, of course; I wear appropriate footwear to all of these occasions—rainbow thongs with "Hawaii" and little palm trees printed on the straps (because this was a formal occasion, I was wearing my white ginger aloha shirt instead of the Magnum, PI one. I also don't get my pants wet, because I wear shorts). There was a huge crowd on the island and they brought down an outrigger canoe decorated with flowers, put the Cardinal in it, and carried him to the church. Again, everyone but me got their shoes wet, although I guess it didn't matter by then. A short church service (no leis for the bus people this time, just a special bench behind the children's choir), and back to our boat. Lambert, my first counterpart, was there, and happy because the Cardinal had touched his baby's head. We tried to find the guy who had made, but not yet delivered, my canoe, but he was still in Vila for the Cardinal's visit (I'll bet he and all the other hundreds of Vao people that made that trip to catch a glimpse of the Cardinal were really put out when they learned that he was making an unplanned visit to their home island). I had brought money and everything, on the chance that I might meet Lambert and get the canoe. Maybe I could have tied it to the top of the bus, or something.

As we left Vao Island, Cardinal Gantin placed his lei on the water.

Back towards Norsup, we stopped by the road at mainland Atchin for a few minutes. These poor people had started up the custom dancing and everything when we came into sight on the way to Vao, only to be left standing open-mouthed when we just rolled on through. This time, the Cardinal stood on the veranda of the store and gave a short talk and led a prayer. I have to admit there was something moving about seeing him there on a dusty old stoop speaking to dirt-poor people who had been waiting a long time to see him.

Cardinal at Atchin Mainland.

Then on to Norsup, where they tried to avoid showing him the disgusting PRV plantation housing by bringing him around the back way to the church. A gate was locked, however, and although he walked the last few yards, they brought the bus around later and took him out via main street, which is a disgrace—ramshackle corrugated iron shacks, some with only a cloth hanging for a door. None of the houses have glass windows, just openings cut in the iron that can be propped open. I had never been inside the Norsup church before, but it is like the town—dirty and worn. There weren't too many people there, because the company hadn't let anyone off work (there wasn't any work done anyway, so they might as well have), and people had given up waiting, since it was late afternoon. The people were disappointed because they were only allowed to sing two songs for him and he just gave his short talk and led the prayer. All along, except at Walarano where we spent a few hours, people had unrealistic expectations of the time allotted them. The priest from

Two Years on Malekula

Vao, who sat beside me in the bus, told me that when the Cardinal was carried up to the church there, women started squeezing coconut milk on fresh laplap (as I've said before, it never pays to let anyone know you are coming). He had to tell them to give it up. Everyone probably had a big party after we left, though.

Apparently, a group of people took it upon themselves to wait at Mae in the hope that the group would stop there. They should have just all come to Norsup, of course, as there wasn't any time to make extra stops.

We all headed to the airport to wait for the plane (the visit was made on regular commercial flights and the other passengers must have wondered what the heck was going on when they saw the crowd and custom dancers all lined up that morning.) The Cardinal posed for pictures with everyone who wanted one, and engaged in small talk. He is from Benin. I really had to look that one up in my atlas. It is really Dahomey, scene of Gerald Durell's "Balfor Beagles" and my gazetteer tells me it is now a "people's republic" (no wonder he wore a red hat). He told one of the sisters next to me that he is 65, and just visited his mother, who is 85. He looked about 45 to me.

Sisters Danielle and Judith with Cardinal Gantin at the Norsup airstrip.
The Sisters were annoyed because the Fijian woman in the centre
kept pushing her way next to the Cardinal.

Anyway, we all lined up to shake hands again (I got a "God Bless"[1] , presumably because I let him use the can first at Walarano) and he got on the plane. As per custom here, we all waited for the takeoff to wave as the plane went past, and then apparently at his request, the plane circled and buzzed the strip, angled so everyone could wave again. I have a theory that, since most airplane accidents happen in extremely close proximity to the ground, it is best to keep events like takeoffs and landings to the bare minimum. Therefore, I think anyone who intentionally makes unnecessary passes near the ground is nuts. Each to their own, though.

-----

[1] As per the title of this section.

Basil and Hanson's Wedding

January 27, 1988:

In early January 1988, Keith Mala and his wife Aslika invited us to the custom wedding of their adopted son[1] , Basil, and his affianced, Hanson, on the family home island of Ambae. It was a three-day affair, but although I laid down some heavy hints, we were not invited to the first day, where the bride killed some pigs in a custom ceremony.

The next day, Thursday January 7, things started out on the family turf of Hanson, the bride. Our three-year-old daughter, Laurel, was sick and intermittently vomited, but fortunately, we were all in the great outdoors, and Aslika just covered the mess up with leaves. We went to the site, and all the men were in and around a shed where kava was being served up; I had a shell, just to be sociable.

Men drinking kava at the start of festivities.

Most of the women were in another shed. In the center ground, a bunch of women were unrolling and stacking mats. On Ambae, mats are used to pay social obligations. Some are about 50cm by 150cm and dyed purple with designs printed with banana leaf stencils on them. Others are left white. This morning was, I think, an affair where the bride's family paid up mats and assorted cargo, all of which was eventually split between the two families. These mats stacked up about 1 metre high.

---

[1] Ni-Vanuatu mix and match children from family to family.

The bride appeared in a red dress and sat on a 5-gallon container of kerosene, which was one of the presents. She held a fan palm leaf like an umbrella over her head (you have to know how they use these leaves for umbrellas) and a sister sat behind her to lend a hand. Then, a whole bunch of mats were stacked on their heads. She had a hanky and cried into it the whole while, as she is supposed to be (and probably is) sad to be leaving her family. Then Hanson distributed some mats to her father and uncles.

Hanson with her family's present mats prior to her sister assisting her to hold up the mats on her head.

After, all the cargo was stacked on the mats It was a large pile of household goods such as washbasins, axes, cloth, dishes, plastic buckets, shovels, etc., etc. Hanson distributed some to her mother and aunts, and then representatives of both families moved in and carted off their shares of the cargo and mats. The bride's family had hired a large truck to haul off their share, and it was needed.

Next, we all moved several miles down the coast to Keith's village. The goings-on here were much more interesting, although there wasn't any kava. (Nominally an Anglican, Keith was also active in the "Holiness Fellowship", which prohibits the use of recreational drugs.)

The women from both families gathered on different ends of the village square. Then, they advanced on each other, hamming it up with ferocious expressions and actions, and engaged in mock combat. They separated, and Basil's side hid in a small shelter, made of palm fronds stuck into the ground, that surrounded a stone that had been planted in the ground; Keith later told me that this stone symbolized that lots of pigs were going to be given away. A banana plant had been stuck into the ground nearby, with a dead snake, head sticking out of ground, buried beneath it, and two or three live snakes, all non-venomous Pacific Boas, had been put up into the tree.

Shooting the snake with a banara (bow and arrow).
It's up there somewhere.

What followed was described variously as a test of courage, or a ritual only Keith's family was allowed to engage in[1] . Basil's aunts advanced from their shelter to the banana plant, with one woman armed with a toy bamboo bow and arrow. After several attempts, starting from two metres and moving progressively to point-blank range, she managed to bounce an arrow off one of the snakes in the tree. Then one of Basil's aunts gave another one a leg up, and she pulled down one of the snakes. One of Hanson's aunts came forward, and the fun commenced.

---

[1] I was never sure about some of these things. People would tell you what they thought you wanted to hear. Also, only some people had the right to disclose some information, and some kastom things were just plain secret to the uninitiated.

Bringing down a snake.

A tug-of-war ensued until the snake broke in half, and the pieces were thrown with gay abandon amongst the crowd. The head half of one snake tried to slither away, but was grabbed and thrown along with the other bits. All ni-Vanuatu are pathologically afraid of snakes, so this was accompanied with a lot of laughter, whooping, and hollering. People also threw around bits of long, wiggly vegetation to add to the fun. All of this was repeated until the aunts ran out of snakes.

The snake tug-of-war. This was the weirdest thing I saw
during more than five years in Vanuatu.

Now, they got down to the serious business of the bride price, which on
Ambae is paid in the social currencies of mats and pigs, preferably those
with circular tusks. First, Basil's male relatives paraded out, each carrying
a mat that is about 30 cm wide and reputed to be 100 metres long—I
would guess more like 100 feet. Each was rolled up from each end into a
double scroll. These were partially unrolled in about three stacks. Then
came the women relatives with hundreds of mats on their heads, which
were piled in stacks lined up behind the first three piles. Keith later told
me that there were 31 long thin mats, 500 red dyed mats, and 1,000 white
mats. Some of the mats were new, and some had obviously been traded
back and forth for quite some time.

After this, the men stuck 18 sticks into the ground and brought out 14
baskets and rice bags, each of which contained the skull of a tusked pig.
On Ambae, a pig skull counts as a live pig until it has been crushed in
another type of ceremony. Four live pigs, ranging from large castrated
males to a weaner, were also brought forward and tied to sticks.

Procession of Basil and brothers carrying bride price mats.

We inquired among the people around us, and were told that this was one of the largest bride prices in living memory. Keith's extended family will probably have to trade for mats for years before another son can get married. I hope they have a few adolescent girls in line.

The Bride Price. Piles of mats in the background, live tusked pigs and tusked pig skulls in bags in foreground.

Two Years on Malekula

Finally, Hanson's family rolled up a couple of trucks, loaded up all the booty, and the party was over. We got a ride back to where we were staying, dropping off various family members with their shares along the way.

Friday was the church wedding, which was a fairly standard Anglican service. The bride wore a traditional white gown, Basil's suit looked borrowed, and our five-year-old daughter, Heather, was a bridesmaid dressed in a long pink dress with white lace gloves and some yellow plastic sandals that Aslika had bought her. We had bought her some white thongs, but I guess they didn't come up to snuff.

The wedding party, with Heather peering out

After the service, the local men's soccer and women's volleyball teams all formed a line along each side of the path from the door of the hall (the local church was too small), and held sticks with streamers to make an arbour for the wedding party to stand in while they shook hands with everyone. Nobody kissed the bride. Then the crowd ate in shifts, by area of island they came from, and we had a couple of hours of speeches from men from both sides of the family. Keith took about 10% of his speech to thank me for coming [1].

After the speeches, at 1600 all of us invited guests got to go back inside the hall to eat a buffet lunch—Holly and Laurel had snuck into the general meal earlier, and I think Heather had something to eat when she was off changing.

---

[1] Another unexpected embarrassing hazard of being the Whiteman "honoured guest" wherever I went.

There must have been two or three hundred people in there, with only about 40 chairs. You can guess who had chairs reserved for them and who had to go eat right after the happy couple. When Basil and Hanson had eaten their fill, they politely gave their plates to relatives to finish up the food.

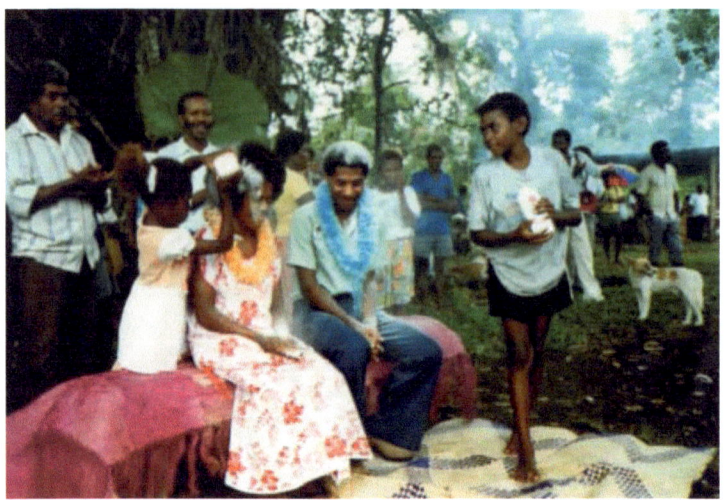

After service, dousing Hanson and Basil with baby powder.

Each guest was powdered as they gave Basil and Hanson their wedding present.

We went home with the girls after that, but I think there were two or three dances in various places all night.

Cyclone Bola

Cyclone Bola merits a special mention, because of the three major cyclone hits during our two years on Malekula, and a further three during another four cyclone seasons in Port Vila, it was the only one that lasted more than twelve hours or so.

For five days, Bola circled south of Malekula and again south of Efate before heading south to give New Zealand a real wallop; winds were less intense there, but New Zealand had lots of built-up infrastructure that was damaged. We had cyclonic winds and rain in Lakatoro for five days. You try sleeping for four or five nights listening to the wind and wondering if the next gust will take your roof off.

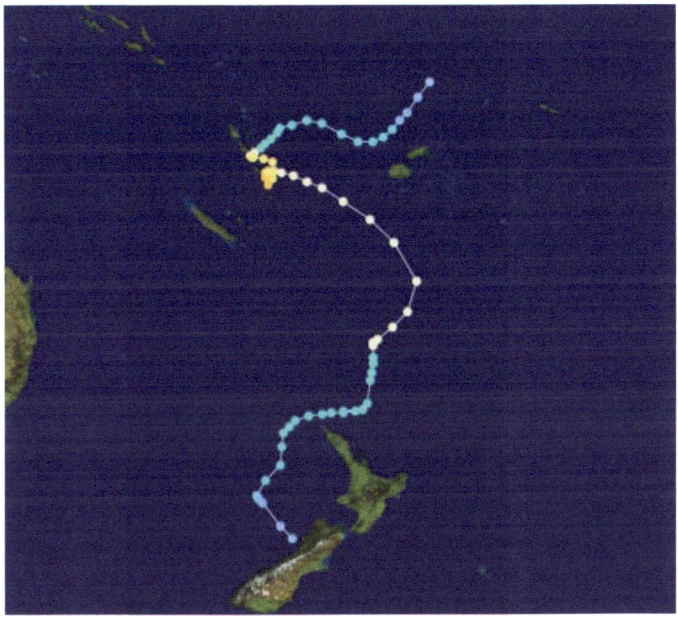

Cyclone Bola's track February 25 - March 8, 1988. Yellower indicates higher winds.

About 50cm of rain fell on Malekula, and for a week the island was covered with water running off to the sea.

Aop River crossing between Lakatoro and Norsup, washed out and impassable. Rebuilding crossings like this put a real dent in the Public Works Department budget. The river spread out substantially down where it entered the sea; that's where I crossed with the motorcycle.

Holly wading through Bola runoff, several days after the cyclone.

Heather Visits Uripiv Island

Uripiv Island was just off Lakatoro; it was the home of Sethy Reganvanu, Cabinet Minister, and several LGC staff. One of those staff had once started building a nice concrete-block house, only to have it torn down by the rest of the village on the grounds that, unless you are a Cabinet Minister or other Big Man, it isn't fair that your house be better than everyone else's. This, rather than emulating the example, is the normal ni-Vanuatu (and the rest of the third world, according to my Father) response to somebody trying to get ahead in the world. A Nepali once told Dad that living in the Third World was like everyone being in a bowl of hot soup, and whenever one person managed to get a leg over the rim to escape, everyone else pulled him back in.

Uripiv was also noted for its strain of chickens, which had tufts of feathers sticking out from the tops of their heads. We'd been over in the Fireball sailing dinghy in its powered form, and seen the old clapboard Presbyterian missionary church with the usual grave of a young English wife outside.

Grave of Helen Gillan, who died in childbirth, missionary wife on Uripiv Island off of Malekula near Lakatoro. Gravestones, sometimes many, of missionary wives and children were a common sight outside old Protestant missionary churches.

Two Years on Malekula

Sethy Reganvanu's sister, Madeline, was a fairly powerful member of the Uripiv community who didn't seem to be averse to attaining further prestige. I only knew her to say "Hi" to and don't know if she thought it would improve her status to have a white child visit or what, but she invited Heather over to the island for the night. Heather went over, and the next morning I was down at the Lakatoro landing stage to pick her up—but no Heather. I was told, "She was down at the beach, but looked like she didn't want to go, so we let her stay." I don't know if they let her get away with this because she was a "smol misis" or because of the ni-Vanuatu family practice of always keeping the youngest child happy. The youngest becoming, in turn, the next-youngest sharing the task of keeping the newborn happy. So, only one of the average 6 children per family ends up really spoiled.

There was no shortage of kids on Uripiv Island.

Perhaps there had been a shortage at one time, though. This cave used to house a tall, skinny, long-haired and -nailed person who ate children. When the villagers went to kill it, it ran to the sea and swam to Paama Island.

Two Years on Malekula

During our year-plus on Malekula we had observed that children are precious to ni-Vanuatu, so I wasn't too worried about Heather's wellbeing, although Holly had some misgivings. Nevertheless, the second day I told the men that if Heather didn't come home tomorrow, she was going to miss her birthday party. That did it. I don't know if the upcoming party motivated Heather to stop looking like she might cry down at the beach, or if the desires of a "masta" overruled those of a "smol misis", but Heather was at the landing stage the third morning.

Of course, we were curious about Heather's experiences on Uripiv. She told us:

"…the best one was one day when some men brought a sea turtle up on the beach. The men put it on its back, and it was waving its flippers, but they cut it up with an ax. Then, they built a fire, cooked the turtle meat, and had a feast. The kids got the best part: first, the kids cleaned out the tubes that the food went through, and then they put the tubes on sticks and roasted them over the fire. The tubes were really yummy!"

For me, this was too good to be true! Not only did we have a story to tease Heather with forever—You Ate Turtle Guts! —but I stored this in my mind in case a teenaged Heather ever came home and started lecturing us on environmental issues: "Yeah, but you ate an endangered species!"

Fason blong father; I don't know why our girls are all screwed up.

Further to Madeline Reganvanu: Shortly before I left Lakatoro, Madeline collected cash from the Uripiv women as their share of a Vanuatu National Women's Centre programme to build women's clubhouses in villages across the nation. She showed up in my office telling me I should forward the money to the Centre, so I did. Eight months later, I returned to Vanuatu and learned that the programme had fallen apart and all the cash sent in by village women's groups had disappeared. Fason blong Vanuatu.

I was then informed by Madeline that I was personally responsible for reimbursing the Uripiv women's money (another fason blong Vanuatu). This I was not anxious to do, not only because I was cheap, but because of the bad precedent of free stuff from waetmen it would support. I told my tale of woe to various friends in Vila. One of my SCUBA buddies, an American women with the South Pacific People's Federation, took it upon herself to tell the Women's Center that I was a bigwig in the National Planning and Statistics Office, and had vowed that if the Centre didn't give the Uripiv women their money back, the NPSO would never approve another Centre programme. The Centre duly sent an equivalent amount of money to Madeline.
Uttering threats was not my mode of operation, I told another friend in the development business. He told me not to sweat it: "Sometimes the ball just bounces your way." I let it go. Fason blong wan samwan we I bin stap long Vanuatu longtaem lilebit (someone who's been in Vanuatu a few years).

Stan DJs a Dance

Lakatoro's Met-Met Club was a large hall built with a frame of local tree branches, walls of woven bamboo, and a roof of palm thatch. It had been built in colonial times under the supervision of Darvall Wilkins, the former British District Commissioner. Mista Wilkin, as he was referred to in reverent tones by all, had requisitioned building materials from Malekula and Pentecost Islands' villages and presumably dipped into colonial government coffers for the concrete floor.

A few changes had been made since independence. In order to restrict unpaid access to events, in this universe lacking the concepts of chance or risk, all doors save one small one had been nailed shut, and strands of barbed wire had been strung in the wide ventilation spaces between the walls and roof. The place gave me the creeps, especially when filled with 300 people. I mentioned once to my ni-Vanuatu co-workers that the Club's roofing material was what I used to light my barbecue, but was assured that there would never be a fire there. You know; "if we don't want something to happen, it won't". Yeah.

One day, I was advised that I had been honoured by having been chosen to DJ the big Local Council anniversary dance at the Met-Met Club. I asked what time it would be, and was told from 9:00PM to 3:00AM. I should have asked for more details, but some things must be learned from experience. I strongly suspect I had been chosen for this task because nobody else wanted to do it and I was both new and ignorant.

Holly and I had been to a previous dance at the Met-Met Club, so I thought I knew what would happen. Music started at 9:00, young women and men had started filtering in about 10:30, and actual dancing commenced at 11:00. The young ladies stood on one side of the hall, with a number of little sisters and brothers sleeping at their feet. Young men stood at the other side. When a song started, men would run across the hall to choose partners and the couples would move onto the floor. As well as couples dancing, there were threesomes of two men with one woman, circles of men, and solitary men roaming the floor. The men were very animated dancers, but the women pretty well stood there and bounced a little—apparently nice ni-Vanuatu girls don't wiggle. When the music stopped, everyone would immediately retreat to their side of the hall.

Some of the taped music played was local "string band" music, recorded by ni-Vanuatu bands playing ukuleles, guitars with the two lower-toned strings removed, a tea-chest bass, and a "shaker" made of bottle caps nailed loosely to wood. One innovative band from Futuna Island added bottles, tuned to a scale with varying amounts of water, that they'd hit with spoons; and some bands included tuned lengths of large-bore bamboo that they slapped across the top

307

with the soles of rubber thongs. To the untrained Western ear, there was not a lot of variation in tunes, but if you understood Bislama, the lyrics kind of made sense. In live performances, the lyrics would be customized to commemorate the event being celebrated or recent happenings. Reggae music was also popular, as was Zouk, a fusion of Calypso and French music set to a Samba beat, which originated in the Caribbean French Antilles Islands.

On this earlier occasion, the manager of the Public Works Department had appeared at 2:45AM and announced that the Lakatoro generators would be turned off in 15 minutes, which broke up festivities pretty quickly.

So, I thought I had a pretty good idea of what to expect this time. I started playing music at 9, and dancing started around 11; so far, so good. Being a smart-ass and culturally insensitive Whiteman, I thought I'd introduce Lakatoro to real Rock n' Roll, so I'd brought a bunch of my tapes to play. **Wrong—Number One**. There was definite dissension in the ranks, with only a few dancers. Soon a guy came up on stage and informed me that my music was not appreciated. He gave me three cassettes out of his bag—one each of string band, reggae, and Zouk. So, I acquiesced to popular demand and for the rest of the dance simply rotated songs from each of the three cassettes. Everyone was pleased and danced away. I did receive one specific request—could I play some slow music so "mifala save holem gel"—we can hold the girls. I complied, and girls were held.

As beer was being sold, it wasn't too long until many of the men were staggering drunk. I was the sole member present of a visible minority that was covertly resented, so I was getting a little nervous that such feelings might emerge under the influence. My fear wasn't allayed much when a guy reeled up on stage and slurred that some of my audience were expressing a desire to beat me up, but not to worry; he'd stay up there and protect me. Great. I was relieved a while later when the beer ran out, as I imagined everyone would now start sobering up. **Wrong—Number Two**. Some of the men simply went up to the house of the Co-op Store manager, woke him up, and demanded he open the store and provide more beer, which he did. The drinking continued.

Finally! Three AM rolled around, and I could wrap things up and go home. I announced the last dance. **Wrong—Number Three**. I could see that a riot was quickly forming—these people expected to "danis kasem delaet"—dance until dawn. What could I do—I immediately re-started my three musical genre rotation and kept it up until the sun came up at six.

What I had neglected to apply here was what should have been my knowledge that if the ladies left the hall while it was dark, many of them would have been raped, or as per the local idiom, "kapsaesem long rod"—flipped on their back along a path.[1]

---

[1] "Pikinini blong rod" (Child of the road) was the Bislama vernacular for "illegitimate child".

Daylight finally came, and with my tapes and hard-won education, I trudged up the hill to our house and hit the hay.

At a Previous Met-Met Club Dance

from a letter home, August 1, 1988:

> I got tired of all this type of music, so I went home and got a bunch of tapes. I asked the DJ if people liked rock and roll, and he said he'd try some. A bit later, Henry, the cute little devil, got on the loudspeaker and announced that he was going to play a new kind of music—Rock and Roll—and that in order to learn how to dance to this new music, everyone should just watch those two white people over there. So, all four hundred people gathered around and watched us do the same dancing they had all been doing all along, to Brian Adam's "One Night Love Affair" (a little Canadian Content there). During the second and third tapes ("The Heart of Rock and Roll" and "Footloose"), a few guys joined in. Holly asked them why they weren't dancing with the girls, and they said that the girls didn't know how to do this new dance. Play that funky music, white boy!

Stan MCs and Competes in a Music Contest

From an August 1, 1988 letter:

> We've just finished a big exciting July 30 Independence Day long weekend. I was delegated to the Music Committee, which organized a local talent music show and the wind-up dance.

> Besides sweeping out the community hall before both events, my main task was to be the MC at the music show Thursday night. Luckily it rained off-and-on over the weekend, so I didn't have to be too paranoid about joining the crowd in the thatch and bamboo hall, which I considered a fire trap. I've told everyone that my mother doesn't consider such places safe, but have been told that a fire will never happen. When it does, I suppose a magician from Ambrym Island will get the blame. Do I sound like I've been here too long?

> We had twelve groups lined up, including me, who were to sing five songs each. Categories were religious pop, choir, pop, break dancing, and a selection of songs from Canada, the Appalachians, and Hank Williams

309

(from guess-who?). Official starting time was 18:30. Don't worry; I didn't really expect it to start on time. People never come to these things unless it is both late and they can hear the event going on. When the hall was still deserted at 19:15, the committee chairman and I started the warm-up act. First, he played a few songs on the keyboard and I tried to strum along on an electric guitar; I got some of the chords right, anyway. Then, I set up a mike and while he played bass guitar, I wowed them all with "Are You A-Walkin' and A-Talkin' For the Lord" and "Why Don't You Love Me Like You Used To Do?" by guess-who, my swinging version of "Michael Row the Boat Ashore" and, for a change of pace, my calypso "Jamaica Farewell". The crowd, jamming the hall by now, was up on their feet, excitedly demanding encores [1], but my first responsibility was to those others who had practiced long and hard over the week since we announced the show, so we had to get started.

First, I read out the order in which the groups were to appear, and then we presented them any which-way that they showed up. I spent my time while each group was playing running around outside looking for people from another group to come on next. We did quite well, as only two groups didn't bother to show up at all.

The Bisal String Band. String bands are Vanuatu's primary indigenous music genre. They typically comprise a tea-chest bass such as this one, two or more guitars, a ukulele, and a "shaker".

I scheduled myself next-to-last. As we only had one mike stand that I used for my guitar, I had Holly come up and hold my voice mike. After a few minutes finding two mikes that worked well and getting the volumes adjusted so both the guitar and I could be heard, I got started. My first number was Joni Mitchell's

---

[1] A 0% truth.

"Circle Game", for which I forgot to use my capo, so I couldn't hit the low notes. I had the words taped to the top of my guitar (an old pro's trick), but I couldn't read them, so after two verses of forgotten words and mixed-up chords, I gave it up and moved on to my next number, Ian Tyson's "Someday Soon". Then, I stumbled through "Sixteen Tons" and did "Four Strong Winds" after starting up in the wrong key. I got "I Saw the Light" pretty well right, though. Everyone was very well entertained, and I got a lot of laughs, as audiences here are pretty honest and seem to have done some training on "The Gong Show". The guys who were looking through holes in the woven bamboo walls and over the walls (approximately same number as paying customers inside) were especially appreciative.

I don't recall winning anything.

An Expedition to the Brenwe River Falls

From an August 1, 1988 letter home:

> I planned to lie in bed all day yesterday, but an Australian couple, whom we had promised to take to the Brenwe falls if the weather was nice, came up to show us that it was sunny (drat). I heard them telling Heather to tell us to come find them when we got up, but pulled the covers over my head. Holly was already up and in the shower, though, and made me get up when she got the message.

Simon and Ros still tolerate us as good friends, amazingly. Simon, the son of the former British District Agent, had grown up on Malekula but for some reason didn't know about these spectacular falls.

> So, we loaded Simon and Ros in our truck (they had paid for gas, as we were broke), picked up Michelle and Daniel Couturier (our French teacher and husband) and Brendan Hanley (the CUSO Doctor) in Norsup, and took off for deepest, darkest Malekula—to the centre of the cannibalistic Big Nambas tribal territory. After an hour or so of trying to find the right path—I had been there once before—we started down one in what we figured was about the right area. The Brenwe River is the one at the bottom of a steep gorge that I saw a while back with a team of New Zealand hydroelectric consultants. I had been telling everyone about this series of fabulous pools and small waterfalls, like a giant marble fountain, coming down from the main falls. When we got to the bottom of the valley, Simon and Ros, whom I don't think are real backpacker types, had just about had it. I didn't recognize that stretch of the river at all; it definitely wasn't what I had promised everyone.

Two Years on Malekula

The Brenwe River below the falls.

Daniel and I left everyone and set off upstream to try and find "the spot". Funny how, when you promise everyone a big deal, after they work hard you never find it. Anyway, we walked and waded and swam in the deep spots up the river.

After, I got ahead and went on alone. I got to a place where it was difficult to pass and had decided to turn back, when along came Daniel. We decided that, having come this far, we would climb this one more place—and there we were where I had come down to from the road last time. So, on we went, balancing on rocks, rock climbing up bits of waterfall, and swimming up deep pools in order to find the bottom of the big falls. Finally, we were about to give up, but decided to climb just one more falls, and we could see the big one through the forest after the next pool. There was a big pool at the bottom of the falls, which really seemed to be only the bottom half of a double falls, with the top half up and around a corner.

We swam over to a rock near the falls, and I climbed up to a small cave at their side to have my photo taken. I had hauled along my underwater camera, which is perfect for this sort of thing. The cave was formed by a sheet of limestone deposit next to the river, and had two stalactites, or whatever you call them, from top to bottom like bars in part of its mouth.

Daniel climbing from one pool to another. I'm not sure what we were supposed to fight off with that knife.

Me in the cave beside the falls.

We had gone back a bit, when up came the rest of the group. Simon and Ros were bringing up the rear, but Simon said that at least he was still speaking to me, when I asked [1]. Most importantly, these guys had the food with them, except Michelle. She and Daniel had left theirs in their car. We all shared.

Daniel and Michelle Couturier, Holly, Simon Wilkins, Me, and Ros Wilkins.

We picnicked and then swam, walked, and climbed back down to the place where I had come down and gone up the valley wall last time.

Starting back down the Brenwe River.

---

[1] Oh, Ros has long since forgiven me and is a good, if sarcastic, Facebook friend.

Two Years on Malekula

One of the Brenwe River pools.

Then, a short forty-minute climb up a slope with the steepness of a ladder, holding on by roots and branches, to the top. After wandering in three different directions through a garden, its owner showed us the way to the road and said we should have just got him in his village to come up and show us the path. He had been our guide last time.

It was the best day we've had in a long time, and we finished it off with a dinner at Daniel and Michelle's, except Simon and Ros, who just flaked out at home [1]. After a couple of tumblers of wine, I amazed myself by actually understanding and participating in the conversation, which as always at their house, was in French. I usually speak Bislama when alone with Daniel, but Michelle (our French teacher, you may recall) won't have any of that.

I hobbled around today, but nobody noticed because they were all recovering from the hike yesterday and big lafet (party) last night.

---

[1] My boss's house just below our little place. They were family friends of his whom they were visiting.

Crisis at the Lakatoro Branch of the Vanuatu Co-operative Credit Union

From an August 1, 1988 letter to my sister:

> Help! We're suffering from a financial crisis here. It's one of those situations that is so typical of here that it hardly deserves comment, but here goes: When I went down to the bank today to make a withdrawal from July's pay, which I swore I wouldn't touch until month's end, the bank was closed. It seems that the manager has lost the only key to the safe. Does the bank where you work ever have this problem? I've yet to see a lock here that has more than one key left. The spares get lost, or someone wanders off with them, or maybe they just throw them away, for all I know. The concept of risk and covering for adverse eventualities doesn't exist here.

> John Kamphorst once told me an ethnic joke that has a lot of truth to it: A famous psychologist performed an experiment in which an Australian, an East Indian, and a Melanesian were each put into bare padded cells with two rubber balls. When he looked though the peepholes two hours later to make his first observation, he found the Australian squeezing the balls to exercise his hands and the Indian practicing his juggling, but the Melanesian had lost one ball and broken the other[1].

> Anyway, if they don't get something fixed up soon, I'll get a friend in Vila to send up some cash on the airplane. Until then, we'll just have to raid the kids' piggybanks.

Note added in margin prior to mailing:

> There's now a sign on the bank door offering a reward if someone finds and returns the key. You have to laugh. A plane was supposed to bring some money in today, but it was raining too hard in Vila for it to take off. Maybe tomorrow. What does the Royal Bank of Canada (my sister's workplace) do in these situations?

Keys just weren't appropriate technology in Vanuatu; they often got lost. I heard once of an expat advisor who went out to a village to inspect a copra storage shed. When he got there, the door was locked, and the local villagers said the owner had gone to his garden. After a few hours of the advisor sitting and

---

[1] Not very PC, but as I wrote, had some truth to it. The Vanuatu National Soccer Team missed a tournament once because they lost their passports and couldn't fly. When it was too late to go, they found the passports under the seat of the car they had taken to the airport.

talking with the villagers, the owner showed up and unlocked the door. They entered to observe that there was no back wall to the shed. In Vanuatu, only certain people have the right to disclose information, and proper form must be observed.

On the subject of the Lakatoro Credit Union branch, the manager was sacked one day for withdrawing money from another person's account. The criminal genius had repeatedly practiced the account owner's signature on the back of the withdrawal slip. He pled that it was all OK because it was a friend's account. What do I know; perhaps it was in a social/cultural sense, but I guess you can't tolerate that sort of thing and keep a credit union going.

Daniel's Nakamal

Daniel and Michelle Couturier were friends who lived in Norsup. Michelle, the local French education advisor, wouldn't believe the stories we told her about Heather and Laurel's schooling (e.g. students got spankings for wrong answers) in Norsup. "But, I never see that when I inspect the school", she said in perfect French, to which I replied in very poor French [1], "That's because you're white." Daniel spent his time hunting, hanging out with locals, and carrying out his profession as hair stylist, including cutting my hair.

From a June 24, 1987 letter:

> While chatting in fractured French with Daniel, I mentioned that I had heard that he had built a nakamal, and got invited to the grand opening on Saturday. It was a good time. We men got to sit inside in the shade (women and pikininis outside, although a part of the wall of the shelter was left off so they could see in), and listen to a chief from north of here give a speech conferring a custom name on Daniel (Lingname), after Daniel gave him 5,000 vatu. Daniel then gave a short speech (from a scrap of paper, as his Bislama isn't too hot) and clubbed a small pig (included in the price of the name). A bunch of us men then retired into the new nakamal to drink kava and storian. Later we had a meal outside (other ranks, i.e. women and kids, got the leftovers [2]—I could get to like it here!), and the chief and friends sang and danced a bit. I had a good time,

---

[1] Michelle's effort to improve my high-school French with lessons were largely fruitless.

[2] This Vanuatu custom was the cause of malnutrition among women and very young children, amongst a plenitude of food. Women, due to a life of malaria, an average of six children, and poor diet, were universally anemic. Holly was amazed they could walk into the hospital lab to have their blood tested for haemoglobin. Kids were well-nourished with a low mortality rate until they were weaned. Then the mortality rate rose until they got to the age of five or so, when they would start scavenging for their own food and their mortality rate dropped.

although Lambert, my counterpart, wasn't too happy about it when I told him. He opined that all of this spoilem kastom blong mifala [1], and was especially upset about the pig killing—he doesn't feel that Daniel has the rank to kill a pig. I'm beginning to see why they have so many disputes here. The officiating chief is from Lambert's island and the nakamal was built with the collaboration of the Norsup chief, so they apparently think the affair fit in quite well with custom, but others have a different opinion of just what custom is.

Daniel (right) at his Nakamal opening.

You sure have to tread carefully here to avoid being lynched or starting a war. According to which story you believe, a CUSO left voluntarily or was held hostage in his house and made a dash for the airport last year when he and his live-in girlfriend moved from Vila to her home village.

---

[1] Was against ni-Vanuatu tradition.

Two Christmas and New Year Seasons in the Combs / Morgan Household
Our First Christmas in Vanuatu: 21 December, 1987:

The house is all flash[1] for Christmas. We got this tasteful set of mini-lights (that didn't even shock us [2] after I wrapped the plug in electrical tape) to drape around our living room shelf. The girls used construction paper and painted old computer paper to make chains that crisscross our ceiling. Holly has hung our six Christmas cards and some stockings on the wall. Friday, I saw a cassette at the co-op with a pirated [3] assortment of carols on it. Among the artists listed were Boney M and Skeeter Davis (the latter singing "Santa Claus Is Coming To Town"), so I thought I had found the ultimate in tacky Christmas albums. Unfortunately, when I got it home and played it, it turned out to contain pretty good music (well, except for Skeeter—she didn't disappoint me).

(Spoiler Alert to any reader under the age of 12) Each year, we'd have the girls write to Santa Claus and send them to my sister, Cindy, who forwarded them to North Pole, Canada H0H 0H0.

Those Christmas Decorations—cards-on-a-string, stockings, paper chains, and stuffed tree—weren't much, but they were ours. They joined our regular collection of bow and arrows, nambugi, nautilus and other shells, tusked pig jaws and a sea turtle shell I scrounged from an abandoned building. I guess I can't claim that no animals or sea creatures were harmed in the decoration of that wall.

---

[1] Anglicization of "flas"—nicely decorated.

[2] Actually, Holly; I always had her plug them in and unplug them.

[3] At the time, Vanuatu was not a party to any international copyright agreements, and pirated music tapes were sold openly in every shop.

Two Years on Malekula

This first year, Heather wrote detailed instructions on how to find her new house—the white one on top of the hill. The retired Canada Post person who responded in lieu of Santa assured Heather "No matter where you live, I will find you." I wish I still had that letter; my gratitude goes to the people who answer those children's letters.

Back in Canada, we played this tape every year in the car until all our vehicles had CD players. Recently, I found all of those songs, by the same artists save one, on iTunes and YouTube and made a CD of them.

Our Second Christmas on Malekula:

January 1, 1989:

> They always shut off liquor sales on weekends and whenever they think there will be trouble; but I cleverly nipped into the store on Monday morning, the 19th, and got this bottle of rum before the store manager had heard that the police had extended the liquor ban because of the attempted coup. I also got some gin the week before, because I heard on Radio Australia (same as on the morning of the 19th) that liquor sales would be banned that day because of the threatened and banned Vila and Lakatoro demonstrations planned for the 16th. See, it really pays to listen to short-wave radio. You have to be on your toes to survive in the third world.

And:

> I came under general ridicule on the evening of the 23rd, when we had friends over and I organized a carol-sing. Holly, of all people, led the general conversation and laughing that went on as a few others and I were singing. Nevertheless, our guests (well, the wife, anyway; you know how sentimental English women are) asked me and Brendan to bring our guitars over to their place the next evening for the Metenesel Christmas Eve party (see, we do get asked to some things over there).

> After midnight at the Metenesel party, these four young ladies (visiting daughters and a son's girlfriend) asked who wanted to go for a dip in the pool, so I volunteered. Unfortunately, I hadn't anticipated that they were going to all find swimsuits, but it was all right, anyway. I just wore my red and green tropical-print boxer shorts, which I had shown to everyone as my "Christmas underwear". Lucky they don't have a fly. We had to clean some frogs and a wayward land crap (sorry, that should have been typed crab) out of the pool first.

Two Years on Malekula

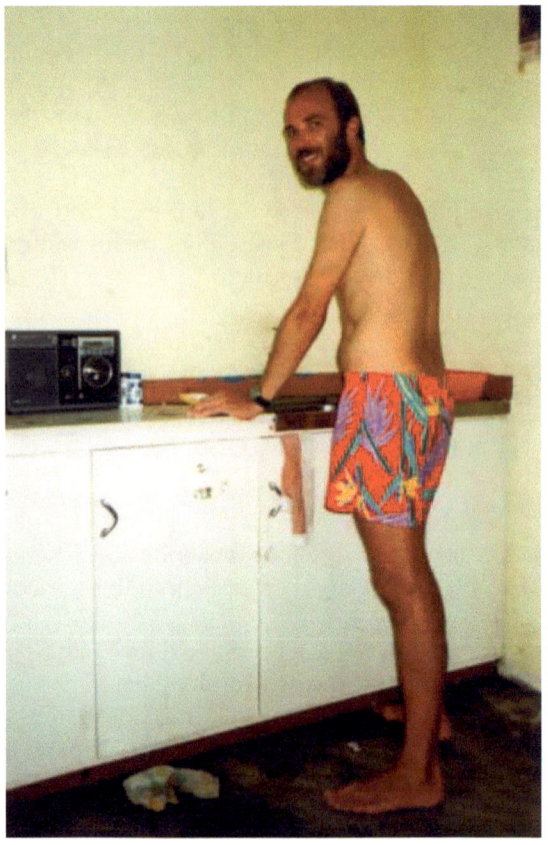

Proudly displaying my Christmas Underwear during our first Christmas Day in Vanuatu. We were visiting fellow CUSOs in Luganville; I brought my shortwave radio.

When I returned, leaving the girls with all that subcutaneous fat in the cold pool, we all sang carols again. Good thing I brought my Readers' Digest Carol Book [1].

We had one of our best trees this year, which is very surprising. Holly insisted that we do what all the other expats do around here and go down to the Agriculture station to buy a Norfolk Pine. You know, the ones that cost a zillion dollars in Canada if you buy a two-foot one in a pot? They planted about 20 of them down there four years ago. Every year, they just cut them off about three feet above the ground if someone wants one, and then another one or two grow back during the next year. They cost 500 vatu. Holly insisted that we go down Wednesday, which I guess was one day earlier than anyone else, because we got the best one.

---

[1] Which, Cyclone Uma-stained, I have continued to use every year at our annual Christmas Parties in Lakatoro and Port Vila, Vanuatu; and Victoria, Kelowna, and Hornby Island, British Columbia.

Two Years on Malekula

It was great going over to the boss's place at Metenesel and looking at his Charlie Brown model, when they had been over the night before and seen ours [1].

This spring some departing CUSOs had given us all their tacky Christmas ornaments, which had been handed down through several generations of CUSOs. As you will recall, we have one lonely string of little lights from last year. The tree was huge, as they always are after you get them home, and we had to cut off a couple of feet from the base to get it under the ceiling. We stuck it into a three-gallon ice-cream bucket full of sand and tied it to the wall, in the traditional manner, with fishing line after it leaned over. It took up about a quarter of our spacious living room. We wound the string of lights around the trunk (rather clever use of a limited resource, in my opinion), and had just enough balls to hang one on the tip of almost every branch that was on the half of the tree away from the corner. A friend in Victoria sends us a box of Rogers Chocolates every Christmas, and the girls made a few extra balls by wrapping the colourful foil wrappers around blown-out eggshells. Then I wound all the yards of about four colours of tinsel garland on the half of the tree that showed. Amazingly, it looked really good. We took it all down today, and bequeathed the decorations to Brendan. Our living room is HUGE now!

Our glorious 1988 Christmas tree. The girls attached a star to a toilet roll for the top of it.

---

[1] OK; I gained great pleasure from one-upping the much-better-paid Metenesel crowd.

Two Years on Malekula

Christmas morning, we had put the plastic beauty sets you sent under the tree from Santa. We were going to put some small dolls in their stockings, but two Barbie dolls I had ordered from Vila on the 23rd (don't like to rush these things, you know), hadn't yet arrived even though I spent most of the 24th at the airport waiting for them, along with a bunch of other people waiting for packages that never came. Quick as a flash, we raided Santa's pack and wrapped the dolls to come from us. Heather and Laurel later asked why Santa was so cheap this year.

The Barbies finally showed on Boxing Day (December 26th for those of a non-British persuasion). We were down at Aop Beach, when I saw a plane land at the strip. I drove over, picked up the package, and the girls opened their late presents on the beach.

I got the girls Barbies because Mom and I had bought a bunch of Snow White and Cinderella Barbie clothes in Jakarta, Indonesia[1] for the girls' Christmas, and all Heather and Laurel had were these real el cheapo fashion dolls they had bought with their savings when we were in Vila last August. For about $3 each, they had got these dolls with Iroquois-cut hair that was supposed to cover the head if you parted it in the middle, and joints that looked like two sticks with a nail through them. As you know, I am virulently anti-Barbie, but I let them buy what they want to with their money. Then, they spent the last few months sewing clothes, often from Chinese toilet paper, for them, so I didn't want to stifle their creativity.

Our daughters' lives being ruined by receiving Barbie dolls because I went soft.

---

[1] Where I had gone for an unsuccessful job interview; Mom and Dad flew in from his posting in Irian Jaya to meet me.

Two Years on Malekula

I loved Christmases in Vanuatu. Best of all, the hoopla only started a week before the day; not right after Hallowe'en like in Canada. If you asked your expat friends on the day to come over for a Christmas Eve party, they all came because they had no extended families there. The Australians were all impressed by the chance to drink eggnog, which they'd always heard about but never experienced. And later, when we were spoiled fully-funded expats in Port Vila, everyone brought a bottle of French Champagne. On Christmas Day, we'd go to a beach with friends and drink Champagne there.

One downside, however, came from the bucket of beach rocks and water that you put your Norfolk Pine Christmas tree into. Little beasties you hadn't realized you'd picked up with the rocks would die and stink. Then, mosquitos would start breeding in there. Life was hard.

Our Second New Year's Eve on Malekula, about a month before we left:

January 1, 1989:

> We really painted the town red last night. Not being members [1], we didn't get invited to the New Year's Gala at the Metenesel Estates Club (I think they sat around the swimming pool and drank). We went over to Dr. Brendan's, who was on call and couldn't drink, and tried to finish off my Christmas rum. We mixed it with a bunch of sour mandarin and pineapple juice that I made yesterday afternoon. We sat around and read until Brendan and Daniel (another CUSO Doctor) finished setting a kid's arm, and then we watched them eat. Then, we played Trivial Pursuit until midnight, when Brendan turned on the radio, and we listened to the Prime Minister, Father Walter Lini, wish everyone a Happy New Year. Daniel wondered if this included the President, who is in jail for "inciting the military and police to mutiny".

> After the PM's message, while they played the worst rendition of "Auld Lang Syne" that I've ever heard, we popped the cork on a bottle of French Champagne that Holly and I were given a couple of months ago when we held a dinner. Dr. Daniel, who is from France, pronounced it undrinkable (I couldn't tell, after the rum), so we poured all of our glasses into a Tupperware container for a use that will shortly become evident. Then, Brendan opened a bottle of Australian fake champagne that he had, and all agreed that it was low quality, but drinkable.

---

[1] We were invited, but were too cheap to join. This was inconceivable to our British and Australian friends over there, who even offered a special low "volunteers rate".

Two Years on Malekula

After, we got into the local New Year's, which is called Bonane (pronounced a bit like banana, from the French "Bonne Année"), celebrations. Groups of people (you can guess in what condition) go from door to door after midnight and sing songs. You come out and douse them with baby powder[1] , they douse you, and then you give them a small gift, such as a kilo of sugar, some rice, a tin of fish, a pineapple, or 100 vatu. Sometime in January, when it is agreed that the New Year's period is over (or the hangovers are gone from the two-week Christmas-New Year's drunk), the singers all get together again and have a party with all the stuff they collected. As you can see, they are socially very well organized here, with each party automatically providing the excuse for the next one. Of course, the Vanuatu Christmas season doesn't really end until messages go out over the radio that civil servants and teachers who haven't returned to their jobs are two weeks late and liable to be dismissed if they don't show up soon.

We had planned ahead for the Bonane singers, with our Tupperware of fine wine, which we shared out like good white imperialists. These guys were already so well lubricated that they could hardly set up their tea-chest bass fiddle, and they seemed to appreciate the fine vintage. They didn't send the bottle back to the cellar, anyway. They sang and danced, and Brendan let them have it with the baby powder and gave them a few tins of meat.

It was about 1 am by then, so we Combs & Morgans went home to Lakatoro and to bed. Of course, at about 3, we heard a gang from Senal, the nearest village, coming up the hill to the Mala's. I figured if we pulled the old Halloween-keep-the-light-off-and-hide-in-the-basement trick, they might not bother coming further up the hill to our place. No such luck. After coming up one side of the house and just about falling into the big hole that has been dug for a new septic sump (but that's another story—mind you, maybe I should go out and check if anyone is down there today), they came back around the other way to our other door. After a brief discussion regarding our chances of being home, they let loose on full volume. Holly wouldn't let me play possum any longer, so we got dressed and went out. They were pretty nice, and not quite as drunk as the bunch at Norsup had been. They sang a song about us going over the sea and them missing us (some of them are Council employees and they know we are soon leaving). More singing, while we all poured baby powder over each other. They were dressed up in grass skirts and had vines wrapped around their heads. Then I gave them a kilo of sugar, and we could go back to bed while listening to them sing their way down

---

[1] Done at celebrations like weddings, birthdays, etc. I don't know the origin of this custom; someone once said that prior to contact, powdered limestone was used. I used to wish I had the baby powder concession for Vanuatu, where a lot of partying goes on.

the hill to the next lucky family. I suppose all of this would lose some of its charms if you had to do it standing in the snow at -30°, but of course, we had to put up with all of those night-time malaria mosquitoes biting us. I hope our maloprim works. Almost every CUSO that has left during our stay, especially the families, have caught bad cases of malaria just before they left. I think we'd better hit the Gin and Tonic [1] hard for the next few days; see, every party does lead to another one here.

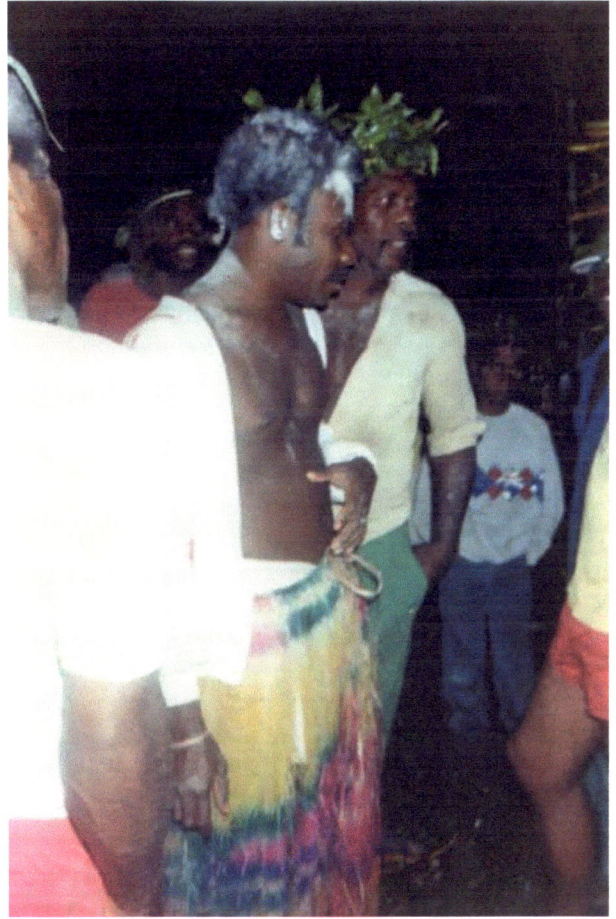

Bonane singers, Lakatoro very early New Year's Day, 1989.

---

[1] Tonic water is flavoured with quinine, the original anti-malarial made from the bark of the Cinchona tree. I used to, and still do, tell people that I drink G&Ts (imagine bad colonial English accent) "for the malaria, you know".

PART 5—LEAVING

Leaving Malekula and Vanuatu

Our CUSO contract was due to finish at the end of January 1988. Most CUSOs took off their last month as holiday and left early, but I worked to the end of the contract and took a month's vacation pay.

Our plan was to spend some months travelling through Australia and then visit my parents in Irian Jaya, Indonesia on the way home.

We had accumulated various things, and didn't want to carry most of the stuff we'd brought with us while we travelled home, so some had to be gotten rid of and some freighted home. Ni-Vanuatu know that when expats leave it's a good time to get their stuff cheap, so we had no trouble shedding Holly's sewing machine, the "ghetto blaster", and various items of clothing—I have a photo of a co-worker proudly wearing one of my shirts.

The bicycles sold quickly—a friend in Australia still has Holly's—but there was a hiccup. I sold my 5-speed mountain bike to a ni-Vanuatu on the other side of the island, but he came back with it a few weeks later; all the bearings in the bottom bracket had come loose and the pedal cranks were just flopping around. He had ridden it in this condition all the way over the hills to our side of the island! He told me that people who had borrowed the bike had been pretty rough with it. Fortunately, because I didn't have any spare bearings of the proper size, all of them were still inside the bracket. I retrieved and cleaned them, and then reinstalled everything. Then, I made an executive decision about appropriate technology. I removed the derailleur, shortened the chain, and turned the bike into a one-speed. The bike's owner seemed pretty pleased with the end result.

Selling the Fireball was more difficult than I had anticipated. I had thought that someone in Vila's dinghy club, which held races on Sundays, would snap it up, but there was no interest. Finally, an Australian in Luganville, whom I never did meet, beat me down on the price, and I put it on a ship to him. He complained that it wasn't in new condition, but with the low price in mind I ignored him.

Then, there was the Land Cruiser. A local insider of the all-powerful ruling Vanua'aku Pati had told me that he expected me to sell it to him when I left. So, I took it up to him, and he arrogantly refused—I wasn't too surprised. But, despite my having pretty well resurrected M-169 from the junk heap and made it run well again, there was no interest in it. Perhaps the villagers thought it took a Whiteman to keep the old thing going; they may have been correct. I have to admit that at the time I was soldering leaks in the radiator every other day. Finally, when we were at the airstrip leaving, our friend and fellow CUSO, the Norsup Hospital doctor Brendan Hanley, said he'd buy it on the condition I send him a new radiator from Australia. I did, and he managed to install it—this only involved four machine screws and two hose connections, but human, rather than automotive, mechanics were Brendan's forte. He later told us he had a great time with it for the rest of his contract. When Brendan left, he sold it to an Australian/French businessman. The last time I saw the Land Cruiser when we returned to work in Port Vila several months later, it was sitting in a business yard with its exhaust system in the front seat; I fear that was the end of the line for that truck.

So, what was left that we didn't require on the road had to be packed for sea freight to Canada. I drove the truck over to Metenesel Estates and bought some lumber from their small mill. Then, I built two crates, and we packed them. I contacted the Atchin Island shipping company and a shipping agent in Vila, and on the appointed day we hauled our crates up to Atchin beach, where the ship's crew put them onto a lighter and took them out to the ship, an ex-Hong Kong ferry if you can believe it. Vanuatu, with its lax regulations, was one of the world's ship graveyards where coastal freighters and this ferry that couldn't be registered elsewhere ended up.

We expected the next time we would see those crates would be some indeterminate future date in Canada[1] .

Our crates go off to the Atchin Star.

---

[1] As Miss Smith taught me in high school English, this is foreshadowing.

Two Years on Malekula

Finally, the day came for us to leave Malekula. The family had all boarded the Vanair Bandeirante, which was about the same size as a Twin Otter. When all were aboard, the pilots determined that the plane was overloaded, and the unsuccessful candidate in the recent national election and his family were ejected. I was sitting in the back row, immediately adjacent to the cargo piled behind me. As the ground crew were having some difficulty getting the large top-hinged cargo door latched, I reached back with my left arm to hold in the cargo. Then, the absolute last thing to happen to me on Malekula occurred. A small weaner pig being transported in the usual Vanuatu fashion, in a woven plastic rice bag with its snout sticking out a hole in the corner, bit me! T'was but a scratch on my thumb, but with blood drawn, I claim it as a legitimate bite. The cargo door was slammed shut, we took off, and by the time we reached the south end of Malekula fifteen minutes later, the plane had lumbered to a higher altitude than the mountains alongside us.

When chatting with new friends and feeling especially obnoxious, I sometimes ask everyone in the room who has been bitten by a pig on a scheduled commercial flight to raise their hands. It's pretty sure that I'll be the only one with my hand up, and then I tell this tale.

During our few days' layover in Vila, we went to the bank to convert our riches into travelers' cheques. What with our last month's pay, our month's vacation pay, the funds from the sale of the truck and sailboat, funds gained by trading our full economy-class ticket for a restricted ticket home, and our resettlement allowance in lieu of unemployment insurance eligibility, we had CAN$12,000, more cash money than we'd ever had! Responsible people would go straight home and add to their retirement savings, of course; we were heading off to tour Australia for four months in a VW minibus camper that we bought when we arrived and sold when we left. The plan after that was four weeks in Manokwari, Irian Jaya, Indonesia visiting my parents and a week in Hawaii with Holly's aunt before arriving home. How often do you have a chance for such an excursion?

While we were buying travellers' cheques from ni-Vanuatu bank staff at the counter, we noticed them looking past us and smiling. Turning around, there were Heather and Laurel squatting on their heels village-style going through each other's hair looking for lice! And not finding any, I may add. Talk about "man bus". This was a sight all of the staff had seen many times before, but not with white children. If you couldn't laugh at this stuff—and dredge it up to embarrass the kids for years to come—you'd die of humiliation.

Another thing I did in Vila was go up to the NPSO office and offer my application for the new Regional Development Planning Advisor position. They said I'd have to send it to the Commonwealth Fund for Technical Cooperation in London, England, which was funding the position. This I did, and received an offer in August. There was a delay because, as I learned later, the non-European CFTC staff put applications from white people at the bottom of the pile, and they sent the NPSO a list of applicants that didn't include me. NPSO had by this time been taken over by people who didn't want more technical "experts" who were ignorant about Vanuatu's regions. It queried right back with: where the heck was the application of Stan Combs, who had two years of regional experience in Vanuatu? A new list with my name included was tendered.

Finally, on the street in Vila a ni-Vanuatu came up to me and said he was a crew member on the ship we had put our crates on at Atchin. He told me that my shipping agent, Captain Klaus, had not picked up our crates yet, and the ship was leaving for Tanna Island in a few hours. This was par for the course dealing with expatriate businessmen in Vanuatu. I rounded up Klaus and his van, and we went down to the dock to pick up my crates. They eventually made it home to Victoria. I always gave Klaus the benefit of the doubt, even though this was not the only time our relations were not up to snuff, because he had saved our bacon two years earlier on the morning after Cyclone Uma. Not that he remembered two decades later when I met him again in Vila.

And with that, we were off on the plane to Brisbane for Australian adventures.

Epilogue

What Did Vanuatu Gain from My Time in Lakatoro?

I'm not sure it gained a lot from my two years in Lakatoro. The Malekula Local Government Council bus ran at a profit—until it was run into a tree. The LGC gained a meager profit from properly-priced concrete blocks and corrugated iron. The Litzlitz wharf didn't use up Aop Beach to make the concrete used in its construction. The LGC had its Lakatoro Resthouse renovated and gained a few vatu from the rental of office space to the Japanese Engineers building the wharf. My counterpart for most of my time in Lakatoro, Kalosak Massing, gained some experience working with me, and I helped him complete an application to attend a course in Japan. Kalosak and a few other people got some schooling in English and Math. Villages in North Malekula got some relief food after crop failures in 1987 and early 1988.

Perhaps the most valuable thing that Vanuatu gained from my time in Lakatoro was my knowledge of rural Vanuatu that I put to use from August, 1989–November 1992 when I was Vanuatu's first Regional Development Planning Advisor. The team of advisors of which I was part may not have had a great impact on Vanuatu's development, because the government and donors basically ignored us. We did write a much more realistic Third National Development Plan, and I attempted to educate development consultants who came through about Vanuatu's realities. Most importantly, when we left the NPSO we felt that our counterparts were prepared to take over our jobs. That, however, came to naught as the government dissolved the NPSO and let our counterparts go.

Hopefully, as stated previously in this memoir, I did less damage than another aid advisor would have, and of course there was the matter of providing entertainment for the locals.

What Did I Gain from My Time in Vanuatu?

This is a completely different matter. In Lakatoro, I gained a wealth of experience in rural Melanesia and enjoyed a multitude of interesting experiences. I learned a lot about the causes of what the West labels as "underdevelopment" and why nations such as Vanuatu do not gain Western-style material wealth. We loved living in the rural tropics, with its fresh fruit and beaches. Although we did not build any close social bonds with ni-Vanuatu, we enjoyed socializing with other Malekula expatriates. Our family spent four months travelling around Australia followed by a month in Indonesia on our way home to Canada; this would not have been possible if we had not been posted as volunteers to Vanuatu. My career was highly enriched by the Vanuatu interlude; I'm not sure I would have survived an unbroken 29-year stint in the British Columbia Ministry of Agriculture. Or, would have the Ministry.

Two Years on Malekula

My Lakatoro years opened the door to my further three-and-a-third years in Port Vila. Professionally, there I did my best for Vanuatu in the areas of aid projects in agriculture, fisheries, tourism, rural water supplies, sanitation (read toilets), energy, minerals and geology, and probably some other areas I've forgotten. I had the unprecedented opportunity to learn about the foreign aid game from the inside.

From a personal point of view, I'm not going to lie. Living in Vila was a time of high income with social and recreational opportunities that my family and I would not have experienced any other way. Although the Commonwealth Fund for Technical Cooperation provided a lower cash remuneration package than other aid donors, like the others they paid for high-quality free housing that I arranged to include a gardener. My salary was tax-free. Medical and dental costs were covered. We could afford a housegirl to keep the house clean. Our daughters' tuition to a high-quality French school in Vila was provided.

A wiser family might have taken the opportunity to squirrel away savings, but we had been warned about doing this in lieu of enjoying new experiences. In Vila, we were able to save about CAN$10,000 each year. The first year, we took out and paid off a loan in that amount to buy capital goods that as recent volunteers we didn't have, such as an automobile and a washing machine. The second year's savings were used on our two-month semi-annual home leave to Canada (aid advisors with other aid organizations received annual home leaves). The third year's savings were used upon our final return to Canada to buy a car and live on while I looked for work—we were not eligible for Unemployment Insurance.

We didn't play golf, squash, or tennis like many other expats, but we became heavily involved with the local riding clubs. Holly and I had previously ridden Western-style, but we took the opportunity to learn English riding and compete in dressage and jumping events. I played Polocrosse, an Australian form of Lacrosse played on horseback. The other sport we enjoyed was SCUBA diving on reefs and the WW II wreck of the SS President Coolidge.

Our social life was rich. Without TV, we had to make our own fun. Many permanent resident expatriates were not especially interested in spending time with short-termers, but we managed to make friends with several of them—it didn't hurt that we had already been in Vanuatu for two years and had shared the Port Vila Cyclone Uma experience. There was also a large contingent of fellow advisors on two-year contracts who were looking for friendship. Many dinners were shared at Vila's large number of restaurants and at private parties. On the beach, French Champagne flowed freely. We gave an annual Christmas Eve party where Australians were introduced to eggnog, of which they had all heard but never had the opportunity to try.

The champion Vanuatu Nation Polocrosse team. We invited some guys down from Espiritu Santo and lent them horses for the game. I'm Number 2 on the right on Pablo-the-Wonder-Horse.

For two years we didn't participate, but we finally started attending the several black-tie balls that the Australians and British threw each year. On our home leave I had bought a tuxedo and Holly had bought a ball gown[1]. Those events were another experience we weren't likely to experience again in Canada.

Near the end of our Vila residency, Holly and I joined the chorus of an amateur production of "The Rocky Horror Show", which was a lot of fun and well-received. Now, where are those photos of me in corset and net stockings? Not in this memoir!

Well, OK. Here I am with some of the scantily-clad women I was forced to share the stage with. I only got into this deal in anticipation of this, but hadn't thought through the part about me having to dress the same.

Of course, all contracts come to an end, even if extended a year and then a final four months—the CFTC was not in the business of providing permanent staff to

---

[1] When we returned to Port Vila and rented the movie "Don't Tell Mom the Babysitter's Dead", we saw it was the same one that Christina Applegate wore in some scenes, albeit a different colour.

Vanuatu. As expected, returning home to a middle-class Canadian existence was rough in some ways. I felt like Eliza Doolittle at the end of "Pygmalion" or "My Fair Lady" when she had been exposed to the high life and then expected to return to the slums. But, we all adjusted and survived. The girls learned to clean their own rooms, and eventually they finished school so I could afford another horse for my last few years prior to retirement.

Bunny-the-Wonder-Horse in Kelowna.

A lasting effect of our six-year Vanuatu interlude was the loss of that length of pensionable time for both of us. So, our retirement income is about 20% less than it could have been. The trade-off has been well worth it—how many Canadians get to enjoy six years of tropical life and travel as a form of early retirement in the middle of their career?

Our Poor, Abused Children

Heather was 5 and Laurel 3 when we went to Lakatoro. We just stuck them in schools where they had to sink or swim by learning French and Bislama. Where, besides not getting a good education, they suffered what would be considered physical abuse in Canada from ancient "whack-'em-if-they-give-the-wrong-answer" teaching methods. For years after, Holly and I ignored their whining about missing McDonalds (where they never had eaten the food anyway, but just played on the toys) and Hallowe'en—apparently going around our living room while we put candies in their bags didn't substitute for real Trick-or-Treating. And, as I've written here, I got a lot of pleasure from teasing the two.

But, later on, we have often caught them telling friends how much they appreciate us having taken them to Malekula. Not only did they have a ball chatting with prison work gangs, playing on the beach, learning kastom dances, and more, but they experienced a different world from Canada. Their horizons were truly expanded, and they appreciate that.

I had six principal educational objectives for our girls; to learn to:

1. Read,
2. Speak Another Language,
3. Read Music,
4. Ride Horseback,
5. Swim, and
6. Downhill Ski.

The first five were achieved in Vanuatu, with even a few days' skiing for Heather when her class spent a week in New Zealand. I don't think numbers 2. and 4. would have been so easily accomplished in Canada. I let conventional schooling cover the rest of Heather and Laurel's academic requirements and enrolled them in ski school when we lived in Kelowna.

I recommend that parents who have the opportunity to take their young children to live in a different universe give it a go.

Holly's Career

While we were in Vanuatu, Canadian medical labs automated, and jobs for highly-trained lab staff such as herself disappeared. Holly adapted into a successful career in environmental lab work, university cooperative programme coordination, and hospital quality improvement.

Two Years on Malekula
My Further International Aid Advisor Career

After my two years in Lakatoro and thirty-nine months in Port Vila, it didn't happen. The Commonwealth Fund for Technical Assistance apparently had no further use for my talents; you may recall that they hadn't really wanted me in the first place.

With my Canadian private sector and development banking experience, I thought the Asian Development Bank would be a good fit, but one of their people in Port Vila advised me that international agriculturalists were out of fashion; the ADB eventually asked me to cease sending in my applications in response to their annual advertisements.

I did get a promising reply from a rather vague organization that had advertised in The Economist, but the project turned out to be an ambitious river re-direction planned by the Libyan government, with which I wasn't anxious to be associated.

Trends in international development were changing in the early '90s — remember how all the aid funding, including Canada's, was redirected to the former Soviet Republics, where it wouldn't be just poured down a rat hole like it was in the third world? LOL, as we write these days; it all went to the Russian Mafia. There was no demand for a Canadian with south Pacific island nation experience.

So, despite having sworn that I would not work in either agriculture or government again, after our savings had run out and a period of minimum wage work with horses in Canada, I ended up with my former employer, the British Columbia Ministry of Agriculture. There were some bad years there, but most of my time prior to an early retirement at age 59 1/2 was interesting and rewarding.

My CUSO Termination Report

At the end of their contract, every cooperant was issued a two-page Termination Report form of several questions, each with a couple of lines for the response, to fill out. During my two-year CUSO contract, I had taken note of some ways CUSO could improve its performance. So, in my way[1], I tossed the paper form, entered the questions into a word-processing document, and submitted fourteen pages of my responses.

---

[1] One of my later supervisors at the British Columbia Ministry of Agriculture told me in a friendly manner that I asked "career-limiting questions", a fact of which I was proud. I was in a union, so they couldn't just fire me without cause, and I had long since reached the career level I wanted — the highest one with technical, but not administrative, functions. And, which paid only a bit less than my supervisor's with all its headaches — like me.

In my report, I gave CUSO praise in the many areas where it was due, but didn't pull any punches regarding areas that could be improved. I offered suggestions for positive changes in those matters.

Back in Canada, everyone with CUSO that I met told me, "Oh—you're Stan Combs—I read your Termination Report." Too bad they didn't do anything with the information. This is the story of my life; nobody wants to take the advice of a pain-in-the-ass.

CUSO Since 1992

CUSO has changed substantially since we were cooperants, and since I assisted in South Pacific Cooperant selection in the 1990s and early 2000s. In 2008, the United Kingdom's Voluntary Service Overseas took over CUSO and implemented its objectives and procedures; it is a very different organization than the CUSO we were part of. Rather than concentrating on technical assistance, it is more concerned with promoting "social justice", a concept I find rather ill-defined and subjective.

CUSO INTERNATIONAL, as it is now called, has withdrawn from Vanuatu, leaving it to an influx of United States Peace Corps volunteers that arrived after we left Lakatoro. When describing CUSO to people unfamiliar with it, I say it is "Like the Peace Corps, but better". Unlike the PC, CUSO's mandate does not include promoting benefits of our home country.

_____

APPENDIX

CUSO COOPERANT - TERMINATION REPORT

Name: STAN COMBS   Country: VANUATU

Location: Lakatoro   Job Title: Regional Development Planner

Employer: Malekula Local Government Council

Placement Date: 1 Feb., 1987   Termination Date: 21 Feb., 1989

1. YOUR JOB.

My professional experience has been very disappointing. After arriving without a clear job description and orienting myself, I decided that the RDP position should have the following functions:

i   Develop a Regional Development Plan that would extend and integrate with the National Five-Year Development Plan.
ii Provide support to Central Government development planners by providing local input into Central Government development project identification, planning, implementation, and monitoring.
iii Support the Local Government Council by providing advice and input to Council aid applications and Council-run businesses.
iv Support local communities by assisting with project planning and funding.
v   Support local businessmen by assisting with business planning.
vi Train a local counterpart.

I have only been able to actually do Numbers iii. and vi. Development Planning in Vanuatu is the exclusive and jealously-guarded province of the National Planning and Statistics Office, which has flatly refused to acknowledge the presence of the RDPs. NPSO has not yet provided any RDP with a copy of the latest Five-Year National Development Plan, so it has not been possible to write a Regional Development Plan.

The former NPSO analyst assigned to the RDPs told me that when the RDP programme was started, NPSO made a policy decision not to cooperate with the programme. He also told me that NPSO considered that almost all projects submitted by RDPs for funding were bound to be of the "cargo" type (i.e. for personal consumption only), or stolen by one member of the community, or would be incompetently administered by the Department of Local Government. I have found most of the NPSO analysts to be completely concerned with large, capital-intensive projects designed to increase Vanuatu's money-economy GNP.

Two Years on Malekula

Their decisions are made without the benefit of any knowledge of the realities of that part of Vanuatu that lies beyond the Port Vila City Limits; they make no attempt to relieve their ignorance by traveling outside Efate or by seeking the input of the RDPs, who are based in the regions where projects will be implemented.

It has been very difficult to work with communities. The political reality in Vanuatu is that the ruling party insists on absolute control of all government and aid funds spent in communities. This means that every funding request, no matter how small, must go through the cumbersome, wasteful, and time-consuming NPSO-NDC-Foreign Affairs-Aid Donor process. I have made very few applications through this channel, since I think that the community enthusiasm needed for project success would be long dead before the funding would arrive. In any case, experience has shown that most RDP-initiated funding requests have been rejected at the NPSO stage.

In reality, though, the funding problem is just a secondary obstacle to achieving community development in Vanuatu through development projects, whether or not they are dependent on outside funding. There is an acute shortage of good-quality community-generated project proposals. Everybody wants mechanical devices, such as power lawnmowers, to increase their already-abundant leisure time, or those, such as video machines, that will fill their leisure time. I recognize that to ni-Vanuatu, much of what whitemen consider leisure is time spent on fulfilling compulsory social obligations, but I think that "development" entails a community grasping control of its destiny. The community can decide to expend its time resources on social functions or on working to obtain leisure-expanding machinery. If, however, the community opts for social functions and still expects outsiders to provide labour-saving machinery, it will not develop. This reluctance to grasp control is also evident when communities implement worthwhile projects. For example, it seems as if community halls must always have aid-funded corrugated iron roofs, rather than the community investing time in producing the same natangura-thatch roof that all their houses have. A century of European churches, colonial governments, and aid donors handing out cargo has resulted in an expectation that industrialized-type goods will be provided gratis to communities.

In theory, a long period of community development work is needed to instill a more responsible expectation, which is necessary to attain CUSO's concept of development, in Malekula's communities. In reality, though, the activities of the Central Government, MP Discretionary Funds, NKDT, High Commission Discretionary Funds, and other aid sources, all of whom freely distribute inappropriate aid, prevent the emergence of this. All of these agencies, with the willing collusion of the people of Vanuatu, are working to continue the present state of aid-dependence. In any case, I did not have the time to devote to effective community development work in any of Malekula's 120-plus villages, and I don't have the skills or background for this kind of work. I have spoken with

Two Years on Malekula

Australian volunteers who did community development work on Santo and felt totally defeated by the system.

I have had a similar scarcity of small businessmen approaching me for business planning advice, although I am satisfied with the talks on the subject I gave to two Women's business workshops, a couple of Ministry of Agriculture short courses, and an accounting short course. This shortage of entrepreneurial ideas will decrease as ni-Vanuatu gain more experience with the money economy.

Regarding my "success" with RDP Functions iii. and vi., I don't think that someone with the education and background of the present RDPs is needed to give general business advice to the LGCs. Some LGCs, although not the Malekula council, may need administrative specialists to help them set up management and administration systems.

I am happy with the results of my counterpart training work. This has been a combination of USP correspondence courses that I tutored for him, other LGC staff, and private sector employees from Metenesel Estates Ltd., along with practical work and day-to-day discussions. I have been fortunate in that the LGC Secretary I worked under has been able to attract and hold good-quality people to work under him. Unfortunately, if he ever leaves this post, my counterpart has said that he and much of the other LGC staff plan to also leave at the same time.

I do not believe that CUSO should replace me or any RDP unless Vanuatu's development planning structure is changed to take full advantage of the RDPs, who are a valuable resource that is being wasted.

2. TIPS FOR NEW COOPERANTS.

> i. Buy a four-wheel drive truck as soon as you arrive. Malekula has a relatively good road system, and mobility will greatly increase your enjoyment of life. You will be able to recharge your batteries during the weekends, making you more effective in your job. This is especially important if you have a family with you. If you are alone, a trail motorcycle will serve the same purpose (but you will get wetter). Two-wheel drive is a poor substitute; you only need 4WD 1% of the time, but that 1% is distributed over a good portion of your trips.

> ii. Learn Bislama as soon as possible and use it exclusively in your work. Insist that CUSO provide you and your family with an introductory course when you arrive in Vila, and force yourself to practice in real-life situations, i.e. whenever speaking with a ni-Vanuatu. Bislama is also handy for communicating with unilingual Francophone Europeans, if you are a unilingual Anglophone, like me. Forget everything all the Vila-based expats have told you, like "you'll pick it up in three weeks", or "you don't have to be able to speak it to understand what is being said". Bis-

lama is not baby-talk English, it is a separate language, and you can expect to just be attaining an idiomatic facility in it at the end of your two-year contract. The best thing that happened to me here was that the LGC Secretary gave me three days to speak English and then spread the word that only Bislama was to be spoken to me.

iii. Do not allow yourself to become or be perceived as being a conduit for aid "cargo". Accept that you may be considered irrelevant when this becomes evident.

iv. Ensure that you get regular trips to Port Vila, even if this means pressuring CUSO to provide bush leaves. The Canadian-Local culture gap here is probably as wide as it gets anywhere in the world, and one needs occasional time back in European society to reset one's cultural gyroscope. Besides, despite what those in Vila tell you, it is not satisfactory to order shopping in by telephone and air freight as, no matter who buys it for you, the order usually gets screwed up. Also, the shopping in Santo is not as good as in Vila. Expect those who live in Vila to fantasize that they are living in the same Vanuatu as you are, and beware their opinions that there is no necessity for you to leave your post. They may also think, incorrectly, that a one-day weekend In-Country meeting held outside Luganville is a bush leave. In the absence of support on this aspect of bush leaves from CUSO, some imagination may be required to insure that bush leaves don't eat up all of your leave time.

Please note that this advice is being written by the CUSO RDP, and perhaps cooperant, who spent the least amount of time in Vila and Santo during 1987-88. It is also worth noting that, of all the CUSO cooperants I met during my contract, every one that spent at least one year in Vila extended his contract, and every one that didn't live in Vila, except three Fisheries Advisors, didn't extend his contract. My point is not that everyone should live in Vila, but that it is useful to occasionally touch base.

v. If you have school-aged children, be aware that Grade 1 here equals European Kindergarten, and this one-year offset extends through primary school. This is because the kids come to their first year of school speaking only their village language, and must learn either French or English during their first few years of school. Our older daughter spent an unnecessary year in Grade 1 because it took us several months to realize this. We put our younger daughter straight into Grade 1 the next year, when she was five, and she did well.

Away from the expatriate schools in Vila and Santo, reliance is placed on learning by rote, with corporal punishment for wrong answers. Frankly, the standard of teaching is not up to Canada's. Heather, as Norsup school's first whiteman student, underwent an uncomfortable initial two weeks as the object of intense scrutiny by all, before being accepted as more-or-less just another kid. For what it's worth, we put the girls into a French school, where we think they learned as much (or little) of the 3 Rs than they would have in the English school, but they did learn some French.

The other expatriate children around here are probably learning more from their Australian and English correspondence lessons, but they seem to suffer from the lack of contact with other children, and they sure don't get the direct contact with ni-Vanuatu culture that our kids got. None of them speak Bislama, either.

3. PERSONAL AND SOCIAL.

Despite my professional frustrations, my personal experience here has been extremely positive. Vanuatu must be the place to volunteer. The people are friendly, the disease risk is minimal, the climate is pleasant, and the beaches beckon. It has been an especially good place for our two daughters, now aged 7 and 5. They have enjoyed a freedom unknown in Canada, where we kept them under eagle-eye and fenced in the backyard. Holly and I have perceived Lakatoro as free of the danger of physical and sexual abuse to children, although we know that sexual abuse is a major worry to adolescent girls and women, and we have heard of cases of incest. Also, this society, unlike Canada's, is oriented towards children; families with children are the norm, and everyone looks out after everyone's children. As a result, Heather and Laurel have attained a degree of independence that they never would have in Canada. I also think that a couple of years of moderate deprivation, as opposed to North America's instant gratification, haven't done them any harm. Other positive experiences for the children have been: attaining fluency in Bislama, being the racial minority, and living in a different culture. They are much more "in tune" with ni-Vanuatu society, at their age level, than Holly and I are.

I think Holly's experience has been positive, but more difficult, as she was culturally isolated without the diversion of full-time work, and her trips to Santo and Vila were spaced about every 6 months, as opposed to 3 months for me. Work occasionally took me to Vila or Santo, but we found the expense of family accommodation to be a major impediment to family bush leaves. Care of Laurel, who was not in full-time school during our first year, and housework kept Holly tied to the house at first. This was especially true during the first few months, when we couldn't afford a housegirl and Holly's days were spent scrubbing clothes and cleaning the house. I think Holly became happier during our second year, when Laurel entered Grade 1, she had part-time work at the Norsup Hospital, and we had a truck that gave her mobility. The strains on Holly put some tension on our relationship, but we seem to have survived as a couple. We do not regret our decision to leave one partner primarily at home to look after the children, rather than have both of us take on full-time work.

Two Years on Malekula

I am sure that my experience here was enhanced because I came as part of a family, which provided a personal and cultural support system. Based on my experience and observations here, I would encourage CUSO to send families to the field when they are available. CUSO is going to find that a growing proportion of the experienced professional cooperants it wants have families, anyway. I would recommend that CUSO not send one-half of a couple to the field, despite a couple's stated willingness to temporarily split. Such splits seem to bring on excessive trips to expatriate centres and Canada, and early returns.

Socially, we did not mix well with ni-Vanuatu. At first, we put this down to the physical location of our house, but we later realized that it was due to the wide cultural gap between ourselves and ni-Vanuatu. We do not have any ni-Vanuatu friends, but as far as that goes, we do not know any Europeans who have ni-Vanuatu friendships that go deeper than the drinking buddy or sexual partner level. This has been somewhat disappointing, but we haven't felt too deprived, since we had moved around quite a bit in Canada and had never become dependent on a large circle of friends. Also, there are several expatriates in the Lakatoro area that we struck up friendships with.

I did gain much enjoyment from storianing with ni-Vanuatu about custom stories. This was a bit difficult, and had to be approached with some sensitivity because whitemen have always ridiculed and discouraged these beliefs, giving rise to a reluctance to discuss the subject with us. Initially, it all sounded a bit silly to me, too. I came to realize, though, that these beliefs are universal here, and not affected by educational level or involvement with Christianity. They represent reality to ni-Vanuatu and thus were well worth the effort required to hear them. As a whiteman, I only got the tip of the iceberg; even ni-Vanuatu men must spend a lifetime in the custom system to be taught the full story.

4. PERSONAL OBJECTIVES

I came here with the objectives of:

i   Assisting the people of Vanuatu to gain greater control over their lives, i.e. "develop",
ii Enjoying a good personal experience, and;
iii Gaining professional experience that would assist me in changing my field of work. In Canada, I was an agricultural development lender, as-sisting people to enter the farming business or expand their farms. I have become convinced, however, that there is too much food produced and too many farmers in North America. I feel that my talents can be better used in the developing world, where there is a shortage of locally-pro-duced food in many places. I hoped that this CUSO contract would give me the developing world experience necessary to enter this field.

I don't think I was very successful at Objective i., although I have heard that this is a common feeling among development workers.

I have met Objective ii., aside from frustration arising from my professional disappointments. Lakatoro is a nice place to live, being somewhat developed compared to rural postings such as Sola or Lolopuepue, but not the expatriate playground of Vila. I have enjoyed observing, albeit at arm's length, the ni-Vanuatu culture, and I think I have learned a lot about village-based, low-tech, animist cultures. Our family experience has been positive.
I feel I have had mixed success with Objective iii. I have gained useful experience in living in the semi-rural third world. Nevertheless, having not been allowed the opportunity to participate in real development planning here, I have not gained the professional knowledge that I had hoped to. Time will tell if I eventually get a satisfying overseas job, if I end up propping up a contracting industry at home, or if I enter a new field of work.

5. CUSO AND YOU

As an organization that provides cooperants to the developing world, a reluctant CUSO is being dragged through a metamorphosis, and it is making this process harder on itself than necessary. When it started, CUSO sent out young, inexperienced, idealistic fresh university graduates to work in the third world on the theory that their education and cultural background would make up for their absolute lack of real-world experience and allow them to provide low-level assistance to developing countries. Now, however, recipient countries are demanding seasoned, experienced professionals and tradesmen. Problems arise because CUSO's administration consists largely of returned volunteers from its early era. These people's minds are still operating on the assumptions of the earlier amateur era, and they are not equipped to deal effectively with the new professional cooperant.

The old-style cooperant, with an exclusive life experience of child- and studenthood, was much more accustomed to accepting authority. Having spent the last 3 or 4 years in an upper-middle class ivory tower, his mind was stuffed with trendy theories un-tempered by experience. He was eager for new experiences, and not yet knowing what he wanted out of life, he wasn't very particular about just what kind of experience he tried. This made him very malleable. The new cooperant, on the other hand, has been around. He's been his own man for 10 or 15 years and is likely to have some sort of career path in mind. He is not as willing to just deliver himself into the hands of an organization to use him as it sees fit. He wants to know what he is getting into, and once he arrives, he expects his situation to somewhat correspond to his expectations. What I am saying is: of course CUSOs have to be flexible, but when they arrive somewhere to set up a carpentry workshop, they probably won't be satisfied if they end up halter-training steers to pull plows. They are also less likely to accept the hair-shirt mentality that their third world experience will be enhanced by unnecessary suffering. Their objective is more likely to focus on providing concrete assistance to the host country, rather than on ridding themselves of developed-world guilt by selfless sacrifice.

I think that as an organization, CUSO puts too much emphasis on the therapeutic benefits to its cooperants of self-sacrifice, both sacrifice to CUSO itself by a cooperant giving CUSO complete control of his future when he signs on, and in the field by living a rougher than necessary lifestyle. I also think that, in practice, this philosophy is used to justify CUSO's unfortunate policy of refusing to accept much of the risk inherent in the cooperant-placement business, i.e. the risk that CUSO will lose its investment in a cooperant because he fails to complete his contract. CUSO does this by pushing an improper amount of risk on the cooperants. For example, after putting a prospective cooperant through a long and what is represented as thorough screening process, CUSO reserves the right to reject a cooperant, who has quit his job, sold his furniture, and rented or sold his house, during the final orientation and right up to the moment he gets on the plane. This is not justifiable by the excuse that accepting its proper share of the risk will cost CUSO money that would otherwise be channeled into its development programmes. CUSO should face up to the fact that this type of risk is inherent in cooperant placement and accept its full fair share, rather than pushing the cost of this risk onto the shoulders of its cooperants, who are already accepting the personal, health, and career risks of overseas volunteer work.

As a practical suggestion, much of this risk of a cooperant being not suitable for the posting could be eliminated by improving the screening process. I think that CUSO confuses "long and time-consuming" with "thorough and efficient". Two of the cooperants who came to our Anglophone orientation didn't speak English and CUSO wasn't aware of it! For example, all of those letters of professional and personal reference are not likely to give CUSO much useful information. First, an applicant is only likely to provide CUSO with people who will give positive references. Second, people do not put negative references in writing. CUSO should phone the references, and follow up verbal clues with hard questions. Besides the references selected by the applicant, it should phone his last few employers, landlords, etc. CUSO should do credit checks on applicants to find out how they have carried out their previous obligations. It shouldn't just accept an applicant's word that he is divorced or whatever, it should require him to submit documentary evidence. All of this is CUSO's right; it is spending money that donors and the Canadian government has entrusted to it. This approach should be more effective than in former times, because CUSO is now dealing with applicants who are older and have track records. Finally, CUSO should expect that there will be occasional failures, and accept that this is necessary if good cooperants are not to be missed.

The degree of support provided by the FSO in assuring that the host government meets its responsibilities to the cooperant is too arbitrary and not strong enough. This type of support is going to become more and more necessary as cooperants are placed in professional positions, such as RDPs, where they must interact with host government bureaucracies. At present, if a cooperant, who isn't getting this backup, decides that the professional conditions of his employment are not being met and decides to terminate his contract, CUSO retains complete discretion over termination benefits. This does not seem fair to me.

I have noticed a couple of other ways that CUSO does not treat its cooperants in an enlightened fashion. Promises made regarding in-country orientation, language training, bush leaves, etc. by the Ottawa office during the application and orientation process are later found by the cooperant to be under the sole jurisdiction and discretion of the FSO. This is dishonest treatment. Administrative flexibility is good, but after a point it can amount to exploitation of cooperants. CUSO should give up some of its flexibility and become more specific, in writing if necessary, in its commitments to its cooperants in order to ensure that there is never a discrepancy between promises made in Ottawa and reality delivered by FSOs in the field.

There is also the matter of cooperant eligibility for jobs within CUSO's administration. During the orientation process, I was warned that in the field, I could expect to be treated with some contempt because I was a "volunteer". I did not expect, however, that CUSO would treat its cooperants in the same manner by denying them the opportunity to apply for permanent jobs within the organization. I have seen two mechanisms used for this purpose. One, CUSO has abrogated its management responsibilities by signing a collective agreement that places positions such as FSOs, which are clearly management positions, under union jurisdiction. This limits openings initially to internal competitions, with appeal procedures available to unsuccessful internal applicants. I find this excessive zeal to unionize ironic in relation to the practices described in the above paragraphs, which if extended to CUSO's permanent staff, would result in strong union action.

Second, positions such as the recently filled Agriculture Desk in Ottawa, that are filled with open competitions, are not advertised to cooperants. Opening these types of jobs to cooperants might cost CUSO some money through early returns, but CUSO should be thinking in terms of long-term advantage to the organization, rather than short-term financial advantage. By closing these opportunities to serving cooperants, CUSO is losing the opportunity to insert good people into its organization. It is also depriving itself of people who have the new ideas needed to help CUSO through the metamorphosis discussed above. At the very least, open competitions should be made known to cooperants nearing the ends of their contracts. I don't think that cooperants, along with present CUSO employees, should be given preference, just that they should be given an equal opportunity to apply.

Another area where CUSO should come clean with its cooperants is in the matter of CUSO's priorities. Cooperants should be plainly told from the outset that cooperant placement is no longer CUSO's top priority and that emphasis has shifted to funding local organizations. Personally, I have had no problem with this, but I have seen almost every other cooperant in Vanuatu become somewhat bitter and disillusioned when they noticed our FSOs devoting a large part of their energy to this type of task. Naturally, everyone thinks that their function is the centre of the universe, and CUSO may have to forcefully get the message through, but cooperants will be happier and more effective if they realize their place in CUSO's priorities from the start.

A positive suggestion I have for the administration of CUSO cooperant placements is for CUSO to adopt the attitude that it is better to have a smaller number of effective placements than the maximum number that can be squeezed out of a budget. I have seen many examples of non-productive penny-pinching during my two years here: personal disputes over bush leaves, exhausted Ottawa personnel on the tail end of a marathon field trip with too much work squeezed into too short a time, a CUSO-sponsored conference sited in the middle of nowhere so nobody could slip away to the bright lights of Vila (with the result that important local participants didn't even show up), two in-country meetings scheduled for weekends so no work time is lost, the same in-country meetings limited to one day so that they are too rushed for any productive interchange to take place, a RDP house built in the wrong village because the FSO didn't buy an air ticket and inspect the site, etc. This management style is sometimes referred to as "stepping over a dollar to pick up a nickel".

My last suggestion is that CUSO should become more active and assertive in its dealings with host governments. CUSO is much too passive and overly concerned with offending host governments, and it is the cooperants, along with CUSO's funders, who pay the price. The concept of a contract is appropriate to CUSO's assistance to a country. Each party should ensure that the other fulfills its obligations. CUSO has not been doing this in Vanuatu. For example, housing should be ready, and inspected by the FSO, before a cooperant arrives. More serious is the situation that has been allowed to exist for the RDPs. The RDPs have been provided, like so much free cargo, to the Vanuatu government, who have not provided the administrative structure to use them properly. We are not being used to anywhere near our potential and are sitting around like excess machinery that has been accepted from an aid donor simply because it is free. For CUSO to meekly accept this state of affairs is for it to fail in its responsibilities to its cooperants and its funders. If a government and an aid donor can't come to a mutually satisfactory use of aid, it should be withdrawn, not continued just to keep up the numbers. At the very least, CUSO should be pressing for a moderately efficient use of its RDP cooperants, but despite my repeated discussions with my FSO on this subject, CUSO has only expressed mild concern to the Director of the Department of Local Government. I would expect the organization who is, after all, paying the shot, to hold discussions with the Prime Minister, who has responsibility for NPSO, and the Minister of Home Affairs, who is responsible for the Department of Local Government. If they can't work out between them a system of using the talents of the RDPs to a reasonable extent, the RDP programme should be canceled or modified to provide cooperants with the skills that are actually being used.

On the positive side of "CUSO and You", I will start with the particular and move on to the general. Financially, CUSO treats most of its cooperants very well. My salary and the family's subsistence allowance have allowed us to live a satisfactory lifestyle. Whenever I have requested a salary advance or a loan, it has been provided immediately. Medical and Dental coverage has been good and in keeping with my belief that a cooperant's risk of developing permanent health problems because of his CUSO service should be minimized. The regular Canadian support payments have allowed us to keep up an adequate level of life insurance and have compensated us for the lower-than-cost rent we receive for our Canadian house. (By the way, I suggest that CUSO save some money by canceling its group life insurance for cooperants. The $25,000 provided is too low by a factor of 10 for those with dependents, and those without dependents have no need for life insurance.) The Resettlement Allowance seems fair. All of this compares very favorably with the financial treatment given by other agencies to their cooperants. In fact, I was pleasantly surprised after arrival to calculate that after taxes, housing, and utilities, my disposable income from all of the above is about the same as it was in Canada, except it is mostly received at the end of my contract. In essence, it has been a period of forced savings where we lived modestly in return for a lump sum at the end. Of course, there is no employment at the end, either.

In general, I think that the idea behind CUSO is a good one. I have had a worm's eye view of international development while here, and it is obvious that the large-scale throw-money-at-the-top approach does not produce benefits that trickle down to a developing country's people. Large-scale infrastructure has its place, but it must be balanced by the bottom-up process, too.

My feeling is, though, that CUSO is an organization weighed down with the baggage of the Sixties. It is much too concerned with ideological form and the repayment of a guilt-ridden sense of debt owed by the developed world to the LDCs. It should be more concerned with functional results leading to real development of real people. To this end, it should shed its proudly-held amateur nature, and become a professional. It should recognize that people who are good cooperants are not necessarily good administrators. It should treat its cooperants, who are its best resource, with more respect and stop expecting them to absorb a disproportionate share of CUSO's risks and costs in the name of rich country guilt and the development cause. It should demand more from its host countries. It should abandon its cost-minimizing approach for a results-maximizing one.

6. YOUR FUTURE

As per my comments in Point 4., I hope to build on my experience in Vanuatu and find further overseas work.

7. PROFESSIONAL CONTACTS

The only professional contacts I have made here are the ones that any successor will quickly make during his first weeks.

8. RESOURCES

i. Constitution of the Republic of Vanuatu. This gives one some idea of what the political objectives of Vanuatu are. It can also help one to follow the tactics used during day-to-day political wrangles in Vila.

ii. Report on the Census of Population 1979, Volume 1: Basic Tables. This gives a general outline of Vanuatu's demographics. I found it worthwhile to read the tables on Malekula in some detail.

iii. National Nutrition Survey Report, October 1983. Concentrates on the vulnerable groups: children and women.

iv. Maternal and Child Health Survey. A bit hard to get ahold of, but the local Rural Health Office should have one.

v. Report on the Agricultural Census, 1983/1984, Part I: The Results. A survey of Vanuatu's real economic activity, although somewhat slanted towards expatriate plantations.

vi. Quarterly Economic Review, Central Bank of Vanuatu. This gives an overview of Port Vila's money economy. Each year's December edition gives a summary of the year.

vii. Tropical Products newsletter from Westpac Bank. This comes out irregularly and gives a good analysis of world markets for tropical agricultural products such as copra, coffee, and cocoa. Westpac Bank has been sending it to me free from their Vila branch.

viii. Second National Development Plan, 1987-1991, Republic of Vanuatu. This Top-Secret document is not even distributed on a Need-To-Know basis, but I have a sneaking suspicion that it might provide valuable information to a Regional Development Planner. Perhaps a midnight armed commando raid on NPSO headquarters might produce a copy at the cost of acceptable casualties. In the meantime, the executive summary has been printed in the December, 1987 edition of the Central Bank of Vanuatu's Quarterly Economic Report.

9. GENERAL

I hope CUSO is secure enough to at least read and consider the suggestions made in this report, and I hope it is passed up the chain of command rather than just filed in Port Vila. I have noticed that CUSO is not very receptive to criticism; it presents a "take it or leave it" face to its cooperants. My FSO told me early on that if a cooperant wasn't happy, she just gave him a ticket home; hardly a policy designed to decrease the risk of early returns, to say nothing of increasing programme effectiveness. In conversations with CUSO administrators, they have usually ascribed cooperant discontent to emotional instability, incorrect ideology, or dishonesty during the application process. This seems to be backed up by an attitude that, as ex-cooperants, they have paid their dues, so why should the CUSO administrators make any effort to improve the system that they suffered through? I would answer, "In order so that CUSO can better meet its objectives", and then ask the question, "What is the major objective of CUSO; to make the cooperants feel good about what they have done, or to actually help the people of the developing world?"

Thank you for considering my views. Feel free to use the information contained in this report for publicity purposes.

January 10, 1989

Stan Combs
CUSO No. 17701-1914

About the Author

Stan Combs was born in the United States in 1951, his family emigrating to Canada when he was 11. Growing up in Edmonton, Alberta, he became an agricultural economist whose non-Vanuatu experience ranged from ranch work to farm lending to crop insurance underwriting to assisting local governments with farm regulation. His career mantra was "Get a Master's Degree, and they'll hire you for anything". Non-work interests included swimming, backpacking in the Rocky Mountains, downhill skiing, competitive horseback riding, and home maintenance. He and his wife have travelled in North America, Australia, the UK, Western Europe, North America, and Mexico's Baja Peninsula. They retired in the early 2010s to a small island between Vancouver Island and the BC mainland.